A HISTORY OF EDENFIELD & DISTRICT

A HISTORY OF EDENFIELD & DISTRICT

JOHN SIMPSON

EDENFIELD LOCAL HISTORY SOCIETY

2003

First published 2003
Edenfield Local History Society

ISBN 0 9516669 1 6

Printed and bound by
SMITH SETTLE
Ilkley Road, Otley, West Yorkshire LS21 3JP

CONTENTS

For Heather, Andrew and Janet

PREFACE

This book is a companion to *Edenfield: Life in a Lancashire village* continuing the story through the Industrial Revolution to the present day. It also includes the neighbouring villages and hamlets of Stubbins, Strongstry, Chatterton, Lumb, Irwell Vale, Ewood Bridge and Turn all of which have interesting stories. I do not claim that this is a definitive history; there is much that I have had to leave out, but I hope it at least gives a flavour of life in the villages in the 19th and 20th centuries.

I would have liked to have thanked all those who helped me individually, but quickly realised that the resulting list would have made Domesday Book look like a raffle ticket. Needless to say I am very grateful indeed to everybody for all the help they have given me and for making my task much lighter.

John Simpson
Helmshore

ILLUSTRATION ACKNOWLEDGEMENTS

British Library: pp.236, 247, 264; Bury Archive Service: B04414, B04541, pp.164, 187; Lancashire Record Office (by permission of the County Archivist): pp.148, 293; Manchester Central Library, Local Studies Unit: pp.68, 157; Haslingden Library: pp.183, 222 (top), 258; Rawtenstall Library: pp.117, 212, 137, 179, 198, 203; Edenfield Cricket Club: p245; Edenfield Local History Society: pp.30, 126, 131, 140, 176, 181 (top), 188, 257, 283 (top); Helmshore Local History Society: pp.32, 110, 130, 150, 186, 195, 214, 223 (bottom), 232, 261; Ramsbottom Heritage Society (at Bury Archive Service): RHS 1714b, 1714a, 1759, 1363, 1536, 1479, 1478, 1280, pp.44, 100, 108, 174, 223 (top), 234 (top), 249 (bottom); Edenfield Parish Church: p.146; Mr. R. Barlow: pp.35, 139, 160, 181, 194, 230, 234 (bottom); Mr. A. Barton: pp.185, 222 (bottom), 264; Mr. D. Belshaw: p.184; Mr. and Mrs. B. Bissett: p.102; Mr. F. Crook: p.167; the late Mr. J. Dewhurst: pp.78, 143; the late Mr. S. Hastings: pp.70, 74, 77, 90; Mr. R. Johnson: p.246; Mr. P. Lonsdale: p.218; Mr. G. Lord: pp.135, 169, 262; Mr. J. Peden: p.119; Mr. I. Summers: pp.32, 110, 130, 150, 186, 195, 214, 223 (bottom), 232, 261; Mr. A. Taylor: p.280; Mr. J. Valentine, p.251; Mrs. E. Whittaker: pp.5, 40, 141; Mr. T. Woodcock: pp.69, 86; Mr. F. Woods: p.149

The remaining pictures are from the author's own collection.

ABBREVIATIONS IN FOOTNOTES

BAS	Bury Archive Service
BT	*Bury Times*
LRO	Lancashire Record Office
MCL	Manchester Central Library
PP	Parliamentary Paper
PRO	Public Record Office
RFP	*Rossendale Free Press*
RO	*Ramsbottom Observer*
RUDC	Ramsbottom Urban District Council
uncat.	uncatalogued

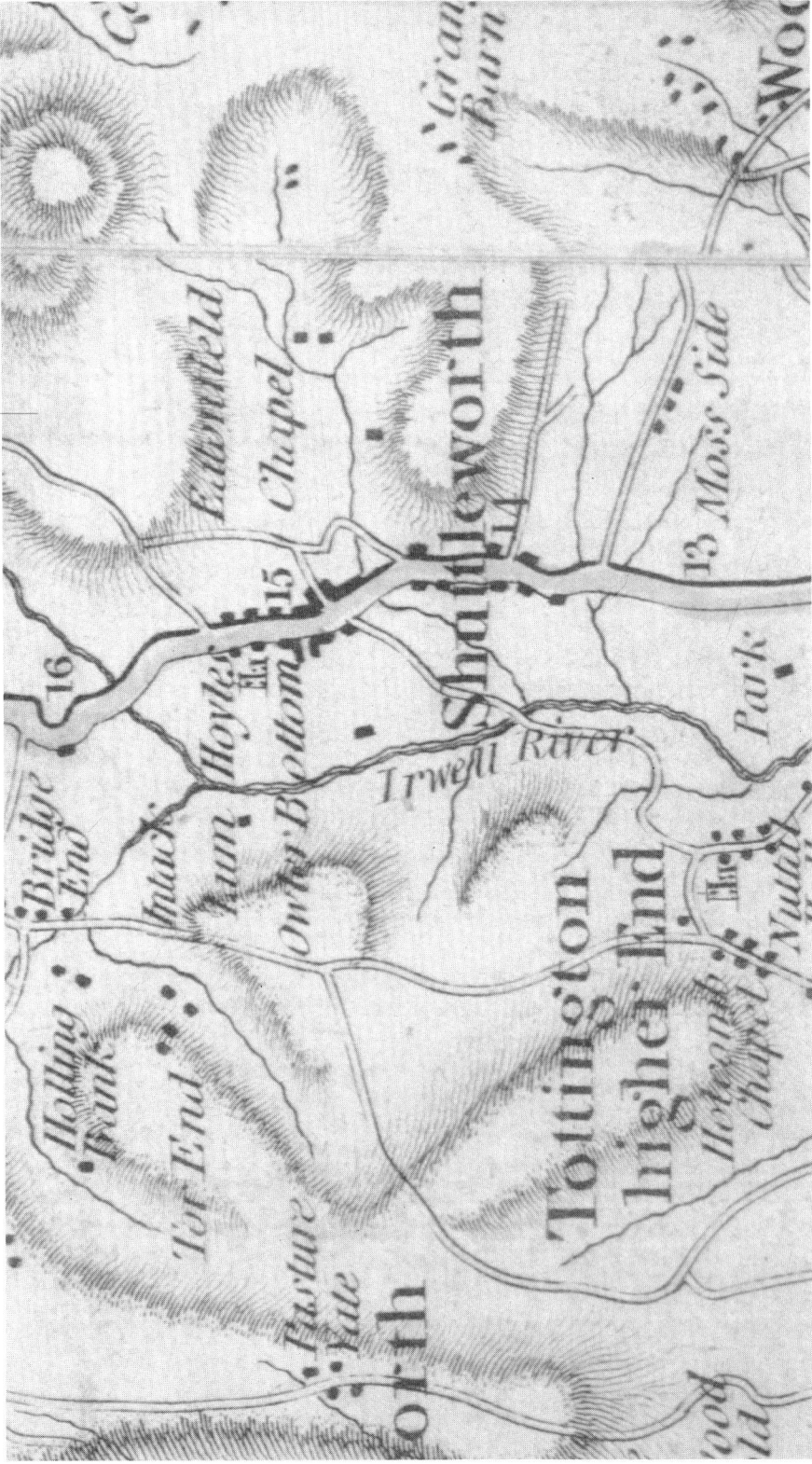

The Edenfield area in 1795, an extract from John Stockdale's *A New Map of the Country round Manchester*. A symbol representing the church is visible below the word 'Hoyles'. At this date, only the main road through the village had been turnpiked.

THE CHANGING VILLAGES

IN 1770, EDENFIELD was the only settlement of any size in the old township of Tottington Higher End. Apart from the church, a school in the corner of the churchyard and two public houses, the village consisted mostly of scattered farms with just a few cottages near the road. Turn, too, was a place of farms spread out across the hillside, although there were some dwellings clustered together at Scout Fold and on Fecit Lane. As for Ewood Bridge, Lumb, Chatterton, Strongstry and Stubbins, these consisted of just one or two substantial farmhouses. In most cases these were once the homes of well-to-do families, but they had slipped down the social scale. Irwell Vale simply did not exist in 1770; another sixty years or so were to go by before it made its appearance.

Edenfield and its neighbours had been changing slowly for generations, but as the 18th century drew to a close the process of change accelerated. The first inkling of what was to come was heralded by the building of a woollen fulling mill at Dearden Clough in the 1760s. By the time officials from the Ordnance Survey were busy mapping the locality in the 1840s, more mills, turnpike roads and the railway had profoundly altered the scene. In later chapters we will look in detail at some of these pieces in the jigsaw puzzle of the local landscape, but let us begin by examining the houses of the people of the Edenfield district and how they have changed over the past two hundred years.

FARMHOUSES

Most of the farmhouses that dotted the local landscape at the end of the 18th century had long histories and they were to continue to be used for several generations, in some cases to the present day. In the 19th century one or two of the old houses were rebuilt either on the same site or nearby. They included Hancock or Hencock Farm, which was demolished to make way for the new vicarage in 1850. Its replacement was erected at the side of Market Street where it still stands (no. 155). Other examples include Plunge Farm, rebuilt in 1884 by its owners, the Misses Wallwork, and Alderbottom rebuilt in 1900 by A.T. Porritt. When offered for sale a few years later the farm was said to bring to mind 'a little residence at the foot of a Tasmanian mountain or a Welsh hill' and to be 'approaching a paradise on a miniature scale.'[1]

When new farms were created, either by taking land from an existing holding or by using some of the former common land on the moors, new farmhouses made an appearance too. This happened when part of the original Hardsough Farm at Pinfold was divided up between 1777 and 1790 and a new farmhouse built at Middle

The farm buildings at Stubbins Vale Mill in about 1880. The barn and stables on the left were demolished in the 1920s to make way for a new weaving shed.

Hardsough Farm (now simply called Hardsough Farm). Changes to some of the Dearden Moor land-holdings saw new farmhouses being built at Four Acre in the 1780s and Whitaker Pasture in the early 1800s. Later in the 19th century some mill owners added farmhouses, barns, stables and shippons to their industrial premises. The Porritts did this at Stubbins Vale, as did their neighbour William Rumney, who ran Stubbins printworks, and who built a house in Stubbins Fold in 1879, which was intended to be used as a farmhouse.[2]

These additions to the local stock of farmhouses were at the same time matched by a number of losses. Many casualties succumbed to changes brought by the Industrial Revolution. Whitaker Pasture, for instance, barely survived the 19th century as its fields were eaten away by Great Height quarry. At the same time some of the houses ceased to be the centre of a farm as their land was absorbed by a larger neighbour or, in the case of some of the farms on Dearden Moor and near Turn, abandoned to rough pasture. In these cases the farmhouses were either deliberately demolished as probably happened in the case of Lower Fish Rake (which disappeared between 1861 and 1881), Bank Nook and Mount Maria (both pulled down between 1891 and 1908) or simply allowed to become derelict. Of course, when one farm swallowed another there were times when the original farmhouse of the smaller farm survived simply as an ordinary dwelling. This happened with Collier Wives Farm (25 and 27, Gin Croft Lane) and Lane Side (Mangle Fold) in Elm Street. Since the end of the First World War, the most rapacious enemy of the old farms has been new housing developments. The first farm to fall victim to them was Higher Chatterton, which stood in what is now Water Lane and whose land disappeared under a tide of council houses between the wars.

COTTAGES BEFORE 1850

The cottages that were built in Edenfield and the surrounding villages before 1770 tended to be attached to, or associated with, farmhouses. In the 1740s, however, cottages that were independent of any farm were built at Pinfold at the north end of the village. Others soon joined them and additions continued to be made to them after 1770. At Crow Woods, to take one example, building had begun in about 1760 and by 1777 there were three cottages and a shippon. In 1796, John Holt, the owner, divided up his property between his three brothers: George received the building that was the predecessor of the old Quarryman's Arms; William got the so-called

3, 5 and 7, Crow Woods Fold in 1938. This was the property acquired by William Holt in 1796.

'Lower House', which stood at the top of Crow Woods Lane; while the remaining share (including a piece of land between the lane and the new turnpike road) went to Ebenezer. By 1837, William and Ebenezer's property consisted of nine cottages, including 'New Row' (15-21, Crow Woods). Another case where additions were made to existing cottages was at Orange Square, near Elizabeth Street. Here four plots of land adjoining the main road were fenced off from Collier Wife Meadow in the 1760s and 1780s and two houses and a barn erected on them. In 1813, John Barnett, one of the village blacksmiths, bought the property. He carried on building on the land (including Barnett Place in 1831) so that by 1837 there were three houses, eight cottages, a shop and a smithy.[3]

As well as the addition of cottages to those that pre-dated 1770, Edenfield's housing stock also grew when completely new rows of cottages were built. Some of these were the result of piecemeal development, where several years might pass between the building of the first and last houses in the row. A good example of this is Temple Row (136-150, Market Street). Today there are eight cottages here, but formerly there were three more at the south end of the row. Two of these were the first to be built and were put up in the late 1780s by John Nuttall, a stonemason. The third cottage was added in about 1804. Of the next four cottages (nos. 136-142), one was built between 1786 and 1790 by Thomas Duckworth, plasterer, and the other three joined on by John Haworth, clothier, who bought the property in 1791. The cottages did not cover all of the land that Haworth bought and after his death in 1804 part of the remaining open space was sold to Robert Barker who promptly built a house (no. 144), which was described as 'lately erected' in 1806. By the time that Barker needed to mortgage his property in 1824 he had added another three cottages. This meant that a row of eleven houses had taken over twenty years to build and consequently display variations in their construction. (No. 144, for example, is the only one with an arched door).[4]

A similar kind of piecemeal development took place in Bury Road. Here the landowner was Thomas Booth. In 1829 he sold off a small plot in one of his fields bordering the turnpike road on the left-hand side going downhill towards Dearden Clough. The buyer, Alice Sagar, built three cottages, which she called Pindle Place (now 47-51, Bury Road). In 1836, Booth began to make long term leases of plots of land on the other side of the road and the oldest cottages there date from that year. For example, Henry Heys, a cotton yarn dresser, leased 194 square yards of land for 999 years in April 1836 and on it were four cottages that he had recently built. These are now 106 and 108, Bury Road with two former dwellings at the rear. By the time the Ordnance Survey map was prepared in 1844-48 several other short rows of roadside cottages had joined those belonging to Henry Heys.[5]

One final example of an early 19th century row of cottages that grew bit by bit was at the north end of the village, where the laying out of new turnpike roads to Haslingden and Burnley created a tapering strip of land at the junction of the two. It was bought in 1815 by John Ramsbottom who had recently built a house, barn,

Early 19th century houses at the Guide Post built by John Ramsbottom and Richard and Robert Pickup, seen towards the end of their life in 1978.

stable and brewhouse on part of it. Two years later he sold the southern end of the land to Richard and Robert Pickup at the same time giving them the right to build up to the end of his house. We do not know exactly when the Pickups started to build on their piece of the land, but by the end of the 1830s their property consisted of a house, shop and two cottages. John Ramsbottom in the meantime had altered and added to his buildings so that they now comprised a beershop and five cottages.[6]

The third way in which cottages were built in Edenfield and its neighbouring villages in the first half of the 19th century was the increasingly common one of a new row being built all of a piece with a uniformity in appearance that some of their neighbours lacked. The earliest surviving example of such houses is at Rose Bank (165-193, Bolton Road North), which was built in about 1807.[7] Other examples include 821-849, Manchester Road, Ewood Bridge; Commercial Row or Bacup Row (4-26, Rochdale Road); and Brass Row (121-127, Rochdale Road, Turn). At Irwell Vale, the entire village consisting of two rows of cottages was built in one go in 1833.

A special example of houses built all at the same time is to be found in Sarah Street and Green Street at the bottom of Gin Croft Lane. Here their uniformity owes something to the peculiar history of their site. In 1761 a small piece of land called The Green was handed over to trustees and the rent from it used towards paying the wages of the village schoolmaster. By the late 1820s a cottage, tollhouse

2-6, Sarah Street, which were built in the late 1830s and were originally back-to-back with Green Street.

and the village lock-up were standing on part of the land and in 1835 the trustees decided to sell the remainder for building. It was divided into lots and auctioned at the Horse and Jockey on 3rd December. Lot one included the toll-house and lock-up (the cottage appears to have been demolished), while the other three lots comprised land which became the sites of Crown House and the buildings at its rear; Sarah and Green Street; and 12, Gin Croft Lane. Strict conditions were laid down for any houses that were built on the land. Each lessee agreed to build houses that were worth twice the yearly value of the ground, such houses to be built within two years and 'to be built agreeably to the plan produced at the time of Letting.' They also had to agree to make and maintain half of the street and passage adjoining their lots, the causeway in front of the houses were to be well flagged one yard wide, while the road between was to be paved with good stones, at least nine inches deep.[8]

It would be easy to think that most of the late 18th and early 19th century cottages were built by mill owners to house their workers. In some cases this was true: nearly all of the houses at Ewood Bridge that were built before 1850 owed their existence to the various people who ran the cotton mill, while at Irwell Vale the whole village was created to house workers at the mill. In Edenfield itself, Richard Rostron (1777-1861) built Commercial Row and seventy-two cottages in Exchange Street for his workpeople between 1812 and 1837. The latter consisted of three rows, of which only Barr Row, nos. 7-15, Exchange Street, survive.

It is clear that apart from the mill owners, other people were busy building houses in the first half of the 19th century. Some of them were craftsmen who had connections with the building trade. For instance, Edmund Nuttall, a stonemason, built two houses between 1785 and 1790 on a site now occupied by 98 and 100, Market Street. Similarly, in 1837, James Pickup, a joiner from Ewood Bridge, built four houses on the opposite side of the road at 115-121, Market Street.[9] Some of the other builders were perhaps first of all concerned with putting up business premises, but at the same time erected a few cottages. John Ramsbottom, who as we have seen built some of the cottages at Guide Post, was a common carrier so began by building a barn and stable for his horses and a house for himself before he added cottages to rent out. His neighbours, Richard and Robert Pickup, were shopkeepers, and they built a shop as well as three houses. At the other end of the village, another shopkeeper, Lawrence Duckworth, built himself a shop and house (Crown House) in 1839, with cottages at the rear in Gin Croft Lane.

A third group of builders were those who built as a speculation or investment where they intended to draw rents from the cottages they built. Badger Row (59-69, Market Street) seems to have been built in this way. They were put up in the 1780s by Lawrence Rostron, landlord of the White Horse (later the Horse and Jockey). In a similar manner in 1837 Edmund Pickup, saddler, bought a piece of land behind his house at the corner of Gin Croft Lane and Market Street (later the Volunteer Inn beerhouse). On this land he built a cottage (1, Gin Croft Lane), which he rented out.[10]

The Edenfield Female Union Society's houses in Eden Street pictured in 1938 when they had been condemned as slums.

Some houses were constructed with a particular set of tenants in mind. They were built by Friendly Societies, two of which put up so-called 'Club Houses' in Edenfield. The first was the Loyal Welcome Lodge of the Independent Order of Odd Fellows who began meeting at the Horse and Jockey in 1820. In 1825 and 1834 they took two building plots at the edge of a field near the junction of Burnley Road and Blackburn Road. Part of the land was used as the site for a timber yard and saw mill, but it was also partly occupied by two, and later three, houses. These became 196-200, Market Street. The Edenfield Female Union Society was formed at about the same time as the Odd Fellows and in 1822 they leased a plot of land on the north side of Eden Street, just off Bury Road. Here they built a pair of houses to which they later added another pair and a slightly larger house. Once completed these houses would have been let to members of the society at a modest rent. (A similar row of houses built in 1824 on the road between Ramsbottom and Holcombe Brook by another Female Union Society were rented at £4 per year).[11]

VICTORIAN TERRACES

From the mid-19th century onwards, terraced houses began to take the place of rows of cottages. One of the first of Edenfield's terraces is numbered 166-172, Market Street and dates from about 1843. In many ways these houses are similar in appearance to the earlier cottages, but they are altogether larger dwellings with higher ceilings and bigger window openings. They were, however, built using the 'watershot' method of construction in which the outer stones of the exterior walls were tilted in order to shed the rain. This way of building was soon to be superseded, and the houses numbered 271-295, Bolton Road North, Stubbins dating from about 1863 are one of the last examples of watershot houses to be built in the locality. From mid-century onwards, it was usual for houses to be built from 'rock-faced' blocks of stone. These had a rough protruding side that had been shaped using a special chisel called a pitcher. The fourteen houses in North Street, Strongstry, built in 1854 by the Porritts at a cost of £1,500 were perhaps the first terrace in the Edenfield district in which rock-faced stones were used. 14-20, Lodge Mill Lane at Turn built in about 1860 are another early example. Further examples from over fifty years later when the fashion for terrace building was coming to an end include 802-820, Manchester Road, Ewood Bridge (1911) and 8-24, Exchange Street (1913).[12]

Like the early 19th century rows of cottages, terraces could either be built in a single go or piecemeal. Examples of the former include Spring Bank Terrace (51-59, Blackburn Road, 1867), Eden Bank (84-90, Bolton Road North, 1882), 30-50, Lodge Mill Lane (1880), 51-63, Bleakholt Road (*c.*1887), and 31-49, Bleakholt Road (*c.*1894). Some of the piecemeal terraces were completed quite quickly, but others grew over a number of years. The long row numbered 102-136a, Market Street, for instance, began life in 1877 as six houses. A further four were added in the 1880s and

19th century terraces in Burnley Road built over a thirty-year period, beginning in 1872.

the remaining eight in the early 1900s. In a similar way, it took almost thirty years to complete three terraces on Burnley Road. These houses were built on plots of land taken from the Elton Banks estate by the Aitken family and left off on long leases to prospective builders. Ivy Cottages (58-60, Burnley Road) were the first houses to be completed in 1872. In 1880, they were joined by 50 and 52, which became the core of Banks Terrace. Further additions were made to both groups of houses in the 1880s and a start was made on what was to become the third terrace. Here the first house (no.76) dates from *c*.1884 and the unfinished state of its front corner clearly shows that it was intended that more houses should be added to its northern side. In fact, a gap, the width of one house was left and separates no.76 from 80-82, which were built *c*.1889. The three houses at the end of this terrace were added in 1894-5. Finally a further three houses were built on to Banks Terrace in the early 1900s.[13]

Whether built all in one go or over a number of years, most of the terraces have a fairly uniform appearance, differing only in details such as window and door surrounds, fascia boards and so on. The exceptions were some of the Porritt-built terraces. Stubbins Vale Terrace (1871) and South Terrace (1874), for example, are three-storeyed houses with steep gables, while the houses in Eden Bank are distinguished by large bay windows on the ground floor. Probably the most important reason for a certain uniformity in the late 19th century terraces was the introduction of controls that governed the layout and construction of new houses.

Porritt-built houses at Eden Bank dating from 1882.

Between 1872 and 1883 most of our area came under the jurisdiction of the Haslingden Rural Sanitary Authority[14] and after 1883 of Ramsbottom Local Board and then Ramsbottom Urban District Council. Each of these bodies had powers to require builders to submit plans to them and to ensure that any new streets and buildings conformed to bye-laws issued by the particular authority.

The Haslingden Rural Sanitary Authority published its bye-laws in July 1876 and thereafter there are several instances in which builders contravened the regulations. For example, in November 1877 the authority ordered that 'the attention of Messrs. Booth [the architects] be called to the infraction of the 12th Byelaw in reference to the premises being erected by Edenfield Co-operative Society.' The architects countered that they were unwilling to put in corbels to support the hearth stones and chimney breasts and the authority responded by withholding the certificate stating that the houses were fit for habitation. Faced with this decision, the architects must have carried out the necessary alterations to bring these houses (Hope View) up to byelaw standard. In the following year, William Rumney was forced to alter the houses he was building in Stubbins Street by making four houses into two, enlarging their flues and re-arranging the joists. Similarly in 1881, James Rostron contravened the bye-laws by having timber too near the flues of the houses he was building in Hardsough Lane.[15]

As well as providing controls to ensure a certain standard in new houses, the Sanitary Authority also employed a Nuisance Inspector and a Medical Officer of

Health who made monthly reports on some of the older properties in the area. In 1876, these officials found conditions were particularly bad at Pinfold and Crow Woods. At Pinfold, for instance, four cottages had no privvies, another three had just one 'broken down, dirty and deficient privy', while a blocked drain outside another cottage caused 'sewage matter' to run down the road. At Crow Woods, seventeen houses had only three privvies between them; there was an open drain and a huge heap of ashes piled at the end of one row of cottages. Conditions were no better elsewhere: a blocked sewer in Exchange Street, open drains in Sarah Street and Green Street, and at Chatterton the occupants of thirty cottages had to share just four privvies, some of which were 'in such a disgraceful condition as to be unapproachable.' Many of the houses dated back to the 18th century, but problems were found in dwellings of a more recent vintage too. The twenty-two back-to-back houses in West View and North Street, Strongstry (built 1864), were singled out because they had only four privvies, while the privvies for the houses on the opposite side of North Street (1854) were built 'on an objectionable system'. Threatened with legal action by the authority, the property owners soon took steps to improve the lot of their tenants by building extra privvies, covering drains and laying down sewers.[16]

Mill owners or other industrialists built many of the terraces as homes for their workers. In some cases the end result was the creation of almost entirely new settlements. The Porritts began this at Strongstry when they built North Street in 1854. They added North View and West View in the 1860s, South Terrace in the 1870s and Strongstry Bridge in the 1880s. Similarly at Stubbins in 1850, there were no buildings between the railway bridge and the river bridge except for the toll bar. Changes began in the 1860s when the Ramsbottom Spinning and Manufacturing Co. built Union Mill and a row of houses at the side of the turnpike road. Over the next twenty years or so they added more houses further along the road and in Dale Street. Their building programme was matched by that of the Rumneys, owners of Stubbins printworks, who began building in Stubbins Street in the 1870s and in Bolton Road North in the 1880s. By 1890, there were nearly ninety dwellings where forty years previously there had been just a single building. Developments at Turn were more scattered than at Stubbins, but here too the character of the community was altered by the terraces built in Rochdale Road, Bleakholt Road and Lodge Mill Lane by the Whittakers (quarry owners), the Nuttalls of Turn Mill and the Ramsbottoms of Lodge Mill. Houses built by mill owners continued to appear until the First World War, some late examples including 802-820, Manchester Road, Ewood Bridge built in 1911 by Anderton and Halstead Ltd., and Holcombe View, Chatterton, built in 1913 by the Cuba Mill Co.[17]

Like the mill owners, the second group of house builders after 1850 had predecessors in the early 1800s. These were the people who built as an investment, drawing an income from the houses that they rented out. In several cases, these people were also building homes for themselves. For example, Jordan Rostron, one of

Hope View, the second row of houses built by Edenfield Co-op. The photograph was taken in about 1904.

the woollen manufacturers at Hardsough Mill, built 57-61, Burnley Road in 1875. He went to live in no. 57, but 59 and 61 were let out to James Gladstone, gardener, and William Butterfield, draper. There was a similar situation just across the road at Banks Terrace where Abraham Casson built two houses in 1881, lived in no. 48 and rented out no. 46. At the opposite end of the village in Bury Road nos. 66-70 were built by Thomas Wolstenholme, joiner and builder, in about 1857. He moved his large family into one house and let out the other two.[18]

Slightly different from those who built as an investment for themselves or their families were the speculative builders who built solely to sell the finished houses. Of course, it was a fine line between the two and there were those who had a foot in both camps. The Wolstenholmes, for instance, as well as building houses for themselves in Bury Road, also built 5-11, Bolton Road North in about 1894, which they then sold. Most of the terraces built by speculative builders were put up in the years just before the First World War. Many were the work of Alfred Worsick (1867-1937) who combined painting and decorating with the building trade. His terraces include 8-24, Exchange Street (1913), 1-9, Bond Street (1914) and 69-89 Bury Road (1915).[19]

The successors to the Friendly Societies as builders in the second half of the 19th century were the members of the Edenfield Industrial and Provident Society Limited (the Co-op). They opened shop in 1859 and by 1868 had become prosperous enough to build their own store and meeting hall. At the same time they built a row

Turnbull and Stockdale's distinctive semi-detached houses in Woodlands Road, built in 1913.

of six houses for their members, which they named Industrial Terrace. In 1877 they added a second row further along Market Street (Hope View, nos. 102-112).

Until the early years of the 20th century, all of the terraces were built of stone, but brick began its rise to prominence at Holcombe View, Chatterton (1913) and Bond Street (1914). An equally significant change also took place in 1913. The Ramsbottom Urban District Council Surveyor's report in July of that year noted:

> A plan for laying out of land in Bolton Road North, above Eden Bank, is submitted on behalf of Messrs. Turnbull and Stockdale. It is proposed to lay this estate out on garden city lines and the initial erection of three pairs of semi-detached cottages is contemplated … The intention in the lay out is to dispense with back streets … The idea of introducing grass verges at the side of the carriageway is one which has been adopted in other towns with success, and when trees are planted in the grass plots, a pleasing effect is obtained.[20]

The houses numbered 1-11, Woodlands Road, were the only dwellings completed under this scheme, but they heralded much of the housing development of the inter-war years and after.

MILL OWNERS' MANSIONS

In the late 18th and early 19th centuries, some of the families who had been land owners in the district for generations decided to rebuild their old homes or to build

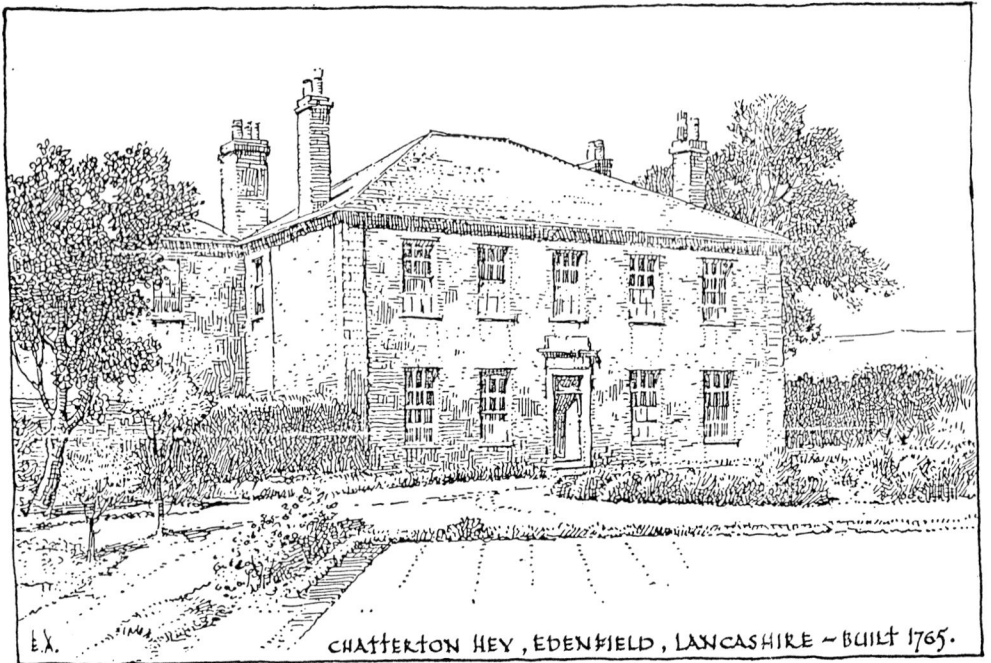

CHATTERTON HEY, EDENFIELD, LANCASHIRE ~ BUILT 1765.

Chatterton Hey.

completely new houses. At Chatterton Hey, for instance, the Haworths replaced their old home with the elegant Georgian dwelling that stands there today. Another branch of the same family moved from their traditional home on the Balladen side of Horncliffe to Horncliffe House, which they built in about 1820. (This was itself replaced by the present Horncliffe House in the 1860s). At about the same time the Elton family abandoned the farm that had their home for at least three hundred years to move to Elton Banks House. This house was partially rebuilt in the 1860s by Captain John Aitken and alterations at some other old houses continued into the early years of the 20th century. They included changes at Mount Pleasant (renamed The Mount) where Edwin Barlow added a billiard room in 1909.[21]

The new mill owners also needed new homes. Brick House (now Hawthorn House) was one of the first, dating originally from the 1770s. It was associated with Dearden Clough Mill and until the second half of the 19th century was generally rented by whoever was running the mill. This meant, for example, that James Porritt lived there from 1837 to 1851, before his business moved to Stubbins Vale. A second dwelling, Dearden Clough House, was built nearer the mill probably in the 1790s and it too became the home of one of the Porritt brothers (Joseph) for a time. Other fairly modest mill owners' houses joined these two dwellings in the early 19th century. Two of the earliest were Edenwood House and Acres House, both dating from about 1806 and both built by the Rostron family. They have been demolished, but still standing is Chatterton House described in 1821 as an 'excellent new-built house standing upon a pleasant eminence at a convenient distance from the works.' Other houses of a similar character include Higher House (47, Market Street), home of the Wallworks of Plunge Mill, built in 1842 and Lumb House built in the 1850s on the hillside above Lumb Mill. More modest still are Hollins Villas, Whalley Road (built in the 1880s) and home to George Ramsbottom, a partner at Lodge Mill and John Clegg, whose family ran Dearden Clough Mill.[22]

While these houses were much larger than the simple cottages in which most people lived, they were themselves dwarfed by the mansions that some mill owners began to build in the 1840s. These houses standing in their own grounds were designed to accommodate large families and a full staff of servants and, at the same time, show off the wealth of their owners. Rose Bank House (now demolished) was the first of these huge houses to be built and dated from about 1840. Stubbins Vale House, The Cliffe and Green Mount, the homes of the three Porritt brothers, followed it in the early 1850s. They cost £2,100, £1,730 and £1,820 to build, compared with a total of £1,500 for the fourteen cottages and a shop built in North Street at about the same time. Considerable additions had been made to each house by the end of the century, but Horncliffe House overshadowed them all. Designed by local architect, Richard Williams, it replaced the older Horncliffe House in 1869.[23]

Stubbins Vale House, the home of James Porritt, pictured in the early 1900s with its huge conservatory at the rear. Stubbins Vale Terrace is just visible in the background.

Details of the rooms found in these houses give us some idea of their scale. At Green Mount in 1859, for example, there were breakfast, dining and drawing rooms, two kitchens, scullery and pantries on the ground floor with cellars underneath, while upstairs were five bedrooms, a dressing room, closet and bathroom. In 1899, Horncliffe House contained an entrance hall, drawing room, morning room, smoke room, dining room, lavatory, servants' hall, kitchen, larder, store room and butler's pantry on the ground floor; five bedrooms, dressing room, day and night nurseries, housemaid's closet, bathroom and WC on the second floor; and four bedrooms and a box room on the third floor. The house even had central heating on the ground floor.[24]

These huge dwellings did not stand alone, but were surrounded by grounds that were as splendid as the houses themselves and which also contained a range of ancillary buildings. In 1880, at Rose Bank, there were stables, harness room and coach house, dog kennels, a fernery, greenhouse, vinery and cucumber house, potting shed and a cellar for mushrooms. Stubbins Vale House had similar out-buildings as well as a conservatory with a 36 ft. high central tower. Horncliffe House could also boast a peach house, underground icehouse, two summerhouses and a serpentine lake in its gardens. As for the grounds themselves, the following description of The Cliffe in 1908 gives us a good idea of what these gardens were like when they had a full complement of staff to look after them:

> The grounds are being steadily cultivated, and in the course of time they will embrace all the appurtenances befitting this charming country estate. There is an orchard in the dell on the left; and nearer the house a tennis court is being laid out. The lawn to The Cliffe is emblematic of a motor-wheel, and is bedded with over a thousand plants, the border to this plot being of blue lobelia. Standard roses circle the edge of the lawn. The main sweep of gravel leading to each residence is avenued with beeches, copper beeches, and silver birches in rare profusion ... The flowering plants and shrubs looked refreshed and diffused the most acceptable perfumes after the rain, and the appearance of a gentle sunshine drew forth the full glory of the flowers. [25]

At the start of the 20th century, those families who fifty years previously might have aspired to a house the size of The Cliffe or Horncliffe House instead erected smaller detached houses. Usually built of brick and stucco, they were more modern and easier to run than the huge houses of the 19th century. Dr. Henry G. Deans was the first to have a 'villa' built for himself. This was 'Newlands' in Market Street, dating from 1909. In the next few years it was joined by 'Highbury' and 'Croft Hey' (both 1910) and 'Crosmoor' (1914), all built by members of the Turnbull family, partners at Rose Bank printworks.[26]

COUNCIL HOUSES

By the end of the First World War there was an acute shortage of houses of sufficient quality for the men returning from the trenches. To remedy the situation, the Housing Acts of 1919, 1923 and 1924 brought in schemes to subsidize local

The height of elegant living: Horncliffe House in about 1910.

Newlands, the newly built 'villa' home of Dr. Deans in 1909. The distinctive chimneys were removed several years ago.

authority building using central government finance. Ramsbottom Urban District Council bought just over eight acres of land near Bolton Road North from Turnbull and Stockdale Ltd. and began their plan to build fifty houses in June 1920. The Ministry of Health provided model designs for the types of houses that could be constructed and which fell into two types: without a parlour (A type) or with a parlour (B type). Thirty-one of the Edenfield houses were B type, the remainder A type. Tenders for building were let to local men Walter Castle and Alfred Worsick and all of the houses were built of brick with pebble dashing above the stringcourse. Work on the new houses progressed rapidly and by May 1921 the first residents could move into their new homes in Oaklands Road and Central Avenue. The *Ramsbottom Observer* noted with approval:

> Good iron baths, white enamel glazed, are being fixed in the houses, and bath and lavatory taps of gun metal, with easy cleaning fittings. Gas cookers and gas boilers are also provided, and in the living rooms care has been taken to install a sufficiency of shelving, together with cupboards and coat hooks.

By the end of the following year all fifty house had been completed and a representative from the *Master Builder and Associations' Journal* who inspected them felt that: 'Altogether the scheme and houses are quite attractive, and have added considerably to the amenities of the town and district.' A further thirty houses were added to the estate in 1926-7 and in the meantime Haslingden Borough Council's house building schemes had included twelve houses in Manchester Road, Ewood Bridge.[27]

No further council houses were built in Edenfield until after the Second World War when under the Housing (Financial and Miscellaneous Provisions) Act 1946, local authorities were paid a subsidy to provide new houses. Ramsbottom Urban District Council restarted its council house programme in 1948 when it announced it intended to build at Acre Meadow, to the north-east of the 1920s estate. The scheme brought protests from the residents of the privately owned inter-war semis in Highfield Road and Eden Avenue, which flanked the site. One lady said 'I strongly object. It will definitely devalue our property and deteriorate it', while another thought that 'Councils put all sorts of folks into their houses and to do so would lower the class of the district.' Despites these protests, the scheme went ahead. Initially the estate was to consist of twenty three-bedroom and ten two-bedroom houses. A series of labour shortages in the building industry put paid to these plans and in June 1951 moves were made to build fifty pre-fabricated houses. Building began in June 1952 and by the end of July 1953 thirty-three houses had been completed in Highfield Road, Eden Avenue and Rawsthorne Avenue. By this date disputes had arisen between Prefabricated Constructions Ltd. (the firm that had won the contract) and some of their sub-contractors and all work ceased. It was not until May 1954 that the last houses (9-15, Eden Avenue) were completed. Further additions were made to the Acre Meadow site in 1965 when flats were built in Highfield Road. In the early 1990s, several of the houses built in the 1950s had to be

Homes fit for heroes: 1920s council houses on Bolton Road North.

demolished or partially rebuilt because the steel strengtheners in the concrete wall supports had corroded.[28]

The second site where council houses rubbed shoulders with private dwellings was on Pin Meadow at Stubbins. The council acquired the site in 1952 and initially planned to build twenty-five houses and four flats. Alterations to the plans in 1956 added six more flats, making a total of thirty-five dwellings in all. Building began in 1957 and the first seven flats were occupied in 1959. In March of that year, the new homes witnessed a ceremony that was probably unique in the history of local authority housing. The Rev. Leonard L. Boulton, vicar of St. Philip's, accompanied by the choir, Guides, other church members and representatives of the Urban District Council, blessed each flat and welcomed the new tenants to his parish.[29]

SPECULATIVE BUILDING AFTER 1918

In the inter-war years Edenfield shared in the revolution in housing that affected the whole country. Private builders took advantage of low wages and the low cost of materials to build houses for sale, while low interest rates made it easier for more people to afford a mortgage and buy their own home. In addition, the 1923 and 1924 Housing Acts introduced subsidies for private builders as long as the houses they built met certain minimum standards. In the village itself private housing was on a fairly small scale in the 1920s: a few houses were built on plots adjoining Bolton Road North, Rochdale Road and Burnley Road as well as in quieter spots such as Gin

Croft Lane and north of Pinfold (Moorlands View). The 1930s witnessed the real housing boom. Further development took place along the main roads, but builders increasingly looked to neighbouring fields and gardens as sites for their houses.[30]

The first of such housing developments was at Acre Meadow where the layout of the new estate was approved in 1932. Building began in the same year and in 1933 the new roads were christened Eden Avenue and Highfield Road. By the end of the decade there were thirty houses on the estate. Building on any scale also started at Pin Meadow, Stubbins in 1933, although a bungalow had been put up on the edge of the site in 1930. Houses were added in Robert Street, Gilbert Street and William Street and two new roads – Meadway and Alderway – were laid out.[31]

Most of the new houses were detached or semi-detached with a basically similar internal plan. 'Character' was added to each house by altering its external appearance, adding bay windows, leaded-lights and so on or by varying the design of windows and doors. One typical example of these houses is 89, Eden Avenue. Built in 1938 of Accrington brick with a blue slate roof and double bay windows, it consisted of a hall with a panelled staircase, lounge, dining room, kitchenette with half-tiled walls and Aga cooker, larder, three bedrooms and bathroom. At Pin Meadow, probably because of the more confined nature of the site, the houses were built in short terrace-like rows of four or five. Bungalows also became popular and appeared scattered around the district in the 1920s and '30s.[32]

As in previous years, some of the inter-war houses were intended as prospective homes for the people who had them built. One example is The Bungalow, Burnley Road built in 1924 for James Cunliffe, managing director of Thomas Aitken and Son Ltd. The vast majority of the new houses, however, were put up by speculative builders and sold once they were completed. A number of local builders, including Alfred Worsick, whom we have already encountered as a builder of terraced houses, erected the semis in Bolton Road North, Rochdale Road, Burnley Road and Gin Croft Lane, but nearly all of the houses on the Acre Meadow estate were the work of Walter Castle from Ramsbottom. Similarly, James Pate who lived at Lumb, concentrated mainly on Moorlands View and Hawthorn Avenue, a new street built in the grounds of Hawthorn House in 1935-6.[33]

After the Second World War very little private housing was built around Edenfield for some years. The odd house or bungalow appeared in the late 1940s and early 1950s, including 'Cockridge', 'The Firs' and 39, Moorlands View, but it was not until the 1960s and 70s that private housing developments on any scale began. Some of the new houses simply filled in the gaps left during earlier developments and found themselves rubbing shoulders with Victorian terraces or 1930s semis. A second group of houses took the place of demolished cottages, farms and mills. The last thirty years or so of the 20th century, however, were most marked by entire fields disappearing beneath new estates. The first of these developments began in a field belonging to Lane End Farm off Bolton Road North where building started in the late 1960s. It was soon joined by Dearden Fold off Rochdale Road, Alderwood

Inter-war housing in Highfield Road. These semi-detached houses were built in the early 1930s.

Grove and, in the early 1990s by Heycrofts View (although these houses were not entirely taking a green field site since they partly stand on the site of Orange Square and Barnett Place). The other villages were not immune to the rash of new houses: between Irwell Vale and Lumb, for instance, 'Meadow Park' was built in the 1970s, while at Ewood Bridge the steep slope above Manchester Road was chosen as the site for a new estate in 1972. Unfortunately the land was unstable and the estate was never fully completed. Nearly all of these houses were built of brick (although not Accrington bricks that were used in the '20s and '30s). Most were quite plain with low pitched roofs and large oblong or square 'picture' windows, although the Georgian style with pedimented porches, small-paned windows and the like was popular too.

SLUM CLEARANCES

As well as encouraging house building, whether by local authorities or private individuals, inter-war governments also turned their attention to the slum dwellings that existed in their thousands up and down the country. Under the 1936 Housing Act, Ramsbottom Urban District Council began a slum clearance programme and in 1938 made a start on doing away with some of the poorest houses in Edenfield. They created clearance areas at Esk Street, Crow Woods and Eden Street. All of these houses were over one hundred years old and were showing signs of their age. Most had sagging roofs, twisted or cracked walls and suffered from rising damp.

Each house also contravened council bye-laws in a number of ways: rooms were too small and badly ventilated, there was insufficient light from the small windows, there were no back doors, rear yards, hot water supplies or baths and all had outside pail closets for their 'sanitary accommodation'.[34]

Before these houses could be demolished the Second World War broke out and they were granted a stay of execution while they were used as temporary homes for refugees. One row of cottages at Lumb was demolished during the war, but others condemned at the same time survived for some time because of the housing shortage that followed the war. They included 94, 94A and 96 Market Street and 3 and 5, East Street, which were not demolished until 1955-56. By the end of the 1960s several other rows of cottages had been condemned and demolished. They included part of Temple Row; cottages near the site of Plunge Mill; Orange Square and Barnett Place; 88-92, Market Street; 71, Rochdale Road; High Street and Bridge Street (Ewood Bridge); Violet Street (Chatterton) and 265-271, Rochdale Road and 1-5, Scout Fold, (Turn).[35]

There were some houses that, although condemned at the same time as these slums, survived in one of two ways. Some, while declared unfit for human habitation, were used for other purposes. Number 20, Kay Street, at the rear of 110, Bury Road, was condemned in 1939, but the council agreed that its owner, John Nuttall,

5-8, Esk Street, Edenfield in 1938.

could use it as a store or workshop. Many other houses were condemned because they were back-to-backs. Here the solution was to break through the dividing wall to make them into through houses. This happened with 171-173, Market Street/2-4, Yew Street; 1-5, Green Street/2-6, Sarah Street; 1-5, The Park/1-5, Mint Street and 4-8, Mint Street/3-7, Well Street North.[36]

NOTES

[1] RO 3rd June 1910

[2] Edenfield parish records: 1777 survey, 1790 survey (MCL: MF PR 117a); Manor of Tottington records (LRO: DDHCL liber Z, folio 581; liber OO, folio 219); BT 8th February 1879

[3] Edenfield parish records: 1777 survey (MCL: MF PR 117a); Manor of Tottington records (LRO: DDHCL liber X, folios 452-453; liber L, folio 92; liber Q, folio 398; liber FF, folio 649; liber HH, folio 196); Tottington Higher End valuation 1837 (LRO: MBH 5/6)

[4] Manor of Tottington records (LRO: DDHCL liber Q, folio 529; liber CC, folio 160; liber R, folio 236; liber DD, folio 337; liber QQ, folio 425); Edenfield parish records: 1790 survey (MCL: MF PR 117a)

[5] Manor of Tottington records (LRO: DDHCL liber TT, folio 162; liber ZZ, folio 390)

[6] Manor of Tottington records (LRO: DDHCL liber II, folio 388; liber KK, folio 555); Tottington Higher End valuation 1837 (LRO: MBH 5/6)

[7] BT 12th February 1859; RO 23rd January 1914

[8] Endowed charities (Lancashire) returns, vol. IV, (1908); Edenfield parish records: 'Conditions ... for letting a close of land in Edenfield called the Green for building ground' (1835) (MCL: MF PR 117a)

[9] Manor of Tottington records (LRO: DDCHL liber Q, folio 528; liber AB, folio 570); Edenfield parish records: 1790 survey (MCL: MF PR 117a)

[10] Manor of Tottington records (LRO: DDHCL liber P, folio 496; liber AB, folio 326); Tottington Higher End valuation 1837 (LRO: MBH/5/6)

[11] PP, Report of the Registrar of Friendly Societies in England, 1875 (408) LXXI; Manor of Tottington records (LRO: DDHCL liber QQ, folio 711; liber XX, folio 388; liber CB, folio 666); Preston Guardian 26th April 1879

[12] Manor of Tottington records (LRO: DDHCL liber AH, folio 271); A. Muir, The history of Porritts and Spencer, [typescript], (1966), appendix XII; Derby estate instruction for leases book, 1856-1861 (BAS: BWO/T1909); Walmersley with Shuttleworth valuation list 1863 (LRO: PUB 8/8); RO 13th December 1912; Haslingden Borough Council minutes 19th June 1911

[13] Haslingden Rural District Sanitary Authority minutes 9th November 1881 (LRO: SAH/1/2); Derby estate instruction for leases books 1878-1882, 1885-1892, 1892-1896 (BAS: BWO/T1911; T1912); 1881 census Tottington Higher End (PRO: RG 11/4136); I. Slater, Royal Commercial Directory of Bury, Heywood, Radcliffe, Ramsbottom and districts, (1888); Ramsbottom North Ward valuation lists 1895 and 1910 (LRO: PUB/8/104 and PUB/8/162); Manor of Tottington records (LRO: DDHCL liber DA, folios 640 & 645; liber DG, folio 744; liber DR, folio 693)

[14] Turn came under Bury

[15] Haslingden Rural Sanitary Authority minute books and letter book (LRO: SAH/1/1; 1/2; 2/1)

[16] Bacup Times 20th May, 17th June, 26th August, 1876;

[17] A. Muir, op. cit., Appendix XII; Lease 13th January 1862 (BAS: GRI/T1676); Walmersley with Shuttleworth valuation lists 1864 and 1876 (LRO: PUB 8/10 & PUB 8/45); BT 20th January 1883; Haslingden Rural Sanitary Authority minute books 1872-1879 and 1880-1883 (LRO: SAH/1/1 & SAH/1/2); Derby estate instruction for leases books 1869-71, 1875-77, 1878-82, 1885-92, 1892-96 (BAS: BWO/T1910; T1911; T1912); Haslingden Borough Council minutes 19th June 1911; RO 11th October 1912

[18] Manor of Tottington records (LRO: DDHCL liber BA, folio 442)

[19] Agreement for lease 29th September 1894 (LRO: DDX/1777 uncat. Box 1); Ramsbottom North Ward valuation list 1895 (LRO: PUB 8/104); RO 13th December 1912, 13th February 1914, 9th July 1915

[20] RO 11th July 1913

[21] Bacup Times 21st July 1877; RO 20th November 1908, 11th December 1908

22 Manor of Tottington records (LRO: DDHCL liber DD, 346; liber AG, folio 351); Manchester Mercury 10th April 1821

23 A. Muir, *op. cit.*, Appendix XII; Bacup Times 26th November 1898

24 BT 31st January 1859; Sale particulars for Horncliffe House 1899 (Rawtenstall library: RC 728 HOR)

25 Poor Law valuations 1880-1882 (LRO: PUH/5/2); RO 28th August 1908

26 RO 8th October 1909, 11th February 1910, 12th June 1914

27 J. Burnett, *A social history of housing 1815-1970*, (1978), pp. 221-229; RO 11th June 1920, 2nd September 1921, 8th December 1922; Haslingden Observer 7th August 1926

28 RO 19th November 1948; Acre Meadow and Pin Meadow estates files (BAS: ARM/T958)

29 Pin Meadow estate file (BAS: ARM/T958); RUDC cuttings book 1953-1957 (BAS: ARM/T967); RO 27th March 1959

30 RO 15th May 1925, 12th June 1925, 9th March 1928, 11th January 1929, 12th April 1929

31 RO 9th September 1932, 12th May 1933, 9th June 1933, 13th October 1933, 14th April 1934, 4th August 1934, 15th September 1934, 10th November 1934, 10th December 1937

32 RO 7th October 1949

33 RO 10th July 1936

34 RUDC slum clearance files 1938 (BAS: ARM/T301)

35 RUDC Health committee minutes 27th July 1944, 8th February 1940; RUDC Register of houses in clearance areas (BAS: ARM/2647/1)

36 RUDC Unfit houses file (BAS: ARM/T956)

FARMING

B Y THE END OF THE 18TH CENTURY, there were more than seventy farms in Edenfield, Ewood Bridge, Turn, Lumb and Stubbins. At one end of the scale were small-holdings like Collier Wives (at the bottom of Gin Croft Lane) of about nine acres and Four Acre on Dearden Moor (about 8¾ acres) – the name refers to its extent in customary acres. In contrast the larger farms extended to as much as ninety-six acres (Lumb Hall) and sixty-three acres (Ewood Hall). In both cases the size of these farms reflected their earlier histories as the centres of estates belonging to the local gentry. New farms continued to appear in the landscape until about the middle of the 19th century. Sometimes these newcomers were carved out of existing farms, a process that had been going on for a few hundred years. At the north end of the village, for instance, Lawrence Elton created a new farm between 1777 and 1790 by taking about twenty-one acres from Elton Banks and putting up a house and buildings at Pinfold. Half a century later in about 1840, an outlying barn on Alderbottom land was converted into a farmhouse to create Mushroom House Farm.[1]

The late 18th and early 19th centuries also saw the high-water mark of the cultivation of the former common land on Dearden Moor, which had first been doled out to local people in the early 1600s. In 1628, for example, Richard Cowpe of Horncliffe had received four acres on the moor 'att a place called Coldwell' and, although the land had probably been enclosed by the mid-17th century, it was not until the 1780s that a house and outbuildings were added to make Four Acre Farm. Another late arrival was Whitaker Pasture, part of whose land was not even enclosed until the early 19th century and where the house, cottage and barn were not built until between 1800 and 1822.[2]

South of Dearden Brook, within the boundaries of the manor of Bury, which belonged to Lord Derby, the enclosure of the commons on any scale did not begin until the mid-18th century and continued into the early 19th century. The first grant of land from the moor was made in 1749 when Richard Booth received almost 106 acres on Scout Moor. In the following year and in 1751, a further thirteen leases were drawn up for pieces of Scout Moor and Shuttleworth Moss. These grants were much smaller than that made to Richard Booth, ranging from about three to about eleven acres. In each case the lessee agreed to enclose the land with a stone wall within a given period (usually three years) and to 'improve all improveable parts so as to render them arable and productive of corn and grass if the same by liming or other common means of husbandry be capable of being so improved.' This work was to be carried out within seven years.[3]

Most of the lessees kept to the bargain and by about 1790 most of Shuttleworth Moss and at least part of Scout Moor had been enclosed. For example, in 1751 Ann

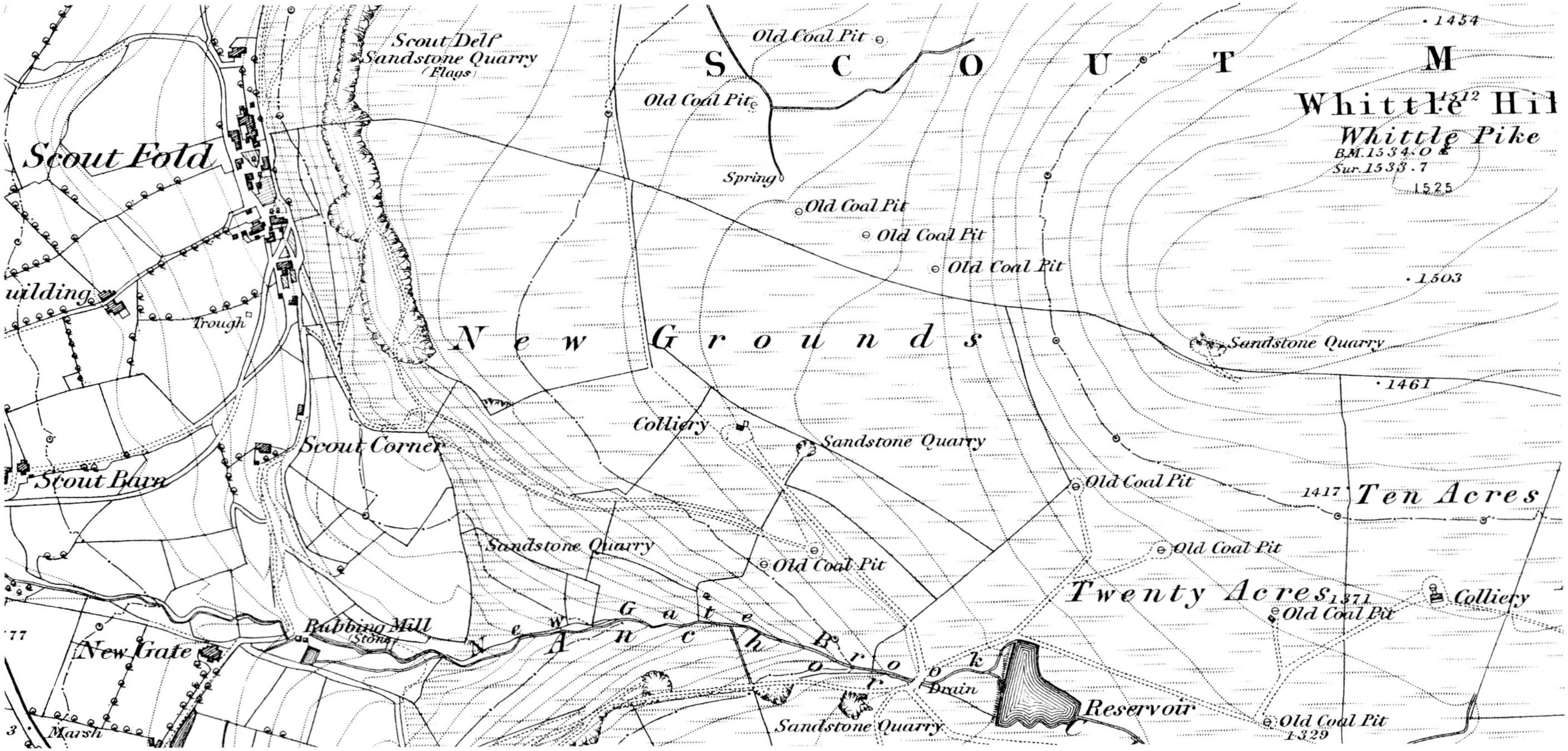

M O U N T

Whittle[12] Hill

Whittle Pike
B.M.1534.0
Sur.1533.7

·1525

·1454

·1503

·1461

Ten Acres

1417

Twenty Acres 1371
Old Coal Pit
1329

·Colliery

Old Coal Pit

Reservoir

Sandstone Quarry

Old Coal Pit

Old Coal Pit

Old Coal Pit

S C O U T

Old Coal Pit

Old Coal Pit

Old Coal Pit

Spring

Old Coal Pit

New Grounds

Sandstone Quarry

Colliery

Old Coal Pit

Sandstone Quarry

Sandstone Quarry

Scout Delf
Sandstone Quarry
Flags

Scout Corner

Scout Fold

Trough

Scout Barn

Buildings

Babbing Mill
Woolen

New Gate

Marsh

18th and early 19th century enclosures on Scout Moor mapped by the Ordnance Survey in the 1840s.

Kay of Walmersley received part of Shuttleworth Moss, which she was to enclose within one year and improve within three. When the land was leased to another tenant in 1798 it consisted of two closes called Lower Moss and Higher Moss. These new enclosures with their straight walls stand out very clearly on the 1848 Ordnance Survey map and on Scout Moor have names like New Grounds, Twenty Acres, Ten Acres and Parts. The process of enclosure carried on until about 1810 when the remaining unenclosed part of Scout Moor was parcelled out to two individuals. John Collinge of Hapton (who later bought several farms on Dearden Moor) got the smaller of the two portions (about 134 acres), which was called Maunder Dyke or Higher Hill. The rest (about 345 acres) went to George Barcroft, an Edenfield shepherd. In both cases the land was to be enclosed with a stone wall within twenty years, although in Collinge's case a second lease later changed this to twenty. Given the height of the land and the poor nature of its soil, there was no obligation to improve it and it continued to be used for rough grazing.[4]

Some of the new farms in Edenfield had relatively short lives and were created when one of the landowners rented a few acres to a tenant who did not live in a traditional farmstead with its accompanying barn, shippon, stable and so on. One example was Cronstadt House (44, Bury Road) where James Brierley farmed a few acres (eight in 1861, three in 1871) when he returned to Lancashire after spending a few years in Russia. Further up the road was Babylon Farm (whose site is now occupied by 88, Market Street). Here in 1871 Ellen Warburton farmed six acres, while ten years later Robert Nuttall had seven acres as well as being a sand manufacturer. Both farms reverted to being ordinary houses in the 1880s. Similarly at Irwell Vale, Abel Hunt is said to have used 24, Bowker Street as a farmhouse, stored hay in 21 and had 26 for a shippon, probably for a few years in the 1870s.[5]

Several of the long established farms also disappeared in the 19th century. Some of them were casualties of changes in the landscape: Lumb Bridge End, for instance, which dated back to the 17th century, was destroyed by the East Lancashire Railway. Several other farmhouses saw themselves reduced to the status of plain dwelling houses as industry expanded. Greaves Farm at Dearden Clough, for example, found part of its land taken as the site for two mills, reservoirs and tenterfields, while the so-called 'Great House' and 'Little House' at Stubbins had their land swallowed up by the printworks and Stubbins Vale Mill and their associated housing. Another example was Hudfield, some of whose fields were sliced up by the new turnpike roads to Rochdale, Bury and Bolton and further reduced as land was taken for Acres House and its grounds, cottages in Exchange Street and the Rostron Arms. Eventually the old farmhouse was left simply as a dwelling at the corner of Exchange Street and Market Place.

Another reason for farmhouses becoming ordinary houses or being lost altogether was one of economics. By the end of the 19th century some of the small farms like Collier Wives or Lane Side (Mangle Fold) in Elm Street had being swallowed by their larger neighbours, leaving their buildings without any land. Holme Meadow, which

Collier Wives Farm, Gin Croft Lane in 1988. The building on the left was demolished in the following year.

stood just north of the bridge over the River Ogden at Irwell Vale, was a farm of about ten acres in the early 19th century, but its land was taken away after the Parkinson family bought it along with the rest of the Ewood Hall estate in 1821. The house was made into four cottages and then demolished when the sewage works were built in the 1890s. Some of the remote, high farms on Dearden Moor and near Turn also began to be abandoned: in the 1891 census Four Acre, Grain Barn, Top of Grain Rake and Dungeon Farms were all uninhabited. The demise of some of the farms like Ringleton Fold and Pike Hill Slacks was hastened in the early years of the 20th century when their land became gathering grounds for the Scout Moor High Level Reservoir and the proposed Scout Moor and New Hall Reservoirs. Some of their neighbours lingered a little longer. Sand Beds, for example, was not abandoned until 1954 (although its land had been farmed separately for some time before that) and Foe Edge was occupied until 1977 and not demolished until 1979.[6]

CATTLE

The district appertaining to the range of hills ... extending to Blackburn and Burnley on the north and Bolton, Bury and Rochdale on the south ... is principally occupied as small dairy farms, there being a great demand for milk and butter.[7]

One of the many farm sale notices that appeared in the *Bury Times* in the 19th century. This one dates from December 1866. Daniel Revett whose stock was for sale at Lane End Farm also used part of Edenwood Mill as a sizeworks.

This comment was written in 1849 by the author of a report on Lancashire farming and it is clear that the farms in the Edenfield locality fitted this general pattern. Our main source of information for the 19th century is the notices that appeared in local newspapers when all or part of a farmer's stock was offered for sale. Using these notices to throw light on farming in the area has some limitations. To begin with, we do not know how many farm sales were not advertised in newspapers, but were instead announced by handbills and posters. Secondly, the sale notices do not always give a complete picture of the stock carried on a particular farm. In some cases, farmers may simply have been selling off surplus animals, while in cases where the farmer was said to be 'declining farming', or in other words was giving up the farm, some stock may have been disposed of prior to the sale.[8]

Despite these limitations, sale notices help to give us a snapshot of farming in the 19th century. Dairy cattle are nearly always first in the list of animals for sale, reflecting their importance in the economy of local farms. Some of the advertisements simply state that a certain number of cattle would be offered for sale. At Strongstry in June 1865, for instance, when the late Robert Duckworth's entire stock was sold, it included three dairy cows. Similarly in October 1880, James Walton, the Horncliffe quarry owner, sold eighteen head of 'milch cows.' Other notices are more detailed as in the case of Henry Whittam of Lumb Hall Farm who in December 1871 sold sixteen cattle, which included two newly calved dairy cows full of milk, two geld cows full of milk, four spring calvers and three promising stirks. A few years later in September 1877 the late William Lambert's stock at Scout Fold comprised five dairy cows (including three present calvers), two promising heifers and one rearing calf. One final example comes from Ashenbottom where Ralph Leeming was giving up the milk business in October 1887. His seventeen dairy cows included six lately calved, two to calve in November, two in December and several 'gelt' cows.[9]

Jordan Rostron, farmer at Hardsough, pictured with a fine shorthorn cow in about 1905.

At the beginning of our period, most, if not all, local farmers would have kept Lancashire longhorn cattle, but by 1815 a change had begun to take place and one agricultural writer noted that 'where milk is the principal object, the short-horned or Holderness sort is often met with (especially near the large towns in the southern and eastern parts of the county.' By the middle of the century, the change was almost complete and a second report from 1849 concluded that 'very few of the native long-horned breed, formerly so much esteemed, are now to be met with.' Many of the Edenfield sale notices in the second half of the 19th century mention horned cattle and no doubt it was the shorthorn they referred to. One advertisement specifically mentions the breed: at Horncliffe, James Walton had a shorthorn cow in calf, which had to be sold following his bankruptcy in 1885.[10]

The milk produced by these dairy herds was either sold around the villages and neighbouring towns or made into butter, which was also sold. There was some cheese making in the locality in the 18th century, which may have continued into the early 1800s but had died out by the second half of the 19th century. Most sale notices list 'dairy utensils' or 'dairy requisites' with some going into greater details. For instance, at Hardsough in 1859, Abraham and James Hindle had a churn and milk and butter basins, while in 1871 at Lumb Hall, Henry Whittam also had butter baskets, milk kits and milking cans. There were winch churns at Plunge (1874), Scout Fold (1877) and Hencock (1887), and in 1888 John Dickenson who was selling up at Chatterton Hey had a patent barrel churn.[11]

Mary Luty who lived at Brown Hill Farm as a child in the late 1880s later recalled butter making on this small moorland farm:

> I can well remember … when the cream was brought out of the cellar and allowed to warm a little, then poured into the tall tapering barrel called the churn. There was a long handle to this churn, fastened to some kind of a hook in one of the beams, to which a sloping handle was fixed almost like a pump handle, and one moved it up and down in the same way until the cream became butter. I can remember being lifted on to a chair, so that I could take hold of the handle and do my share on churning days. I was not allowed to help in any other way in the making of the butter, and this disappointed me. For the real excitement, I thought, came when the butter was being washed in icy cold well water, and the salt being added, my grandfather would call out, "Not too much salt now. I don't like to see butter crying."
>
> How I longed to able to pat the pound shapes or to put the stamp of the cow on each; but no, only sometimes I could persuade my mother to let me do this on the last pat, which would not weigh a full pound and, of course, would be used in the farm house.
>
> As the shapes of butter were complete, each would be stood on cool blue slates, and carried down into the cellar and stood on stone benches until someone took the butter to the town to be sold.[12]

Some farmers reared cattle for slaughter. Usually there were only one or two such animals on each farm. Typical examples included James Rostron with one fat calf in addition to ten calvers and milch cows at Chatterton Hey in 1858; John Taylor who had a fat heifer at Foe Edge in February 1881 and Joseph Kershaw of New Hall whose stock of twenty-six head of cattle included one fat cow in April 1886. Ralph Leeming at Ashenbottom had an unspecified number of beef cows as well as seventeen dairy cows and there were three beef cows at Hencock in the same year. Only one sale notice hints at beef rearing on a larger scale. This dates from September 1871 when William Rumney, the Stubbins calico printer, sold thirty fat 'Scots' three year olds, four fat heifers and one fat bullock at his Chatterton farm.[13]

SHEEP

Several farmers kept sheep as well as dairy or beef cattle. On some farms they apparently played only a minor part in the farm economy and were kept in small numbers. Joseph Kershaw's flock at New Hall in April 1886, for instance, consisted of only thirteen hogs (one year olds), compared with twice as many cattle of one kind or another. On the other hand, there were some farms where sheep were the most important livestock. These included Foe Edge with a flock of thirty-four in February 1881 and sixty-four in September 1888 and Pike Hill Slacks where there were eighteen sheep in March 1889. The numbers of cattle on the same farms in those years were seven, ten and three respectively. Both these farms were high moorland farms with poor fields and access to the moor for rough grazing. All of the

Sheep-shearing at Nuttall's Pack Horse Farm, July 1998.

flocks referred to in the sale notices were dwarfed by that kept by James Rostron, mill owner, at Chatterton Hey: in April 1858 he had 145 sheep. These animals could have grazed not only on the fifty-eight acres or so of land near the house, but also on another seventeen acres on Dearden Moor, which were associated with the farm.[14]

Only one breed of sheep, the lonk, is referred to in the sale notices. For example, John Taylor at Foe Edge in 1881 had twenty-five strong lonk ewes, eight one-year-old hogs and one lonk tup. Similarly at Pike Hill Slacks in 1889 there were seventeen strong lonk ewes and one lonk tup. The lonk, or Haslingden breed as it was also known, was said to be 'a hardy mountain breed of fair size, which make excellent mutton when fat ... They are horned, and have grey faces. Their wool is quite as good in quality as the Cheviot, and produces as heavy a fleece.'[15]

POULTRY

Poultry were kept to supply not only the needs of the farmhouse, but also as another source of income to add to takings from selling milk and butter. They were also kept by non-farmers like George Hoyle, greengrocer and beerseller, in Bury Road in 1881 and Dicky Bramoley, landlord of the Coach and Horses who died in 1884. Numbers ranged from just a handful, like the six kept by Henry Whittam at Lumb Hall in 1871, to sizeable flocks such as the seventy-four which Robert Duckworth had at Strongstry in 1865 or seventy at Sand Beds in January 1883. Some sale notices simply say that so many head of poultry or 'choice barn fowls' were on offer, but others are more specific. Ducks and geese were on several farms including Scout Fold (eight Muscovy ducks in 1877), Sky House (seven English geese in 1885) and Hencock (two breeding geese and a gander in 1887). Other farmers went in for ducks or geese in a bigger way: James Whittaker at Higher Ashenbottom in 1878 had twenty-four geese, six ducks and one drake as well as sixteen barn fowls. Only one farmer, George Nuttall at Gin Croft, had anything more exotic than hens, ducks or geese: his stock included several turkeys when he sold up in August 1876.[16]

PIGS

Most farmers kept two or three pigs, but again there were those who kept more. They included Daniel Revett who had five 'good store pigs' at Lane End in 1866 and John Dickenson with six store pigs and a breeding sow at Chatterton Hey in 1882. Recalling her childhood at Brown Hill at about the same time Mary Luty, declared that 'pigs were born to be killed and eaten.' Her recollections of what happened when the pigs were slaughtered could no doubt have applied to nearly any farm in the district at the time:

> I remember thinking my mother was rather foolish because she took me to the next farm so that we could not hear the awful shrieks and squeals of the pigs as they were caught and fastened on to a bench, where they were stabbed with a sharp knife and their throats slit to

allow the blood to be caught, which was mixed with barley and herbs and made into black puddings. I was keen to get back again to the farm and watch the boiling water being poured over the pigs as they lay on the stone bench out of doors. Then the men would take the shiny steel candlesticks used on the farm and scrape the hair from the pigs' skin. How nice and clean and pink the pigs looked when they were hung up in an outhouse and left there a day, or perhaps two, before being cut up and laid in salt…All kinds of different dishes were on the table after pig-killing. There would be for dinner one day "Black Dish" – liver and heart with sage and onions; then spare-ribs another day, and potted meat made from the head…Bacon was a staple item of diet in those days on the farm and provided many savoury meals during the cold winter days.[17]

HORSES AND DONKEYS

Until after the Second World War, most local farmers used horses as their motive power or for getting about their farms. They generally did not need more than one or two horses, unless they made part of their living from another business. For instance, James Whittaker had eleven 'valuable young cart and harness horses' in April 1878, but as well as farming at Higher Ashenbottom he had been a partner in the carrying firm of John Whittaker and Brothers until June 1875. Sale notices usually specify whether horses were for riding or for draught purposes. Hackneys and cobs for riding were offered for sale at several farms, while people like William Hopwood at Ewood Hall in 1876 had a brown mare bred 'for agricultural purposes.' Horses could, of course, be used both for riding and pulling carts or farm machinery. John Scott at Turn in 1873 had a pony 'for saddle or harness'; while in the following year John Ashworth at Plunge sold a 'very promising' iron-grey pony 'fit for cart or harness.'[18]

Some of the farmers who lived on the high farms did not have any horses at all, but relied instead on donkeys. These animals were found at Foe Edge in 1881 and Sky House in 1885. At Brown Hill, James Ramsbottom, Mary Luty's grandfather, used donkeys to carry goods to and from Waterfoot:

I do not remember ever being allowed to go shopping. But I used to watch as the donkeys were loaded up with baskets of eggs and butter. Farmers would sometimes borrow each other's donkeys. My grandfather had one known as "Owd Jennie", having the reputation of being bad tempered and cunning. At a certain point on the homeward journey she would frequently stop, kick up her heels like a Wild West broncho until she got the load off her back. This was a difficult task for the women folk to get it on again. Only the women folk drove the donkeys to town, which sometimes would be over the fringe of the moor, down by Borders and Lower Cowpe to Waterfoot, or down the other side of the moor to Edenfield.[19]

CROPS

Grass continued to be the most important crop grown by farmers in the Edenfield area and as the 19th century wore on arable was almost completely abandoned. In 1838, out of a total of 3,686 acres, there were nearly eighty-one acres of arable

Jim Nuttall from Pack Horse Farm and a group of village youngsters haymaking in a field off Market Street in the 1930s.

within the township of Tottington Higher End (which included most of the area we are looking at, except Turn), but by 1906 just seven acres of arable were to be found in the Ramsbottom area.[20]

Traditional methods of haymaking by hand using scythes, rakes and pitchforks were used on most farms until the 20th century, partly because new improvements cost money. However, by the mid-19th century a few machines for haymaking had begun to creep into sale notices. They included one for Lane End Farm in 1866 where Daniel Revett not only had a mowing machine, but also a hay-shaking machine to shake up and open out the drying grass, and a horse hayrake to gather the hay into swathes. William Hopwood at Ewood Hall in 1876 similarly had a single horse mowing machine and a single horse hay-shaking machine.[21]

Haymaking on most farms would have followed the more traditional pattern described by Mary Luty at Brown Hill:

In the summer time, when the grass had grown and, as they said, "ripened," a number of Irishmen would usually appear at the farm ... Those were the "good old days" before mowing machines were popular. Two, or perhaps more, of the gang would be known as mowers. How fascinating it was to watch them stand, the handle of the scythe resting on the ground and the shining blade held over the shoulder, as they whetted or sharpened it by means of a sandstone, round in shape, almost like a rolling-pin ... Then one would hear the steady swift stroke of the scythe as it moved through the grass, and the snake-like swathes would fall to the ground ... The whole family had to help with hay-making. After the grass was cut it was spread abroad by hand. Then, after being allowed to dry in the sun and wind, it was raked into long rows, and later stacked into heaps or "cocks." Another day it was spread abroad again, then raked into bigger rows and stacked in much larger "cocks", which were lifted, or forked, on to the hay wagons ready for the barn.

We children had sometimes to follow those who raked up the leavings from these larger "cocks" and carry the hay to one big pile. We soon tired of that job, but thought we were greatly privileged and very important if we were allowed to go on the hay mow and help to trample down the hay into a neat pile.[22]

In the first half of the 19th century, some local farmers continued to cultivate other crops on part of their land. Although potatoes and barley were grown in parts of Bury parish, the farmers around Edenfield concentrated on oats. There could be difficulties in growing even those. In November 1838, for example, Thomas Martin who visited Edenfield to report to the Tithe Commission noted,

The farming is not good, & the Crops, nearly altogether Oats, are usually late. This year, various fields were out on the 8th of November, & the Harvests are said to be frequently as late as in the present year.[23]

The cultivation of crops in the second half of the 19th century seems to have been confined to a few of the high farms. Mary Kershaw who sold up at New Hall in 1878 had a plough among her machinery (although, of course, it may not have been used for many years), while her neighbour at Sand Beds in 1883 not only had an iron plough and harrows, but also three stacks of oats.[24]

FERTILIZERS

For generations, local farmers had applied manure, marl and lime to their land to keep it in good heart and they continued to do so in the 19th century. At Lumb Hall, 3,000 loads of lime were put on the land before the tenant, James Crawshaw, took over the farm in 1828. Another 1,500 loads were spread in that year and Crawshaw agreed to apply sixty loads every year. Under the terms of another tenancy agreement in 1832 he promised to put fifty-three loads of lime on every acre he ploughed, but he was to confine his ploughing to one field a year. Lime was used on the moorland farms too. Once a year a team of lime 'gals' brought sacks of lime to a point near farms like Brown Hill and it was then carried to the surrounding fields on the backs of donkeys. After the tramway opened from Cloughfold to Ding Quarry, this was used to carry lime up to the farms instead of horses.[25]

As well as marl and lime, farmers continued to spread farmyard manure supplemented with 'night soil' from the privvies in the neighbourhood. Until after the Second World War, manure was usually spread from a cart using hand tools, but some farmers like James Whittaker of Higher Ashenbottom also discovered the value of liquid manure. In 1878 he had a liquid manure cart, which consisted of a large cask (containing about 150 gallons) mounted on wheels and supported between shafts so that it could be pulled by a horse. The manure was spread from a perforated tube at the back.[26]

One of the mid-19th century reports on Lancashire agriculture recorded another method of fertilizing the land that seems to have been unique to the area north from Bury to Haslingden, Rawtenstall and Bacup. The author said:

> In these localities, great attention is paid to this mode of fertilizing the land, and very early and abundant crops of superior hay are every season produced. Often cut the latter end of May or early in June, and frequently two or three crops in a season. Water is conveyed from higher land, or diverted from rivers, brooks, or other streams, and by grips made to flow over the surface of grass land, and taken off again at a lower level.[27]

FARMING IN THE 20TH CENTURY

A new century did not bring any great change in farming in the Edenfield district. Visitors to Lancashire agreed that the production and sale of milk, eggs and poultry was the usual way for East Lancashire farmers to make their living. In 1910, one commentator noted that all the farms 'depend on the sale of milk; they are mostly small, and the living is earned as much by the retailing as by the production of the milk.' Similarly in the 1930s, John Orr, a Manchester University lecturer said:

> The farms, villages, and towns are so intermingled among these hills that the market for milk is brought close to the cows. Scores of milk floats enter each of the East Lancashire towns and villages. In their capacity of salesmen, farmers get rid of their milk and eggs to the best advantage. Competition is keen.[28]

The detailed evidence available to us, dating mainly from the war years, confirms that the farms in Edenfield and its neighbourhood fitted this general pattern. During the Second World War, a National Farm Survey was carried out, partly to provide information for the ploughing-up campaign, which was designed to increase food production, and partly as the basis for post-war agricultural planning. Farms had to provide details of numbers of livestock, crop acreages and so on.[29]

The Edenfield returns show that nearly all farmers concentrated on keeping cows and poultry. At Kay Close, for example, Herbert Trippier had nine cows, five of which were in milk when he filled in his form, and fifteen hens. He spent two or three hours a day selling milk. In the village itself, Arthur Berry at Lane End was milking twelve cows and had twenty hens; Annie Crofts had nineteen cows in milk and 160 hens at Chatterton Hey; while Christopher Guy at Hollins Lane was milking twelve of his sixteen cattle and kept seventy hens. The largest dairy herds were those belonging to Richard Holt at Chapel House (thirty-eight cows in milk) and Frederick Nelson at Chatterton (thirty-two cows in milk). Both these farmers occupied land in addition to their home farm: Hey Meadow and Pinfold Farms in the case of Richard Holt and Dundee Lane Farm, Ramsbottom, in the case of Frederick Nelson.[30]

Richard Holt at Chapel House also had a large flock of hens (205). Other large poultry keepers included John Ormerod at Brook Bottom (150), James Whitworth at Elton Banks (124), Rosanna Rowles at Gin Croft (215), William Grimshaw at Acre Nook (100) and Henry Chadwick at Alderbottom (250). Joseph Pye at Grime Cote was by far the largest poultry keeper in the area with a flock of 380 hens. Other poultry included ducks at Kay Barn, Scout Barn, Great Hey and Alderbottom, and geese at Acre Nook and Alderbottom.

The wartime returns do not specify what breed of cattle local farmers kept, but they were almost certainly still shorthorns. James and Joseph Kay, who were well known as butchers in Edenfield and Ramsbottom in the inter-war years, made a speciality of breeding and showing pedigree shorthorns. At the Royal Lancashire Show in 1925 they 'had the distinction of being second to the King' in the class for short-horned heifers calved in 1923 with Edenfield Lady Geneva. Two other cows, Edenfield Mary and Edenfield Nanette, carried off twenty-three first prizes in 1928 and Nanette also won the Milk Recorded class at the Royal Lancashire Show at Oldham.[31]

Edenfield Mary and Edenfield Nannette, two prize winning cows belonging to J. and J. Kay.

The Kays owned several farms around Edenfield on which they raised cattle to supply their shops. The 1941 returns also show that some other farmers were raising beef cattle, although this may have been due to the special circumstances of the war. Such animals were kept in ones or twos, except at Pack Horse Farm where Richard Nuttall and Sons had twenty-one steers and heifers being fattened for slaughter before the end of November 1941 and at Scout Barns where Henry Holt similarly had nineteen steers and heifers bred for slaughter.

Of the twenty-five farms that were surveyed in Edenfield, Turn and Chatterton in 1941, only eight had any sheep. Most of these had access to rough grazing on the moors. George Foulds at Brown Hill had the largest flock consisting of 280 ewes and lambs and two rams, which he ran on Scout Moor. On the other side of the Dearden Brook, Henry Holt at Scout Barns also had grazing rights on Scout Moor, which allowed him to keep 152 ewes and lambs and two rams. Smaller flocks were kept at Elton Banks, the Pack Horse, Chatterton, Hardsough, Great Hey and Acre Nook.

Apart from horses, pigs were the only other animals recorded in the 1941 survey. They were kept on only eight farms and in small numbers. Joseph Pye at Grime Cote had the most with ten, but this included eight piglets. Some sows were in pig or were kept for breeding purposes, but there were two barren sows that were being fattened up and no doubt some of the two to five month-old piglets were being reared for the same purpose.

In normal circumstances, growing any other crops apart from grass almost entirely disappeared. In 1926, for example, when Lord Derby sold many of his farms in Turn and the surrounding area only part of one field at Bleakholt was classified as arable. The rest of the land was meadow, pasture or rough grazing. As we shall see in a later chapter, cereals and fodder crops were grown on several farms during the Second World War.[32]

THE LAST FIFTY YEARS

Since the end of the war, the decline in the number of farms has continued. Of the fifteen farms in Edenfield itself that sent in returns in 1941, only four are still working farms. The land of some of the farms that have disappeared or have become ordinary houses has usually been added to a neighbouring farm to create larger and more economic holdings. This was already happening in 1941. For example, Richard Holt at Chapel House also farmed land at Hey Meadow and Pinfold, while Robert Barker at Hardsough rented an additional thirty-three acres at Lumb Hall. Some of the farms like Brown Hill whose lands were stripped away have been demolished, while others like Windy Harbour and Ashenbottom have become simply dwelling houses. Others have fallen victim to the demand for new houses: Chapel House, for example, made way for Church Court in the early 1980s, while at Lane End the fields began to disappear beneath bricks and mortar, roads and gardens in the 1960s. The farm lingered on until the 1990s when the cottages were renovated and the barn converted into houses.

Chapel House, one of Edenfield's lost farms. Church Court now stands on the site. The name of the farm refers to its proximity to Edenfield chapel-of-ease (now the Parish Church).

There have been two great changes on the farms over the past half-century, whether or not they are still working today. The first of these is mechanisation. During the war this had barely begun. Most farmers had one or two horses 'for agricultural purposes.' Those that did not, tended not to concentrate on dairy farming and included Henry Chadwick at Alderbottom (poultry) and George Foulds at Brown Hill (sheep). Only two farmers had tractors: Richard Holt at Chapel House had a twenty horse-power Fordson and George Davies at Smithy Carr had a sixteen horse-power Hupmobile. Mr. Davies was classified as a part-time farmer who earned part of his living as a ploughing contractor. No doubt this explains why he had a tractor since his farm was only 9½ acres with ten acres rough grazing on which he kept ten cows, sixty hens and one pig. Within twenty years of the wartime survey, Edenfield, like most other places, saw the end of the horse's reign as the chief motive power for farming as tractors became commonplace. The survey also revealed that many farms had no supply of electricity and even those that did have power laid on used electricity for lighting purposes only. Again, the post-war years have seen the spread of the use of electricity for many purposes on the farm, in particular milking.

The second important change of the last fifty years has been to farm stock. Pigs and poultry have largely disappeared from local farms, although some farmers did specialize in these for a time. For example, in August 1955, William Smith at Ashenbottom had sixty store pigs, which he was fattening for sale to the Ministry of Food's Bacon Board and he intended to have 200 pigs. Dairy farmers have switched from the old shorthorns to Friesians, but have found their output restricted by milk quotas introduced in the 1980s. Today, most farmers in the Edenfield area concentrate on sheep farming.[33]

NOTES

1   Edenfield parish records: 1777 survey, 1790 survey (MCL: MF PR 117a)
2   Manor of Tottington records, Easter 1628 (LRO: DDHCL 3/110); Edenfield parish records: 1790 survey (MCL: MF PR 117a); Manor of Tottington records (LRO: DDHCL liber Z, folio 581; liber OO, folio 219)
3   Manor of Bury leases (LRO: DDK Boxes 214 and 260)
4   Manor of Bury leases (LRO: DDK Boxes 206, 214 and 260)
5   1861 census Tottington Higher End (PRO: RG 9/3059); 1871 census Tottington Higher End (PRO: RG 10/4139); RO 7th July 1933
6   Tottington Higher End tithe award and plan 1838 (LRO: DRM 1/97); Ewood Bridge deeds (Helmshore Local History Society collection); 1891 census Tottington Higher End (PRO: RG12/3352); Rossendale Free Press 29th September 1973
7   W. Rothwell, *Report of the agriculture of the county of Lancaster*, (1849), p 20
8   For information on the nature of sale notices see R. Dalton, 'Farm sale advertisements as a data source in historical agricultural study: possibilities and limitations', *The Local Historian*, (February 1998) 36 - 49
9   BT 17th June 1865, 9th December 1871, 29th September 1877, 16th October 1880, 1st October 1887
10   R. Dickson, *General view of the agriculture of Lancashire*, (1815), p. 542; G. Beesley, *A report of the state of agriculture in Lancashire*, (1849), p. 47; BT 3rd October 1885
11   BT 25th February 1859, 9th December 1871, 3rd January 1874, 29th September 1877, 5th November 1887, 5th May 1888
12   M. Luty, *A penniless globe trotter*, (1937), pp. 10 -11
13   BT 24th April 1858, 19th February 1881, 17th April 1886, 1st October 1887, 5th November 1887, 16th September 1871
14   BT 17th April 1886, 19th February 1881, 15th September 1888, 23rd March 1889, 24th April 1858
15   BT 19th February 1881, 23rd March 1889; W. Rothwell, *Report of the agriculture of the county of Lancaster*, (1849), p. 105
16   BT 10th December 1881, 8th November 1884, 9th December 1871, 17th June 1865, 27th January 1883, 29th September 1877, 9th May 1885, 5th November 1887, 20th April 1878, 19th August 1876
17   BT 8th December 1866, 30th September 1882; M. Luty, *A penniless globe trotter*, (1937), pp. 13 - 14
18   BT 20th April 1878, 23rd December 1876, 20th September 1873, 3rd January 1874
19   M. Luty, *My life has sparkled* [typescript], (1967?), p.7 (Rawtenstall library: RC 921 LUT)
20   Tottington Higher End tithe file (PRO: IR 18/4284); W. Farrer and J. Brownbill (eds.), *The Victoria history of the county of Lancaster*, vol. V, (1906), p.123
21   BT 8th December 1866, 23rd December 1876
22   M. Luty, *A penniless globe trotter*, (1937), pp.15 - 17
23   Tottington Higher End tithe file (PRO: IR 18/4284)
24   BT 30th March 1878, 27th January 1883
25   Estate memoranda book (LRO: DDFo/44/16); M. Luty, *My life has sparkled* [typescript], (1967?), p.7 (Rawtenstall library: RC 921 LUT)
26   BT 20th April 1878
27   W. Rothwell, *Report of the agriculture of the county of Lancaster*, (1849), p. 88
28   A. D. Hall, *A pilgrimage of British farming 1910-1912*, (1913), p. 233; J. Orr, 'Lancashire and Cheshire', in J. Maxton (ed.), *Regional types of British agriculture by fifteen authors*, (1936), pp. 60-61
29   W. Foot, *Maps for family history – a guide to the records of the tithe, valuation office and national farm surveys of England and Wales, 1836-1943*, (1994), p. 53
30   National Farm Survey, parish of Ramsbottom (PRO: MAF 32/564/94)
31   RO 31st July 1925; Diocese of Manchester – Parish church, Edenfield blotter 1929 (author's collection)
32   Sale particulars of the Bury and Pilkington Estates, 1926 (author's collection)
33   Haslingden Observer 27th August 1955

TEXTILES

IN 1770, EDENFIELD'S TEXTILE INDUSTRY was much the same as it had been for generations. Textile workers ranged from small-scale spinners and weavers to clothiers and chapmen. Clothiers bought raw wool, put it out to spinners and weavers, and sold the finished lengths of cloth to merchants in places like Rochdale and Manchester. They included John Haworth who lived at Stocks (the Yew Street area) at the end of the 18th century. He used some of the profits of his business to build additional houses at Stocks and in Temple Row and by the time he died in 1804 he also had a warehouse. This may have been part of Temple Row itself. There is a blocked taking-in door in the gable end of 150, Market Street through which raw materials and finished cloth could have been hoisted into and out of the working area, avoiding the living quarters. The very name of this row of houses suggests that it was used for handloom weaving since a temple was a device used to keep cloth taut in the loom. Chapmen brought supplies of wool and yarn to independent weavers and clothiers and also helped them to market their goods. There were at least two chapmen in the village in the late 18th century and, like John Haworth, they invested their money in property: James Heyworth bought Bank Nook Farm and property in Orange Square in 1774-5 and Robert Whittaker also bought some of the Orange Square houses in 1784.[1]

No doubt many other cottages in Edenfield and district were used for handloom weaving, first of wool and then of cotton, even though they have no distinctive architectural features such as long rows of windows or taking-in doors. Badger Row (59-69, Market Street) may have had handloom weaving in its upper storey, for example. In addition, there were purpose-built loomshops. That at the bottom of Fish Rake Lane adjoining the old Quarryman's Arms was demolished when the beerhouse itself was rebuilt in 1894, but still standing is Lime Leach at Turn. This three-storey building has a taking-in door in the eastern gable approached by an external staircase.[2]

By 1770 Edenfield had already taken its first step towards the mechanisation of its woollen textile trade with the building of a fulling mill at Dearden Clough in the mid-1760s. By about 1800 this mill had been joined by others at Chatterton, Plunge and Hardsough. Water-driven carding engines were often associated with these fulling mills. Thomas Booth, for instance, installed one at Dearden Clough in the 1780s and Dearden Clough Lower Mill, Hardsough Mill and Lumb Mill were also carding by waterpower in the early 19th century. The transfer to power spinning and weaving of wool took place more slowly, but Chatterton Mill was spinning wool by 1821 and woollen powerlooms had been introduced at Dearden Clough by 1836.[3]

With the meteoric rise of the cotton industry in the 19th century, wool declined in importance and many woollen mills were converted to cotton manufacture. The

The handloom weaving shop at Lime Leach, Turn, with an external staircase giving access to the workshop that ran the length of the top storey.

change took place gradually, however, and wool was never entirely ousted from the district. It continued to be used at Hardsough Mill, for example, for most of the 19th century and was central to the prosperity of Stubbins Vale Mill, which produced all sorts of woollen felts and cloths. At some of the other mills like Plunge, woollen fulling and cotton spinning were carried on in the same building.

Woollen workers at Stubbins Vale Mill in the early 20th century. The photographs show felts being washed (*above*) and thickened. In the latter process they were stitched into long loops and passed between weighted rollers in rotary milling machines.

THE INTRODUCTION OF COTTON AND THE POWERLOOMS RIOTS

By the beginning of our period, cotton had started to appear in the locality. In 1778, for instance, the Rev. John Smith noted that the 300 or so houses in Edenfield chapelry were inhabited by yeomen 'and manufacturers of cotton and woollen goods.' By 1804 he could report that the chapelry had four cotton spinning mills as well as a calico printworks and a bleaching ground. As with wool, waterpower was first applied to the preparatory processes in producing cotton cloth so, for example, in 1815 Ewood Bridge Mill had water-driven carding engines and drawing, slubbing and roving frames. Within a few years two firms – Lawrence and John Rostron at Bridge Mill and Aitken and Lord at Chatterton – had taken the next step and installed powerlooms for weaving cotton.[4]

The severe trade depression at the beginning of 1826 threw many handloom weavers out of work or allowed them to work only half time. One Haslingden youth later recalled:

> Cotton weaving got to starvation work in 1826. I don't think anyone could make above 9s a week, work as hard as they could … Salt was 4d a pound, broken sugar 8d and lump sugar 1s. But then working people didn't use much sugar. They had porridge and milk. I have had porridge twenty-one times a week … Powerlooms were getting into vogue … and farmers thought it was making trade so bad. [They] fancied the powerloom was going to starve them to death and they and other people turned out and broke the powerlooms.[5]

In Edenfield itself a woman said that she had been reduced to washing and boiling potato peelings that her children had picked up from an ash heap and that this was the only food the family had had to eat for two days. At the same time, an Edenfield weaver found that he was unable to sell the thirty-yard length of cloth he had woven, but had to exchange it for twelve herrings.[6]

On 26th April 1826 a mob estimated at between 3,000 and 4,000 people made its way from Rawtenstall to Edenfield intent on destroying any powerlooms in the village. At Bridge Mill, the Rostron brothers had had news of the approaching attack and, helped by a few loyal workers, had removed as many warps from the looms as possible so that the women in the mob could not slash them. John Rostron stood at the mill doors with the keys in his hand and tried to prevent the rioters from entering. One of the men struck him on the hand with a club and took the keys from him. Once inside the mill, the crowd quickly dispatched the fifty-eight looms as well as some of the spinning machinery. Two of the mob were sent to Dearden Clough Mill, but soon discovered there were no looms there. After Edmund Sagar, the mill owner, had given them some money and sent them on their way they turned their attention to the mill at Chatterton.[7]

William Grant, the Ramsbottom factory owner and JP, and a detachment of soldiers met the mob as it made its way down Chatterton Lane. Grant appealed for calm but to no avail and he decided to read the Riot Act. This meant that any

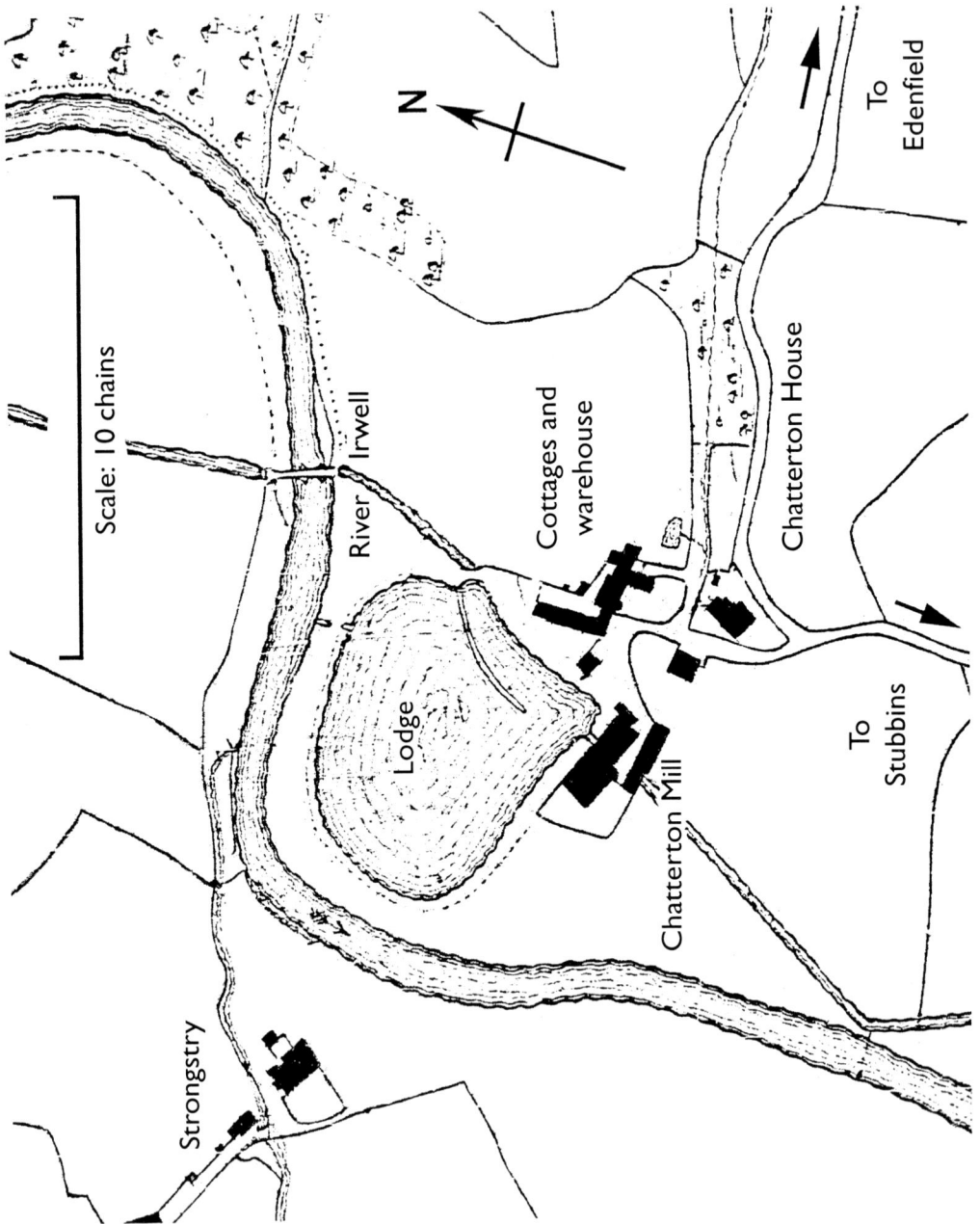

Chatterton at the time of the powerloom riots in 1826.

actions the crowd now took could be seen as a felony, punishable by death. The soldiers still barred the way down the lane so the rioters climbed over the wall and ran across the fields to the mill. Here they were faced with closed and barred factory gates and the mill owner, Thomas Aitken, standing before them. Some of the rioters demanded money and food from him, but when he made no reply one man shouted, 'Damn thi' then, thi mun tek care of thi'sel' afore two hours end! We'll finish thee before we leave.' Much alarmed, Aitken collected his family from his nearby house and fled the scene, not returning for two days. Mrs. Aitken is said to have been thrown into 'violent hysteric fits' by the experience.[8]

Some of the mob managed to break into the mill through the windows at the rear and began the task of destroying the looms. The remainder turned their attention to the soldiers, pelting them with sticks, earth and paving stones that were lying nearby. When the soldiers retaliated by opening fire on their attackers, the onslaught did not slacken. One man gave an indication of the mood of the crowd when he shouted, 'I'd rather be killed on this spot than go home to starve. I'm not leaving this place until every loom is destroyed.' Soon five people lay dead and many were injured, including Edward Hunt from Hollins Lane [Fish Rake Lane] in Edenfield who was shot in the abdomen. By this time all of the looms had been smashed to pieces and the mob started to disperse. But there was to be one more death. James Waddicar, an employee of the Rostrons, lived at Alderbottom and had earlier helped to remove warps at Bridge Mill. His death in somewhat controversial circumstances 'excited much interest and sympathy in the neighbourhood.'[9] Early in May 1826 the *Morning Herald* sent a reporter into Lancashire and he visited Edenfield to collect information on the riot and Waddicar's death. This is his account of what took place:

In a cottage near the mill lives Betty Upton, a young woman with one child, having buried her husband a few weeks before the catastrophe. One of the mob having sought refuge in her house, concealed himself under the bed upstairs, and two women also fled to her chamber for safety during the firing. The door was afterwards made fast with a nail, and poor Whataker (who was an amiable man and a neighbour) was trying to get in, when he received the shot which caused his death. One of the riflemen then came up, smashed the window with the butt of his gun, and swore he would shoot her if she did not let him in; being terrified, she opened the door, and then again he swore most tremendously he would put her and the other women to death. Widow Upton then screamed, and clasping the ruffian round the arms, begged he would not take her life, and her terror causing desperation and strength, she held him fast, saying, "I will not be shot in my own house, I am a poor woman and unprotected. I have not stirred from home; I am Mr. Aikin's neighbour, I have nothing to do with the mob, and you cannot – nay you shall not shed my blood upon my own floor." Her cries and screams perhaps alarming the fellow, or causing some compunction, he promised not to do her harm if she would loose her hold. He then went upstairs, seized the man who was under the bed, and led him away. The other woman then helped to bring Mr. Whataker into the house; he bled fast, and died in about an hour. The ball passed through him, through the door, and to the further end of the cottage, and is at present in widow Upton's possession.[10]

The jury at the inquest on James Waddicar gave a verdict of murder by a rifleman unknown.

In the days that followed the so-called 'Chatterton Fight', the rioters destroyed more looms in the Rossendale valley and in Bury, but all to no avail. The Rostron brothers and Aitken and Lord received compensation (£1,500 and £568 respectively) and by 1836 they had 517 powerlooms at Bridge Mill and 107 at Chatterton. In addition there were fifty looms at Lumb, seventy-eight at Ewood Bridge and fifty-five at Dearden Clough (where they were used for weaving woollen cloth).[11]

The 1826 riots were not the last occasion of industrial unrest that Edenfield witnessed. The trade depression in 1842 and its accompanying distress among the working classes again saw gangs of workers roaming the district. This time they brought mills to a standstill by removing the plugs from the boilers. The rioters visited Bridge Mill and Ewood Bridge Mill before making their way to Haslingden.[12]

THE HANDLOOM WEAVERS

The introduction of powerlooms did not do away with handloom weaving overnight. To begin with, the early powerlooms were too crude to weave anything but coarse cottons in a satisfactory manner. All the powerlooms in the village in 1836, for example, were weaving either fustians or calicoes, except for those belonging to Stott and Smith at Dearden Clough, which wove woollens. However, by the 1850s improvements to powerlooms had swung the balance as far as cotton weaving was concerned. In the 1851 census there were only two cotton handloom weavers in the village, one of whom, Thomas Eccles, was still weaving gingham by hand in his house at Crow Woods in 1871. Woollen handloom weavers continued to be employed by the Porritts into the 1870s. There were nineteen in the 1861 census, most of whom lived in Chatterton and Strongstry, not far from Stubbins Vale Mill. This was not an ageing workforce at the end of their working lives. The brothers Henry and James Ramsbottom, for instance, were aged only nineteen and seventeen, while several of their co-workers were in their twenties. Ten years later only seven of the same men are still listed as woollen weavers, although it is not clear whether they were using handlooms or powerlooms.[13]

CHILD LABOUR

In 1819 James Watkins, a magistrate for the Bolton district, visited two Edenfield mills. At Edmund Sagar's fulling mill at Chatterton he found that out of a total workforce of thirty, seven were children aged under fourteen, while at Edenwood Mill there were ten children of a similar age out of a total of forty workpeople. The hours of labour (excluding mealtimes) were thirteen at Chatterton and fourteen at Edenwood. He found both mills to be very filthy with little ventilation and the children were 'puny and sickly.' A little over twenty years later twelve-year old

In the 18th and early 19th centuries, cotton mill owners often used pauper apprentices to tend their machines. In this advertisement from 1792 the Ewood Bridge firm of Morris and Staveley seek one of their apprentices who had run away.

Thomas Parkinson who worked at Rose Bank printworks said that he had recently come to work at four o'clock on a Saturday morning and stayed until ten at night. He admitted that this did not happen often and said that the usual starting time was six o'clock in the summer and seven o'clock in winter. He was allowed three-quarters of an hour for breakfast, but he usually went back to work after quarter of an hour or twenty minutes.[14]

For one Haslingden boy the hardships of working at Bridge Mill in the first half of the 19th century were made much worse by the long walk to and from work that he and his brother faced each day. He later recalled:

> When I was a boy, my younger brother, who was then under six years of age, and I worked at Pinch Dickey's mill at Edenfield. We lived in Haslingden and had to make the journey of about four miles every morning and reach the mill by six o'clock, winter and summer, wet or fine. Sometimes we had to fight our way through snowdrifts during a winter blizzard, and my younger brother often dropped from fatigue and exposure. Then I had to carry him on my back and at the end of the journey we were both dead beat before commencing work. Imagine our condition during the long day, soaking wet or half frozen: and when work was finished the long journey home through the snow and mud – and no lamplights. A hurried meal and off to bed, sometimes having to be carried up asleep – shirt, stockings and every patch of clothing drying before the fire – and to be awakened again for another agonising day before we had obtained half the sleep we required. Before I reached my 21st birthday I felt like an old man and have been denied good health because of the hardships of my early youth.[15]

Successive Factory Acts did much to improve the lot of such children by fixing the minimum age at which they could be employed and by limiting the number of hours they could work each day. Inspectors regularly visited local mills and imposed fines on owners who had breached regulations. In December 1836, for example, John Parkinson was fined £5 for having employed people under the age of eighteen for more than twelve hours a day at Ewood Bridge Mill. In the following year he was fined again for employing two children under the age of eighteen during the night and at the same time Henry Kilshaw of Irwell Vale Mill was fined 10s for employing young people more than twelve hours a day and children more than nine hours a day. The 1844 Factory Act also established the 'half-time' system that ensured that children under thirteen received at least three hours schooling every day. At the same time, however, it lowered the minimum age at which a child could be set to work so that the working lives of thousands of children in 19th century Lancashire started when they were aged just eight.[16]

Typical of such children was Alice Holden of Scout Moor who began work as a half-timer at Lodge Mill in 1853 aged eight, going full-time when aged eleven. Similarly Edward Pyzer Smith (born 1856) was eight years old when he started at Ewood Bridge Mill, but did not go full-time until he was thirteen. He worked from six in the morning until six at night, with an hour for dinner, although later his clocking off time was changed to 5.30pm. In the 1860s, John, son of Alexander Barlow, started work at his father's mill at Shuttleworth at six o'clock in the morning and worked until breakfast time when he walked the two miles to school. Leaving school at four o'clock he had to hurry back to the mill to continue working until six o'clock. In the 1870s the minimum age was raised so that children like Edwin Rogers (born 1877) were starting work when they were ten years old. Edwin went to work at Union Mill, Stubbins on a wage of 2s 9d a week. This rose to 5s 6d when he went full-time aged thirteen.[17]

The wages of children, especially in the spinning side of the cotton trade, were usually paid directly by the adult workers who employed them to mend broken threads, clean machinery, sweep up, and so on. This system could be easily abused as Michael Davitt found when he went to work at Ewood Bridge Mill in 1856:

> I only remained there a month as the man for whom I was working as a 'bobbin tenter' drank my wages (2s 6d) on the third week, and not being big enough at the age of ten, to give him a taste of my clogs, I left him.[18]

THE COTTON FAMINE

By 1860 Lancashire's cotton mills were largely dependent on the southern states of America for their raw material, a state of affairs that proved disastrous when the American Civil War broke out. At first its effects were not widely felt in the county because stocks of both raw cotton and cloth were high, but by the autumn of 1861 the blockade on American ports had begun to bite. At the beginning of 1862 the *Blackburn Standard* reported that an increasing number of mills in the Haslingden Poor Law Union (which included Edenfield and district) were going on short time. Irwell Vale Mill closed completely for a time and other mills probably did likewise. By the beginning of 1863, out of a total of 1445 cotton workers in Tottington Higher End, only ninety-six were working full time, 471 were on short time and the remaining 878 were out of work altogether.[19]

The unemployed were forced to seek relief from the Poor Law Guardians who in the summer of 1862 introduced a new scale of relief allowing 2s 6d per week for one person, 4s 6d for two, 6s for three, 8s for four, 9s 6d for five, and 11s for six. They allowed an extra 1s 6d a head for families of more than six people. By the end of the year the Guardians had been forced to increase the poor rate to 9s in the pound, 800 per cent more than it had been in the first quarter of 1862. The distress had deepened to such an extent that relief committees depending on voluntary contributions were set up. The Edenfield Relief Committee consisted of John Aitken (cotton manufacturer at Irwell Vale), James Porritt of Stubbins Vale, Lawrence Duckworth, the Rev. Matthew Wilson and Edmund Pickup. They administered funds donated locally as well as grants that came from elsewhere. In May 1863, for instance, the Manchester Central Relief Committee made a grant of £100 to Edenfield to cover a period of four weeks. Relief payments or 'dow' as they were known, were made from Edmund Pickup's house at the corner of Gin Croft Lane (later the Volunteer Inn beerhouse).[20]

The Relief Committee also set up a sewing class at Bridge Mill superintended by James Porritt's wife, Mary Hannah. Those who attended were paid a small amount each week and the finished articles were distributed to the most needy families in the area. For the men of the village a school was started in the large room over 11, Market Street. One of the teachers, James Pickup, later recalled:

> I should think there would be something like forty persons attending the school … The scholars who attended the school included young men of different ages, and they were paid 5s per week, the teachers receiving 7s 6d per week. They had nothing coming in in the shape of wages, and those who attended school, during those trying times were paid for doing so.

In March 1863 it was decided to fill in part of Horncliffe Quarry and some of the older scholars went to work on that project. Some of the local mill owners were able to help in other ways too: James Porritt, for example, employed about thirty extra men to work in his grounds at Stubbins Vale House.[21]

Conditions gradually returned to normal in 1864 and 1865 and the Relief Committees were wound up. Members of the Ramsbottom Committee decided that they would use the small sum of money left in their hands to treat the aged residents of the district.

> Wednesday the 7th of February, 1866, will be long remembered by the old folks of Ramsbottom, as the day on which a splendid treat was given them by the members of the Relief Committee, or, as they were more commonly known, "t' dow chaps."

said the *Bury Times*. One hundred and sixteen guests with an average age of seventy-six enjoyed a meal at the Railway Hotel, Stubbins. The oldest couple were Dick and Alice Brierley from Lane End in Edenfield.

> This ancient couple are each eighty-two years of age, having been man and wife above sixty years, and strange to say, during the whole time, they have both eaten from one plate. Considerable amusement was caused by one of the waiters endeavouring to persuade them each to have a plate; but they resolutely declared their intention of doing as they had always done.

After the meal, punch, pipes and tobacco were provided and the rest of the afternoon was spent singing, gossiping and dancing to the strains of a quadrille band.[22]

KNITTING

For a few years towards the end of the 19th century a handful of Edenfield people were employed making knitted clothes. Simeon Chattwood set up the business in the buildings behind his grocer's shop at 4, Market Place. A visitor to his works in the late 1880s said:

> The hosiery manufacture is in Gin Croft Lane and the goods in this department are far too numerous for detail. The specialities include cardigan jackets, boys' suits, Tam o' Shanter caps, ladies' skirts, children's skirts, children's dresses, under vests, ladies' stockings, gentlemen's stockings, socks and all classes of wool work. They are machine-made and for both wholesale and retail trade. Mr. Chattwood's motto is that 'small profits' will bring 'quick returns', and he therefore supplies his numerous customers with the very best quality of goods at the lowest reasonable price. His system of conducting the business is doing much to secure an even greater connection in the future than he has enjoyed in the past.

Mr. Chattwood's two daughters, Elizabeth and Gertrude, worked in the knitting factory and the 1891 census lists three other women in the village who were probably employed there too. Some seventy years later, the knitting industry returned to Gin Croft Lane when Eden (Knitwear) Ltd. took over the old Working Men's Club. For just over three years the company produced knitted pullovers and cardigans in the building, employing about twenty-five people.[23]

Simeon Chattwood's knitting workshop in Gin Croft Lane pictured in 1990 before the building was renovated.

NOTES

1. Manor of Tottington records (LRO: DDHCL liber CC, folio 358; liber M, folio 567; liber N, folio 152; liber Q, folio 398)

2. *pers. comm.* W.J. Smith; Tottington Higher End valuation 1837, entry for Green Head (LRO: MBH/5/6)

3. Edenfield parish records: 1777 survey, 1790 survey (MCL: MF PR117a); Manor of Tottington records (LRO: DDHCL liber KK, folio 207); Royal Exchange fire insurance policy (Guildhall Library: No. 179638); E. Baines, *History, directory and gazetteer of the County Palatine of Lancaster*, vol. II, (1825); Manchester Mercury 10th April 1821; PP, *A return of the number of power looms used in factories ...* 1836 (24) XLV

4. Articles of Enquiry preparatory to Visitation 1778 and 1804 (Cheshire Record Office: EDV7/1, vol. 2; EDV7/3, vol.2); Manchester Mercury 14th March 1815

5. Haslingden Gazette 3rd June 1916, 10th June 1916

6. Bolton Chronicle 6th May 1826, 8th April 1826

7. W. Turner, *Riot! The story of the East Lancashire Loom-Breakers in 1826* (1992), pp.41 – 47; Leeds Intelligencer 4th May 1826

8. Bolton Chronicle 29th April 1826

9. Morning Herald 4th May 1826

10. Morning Herald 9th May 1826

11. PP, *A return of the number of power looms used in factories ...* 1836 (24) XLV

12. C. Aspin, *Haslingden 1800-1900*, (1962), p. 21

13. 1861 census Tottington Higher End (PRO RG 9/3059); 1871 census Tottington Higher End (PRO: RG 10/4139)

14. PP, *House of Lords Committee on the state and condition of the children employed in the cotton manufactories of the United Kingdom*, 1819 (24) CX; PP, *Children's employment commission: appendix to the second report of the commissioners, part II: reports and evidence from sub-commissioners*, 1843 (432) XV

15. C. Aspin, *Lancashire. The first industrial society*, (1969), p. 65

16. PP, *Persons summoned for offences against the Factory Act 1835-36*, 1836 (278) XLV; PP, *Number and names of persons summoned for offences against the Factory Act*, 1837-38 (120) XLV

17. RO 5th November 1915, 13th August 1937, 25th December 1959; Accrington Observer 25th July 1925

18. RO 1st June 1906

19. C. Aspin, *Haslingden 1800-1900*, (1962), p. 126; RO 5th November 1915; *Fund for the relief of distress in the manufacturing districts - return from local relief committees, week ending 31st January 1863* (MCL: P3339)

20. C. Aspin, *op. cit.*, pp. 127-128; RO 21st August 1914; BT 9th May 1863

21. RO 21st August 1914; A. Muir, *The history of Porritts and Spencer* [typescript], (1966), p.77; Haslingden Guardians' minute book, 27th March 1863 (LRO: PUH/1/7)

22. BT 17th February 1866

23. *Lancashire. Part First. The premier county of the kingdom. Cities and towns, historical, statistical, biographical, business men and mercantile interests, wealth and growth. An epitome of results.* (1889-90), p. 209; RO 11th August 1961, 1st January 1965

MILLS AND WORKSHOPS

EDENFIELD TOOK ITS FIRST STEP into the industrial age in 1765 when the waters of the Dearden Brook were harnessed to power a woollen fulling mill. By the 1820s, there were no fewer than seven mills within the space of about a mile using the brook to turn water wheels, supply steam engines or as part of the bleaching and printing processes. The Dearden Brook mills were joined by others at Stubbins, Chatterton and Ewood Bridge at the end of the 18th century, and at Irwell Vale, Lumb and Turn in the first half of the 19th century. Mid-century was marked by the completion of the first of the Stubbins Vale Mills, but only two new mills – Union Mill and Hope Mill, both dating from the early 1860s – were put up in the second half of the 19th century. The Chatterton Weaving Shed dating from 1908-9 was the only completely new mill to be built in the 20th century.

The story of the mills, which is recounted in some detail below, not only throws light on the rise and fall of the textile industries, but also tells us much about the people who ran them or spent their working lives in them.

DEARDEN CLOUGH MILL

Thomas Booth, a prosperous landowner who lived at Mount Pleasant (now The Mount), built Edenfield's first mill between 1765 and 1767. Booth's fulling mill, as it was known, also included a house, 'perching mill or gigg' and nine seams of tenters.[1] Its first tenants were three Manchester merchants: John Booth, Benjamin Greaves and Joseph Mather. Booth moved from Manchester to Brook Bottom in Shuttleworth no doubt to supervise the day to day running of the mill, while his partners looked after the Manchester end of the business. Their tenancy of the mill did not last many years and by 1774 they had been replaced by William Wallwork. This man was still at the mill in 1777 when the leasehold was offered for sale, but was himself replaced by new tenants in 1783. The 1777 sale notices state that in addition to the mill there were also a mill house, thirteen seams of tenters and extensive warehousing, which were leased from Thomas Booth for £64 10s per annum.[2]

The men who took the mill on a fifteen-year lease in 1784 were two brothers, John and Lawrence Hoyle, from Haslingden where they had a flourishing woollen business. The Hoyle family were to work the mill for nearly thirty years and were responsible for an important change to the site. By 1792, when a new lease was granted to John because Lawrence had died, they had built a second fulling mill (Dearden Clough Lower Mill) and a stovehouse or dryhouse.[3] In the following year, John insured the original mill and an adjoining warehouse for £300, machinery and stock for £1,200, the new mill for £100 and its machinery and stock for a further

The leasehold of Dearden Clough Mill offered for sale in the *Manchester Mercury* for 25th March, 1777.

£100. Added to this, his warehouse in Haslingden and its contents were insured for £750, making £2,450 in total, a huge sum in today's prices.[4]

Following his brother's death, John Hoyle took his son (also called John) into the business. They negotiated a thirty-year lease on the mills in December 1798 and continued to make additions to them until 1812. In May of that year new tenants took over. They were three local men: Lawrence Duckworth, fulling miller, who lived at Dearden Clough, John Wallwork who had another fulling mill in Ramsbottom, and Thomas Elton, an Edenfield butcher. Their lease was for seventeen years and covered both Dearden Clough Mills, but they sublet first the lower mill and then Dearden Clough Mill itself. By the time the mill was offered to let again in March 1828 it had been taken over by Edmund Sagar, who, as we shall see, had become tenant at the lower mill in 1816.[5]

James Stott and Thomas Smith, Methodist flannel manufacturers at Flaxmoss near Haslingden, took over the original mill in 1829. In January 1830, Stott noted,

This year we have taken a little Mill at Dearden Clough which [we] have not yet quite fill'd with Machinery. We begun to card in Oct. last & thinks by proper management & the favour of providence it may ans' well for us.[6]

The partners not only used the mill for carding, but also began powerloom weaving on a modest scale and by 1836 they had fifty-five looms.[7] In the same year Stott and Smith transferred their business to Sykeside where they had built their own mill.

Dearden Clough Mill did not long remain empty. On 2nd January 1837 it was let for fourteen years to Joseph and James Porritt, manufacturers of industrial felts. Their business had outgrown its premises in Bury and they had decided to move to a larger mill. The property they rented at Dearden Clough included not only the

Joseph Porritt (1808-1868), senior partner in the firm that ran Dearden Clough Mill from 1837 to 1852.

mill with steam engine and water wheel, but also two warehouses, three cottages, a stable and shippon, a house with brewhouse, garden and orchard and a few acres of land. As well as an annual rent of just over £200, they agreed to pay £7 10s for every £100 that Thomas Booth, grandson of the man who built the mill, might spend on a new water wheel.[8]

The Porritts soon settled at Edenfield with Joseph at Dearden Clough House next to the mill, James at Hawthorn House and Samuel (who joined the partnership in 1838) on Market Street. At first they used the mill for carding only, but quickly decided to finish their pieces as well and installed new fulling stocks, enabling them to run the mill night and day. At the beginning of 1838, the firm's equipment, stocks of wool and manufactured goods were valued at £2,700 18s 0d. Three years later the figure had more than doubled. In the 1840s, the Porritts took another partner, John Austin, James's brother-in-law, and a lease on another mill in Ramsbottom. By the time they left Dearden Clough for their own mill at Stubbins Vale they were employing 167 people.[9]

The Porritts' departure from Dearden Clough marked an important break in the mill's history: for the first time it was used for cotton manufacturing rather than wool. It began to specialise in 'hard waste' spinning and weaving. Its raw material, a by-product of mule spinning, consisted of tubes of hardened cotton yarn formed when mule spindles were coated with starch paste before spinning began. These so-called 'cop bottoms' were broken down by machines called devils, the fibres carded and re-spun and the resulting yarn used in the manufacture of coarse sheetings, twills and similar cloths. It has been suggested that the idea of using cop bottoms as a raw material actually originated at Dearden Clough Mill and later spread throughout the Haslingden and Rochdale districts.[10]

John and William Cronkshaw, members of an old Helmshore family, were the first cotton men at the mill, but went bankrupt in 1858. Afterwards the mill was divided into two. Part was rented by James Emmett, a small-scale cotton manufacturer, (he was employing just nine people in 1861) and the remainder was taken over by Eastwood, Clegg and Co., cotton spinners and manufacturers. The partners in the firm were William Eastwood and George Clegg, a man who had spent some time prospecting for gold in Australia. Though larger than James Emmett's business, Eastwood and Clegg's concern was still fairly modest, employing thirty-one people in 1861.[11]

By 1865, James Emmett had moved to Bridge Mills, and the other firm became the sole occupant at Dearden Clough Mill. There were several changes in the partnership until George Clegg took sole control in 1873.[12] His name was to be associated with the mill until the end of its days. For more than twenty years his business seems to have prospered, but failed early in 1899. A private limited company bearing his name was set up in the following year by a group of Bury and Tottington businessmen, including George Clegg's son, John, who became secretary and manager. It was reconstituted some twenty years later as George Clegg (1920) Ltd. The directors of the second company decided to do away with the weaving side of the business and concentrated solely on cotton winding and spinning, using first mules and later ring frames.[13]

Like many hard waste mills, Dearden Clough caught fire a number of times, most seriously in October 1871. The main part of the mill was five storeys high and contained the carding and spinning rooms and the weaving shed. The fire broke out one Saturday dinner time in the carding room on the second floor and was immediately tackled by the mill workers while they waited for the fire engine to arrive from Grants' mill at Ramsbottom. 'The fire, however, had got fairly hold of the combustible material, and bade defiance to the anxious endeavours of its opponents, who were obliged to give way on the score of personal safety.'[14] By the end of the afternoon the mill lay in ruins, although the adjoining breaking up room and engine house were saved. The mill was rebuilt in the following year, but was reduced to three storeys.[15]

A fire played a part in the final demise of the company and of Dearden Clough Mill. As a result of the general recession and the long-term decline in the Lancashire

Dearden Clough Mill during demolition, 1990.

cotton industry, the mill was scheduled to close at the end of 1982, but was given a last minute reprieve when its staff was cut from thirty-six to seventeen. The smaller business continued until 1987, spinning about five tons of cotton a week. In June of that year the shareholders sold out to a single individual and under his guidance more staff were taken on and by November they were spinning twenty-two tons a week. Problems began on 29th November when a fire caused extensive damage and meant that production was reduced by two-thirds. When it became clear that the mill had been under-insured, additional finance had to be sought by borrowing from the bank but this did not solve the problems. Orders were unfulfilled and customers were lost. Staff were gradually laid off until by the middle of 1988 there were just ten workers employed two days a week. At the beginning of the following year it emerged that creditors were owed more than £127,000. The company was wound up early in 1990 and the mill subsequently demolished.[16]

DEARDEN CLOUGH LOWER MILL

As we have seen, Dearden Clough Lower Mill, which stood a little further downstream from Dearden Clough Mill, was built by the Hoyles of Haslingden in about 1792. The two mills shared the same tenants until 1816 when Lawrence Duckworth, John Wallwork and Thomas Elton sublet the lower mill to Edmund Sagar. Sagar, a woollen merchant, was in business with his father at Chatterton, and used Dearden Clough Lower Mill for carding and slubbing. He also had the use of the highest chamber in the dryhouse at Dearden Clough Mill and the seams of tenters it contained.[17]

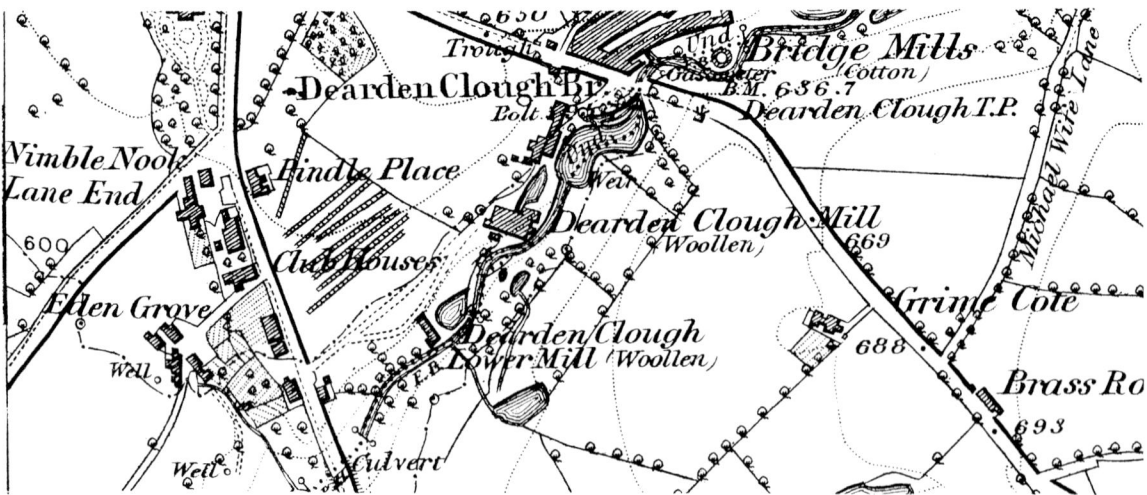

The two mills at Dearden Clough in the 1840s. Note the seams of tenters on the hillside just above the lower mill.

Sagar's lease was not renewed in 1829, but instead the mill was taken over by Thomas Entwistle and his brothers and converted to cotton manufacture. The mill was quite small – it had just five rooms when offered to let in 1849 – and was powered by a sixteen-foot diameter water wheel. By 1868 this had been replaced by a 14 horse-power vortex turbine, which was later coupled to a small steam engine. From the time that Thomas Entwistle took the mill in the early 1830s until the early 1880s, Dearden Clough Lower Mill was occupied by a succession of small hard waste spinners and manufacturers. For example, Thomas Walsh who ran the mill from 1859 to 1870 employed thirty-eight people, while John and Hitchon Hitchon who were there in 1881 found work for just six men and one girl. For a few years in the 1870s, Haworth and Co., soap and soda crystal manufacturers, also used part of the mill.[18]

A more settled period in the history of the mill began in the early 1880s when it was taken over by Richard Taylor from Bury who used it to make healds and reeds. Since a heald was known as a 'yell' in Lancashire dialect, the mill soon became known simply as 'Th' Yell Shop'. Richard Taylor died in 1898 but his widow carried on the business. She was followed by her son-in-law, Harry Minton, who later became one of the directors of George Alty Ltd. at nearby Hope Mill, but the name of Richard Taylor continued to be associated with Dearden Clough Lower Mill until its closure in the early 1960s.

Richard Taylor's name had a long association with Dearden Clough Lower Mill. This advertisement dates from 1923.

CHATTERTON MILL

In the 1780s, a second watercourse, the River Irwell, was set to work driving the wheels of another of Edenfield's early mills. The site chosen was at Chatterton, where a fulling mill was built between 1787 and 1790 on flat land just south of a great loop in the river.[19] A weir was thrown across the river near Chatterton Hey Wood and the water carried in a goit to a small lodge behind the mill. Considerable alterations were made to this simple arrangement in 1818 following the settlement of a dispute about the use of water from the river. A new weir was built upstream of the old one and the water carried from one side of the meander to the other in an open goit. Then it was taken over the river in an aqueduct before finally emptying into the mill lodge. Once it had done its work at the mill, its journey back to the river was no less complicated: it flowed to the end of the Chatterton Mill race into a new goit through the meadows to a point just north of the bridge at Stubbins, crossed the river in a wooden tunnel, passed under the turnpike road and finally poured into the headrace of Ashton's mill at Ramsbottom.

For the first sixty years or so of its life, two families worked Chatterton Mill. Edmund Sagar was the original tenant and at first ran the mill as a woollen fulling mill. He later added cotton spinning to his enterprise and was joined in the business by his sons, Edmund, William and Richard. By the early 1820s, like several other

The ruins of Chatterton Mill in the early 1890s shortly before their demolition.

local woollen firms, the Sagars were exporting to America and Richard had gone to live in New York to deal with the business there. The firm went bankrupt in 1821 and the mill was offered to let.[20]

The four storey fulling and spinning mill, dyehouse and dryhouse were taken by Thomas Aitken (1789-1858), son of a Haslingden cotton manufacturer, who had previously run a mill at Sunnybank, Helmshore. Under his control Chatterton became solely a cotton mill powered by a water wheel fourteen feet wide and just over fourteen feet in diameter.[21] By 1826 the mill was weaving as well as spinning using forty-six newly installed powerlooms. In April of that year it was attacked in the powerloom riots and was the scene of the infamous 'Chatterton Fight'. Aitken was paid £568 compensation for his smashed looms, which enabled him to buy new ones and restart the mill. In the early 1830s he took his son, John, into the partnership and expanded the business into Irwell Vale Mill, a short distance upstream. By 1851, Chatterton Mill was employing 110 people, but in the following year Aitken transferred all of his business to Irwell Vale and the Chatterton estate was sold.[22]

The purchaser was Richard Bridge, a cotton spinner from Dunnockshaw. He paid nearly £7,500 for the Chatterton estate, although he in fact bought the property on a mortgage from the original owner. His business was not a lasting success and he was declared bankrupt in 1857. Another man named Bridge, although not apparently related to Richard, bought the mill. William Bridge was a Manchester commission agent whose business was more successful than his predecessor's. By 1863 he had paid off his mortgage on the property, but in the following year he decided to rent out the mill to another firm, Kershaw and Newbigging. Theirs was a fairly modest concern and when they sold up in January 1868 the bulk of their machinery consisted of ten throstles, two mules and eighty-seven powerlooms.[23]

Kershaw and Newbigging were the last cotton men to rent the mill. It stood empty for some time until William Bridge could find new tenants. Thomas Brogden and William Haworth were mineral water manufacturers who were at Chatterton for a few years before they too went bankrupt in 1881. Their successors, Thomas Butterworth and William Blackburn, produced mineral water at Chatterton until 1892 when they were taken over by the Ramsbottom Mineral Water Manufacturing Co. Ltd. Butterworth and Blackburn occupied only part of the mill and by the early 1890s much of it was dilapidated. Richard Porritt bought it in 1895 and soon demolished the buildings and some of the adjoining cottages. It was Richard's son, Austin, who some twenty-seven years later presented the mill site to the people of Ramsbottom and district as a recreation ground.[24]

STUBBINS PRINTWORKS

The early fulling mills at Dearden Clough and Chatterton were joined in the 1780s by two calico printworks. One of these was at Stubbins where there was sufficient flat land for a mill and a supply of water from the stream in Ox Hey Clough. Charles

A notice for printers at Stubbins that appeared in the *Manchester Mercury* in February, 1788.

Leigh rented part of the old Stubbins estate and began calico printing there in 1785.[25] The end of the 18th century was a period of great change in the printing and bleaching industries with the introduction of the cylinder-printing machine and of bleaching powder (chloride of lime). Many fortunes were made, but many were lost as people rushed to invest. The industry required a considerable outlay of capital, particularly in keeping a stock of raw, finished and semi-worked material for a long time. There were many bankruptcies and Charles Leigh was no exception: his business failed in 1789. His successors, John and Charles Johnston, fared little better and they too went out of business in 1792.[26]

The printworks remained empty until 1795 when a more settled period in its history was ushered in by the granting of a twenty-one year lease to Samuel Milner of Manchester and Thomas Sandiford of Witton, near Blackburn. The partners were allowed to 'cut such sluices, drains and reservoirs as may be needful and necessary for the further, better and more advantageous use and occupation of the said premises.' They got the right to take water from the streams in a neighbouring property and divert it to the printworks. Soon the hillside between Buckden and Ox Hey Cloughs was crossed by a series of goits and small lodges. From the same period (1795-7) dated the White Croft bleachworks, built by Milner and Sandiford on a site now occupied by The Cliffe.[27]

Over the following twenty years or so the Stubbins partnership underwent several changes, either through death or retirement, but in 1814 Thomas Sandiford took sole control of the business. We can get some idea of the scale of the enterprise from a valuation dated 31st December 1805, which calculated the total shares of the four partners as £53,186 3s 1¼d. (This excluded a newly built warehouse in Cannon Street, Manchester and the leasehold property at Stubbins).[28] Thomas Sandiford ran the printworks until 1833 when he handed over to his son, also called Thomas, and died in 1837. The younger man carried on the business for only a few years, for he died in 1840 aged forty-five. In the previous year he had let the printworks to John Brown and Thomas Powell, two Manchester calico printers, for a term of fourteen years. Bankruptcy soon claimed their business and the works were taken for just a year by John Wardley who was setting up his own mill at Darwen. His successors, John and Watson Losh, who traded as John Losh and Co., worked Stubbins until about 1851. During their time there the Stubbins works were described as 'a small, old place', printing 'mostly furnitures of low quality.' A twenty horse-power steam engine supplied power for three printing machines and there were also seventy-eight tables for block printing.[29]

In 1851 a new firm took control at Stubbins. David Greenhalgh, a Manchester born calico printer who had been living in Barcelona for some years, formed a partnership with Thomas Kenyon, another printer originally from Accrington. Kenyon's place was taken in 1853 by William Rumney, a man who was to have a decided influence not only on the printworks, but also on Stubbins as a whole. He was born in Leck, near Kirkby Lonsdale, in 1823 and went to Manchester when aged fifteen. There he found work with Wilson and Graham and stayed with them until taken into partnership by David Greenhalgh.[30] By 1861 Greenhalgh and Rumney were employing 274 people, but the partnership was dissolved in the following year. A tradition in the Greenhalgh family says that the alliance between the two men was not a happy one because Rumney insisted on buying inferior goods and shipping them abroad as the firm's own product. There was certainly a lengthy court case after the partnership was dissolved in which

William Rumney (1823-1882), for over twenty years sole proprietor of the calico printworks at Stubbins. His obituary noted that for many years he 'exhibited a wonderful amount of energy and indomitable perseverance.'

Greenhalgh maintained that Rumney had kept books and accounts that should have been handed over to the accountant to be audited. The case dragged on for some years and was not settled until 1870.[31]

Once Rumney had taken control at Stubbins he set about expanding the business, enlarging the printworks and taking over mills in Shuttleworth, Ramsbottom and Bury so that he could produce his own cloth. He also started to change the face of Stubbins by building houses for his workers in Stubbins Street and Stubbins Fold. In 1878 four of his senior employees were taken into partnership and the firm of William Rumney and Co. formed. Rumney himself died in 1882 leaving a firm that employed 1,500 people and a personal fortune of nearly £229,000. In 1899 many Lancashire calico printing firms (including William Rumney and Co.) joined together in a combine called the Calico Printers' Association in an effort to reduce unnecessary competition between them. The enterprise was not an immediate success and in the early 1900s steps were taken to close some of the works that had been acquired by the CPA. It was announced in February 1903 that the Stubbins printworks would close for 'remodelling' but in fact they never re-opened. About

300 people were thrown out of work and had to leave the district. Commenting on the closure a few years later the *Ramsbottom Observer* said:

> Ramsbottom township suffered a depopulation from which it has not since been able to recover, and the consequent withdrawal of several hundreds of pounds in wages must have been keenly felt by shopkeepers generally.[32]

In the following few years, much of the huge complex of buildings was demolished, but in 1905 part of what remained began to be used by James Booth, trading as the Japa Blind Co., for the manufacture of paper window blinds. Barnes and Hargreaves had a chemical works in another section and after Richard and Austin Porritt bought the buildings in 1906 they also used some of them as offices. J.R. Crompton Bros., papermakers of Bury, bought the main part of the site from the Porritts five years later and produced their first sheet of paper at Stubbins on New Year's Eve 1911. Their first papermaking machine was joined by another in 1915 and a third in 1920 and the works were considerably enlarged. During the First World War they started to make cigarette paper and soon the mill was running night and day to supply all the main cigarette manufacturers.[33]

Expansion continued after the Second World War with a new papermaking machine installed in 1949 and the addition of several buildings costing many thousands of pounds. The works suffered a set back in November 1962 when a warehouse containing £18,000 worth of raw materials was destroyed by fire, but a more serious blow fell in 1967. In April of that year the Wiggins Teape Group (the

The huge bulk of Stubbins papermill in 2002. The buildings occupy one of the oldest industrial sites in the district.

owners) announced that as part of their rationalisation programme they intended to close Stubbins. Two hundred and thirty-six employees were either made redundant or found jobs elsewhere and the plant was dismantled.[34]

The mill stood empty until the following year when it was bought by Sterling International (UK) Ltd. A new company – Sterling Stubbins Ltd. – took over running the mill and installed a new machine to make toilet, facial and serviette tissue. Production started in March 1970 with a workforce of about seventy people. This figure rose as the works grew, culminating in a £70 million expansion programme that was completed in 1993. The company running the mill had become Fort Sterling in 1984 and when this business amalgamated with an American firm – the James River Corporation – in 1997 the name was changed to the Fort James Corporation. Three years later, Stubbins became part of the world's leading manufacturer of tissue products when the Georgia Pacific Corporation acquired Fort James.[35]

EWOOD BRIDGE MILL

The second printworks that began working in the 1780s was at Ewood Bridge. William Morris and William Staveley, Manchester fustian manufacturers, started printing there in 1786, probably using the old corn mill. In 1791 they took several plots of land on a 999-year lease, raised a weir across the Irwell and built a printing shop, dye house and calendar house. The Morris-Staveley partnership was dissolved in January 1792 and a new one formed between William Morris, William Clark (who took up residence near the mill) and James Steel of Hollins, near Whitehaven. James Steel's son, John, had been bound apprentice to Morris and Staveley and on several occasions Steel expressed a wish to invest money in the printing trade. Morris had invited him to join the new partnership and it was agreed that Steel's second son, Anthony, would be brought up in the business and made a partner when aged twenty-one. The articles of partnership were signed on 1st May 1792 and trade began as Morris, Steel and Clark.[36]

To Masons, Carpenters, Millwrights, and Diggers.
To be LET,

THE Building or Raising a WEIR over the River IRWELL, above Ewood Bridge, in the Parish of Haslingden, and County of Lancaster.

Also the Cutting and Banking a MILL DAM and GUTTER.

Further Particulars may be had by applying to Mr. John Schofield, at Ewood Bridge, and Proposals will be taken in at Mr. John Kay's, the New Inn, Haslingden, on Saturday the 30th Instant, between the Hours of two and five o'Clock in the Afternoon.

Preparations for the new mill at Ewood Bridge in 1791 included the raising of a weir across the Irwell. The 'gutter' (head race) and mill dam can still be seen today.

James Steel soon regretted his decision to invest money in the business and withdrew. The articles of partnership were cancelled and it was agreed to pay him £1,000 in instalments as his share of the capital. Not many months later Morris and Clark were declared bankrupt with debts of about £10,000 and in the autumn of 1793 Ewood Bridge was offered for sale. Lot one included the main part of the mill buildings, including printing shops, dyehouses and a calender house. South of the bridge, next to Ewood Hall, was another printing shop and dryhouse, which formed part of lot three. The remaining lots comprised ten newly built cottages at Ewood Bridge and a factory in Manchester.[37]

The main part of the mill stood empty for some years, but William Cockshutt of Bolton took the buildings near Ewood Hall. Cockshutt ran several mills, including a handloom weaving factory that he built at Horncliffe Wood and which survives as a row of cottages. At Ewood Bridge he filled the old printing shop near the Hall with hand operated spinning mules, but was forced to sell up in 1799.[38] The mill continued to stand empty and advertisements drafted to sell or to let it sound increasingly desperate. One dating from 1802 said that the buildings were:

> … peculiarly well situated for any person who is inclined to carry on the calico printing business, by which immense fortunes have been lately acquired … They also afford an advantageous situation for a cotton spinner, who may avoid the heavy expenses of purchasing and maintaining steam engines, and providing coal at its present enormous price, by working his machinery by means of this powerful river.[39]

In fact, cotton gained the upper hand at Ewood Bridge and by 1805 the mill had been taken over by the firm of Chorley, Gorton and Potter. Joshua Chorley, a Manchester merchant, had gone into business with John Gorton from Tottington in the 1790s. Together they had built a cotton spinning mill at Kirklees on land acquired from John Nuttall of Bury, who also owned the Ewood Bridge estate. James Potter, another Manchester merchant, who had links with the Tottington area and whose descendants were to include Beatrix Potter, joined the partnership. The three men built a new mill on the site and ran it until November 1814 when John Gorton withdrew from the partnership. In the following year Chorley and Potter put the mill up for sale.[40]

For the first time, the sale notices give us some idea of its size. Four storeys high, it was twenty-five yards long by thirteen yards wide and had a blacksmith's shop adjoining. Inside were throstles (totalling 3,000 spindles) and mules (900 spindles) as well as carding engines and drawing, slubbing and roving frames. The mill was powered by a single water wheel. The new owners were Thomas Ratcliffe and his brothers, James, John and Robert, calico printers from Loveclough. Thomas and John moved to Ewood Bridge, while James and Robert lived in Manchester to deal with the business there, including the warehouse in Cannon Street. At Ewood Bridge they converted the four storey spinning mill into a calico printing shop and also had a smaller printing shop and a range of ancillary buildings including joiners' shop and block shop, madder room, cutting shop, drawing shop, hanging room, colour shop, dye house and warehouse.[41]

The Ratcliffes seem to have begun well enough with a capital of £12,000 but their success was short-lived. They were declared bankrupt in 1819 and the mill was on the market again. When it was eventually sold in 1821 it reverted to cotton and there followed a more settled period in its history. John Parkinson (1778-1862), the purchaser, came from Goodshaw and he and his sons ran the mill for fifty years. By the early 1830s they had installed a second water wheel and a thirty horse-power steam engine and were spinning about 3,000 pounds of cotton each week. A few years later John Parkinson told a visitor that he and his wife would go into the mill during the dinner hour and continue to work until their employees came back. By this means they could make between them an extra twenty shillings a day. [42]

Naturally, the Parkinsons' time at Ewood Bridge was not totally without incident. In 1829, Henry, John Parkinson's eldest son, fell to his death while hoisting a bale of cotton into the fourth storey of the mill, while in 1842 the mill was one of several in the locality attacked during the 'Plug Riots.' However, the biggest set back came in 1844 when most of the mill was burnt down. The *Blackburn Standard* for 8th May recounted the events of a few days previously:

> On Saturday night last, about a quarter past nine o'clock, the extensive cotton factory of Messrs. Parkinson, situate at Ewood Bridge, near Haslingden, was observed to be on fire. The fire spread with fearful rapidity and the whole building from one end to the other in less than half an hour was completely in flames. About ten o'clock the roof fell in with a tremendous crash, and floor after floor gave way in rapid succession, till the whole reached the bottom floor. By half past ten, the factory was a complete ruin and part of the outer walls had fallen … An attempt was made at first to put the flames out by carrying tinfuls of water and throwing it on the burning materials; but no good could be done and a messenger was sent to Messrs. Turner of Helmshore, and Messrs. Hoyle, Ashworths and Co., of Newhall Hey, at whose works engines are kept. Messrs. Turner's engine was shortly on the spot and was followed soon after by Messrs. Hoyle and Co's. The engines were immediately set to work, but the fire had made too much progress, and it seemed impossible to save any part of the factory or the buildings around it …[43]

The damage was estimated at between £8,000 and £10,000, while the Parkinson were insured for only £3,000. Nevertheless, they rebuilt the mill on a larger scale and were soon in production again. By 1861 when John Parkinson the younger was in charge, the mill employed 224 people. The Parkinsons withdrew from running Ewood Bridge in the early 1870s, although they still owned it until the mid-1890s. A new company – the Ewood Bridge Mill Co. Ltd. – took over the mill. The company was set up by a group of mainly Haslingden cotton manufacturers and businessmen, including John and John George Dean who already had mills at Sykeside and Grane. The company ran the mill for twenty years, but sold up in 1894 when the building contained 12,000 spindles and 300 looms. It was powered by a steam engine newly installed in 1893, but also had two water wheels twenty and twenty-one feet in diameter. Indeed one of the selling points of the mill in 1894 was that the water wheels were powered by the River Irwell 'thus reducing coal consumption very materially.'[44]

Ewood Bridge Mill photographed in the summer of 1942 by Dr. G.H. Tupling.

The purchasers of the mill in 1894 were Anderton and Halstead, an old Haslingden firm, begun by John Anderton and his brother-in-law, Richard Halstead, in the late 1850s. The partnership became a private limited company in 1895 and for sixty-five years was the main employer in Ewood Bridge. In 1901 they extended the mill by building a warehouse and weaving shed at the side of the existing buildings, standing partly on the end of the lodge. The firm fell victim to the gradual contraction of the Lancashire cotton industry and closed Ewood Bridge Mill in 1959. Within a couple of years the oldest part of the mill, including the three-storey spinning section and a weaving shed, which had latterly been used as a carding room, were demolished. The remainder was taken over by Durie and Miller Ltd., carpet underlay manufacturers, who stayed there until 1975. After their departure the mill was divided into units.[45]

On the other side of the Irwell from Ewood Bridge Mill a new industrial building made its appearance in 1973. Mayfield Chicks Ltd., a firm set up in Colne in 1966, built a chicken hatchery in a field belonging to Ashenbottom Farm. The company specialises in rearing day-old chicks and has extended its buildings several times since the early 1970s. On the 16th July, 2002, most of the hatchery was destroyed by a fire that caused damage running into millions of pounds.[46]

EDENWOOD MILL

The early years of the 19th century saw a new phase of mill building and within a short time four new mills had been added to those that were already working. Edenwood was one of the new arrivals and was built in about 1801 by Lawrence Rostron, landlord of the White Horse (now the Horse and Jockey). In August 1806 he transferred much of his property, including two mills (one of which was Edenwood), to his sons, John and James, who were in business together as cotton spinners. The two brothers also got a warehouse, stable and shippon and seven cottages from their father. They stayed in partnership until 1831 when James withdrew and made over his share of the property to John. At the same time, John's son, also called John, took over running the mill itself. By the mid-1830s, Edenwood was powered by a thirty-six foot diameter water wheel and a sixteen horse-power steam engine and contained seventy-five calico powerlooms. In the late 1830s, the Lancashire cotton trade entered one of its periodic depressions and many businesses failed. Edenwood Mill closed early in 1841, throwing about one hundred people out of work.[47]

John Rostron the younger died in 1843, but in the meantime his father had been able to let the mill for seven years to Edmund Seddon, a cotton spinner from Shuttleworth. The mill was partially destroyed by fire in July 1849, but it was well insured and had been rebuilt by the spring of the following year when John Rostron sold it to his nephew, another John Rostron. As we shall see, this man had previously

The Rostron Brothers, James (1779-1849) and John (1775-1853), who ran both Edenwood and Rosebank Mills until 1831.

Edenwood Mill in 1906, with the now demolished Edenwood House on the right. In the 1880s, the building at the front with three large windows was a dining room for the mill workers.

had a share in another Edenfield mill, but following a bankruptcy had emigrated to Australia for a few years. His new enterprise at Edenwood employed eighty-two people, but lasted only a few years and in 1856 the mill changed hands again. This time the new owner was John Rostron's cousin Richard, son of the man who had sold it in 1850.[48] By the early 1850s the mill was no longer run by any of the Rostrons, but was let out to other manufacturers. In 1854, for instance, it was shared by Hicks and Pilling, sizers, and Anderton and Co., cotton spinners and manufacturers and by the early 1860s there were three separate firms in the mill: Daniel Revett and Co., sizers, and George Tattersall and Butterworth and Riley, cotton manufacturers. Revett's size works employed about twenty people and George Tattersall had a workforce of between fifty and one hundred.[49]

At the beginning of 1868 the mill reverted to being run by a single concern when the newly formed Edenwood Mill Company took over. The new enterprise was set up by William Rumney, the Stubbins calico printer, and two men from Manchester. The senior partner was Alfred Watkin, head of his family firm of Absalom Watkin and Son, commission agents, and a future mayor of Manchester. The second Manchester partner was Charles Ratcliffe who moved from the city to Edenwood House to manage the mill. The reopening of the mill under the new company was marked with a dinner and ball in January 1868 at which 'the refreshments &c. comprised all the delicacies of the season ... dispensed with a liberality which will be long remembered by all who partook of them.' Alfred Watkin died in 1875, but it was not until after William Rumney's death in 1882 that the company was wound up. By then ownership of the mill had passed to the Fielden family of Todmorden and they leased it to Charles Ratcliffe, the surviving partner, for fourteen years beginning on Christmas Day 1882.[50]

Ratcliffe did not live to see many years of the lease elapse – he died in 1884 – but his widow, Susan, and son, Frederick, carried on the business in his name until 1901. In the previous year Edenwood had been sold by the Fieldens to Turnbull and Stockdale Ltd., calico printers, who had moved to Rose Bank printworks in 1896 (see below). They transformed the mill into a dyeworks and ran it until 1968, making additions in the 1920s and modernizing it in 1955-56. A programme of rationalisation by Arthur Sanderson and Sons Ltd., which had taken over Turnbull and Stockdale, saw the closure of Edenwood in the autumn of 1968. Its links with the past were not severed entirely, however, for it was bought by Edward Turnbull, great-grandson of one of the founders of Turnbull and Stockdale, whose company still runs the mill, producing cloth printed in the traditional method using wooden blocks.[51]

ROSE BANK PRINTWORKS

Rose Bank printworks were built at the same time as Edenwood and were also run as a cotton mill by the Rostron brothers, James and John, until James's withdrawal in 1831. John then had the Lower Factory (as it was called) converted into a printworks and rented it out to Joseph Jackson and David Watson of Manchester and Thomas Greig from Ramsbottom. In 1834 the partners renewed their lease for another twenty-two years at an annual rent of £290. Apart from the mill, which had a water wheel and an eighteen horse-power steam engine, the property included four cottages and rights to the stream flowing out of an old quarry at Sheep Hey.[52]

Joseph Jackson withdrew from the partnership in the early 1840s, leaving the Watson and Greig families in charge of a works described as 'a small tidy concern capable of doing a middling business' and that produced good cloth and paid better wages than their neighbours. They had five printing machines with their own engraving shop where patterns were cut into the cylinders, but also employed hand block printers. By this date Rose Bank was finding work for 142 people. Thomas Greig settled at Rose Bank House and saw to the day to day running of the works. He was born in Leven in Fifeshire and came south to work for the Grants of Ramsbottom. His brother, Bennett, later joined the business at Rose Bank but died in 1854. Thomas had retired a few years previously and had returned to Scotland where he bought an estate at Glencarse in the Carse of Gowrie. Here he lived the life of a country gentleman until his death in 1884.[53]

Lawrence Rostron
(1751-1812)
innkeeper
The White Horse (Horse and Jockey)

John Rostron	Richard Rostron	James Rostron
(1775-1853)	(1777-1861)	(1779-1849)
cotton manufacturer	woollen manufacturer	cotton manufacturer
Edenwood & Rose Bank Mills	Bridge Mill	Edenwood & Rose Bank Mills

John	Richard	Lawrence	James	John
(1804-1843)	(1795-1868)	(?-1854)	(?-1858)	(1806-1883)
cotton manufacturer	merchant	cotton manufacturer	cotton manufacturer	cotton manufacturer
Edenwood Mill	Owned Edenwood & Rose Bank Mills	Bridge Mill	Bridge Mill	Bridge Mill

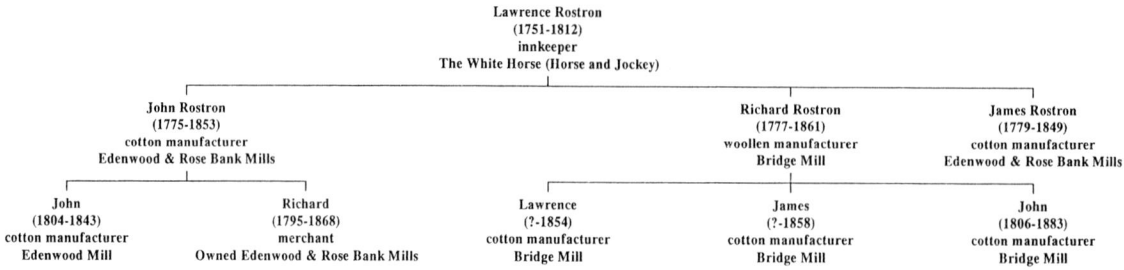

The Rostron family had an important influence on the development of Edenfield in the first half of the 19th century. This tree shows the relationship between the various members of the family who built and ran mills in the village.

At Rose Bank a third family, the Starks, who were related by marriage to Thomas and Bennett Greig, joined the partnership in the 1850s and the name was changed to Watson and Stark. When the Watsons withdrew from the partnership in 1879, Thomas Greig Stark became the sole proprietor and ran the business until he died in Egypt in 1891. His son, Lieutenant John Stark of Hanworth Hall, Norfolk, took no interest in the business he inherited, preferring to spend his time gambling, horse breeding and exhibiting dogs. He moved to Croston Towers, Alderley Edge in 1892 following his marriage to Jessie, daughter of John A. Porritt, and for some years kept a staff of seventeen servants. However, he went bankrupt in 1905 with liabilities of nearly £3,900 and assets of a mere £270.[54]

The printworks had never belonged to the Greigs, Watsons or Starks. When John Rostron, one of the original owners, died in 1853 he bequeathed Rose Bank to his son, Richard (1795-1868). Richard Rostron was a very successful Manchester merchant who specialised in selling to the South American market. He was a partner in a number of firms with branches in Rio, Pernambuco and Bahia. From the 1830s onwards he had close connections with the Fielden Brothers of Todmorden and one of his firms acted as their agents in Brazil. In 1857 the two firms collaborated on a joint venture to build a gas works in Pernambuco. However, Richard's business failed in the early 1860s. He owed Fielden Brothers no less than £134,349 and his Edenfield property, including Rose Bank and Edenwood, passed to Thomas Fielden. Richard himself left Edenfield and made his home in Portugal where he died in 1868.[55]

It was the Fieldens who leased Rose Bank to Watson and Stark and in 1896 to Turnbull and Stockdale. Four years later, John Ashton Fielden sold the Rose Bank estate to this second firm for £22,000. The company began life in Bury in 1881 as W. Turnbull and Co. William Turnbull, one of its co-founders, had served his apprenticeship with William Rumney and Co. at Stubbins before becoming foreman printer at their Blackford Bridge works. He took into partnership William Stockdale of Bury, a friend he had met while studying at the Mechanics' Institute. It was

William Turnbull (1846-1915) (*left*) and William Stockdale (1851-1923), founders of the calico printing firm that played such an important part in the history of Rose Bank.

Stockdale's idea that the firm should not only bleach, dye and print cloth for merchants on a commission basis, but should also print cloth with their own designs for sale direct to the retailers. 'Rose Bank' designs became world famous and were exhibited at the St. Louis World's Fair in 1904 (where they won two gold medals), the British Empire Exhibition at Wembley in 1924 and the Paris Exhibition in 1937. By the early 1950s, some of the company's fabrics, including 'Hollyhock' and 'King's Navee' graced the homes of Queen Mary and the then Princess Elizabeth.[56]

Turnbull and Stockdale's purchase of Rose Bank in 1900 allowed them to make additions and alterations to the buildings as they chose. They began in 1905 with a four-storey extension and later added a new warehouse and offices. From 1906 the works were supplied with electricity by the Lancashire Electric Power Company. By 1931, the year of the firm's golden jubilee, the plant at Rose Bank had more than trebled in size. The only major setback that the works suffered was a fire in 1945. The four-storey distributing centre caught fire in the early hours of 13th January and soon the light of the flames could be seen over four miles away in Bury. The fire brigades from Ramsbottom, Rawtenstall, Bury and Bolton worked hard through the night and managed to confine the blaze to one section of the works. By the morning only the shell of the building remained, its machinery and large stocks of finished goods having been completely destroyed.[57]

Despite this setback, the firm continued to prosper under the descendants of the original founders until 1964 when it was taken over by Arthur Sanderson and Sons

Ltd. The change of ownership initiated a period of reorganisation and installation of new plant, including a fourteen-colour printing machine in 1966. By July of the following year, however, increasing losses forced the company to close several departments. Contraction continued in 1968 and soon Rose Bank was used solely for making up curtains, stretch covers, bedspreads, cushions, quilts and tea cosies. Eventually production was transferred to Bolton, bringing to an end Rose Bank's long association with the textile industry. Until the closure of the works on 1st February 1974 the tolling of a bell marked the end of each working day. As a twelve-year old boy the author was taken to witness this tradition for the last time and was allowed to pull the rope that rang the bell in its cupola high on the warehouse roof.[58]

At the end of 1974 part of Rose Bank was destroyed by a huge fire that broke out at the same time as another blaze at nearby Cuba Mill. The remaining buildings were divided into about ten units. One of the occupiers was the Two Rivers Paper Company, a one-man business set up by Robert Partridge of Ramsbottom to produce special paper for watercolour artists. His improvised plant included an old washing machine, a beer keg and a spin dryer. Another business in the mill recycled plastics and a fire in their premises in June 1980 caused thousands of pounds worth of damage and destroyed three units. In the late 1980s the mill fell empty and plans were put forward to use the site as a 'craft village' with workshops, studios, offices, a hotel, restaurant and residential flats. When nothing came of this idea, the mill was demolished and houses built on the site.[59]

THE CROFT BLEACHWORKS

Just before the hard-worked Dearden Clough Brook joined the River Irwell near the New Bridge at Stubbins it was turned from its course one last time to supply water to a small bleach and dyeworks. This mill was built in about 1801 by Thomas Sandiford the elder and his partners at Stubbins printworks and in its early days was known either as New Bridge or Rose Bank bleachworks. Sandiford negotiated a new sixteen-year lease on the property in 1813 at the same as he was taking sole control of the printworks. A few years later the works were bought by John Rostron who was then still running Edenwood and Rose Bank in partnership with his brother James. In 1834, John leased the bleach croft to Jackson, Watson and Greig who had taken over at Rose Bank, thus beginning a long association between the two mills. By the mid-1870s, the two buildings were linked physically by an aerial tramway that carried lengths of cloth from the bleach croft to the white room at Rose Bank.[60]

Facing page: Two photographs of Rosebank printworks at the beginning of the 20th century. That at the top was taken in 1905 when work had just begun on a large extension. It shows very clearly the complex of buildings that made up the printworks. Those in the centre were part of the original early 19th century cotton mill. The other photograph shows the completed extension in 1906.

The most dramatic moment in the history of the bleachworks came in 1873. On the evening of the 7th April, most of the workforce finished for the day at six o'clock. Nine men remained behind to work until eight o'clock. On the ground floor of the mill stood four huge boilers or kiers, two of which were worked under high pressure. Shortly after half past six, one of these kiers (containing 700 pieces of cloth) exploded, badly damaging the building and its machinery and injuring three of the workmen. The *Bacup Times* for 12th April described the scene of devastation:

> A portion of the roof was completely blown off, a quantity of slates and stones being hurled in a field upon the opposite side of the road. The greater portion of the wall

The aftermath of the explosion at The Croft bleachworks on 7th April, 1873. A workman stands next to one of the damaged kiers and it is just possible to make out the figure of a policeman standing behind it.

fronting the high road was blown down, while some portion of the roof and the flooring of the second storey, with a large quantity of machinery, fell upon the machinery upon the ground floor, tearing down the gearing and piping in its descent, and making the whole place a mass of wreck and confusion. The kier which exploded was estimated to weigh four tons, and the sides of it, which are circular, were rent asunder, and blown in long straight pieces. The top of the kier was hurled through the roof, and descended through another portion of the roof, some yards distant, smashing everything in its course.

Like Edenwood and Rose Bank, the bleachworks passed through the Rostron family to the Fieldens and from them to Turnbull and Stockdale in 1900. They closed in 1968 as part of the programme of rationalisation begun by Arthur Sanderson and Sons Ltd., who had taken over Turnbull and Stockdale's. A new company – the Ramsbottom Bleaching and Dyeing Co. Ltd. – was set up by some of the former Turnbull and Stockdale employees, including Herbert Hall and Eric Rostron, respectively works manager and technical director for Turnbull and Stockdale. With a workforce of about thirty, the company ran the mill for twelve years. The only incident of note was a fire in August 1971 that destroyed the dyehouse in the centre of the building. By 1980 the firm had become a subsidiary of the Woodhey Dyeing Company and was badly affected by the terminal decline of the Lancashire cotton industry. Although the mill closed, this was not the end of the story. In a move which re-established ties with the past, the bleachworks were taken over by Edward Turnbull and Co. Ltd., the Edenwood block printers.[61]

Turnbull and Stockdale's bleaching croft in the late 1940s.

The last of the mills to be built on Dearden Brook in about 1801 was also the furthest upstream. It was built at Plunge by Giles Hoyle, clothier, from the New Inn at Cheesden. He took a ninety-nine year lease on part of the New Hall estate and was given the right to put a weir across the brook and divert the water to power his newly built fulling mill. Hoyle had gone bankrupt by the beginning of 1812 and his lease on Plunge Mill was taken over by John Wallwork who had previously had a mill at Holme, just north of Ewood Bridge. The Wallwork family were to have a long association with Plunge Mill.[62]

John Wallwork died in 1836 and ordered that his leasehold interest in the mill should be sold and the proceeds divided among his eight children. His son, Thomas, agreed to buy the lease for £1,150. Eight years later he paid a further £1,650 to Lawrence Rawstorne, owner of New Hall, to buy the mill outright as well as Plunge Farm and about eighteen acres of land. By 1851 Thomas had branched out into cotton spinning and manufacturing as well as fulling woollen cloth and was employing forty people at his little mill. When he died in 1862, the mill was taken

The ruins of Plunge Mill in the 1920s. This part of the building housed the waterwheel.

over by his daughters Elizabeth and Jane. They ran it on their own account as a hard waste cotton mill until 1867, after which they rented it out to a number of tenants.[63]

Robert Heyworth and John Wrigley were the first people to rent the mill from the Wallwork sisters. Their lease began in June 1867 and was supposed to run for seven years, but their business failed early in 1869 and their machinery was put up for sale. Later in the same year John Wadsworth, a Haslingden mill manager, and Joshua Cunliffe, a book-keeper from Helmshore, who traded as John Wadsworth and Co., started making felts at the mill. Their success too was short-lived: just over a year later they had gone into liquidation. The third set of tenants who rented the mill were Walter and John Rushton who changed the mill back to cotton manufacturing in 1874. John took sole control of the mill in 1875, but went bankrupt in 1879 with liabilities of over £8,000.[64]

The mill seems to have remained empty after John Rushton's departure. It was offered for sale in 1887 and its contents put up for sale in 1889, but it was not until after the deaths of Elizabeth and Jane Wallwork that it was sold. The purchasers in 1904 were Alexander Barlow and Sons at nearby Bridge Mills. The buildings at Plunge fell into ruins and were gradually demolished, the chimney getting the long drop in March 1909. One corner of the mill – the cloth warehouse and winding place – survived as an outbuilding next to a row of cottages until the 1950s when it was demolished after the cottages had been condemned.[65]

HARDSOUGH MILL

The second fulling mill in the Edenfield district that dated from the early years of the 19th century was built at Hardsough next to the River Irwell. In 1798 John Bowker of Bowker Bank, near Manchester, merchant and baize and flannel manufacturer, bought part of the Hardsough estate. It included a large flat meadow on which he built a stone fulling, scribbling and carding mill, dryhouse and dwelling that he insured for £600 towards the end of 1801. The water wheels and other machinery he insured for a further £200. Bowker's partner in the business was John Haworth, an Edenfield clothier, who would no doubt have been responsible for the day-to-day running of the mill. He died in 1804 and the mill was let to various tenants, including William Hutchinson and Sons, woollen manufacturers, who were there between 1816 and 1826. By the beginning of the following year, the mill was being offered to let in the Manchester papers and was sixty-six feet long, fifty-one feet wide and three storeys high 'besides a floor in the roof' and was 'capable of being used as a cotton mill or for printworks.'[66]

The mill was let to William Sagar, fulling miller, who ran it for the next twenty years or so. He was almost certainly the same man who had previously been in business at Chatterton Mill and who had gone bankrupt along with his father and brothers in 1821. Three water wheels, each six feet wide and twelve feet in diameter powered the machinery, while the finished cloth was tentered out of doors on the rising ground east of the mill. Sagar retired in the late 1840s and his place at Hardsough was taken by James Hindle from Haslingden. His small business – he was a cotton spinner as well as a fulling miller – employed seventeen people, including his sons, Abraham and James. They took over the mill when their father died in 1857, but soon decided to concentrate on dealing in cotton waste.[67]

Selling off the machinery of the Hardsough Spinning and Weaving Co. Ltd. after the business had gone into liquidation in 1870.

In 1861 Hardsough Mill changed to cotton completely when the Rawtenstall and Hardsough Spinning and Manufacturing Co. was established. It was formed by a group of workmen mainly from Rawtenstall who included three carders, a tackler and a grocer. The early 1860s was not a good time to start a new cotton company and the Cotton Famine ruined the business. It went into liquidation at the end of 1864 and the machinery was sold off. Trade was beginning to revive in the following year and a new firm, the Hardsough Spinning and Weaving Co. Ltd., started to work the mill. They did not last much longer than their predecessors and went into liquidation in 1870. By the end of the year the mill was empty and was being offered to let.[68]

A more settled period in the history of the mill began in 1872 when James Rostron, a woollen manufacturer at Tunstead Mill, Stacksteads, bought it. For a couple of years he ran both mills, but retired in 1874 and leased Hardsough to his sons, William, James, Edmund and Jordan, at an annual rent of £750. The Rostron family made considerable additions to the mill, extending it to cover most of the adjacent field. They also built rows of terraced houses in Hardsough Lane and a detached house called The Grange to replace an earlier dwelling. By the early 1880s the mill had three steam engines, but also still took part of its power from two water wheels, one of which drove six pairs of fulling stocks.[69]

Jordan Rostron took sole control of the mill in 1889 and ran it for another thirteen years. He then sublet it to John Stansfield, a Rossendale felt manufacturer. Before many years of the lease had elapsed the mill had been sold to Mitchells, Ashworth, Stansfield and Co. Ltd., a combine of the largest woollen firms in Rossendale, including that owned by William Stansfield, John's uncle. MASCO used Hardsough for about ten years, but by 1916 had rented it out to the Lancashire Book Cloth Co. At this date it was described as a modern, stone built mill with ample spare ground for extension, powerful water wheels, a constant fresh water supply and 'lastly, but most importantly, a Private Siding for receipt and dispatch of goods.'[70]

As the First World War was drawing to a close, George Chapelier, a Belgian paper merchant living in London, took over at Hardsough and in May 1919 set up Pulpine Ltd. to use the mill for making paper pulp. Two of the shareholders in the new company were Constance Milne and her son, John Rothwell Milne who was a great-grandson of John Bowker, the mill's original owner. The business was not a success: a receiver was appointed in January 1920 and the machinery sold off. Hardsough Mill remained empty for the rest of its days, although it was not demolished until 1938-39. The *Ramsbottom Observer* commented in May 1939, 'The removal of the Hardsough Mill has altered the whole landscape at Irwell Vale, viewed from the train at any rate. You now get a full view of the village when passing on the railway.' Indeed, walking through the field where the mill stood it is hard to imagine that it once contained such a large building.[71]

This engraving of Hardsough Mill dating from about 1910 shows the extent to which the mill had expanded to cover most of the field behind the original site. The long two-storey building on the left was the dry house where lengths of cloth were dried on tenterhooks in steam-heated rooms.

LUMB MILL

Towards the end of the 18th century, the Formby family of Formby Hall, who owned the Lumb Hall estate, made several attempts to use part of their land as the site for a mill. They had a flat riverside meadow to offer and advertisements placed in the *Manchester Mercury* in 1791, 1792 and 1801 stressed the advantages of the site: it was suitable for a bleaching ground, the fall of water had sufficient power to turn the largest machinery and if, necessary, the owners were prepared to lend 'any sum of money, requisite for the building of a Factory.' However, it was not until the early 1820s that the Rev. Richard Formby built a mill himself and installed water wheels and associated heavy gearing. The mill was almost complete by February 1824 when it was leased for twenty-one years to Robert Barker, an engineer from Holme, north of Ewood Bridge. Barker was also allowed to raise a weir just above Lumb Bridge and carry water from the Irwell in a goit cut through the grounds of Lumb Hall.[72]

Robert Barker ran the mill in partnership with his son, William, part of it being used for woollen carding and part for cotton spinning and manufacturing. A few years after starting at the mill, Barker tried to sublet part of it and offered leases on two rooms each with power from the water wheels, but nothing came of this plan. He added an extension in about 1832 with iron doors between it and the original building to prevent fire spreading from one to the other. The first of a series of lodges was also made in the hillside above the mill.[73]

By 1835 the property comprised:

> Two Factories for spinning cotton; one 30 yards long by 14 yards wide, and four stories high; the other 11½ yards long by 10¼ yards wide, three stories high, with three water wheels and mill gearing ...[74]

The water wheels were fifteen feet in diameter, two being eight feet wide and the other ten feet. There were also five cottages, a stable and smithy near the mills, five cottages in the lane between the mill and Lumb Hall, and five more cottages at the end of Lumb Bridge. Robert Barker had retired from the business by 1841 and died in 1847. His son continued on his own for a few years, but left to farm at Great Hey in 1846.

A new chapter in the history of the mill then opened when it was converted to papermaking, using cotton rags and waste as a raw material. The first papermakers at Lumb, William Round and George Hadley, did not stay long and were replaced in 1848 by James Newbold and James Park, ironfounders from Bury. The latter kept an interest in the business until about 1860, but the mill was run by another partner, John Stones, and after his death in 1856, by his sons, James and John. In 1860 another papermaker took over at Lumb: Samuel Holker came from Bury and was soon employing about fifty people. He bought the mill, cottages and about twenty-five acres of land in 1867 for £9,575. Seven years later he added a second mill with its own steam engine on the opposite side of the Irwell from the original site. Holker's business may have been getting into difficulties in the early 1880s (he mortgaged his property to his brother, Sir John Holker, for £10,000 in 1882) and by 1886 he had put the mills up for sale. The sale notices said this was due to failing health, but in the following year the business collapsed and Holker's creditors were being paid a final dividend. By this date the mills had seven steam engines between them as well as two water wheels. The paper making equipment included three paper machines (capable of producing fifty tons a week of brown glazed, fine glazed and cartridge paper), six glazing calenders, twenty-three washing and beating engines and four revolving boilers.[75]

When the mills were eventually sold in 1889, the change of owner brought another change of use. The Manchester Cop Dyeing Co. Ltd. dyed twist and weft thread on the cop, claiming that since this cut out the need for reeling and winding it saved time and wages. It was given the right to use an invention that improved the process of treating yarn on the cop and that had been patented by August Graemiger, a Swiss born inventor who came to live at Lumb. Among the first directors of the company were Sir Edward Tootal Broadhurst, a partner in Tootal Broadhurst Lee Co. Ltd., one of the largest cotton firms in Lancashire, and Edward Hoyle of Joshua Hoyle and Sons Ltd. who had a mill a few miles downstream from Lumb at Summerseat. The new owners demolished some of the oldest buildings at Lumb, but additions were also made to the complex on the east bank of the Irwell.[76]

The Manchester Cop Dyeing Co. Ltd. ran Lumb Mill for just over ten years, but at the end of 1903 the directors took the decision to wind up the company. There then followed a somewhat unsettled period in the history of the mill. By the summer of 1904 another company – the Electrical Bleaching Co. (1904) Ltd. – had taken over. It paid £13,000 for the buildings and installed new machinery for washing and

Lumb Mill in 1898 when it was run by the Manchester Cop Dyeing Co.

dyeing hank yarn, a fifty horse-power vertical water turbine and a fifty-kilowatt dynamo. This company went into receivership in 1906. One of the shareholders, Charles Martin, a Nottingham merchant, felt that the company had not had sufficient chance to fully exploit the patent rights it owned and paid £26,000 for its assets so that he could reform the company 'on such a basis as to ensure it having a fair prospect of paying dividends in future, saving patents and giving old share-holders the chance to recoup themselves for some of the loss they have sustained.' In January 1907 Martin agreed to sell to the new concern (called the Lumb Electrical Bleaching Co. Ltd.) the mill buildings, plant, stock in trade and several patents relating to the electrolytic bleaching of cotton. Hopes for lasting success for the new business were short-lived and a liquidator was appointed in 1909.[77]

The mill fell empty after this last failure and was bought by A.T. Porritt in 1912. When war broke out in 1914, he immediately offered it for use as a barracks, but in 1917 a new company, J.B. and W.R. Sharp Ltd, set up in business there. The firm was founded by James Booth Sharp, a Manchester dye manufacturer, and made aniline dyes at Lumb until the early 1920s. The company went into receivership in December 1922 and the directors took the decision to wind up the firm in October 1923, although the final winding up meeting was not held until 1928. In the same

The last of Lumb Mill: a derelict calender house and engine house pictured in 1986.

year the mill was briefly considered as a possible site for making artificial silk. Nothing came of the plan and it stood idle throughout the 1930s, but again saw service during the Second World War, first as a barracks and then as a Ministry of Supply depot.[78]

With the arrival of Thomas Aitken and Son Ltd. of Irwell Vale Mills after the war, Lumb was given something of a new lease of life. It was renamed Lumb Vale Mill to match Irwell Vale, Wood Vale and Spring Vale, the firm's other mills, and was used until the early 1960s. For a few years afterwards, Durie and Miller, the carpet underlay manufacturers who were already using Ewood Bridge Mill, moved into Lumb but when they left in about 1974 the mill was coming to the end of its life. Most of it was demolished in the following year, although a smithy, calender house and small engine house dating from 1872 survived until 1990. A chemic shed, mixing shed and pump house, also dating from the papermaking days, still stands on the hillside overlooking the site and is now a private house.[79]

BRIDGE MILL

Bridge Mill was the last of the mills on the Dearden Brook and the third mill in the village that owed its existence to the Rostron family. On 8th May 1824 Richard Rostron (1777-1861), woollen manufacturer, took a 999-year lease on a piece of land next to the bridge that carried the Edenfield-Rochdale turnpike road over the brook. To supply his intended fulling mill with water he was given the right not only to take water out of the brook, but also to build a covered drain to carry water out of the adjoining Gin Croft Farm. Rostron's nickname was 'Pinch Dickey', an allusion to his penny-pinching ways. In about 1808, for instance, he began putting out work to handloom weavers in Rochdale because he could pay one third less wages there than elsewhere. He is also said to have 'watered' his cloth to make it up to the required weight and thickness before it was sold.[80]

Once the buildings at Bridge Mill were complete, they were used not only for fulling woollen cloth, but also for cotton spinning and weaving by Richard's sons, Lawrence and John. As pioneers in the use of powerlooms the brothers suffered in April 1826 when their mill was attacked by the rioters. All fifty-eight of their looms were destroyed. In spite of this set back, the mill was soon running again and the cotton business prospered. Ten years after the riot there were no less than 517 fustian powerlooms in the building, by far the largest number in any mill in the district. A visitor to the mill in February 1833 noted that not only did it have a twenty-three foot diameter water wheel and an eighty horse-power steam engine, but also that another fifty horse-power engine was being installed.[81]

As the business grew, another brother, James, was taken into the partnership in about 1830. He went to live in New York to look after the company's affairs on that side of the Atlantic. Lawrence made his home in Manchester so that he could oversee the Manchester warehouse, while John stayed in the village to keep an eye on the

Richard Rostron (1777-1861) otherwise known as 'Pinch Dickey'. The stretch of Rochdale Road that slopes past his mill is still known locally as 'Dickey Broo'.

day-to-day running of the mill. Although the early 1830s seem to have been prosperous years for the three brothers, they ran into difficulties when the cotton trade fell into one of its periodic depressions. A fiat of bankruptcy was issued against Lawrence and John in January 1836 and against James in the following year. Their assignees continued to run Bridge Mill until August 1841, but the failure of the Rostrons' business was a very serious blow to the village. When Leonard Horner, the factory inspector, visited Edenfield on 5th October 1841 he was told that the three brothers had employed 550 people, paying out £280 a week in wages. Since the stoppage, about half of the employees had left the village to look for work elsewhere. Richard Pickup, relieving officer for Tottington Higher End, said that twenty families were receiving poor relief at the rate of 2s per week for each person and when Horner spoke to William Turner, chairman of the Haslingden Board of Guardians, he 'fully corroborated all I had heard from the relieving officer of the state of destitution of many most respectable people by the stoppage of Messrs. Rostron's mill.'[82]

Bridge Mill was put up for sale. The sale notices reveal that it had in fact grown into two separate buildings – the old mill, four storeys high, and the new mill, five storeys high, – as well as a weaving shop (two storeys), weaving shed (212 ft. long by 56 ft. wide) and various ancillary buildings, including a gas making plant with nine retorts and pipes and burners for 400 lights. The machinery included carding engines; drawing, slubbing and roving frames; throstles, mules and twisting jennies, 508 fustian looms and five sets of fulling stocks. Along with the workers' cottages, the whole property was valued at £20,000, but attracted one bid of only £4,500. Eventually the mills were bought by William Turner, the man who had spoken to Leonard Horner. He was an extensive woollen manufacturer at Helmshore and father-in-law to James Rostron, one of the partners in the bankrupt firm. Turner tried to find new tenants for the mills and one of his advertisements in the *Manchester Guardian* in 1845 shows that the Rostrons' failure continued to affect the village since it states that the mills were 'close to the village of Edenfield where there is an abundance of empty cottages.' When the 1851 census was taken there were still forty Rostron-built cottages standing empty in Exchange Street.[83]

By this date James Rostron was back in business at Bridge Mills in a small way: he was employing just forty-nine people. Although we cannot be certain, it seems probable that his father-in-law had helped him to re-establish himself as a cotton spinner and manufacturer. He ran the mill until his death in 1858 with only one further setback: a fire in 1857 caused £1,000 worth of damage. James's widow, Sarah, carried on his business after his death and also rented some of the buildings to other small concerns. For example, two brothers Edmund and Richard Emmett, who were there in 1861, employed thirty and twenty-three hands respectively. They were later joined by a third brother, James, who moved across the road from Dearden Clough where he had had just nine workpeople[84]

Prosperity seemed to be returning to Bridge Mills, but the 1870s saw further reversals of fortune. In October 1871 work was in progress on the bed of a large boiler on the ground floor of one of the mill buildings. During the course of the work an iron column supporting the floor of the roving room above gave way, bringing part of the ceiling with it. This broke a four-inch pipe out of which steam blew at a tremendous force. Two workmen – a labourer known only as 'Jack Navvy' and Richard Wallwork, eighteen-year-old son of the village greengrocer – were scalded to death and a third man, Robert Green, was badly injured. The women working in the roving room managed to escape unharmed. The explosion happened on the same morning as the big fire at Dearden Clough Mill and the combination of the two catastrophes attracted huge crowds of people to the village. The *Bury Times* in a special edition for 24th October said:

> The news of the fire and explosion spread like wild-fire on Saturday afternoon and evening, when there was a large number of visitors to the vale in which the lamentable events trans-pired. Sunday, however, was *the* day. As early as six o'clock in the morning people began to flock into the village, bent on satisfying their curiosity; to and fro they went till eleven

o'clock in the evening, and it is computed that over 30,000 passed in and out of the village during the day, as many as 1,000 persons passing a given point, at one time, in ten minutes.

The second disaster took place on Christmas Eve 1875 after the mill had closed for the holidays. The buildings stood in two blocks separated by a narrow passage four or five yards wide, but communicating with each other by a wooden bridge on the third storey. The smaller of the two blocks nearest the brook was occupied by Sarah Rostron, who used it for preparing cotton for spinning, and George Duckworth and David Wallwork who had a small weaving shed containing about seventy looms. A fire broke out in the middle of this building 'and the premises being old, and the timbers exceedingly dry, the fire had complete possession of the place within half an hour.' Edward, Sarah Rostron's son, and P.C. Rae, the village policeman, smashed down the interconnecting bridge, thus preventing the blaze from spreading, but by the early hours of Christmas Day the building where the fire had started lay in ruins. About £13,000 worth of damage was caused and some 250 people thrown out of work.[85]

Almost exactly two years later the second part of the mill was burnt down. It was stone-built, five storeys high with walls a yard thick and had just had new floors put in and new machinery installed throughout. The fire was not discovered until it had a firm hold on the building. Fire engines were sent for from Haslingden and Bury, but by the time they arrived nothing but the walls were standing. At the height of the fire the light from the flames could be seen for miles around, even as far as Accrington. About 100 people lost their jobs as a result of the fire and the damage was estimated at between £15,000 and £20,000.[86]

This second fire probably persuaded Sarah Rostron and her son (who was running the business) to dispose of what remained of the mill in 1878. The engine and boiler house, weaving shed, warehouse and site of the burnt out buildings were bought by Alexander Barlow (1824-1897). He began work at the age of eight at Plunge Mill and had worked at Bridge Mills themselves when the Rostron brothers were there. After working as a tea-dealer and draper, he entered the cotton trade on his own account by leasing part of Edenwood Mill in the 1850s. In about 1860 he moved to Twine Mill, Shuttleworth, in partnership with his brother-in-law, John Ramsbottom and Richard Pickup. For the next twenty years or so the Barlow family lived at Top o' th' Lee, which Alexander farmed as well as running Twine Mill.[87]

Alexander Barlow set about rebuilding Bridge Mills and installed 300 looms. When he added a completely new weaving shed in 1893-4, the mill became the first in the district to be lit by electric light. Power from a generator installed by village man John Henry Hindle supplied about 300 lights in the three weaving sheds and winding and preparation rooms. Shortly before Barlow died in 1897 he took his four sons, John, Thomas, George and Edwin, into partnership and acquired another mill at Church, near Accrington. The Barlow brothers continued in their father's footsteps by adding another mill – at Blackley – to the two they already owned and by continuing to expand at Bridge Mills. A new weaving shed in 1905-6 was built to hold an additional 400 looms and was followed in 1911 by a second shed, storeroom,

Bridge Mills from Dearden Clough in about 1907, with The Mount, then the home of Edwin Barlow, at top right.

offices and cloakrooms for the workpeople. By this date the mill housed 1,100 looms. A few years later the bad luck that seemed to have plagued Bridge Mills struck again when a fire destroyed the warehouse, winding room and preparation room and caused about £60,000 worth of damage.[88]

John, Thomas and Edwin Barlow retired in 1919 (George had died in 1904) and Alexander Barlow and Sons became a private limited company run by their nephews Tom and Alexander Barlow Hillis. The Hillis family saw the mill through the difficult years of the '20s and '30s, including the strikes and lockouts of 1929-1932. These culminated in a county-wide strike at the end of August 1932 that was called as a protest against proposals to cut costs by increasing the number of looms operated by each weaver. At the beginning of 1934 a 10% reduction in wages was suggested as an alternative to the 'more loom system', but eventually six looms per weaver were introduced at Bridge Mills. One male weaver later recalled that his income from four looms was sufficient to keep his family, while the other two looms provided 'beer and baccy money.'[89]

Changes continued after the Second World War: the old weaving shed was demolished and in the new shed the number of looms reduced to 600. In the early 1950s, the cotton industry as a whole was facing a slump in demand and in March 1951 Bridge Mills went on a three-day week. Prospects improved a little in 1953, but in the years that followed more and more Lancashire cotton mills were forced to

Weavers and tacklers of Alexander Barlow and Sons at Bridge Mills in 1917. George Barlow (*standing left*) was inside manager of the mill for many years.

close. Bridge Mills joined their number in December 1956 throwing 130 people out of work. The mills were offered for sale early in 1957, but no buyer could be found so the contents were sold off piecemeal. The empty buildings were taken over by a new business, the Technical Felt Company, which began making stiffened felt for the slipper trade in the autumn of 1958. Their stay in Edenfield was short-lived since they went into voluntary liquidation in January 1960 and once again the mills and their machinery were on the market. The new occupants of the mill were also felt makers. Prefabricated Felts Ltd. ran Bridge Mills until the early 1970s, after which they joined the ranks of textile mills that were converted into industrial units. Various businesses moved into the divided mills offering a variety of products and services including moulded polythene containers, MOT testing, and auto-electrics. One firm – John Schofield (Textile Machinery) Ltd. – even maintains the mill's links with its origins. The saga of misfortune that dogged Bridge Mills was not over, however, for in 1977 the premises of Bladesville Ltd, a haulage firm, were wrecked by a £20,000 blaze.[90]

TURN MILL

Turn Mill stood at the side of the main road through the hillside village, near its junction with the lane leading to New Gate. It was powered by water taken from New Gate Brook and stored in two lodges behind the mill. It seems to have been

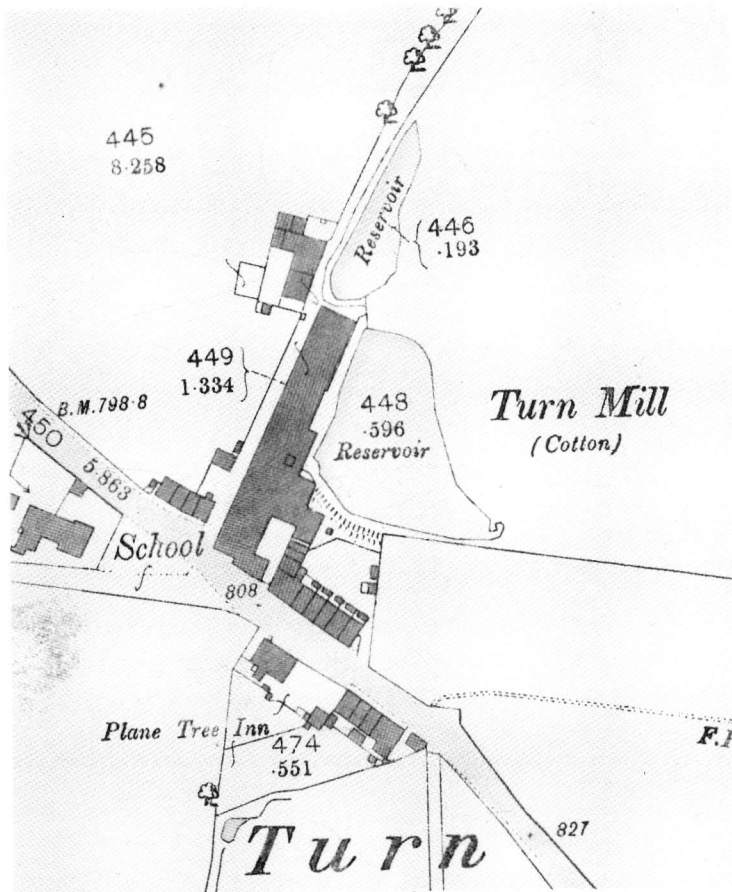

Turn Mill in the early 1890s.

built in about 1822-23 by Richard Haworth of Croston Close who ran the mill with his younger brother, George. By the time Richard died in 1844 the property included not only the mill itself but also warehouses, a shippon and four cottages. George Haworth outlived his brother by sixteen years, but a new chapter in the history of the mill had already begun in 1854.[91]

From 24th June 1854, John Nuttall, a Shuttleworth farmer, took a 99-year lease on the property. He demolished the old mill and built a new one in its place, complete with steam engine. Nuttall was joined in the business by his four sons, John, Richard, James and William, and the firm continued as John Nuttall and Sons even after John the elder's death in 1861. The sons dissolved their partnership in 1875, from which point Richard carried on in his own name until his own death in 1896. He converted the spinning portion of the mill to weaving and later added a new weaving shed so that when he died there were over 300 looms in the mill. His obituary noted that:

As an employer Mr. Nuttall has possessed in quite an unusual measure the good will of his work people to whom he has been familiarly known as "Dickey". Perhaps this is scarcely to be wondered at seeing that some were friends of a lifetime, and had been in his service for the last 20 or 30 years. The employees at Turn Mill have had regular work and it is stated that since the firm commenced there have been no stoppages except for breakdowns or holidays.[92]

Richard's son, Edward, took over from his father and ran the business until he died in 1907. His son was just fourteen years old, so the mill was sold to Richard Ryden, a Blackburn cotton manufacturer, who did not keep it very long. The Turn Manufacturing Co. took over in 1909 and was soon weaving printing and bleaching cloths on 300 looms. The directors of the new company included John Fort (later one of the directors of George Alty Ltd. at Hope Mill), Alexander Fearfull, a director of the Grane Manufacturing Co., Haslingden, and James and Jonathon Haworth of Bleakholt Road. After the company was wound up in 1930 the building stood empty for a while. A complete change came in 1933 with the advent of J.D. Kerr, manufacturers of paints, varnishes and lacquers, from Blackheath in London, who wished to use the mill for making cellulose lacquers. Their arrival was heralded as good news for the village, but they did not stay long at Turn and the old mill was demolished in the summer of 1937. Only a few foundation walls and two overgrown lodges remain to remind us of its presence.[93]

IRWELL VALE MILL

The second mill in the Edenfield district built by John Bowker, the Manchester merchant, was at Irwell Vale. On the opposite bank of the Irwell from his Hardsough Mill, it stood on part of the old Ravenshore estate that Bowker had bought in two parts in 1806 and 1813. It was not until the 1830s that he decided to build a mill near the confluence of the Ogden and Irwell. The new mill was offered to let in the *Manchester Guardian* in January 1832:

> WATER POWER MILL – TO BE LET, with immediate possession, a New Substantial STONE BUILDING four stories high, 41 yards long by 16 yards wide, with water wheels, &c., a supply of water equal to 30 horses' power in the dryest seasons. Situated in the Vale of the Irwell, near Edenfield, fifteen miles from Manchester – For further particulars apply to Mr. Bowker, Prestwich.[94]

Bowker also built two rows of workers' houses next to the mill and in doing so created a completely new village. To supply the mill with water required considerable effort and expense. Some distance upstream on the Ogden a large stepped weir was built to divert water into a goit. This tunnelled through solid rock before emerging into a field and contouring around the side of the hill to the back of the mill, covering a distance of more than a third of a mile.

Bowker's first tenant at Irwell Vale was a cotton spinner called Henry Kilshaw. In 1836 he was one of the local textile manufacturers who took advantage of the scheme promoted by the Poor Law Commissioners that encouraged families from depressed agricultural areas in the south of England to move north to work in the mills. James Bew, his wife and seven children came from Bucklebury in Berkshire to work at Irwell Vale Mill in April 1836. James was to receive a wage of 10s a week, his daughter Harriet (aged 14) 3s 6d and his sons, James and Thomas (both aged 12) 3s. Unfortunately for the Bew family, Henry Kilshaw was one of the many bankruptcies of the trade depression in 1837 and they left the village. Kilshaw too left the area, eventually ending up in Belgium. He had married Isabel Aitken and it was her father, Thomas, from Chatterton who took over at Irwell Vale, thus beginning a long association between the mill and the Aitken name. For a short time he ran the mill in partnership with James Stott and Thomas Smith, the Haslingden woollen manufacturers whom we have already encountered at Dearden Clough. The partnership was dissolved in 1839 and Aitken carried on the business with his son, John. In 1851 they were employing 152 people at Irwell Vale. When Thomas Aitken died in 1858 his younger son, also called Thomas, joined his brother in the concern, although it continued to be called Thomas Aitken and Son. John Aitken retired in 1875 leaving the younger Thomas in sole charge of the business. He ran Irwell Vale until his death in 1911 and in 1905 bought not only the mill but also most of the village from the descendants of John Bowker. [95]

Thomas Aitken, junior, (1833-1911), who ran the family business at Irwell Vale from 1875 until his death.

The mill had two water wheels, but was also partly steam driven. By the early 1880s it had three steam engines altogether, and in 1912 a 'magnificent and up-to-date new engine … appropriately housed in a new building, of ample proportions and with large windows giving an abundance of light' was installed and christened 'Thomas and May Aitken' by Mrs. Aitken. Following Mrs. Aitken's death in 1915 the business passed to her cousin, Margaret Gray. Miss Gray transformed Thomas Aitken and Son into a private limited company in 1918 with herself as governing director. The other shareholders were James W. Cunliffe, general manager at Irwell Vale, who became managing director; William Haslam, cashier, who became company secretary, and Samuel Woodcock, solicitor.[96]

Margaret Gray died in August 1930. The *Daily Dispatch* described her as 'God-mother of the Mill' and noted that she was,

... already a wealthy woman when the mill was left to her ... and she did not look to the mill to add very considerably to her fortune. Instead, she spent big sums in improving the conditions of the workers. She started a scheme of profit-sharing among them, gave large sums to their local hospital and was always doing good deeds. If any worker fell ill or became permanently incapacitated she at once pensioned him off comfortably for the rest ˙of his life.

Among the legacies that Miss Gray left was one of £10,000 to be shared by employees at Irwell Vale who had worked there for more than two years at the time of her death. Unfortunately, the slump in the cotton trade and a fall in the value of Miss Gray's securities and property meant that no money was paid out until Christmas 1936 when each legatee received £4 as part of their share.[97]

During the inter-war years several additions were made to the mill buildings, especially on the north bank of the Ogden and over the river itself. This caused problems in December 1936 when there were over twelve hours of continuous rain. The swollen river flooded into the weaving shed, big loom shed, warehouse, doubling and winding rooms and offices. There were similar scenes in September 1946 when the floodwaters passed the high level mark of 1936.[98]

James Cunliffe died in 1933 and new directors were appointed, including his son-in-law John Dewhurst. This man and his sons, Tom and Geoffrey, were to run the company for the rest of its life. The mill saw several changes in the Second World War and the immediate post-war years. They included an extension to the offices, the building of a canteen and a warehouse, stretcher room, doubling room, pirn room and weaving shed on the north bank of the Ogden in 1952. A few years later, in 1957, most of John Bowker's original mill was demolished. Thomas Aitken and Son

The end of John Bowker's original mill at Irwell Vale, a picture taken during its demolition in 1957.

were running four mills in the late 1950s, but production was gradually concentrated at Irwell Vale until that too closed. The buildings were bought by a Ramsbottom soap making firm, W. and E. Products, who stayed until the early 1990s. In 1985 the company was at the centre of an investigation carried out by the BBC's *Newsnight* programme into the manufacture and sale of soap with a high mercury content. The soap was exported to Africa where it was sold as a skin lightening aid. The programme highlighted the concerns of women soap-packers who were found to have high levels of mercury in their hair and nails after working with the soap. Edenfield Soap and Toiletries Ltd. took over from W. and E. Products at Irwell Vale in 1993 and ran the mill until 2001 when they too were replaced by Sigma Soap Ltd.[99]

ELTON BANKS MILL

Elton Banks Mill had the shortest life of any of the Edenfield mills. It was built in 1838 by Lawrence Elton in a field below Elton Banks Farm and was powered by a small twenty horse-power steam engine. At first Lawrence's son, also called Lawrence, ran the mill, but later he leased it to Charles Somerset.[100] Its end came early in 1851 and was recorded by the *Blackburn Standard* for 12th February:

DESTRUCTION BY FIRE OF A FACTORY NEAR EDENFIELD – On Sunday last, early in the morning, the factory situate near Edenfield, generally known by the name of

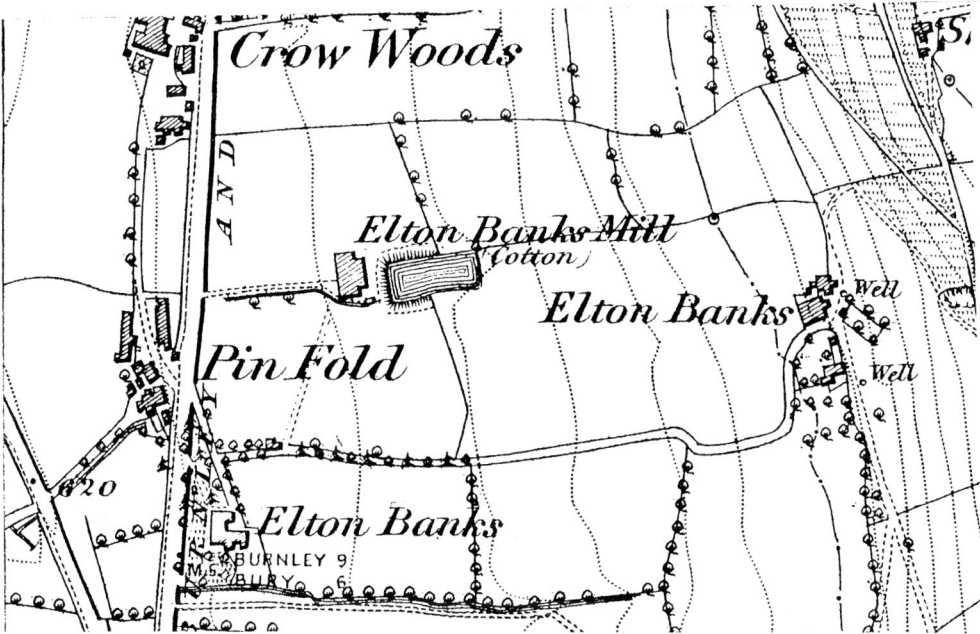

The brief existence of Elton Banks Mill was captured by the Ordnance Survey on the first edition six-inch map, which was surveyed in 1844-48.

"Elton's Factory", and which is in the occupation of several parties, was destroyed by fire. The engine belonging to Messrs. Hoyle and Hardman was got to the premises, and was the means of saving the engine and boiler. The origin of the fire is not known. Some part of the mill, if not all, was, we understand, insured at Christmas last.

The mill was not rebuilt and today only the lodge remains to remind us of its existence.

LODGE MILL

Two brothers, John and Henry Ramsbottom, whose family also built and ran several mills in the Cheesden valley, built Lodge Mill in 1845. Their new mill stood between Shuttleworth Brook and Riding Head Lane and, like Turn Mill, was supplied with water from New Gate Brook. The brothers worked in partnership for some time, building houses near the mill in 1856, but by the early 1860s Henry was running the mill on his own as a cotton hard waste spinner and manufacturer. His business failed, perhaps because of the Cotton Famine, and his machinery was put up for sale in January 1863. It included eight hard waste devils, five carding engines, two billys, two pairs of mules and forty-eight powerlooms.[101]

The mill was taken over by James Ramsbottom, second cousin to John and Henry, who set up in business with his sons. This was another occasion where one firm and one mill were to be linked for a long time. The name 'James Ramsbottom and Sons' was associated with Lodge Mill for almost exactly one hundred years. Henry Ramsbottom had made some additions to the original mill and James Ramsbottom continued the process of enlargement. By the late 1860s the mill consisted of two main blocks with various ancillary buildings. The firm also built more workers' houses in Lodge Mill Lane. Until 1889, part of the mill was worked by water, but the old water wheel was taken out when alterations were made to the steam engine.[102]

Lodge Mill standing empty in April, 2000.

James Ramsbottom died in 1880, leaving his sons, George, Joseph Henry and Dennis, in charge. They made the firm into a private limited company in 1899. Joseph Henry outlived his brothers – he died in 1923 – so that the business passed to his sons. Like many mills that used cotton hard waste as a raw material, Lodge Mill caught fire several times, most seriously in September 1923 when sparks from grit in the cotton waste that was being broken up set fire to the waste itself. The resulting fire destroyed the two storey breaking department and caused £11,000 worth of damage.[103]

In 1938, James Ramsbottom and Sons Ltd. were taken over by William Kenyon and Sons Ltd. of Dukinfield who ran Lodge Mill until its closure in February 1966. Twenty of the thirty-five workers at the mill were made redundant, while the remainder found work in another company in the William Kenyon group. The mill buildings were divided into units and sold. There are currently (2002) plans to demolish the mill and build houses on the site.[104]

STUBBINS VALE MILL

As the business of the firm of J. and J. Porritt expanded steadily throughout the 1830s and 1840s, it became clear to the partners that Dearden Clough Mill at Edenfield and Springwood Mill at Ramsbottom would soon be too small. In addition, the lease of Dearden Clough was due for renewal in 1851 and the brothers felt that they might not be able to renegotiate it on favourable terms. Instead, they determined to become mill owners themselves and began looking for a suitable site. In the summer of 1850 they bought two adjoining properties – Lower Stubbins and Lower Strongstry – for £3,000.[105]

Work on building the new mill began immediately using stone from a quarry on the hillside and had been largely completed by the end of the year. Stubbins Vale Mill was designed by James Porritt, the second of the three brothers, and was sixty yards long, twenty yards wide and four storeys high. As it rose from its foundations James carefully oversaw the work, climbing the scaffolding

James Porritt (1810-1896), one of the senior partners in the firm that ran Stubbins Vale Mill, and architect of the original mill buildings.

each day. The boiler house and chimney were added in 1851 and were also designed by James Porritt. He later recalled that he had travelled to London to take stock of Nelson's Column so that his chimney could be built on similar lines. When it was complete he climbed to the top to fix the lightning conductor himself.[106] The machinery at Dearden Clough was moved to Stubbins Vale in February 1852 and production began under the new name of Porritt Brothers and Austin. (James Porritt's brother-in-law, John Austin, had been taken into the partnership). The firm's assets were valued at £21,000 and as well as continuing to manufacture paper-makers' felts, they began cotton spinning and weaving to supply specialist fabrics to sugar refiners and calico printers.

As well as the mill, the Porritts built houses for themselves and their workpeople. Stubbins Vale House, James's home, was nearest the mill; Samuel had The Cliffe on the hillside above, while Joseph lived at Green Mount near the old farm at Strongstry. They built eight cottages and a shop in East View at the same time as the mill and added fourteen cottages and a shop in North Street in 1854. These were joined by North View (1860), West View/North Street (1864), Stubbins Vale Terrace (1871), South Terrace (1874) and Strongstry Bridge (1881). There were also Springfield Cottage (1870) for the mill manager and farm buildings and cottages.

Considerable additions were also made to the original mill. A second mill three storeys high with attics was built to the south of the first mill in 1862 at a cost of £4,600, while in 1874 the Fireproof Mill was added linking the two earlier buildings so that they enclosed three sides of a square. Substantial stone offices and a gatehouse completed the fourth side, while in 1866 a castellated tenter tower was put up on the hillside behind the mills. It was used to house long lengths of wet woollen cloth that had been taken out to dry on rows of tenterhooks in the nearby field. The 1870s also saw the construction of a new weaving shed and a block of buildings on open land between Stubbins Vale Road and the railway. These comprised store rooms, cooling and making up rooms and an oil extracting shed. There was also a building put up especially to house male and female dining rooms and a newsroom. The latter was supplied with the London and provincial daily news-papers and housed a library of about 200 volumes that had been established in 1863 and moved to its purpose-built home towards the end of 1873. By 1877 total expenditure at Stubbins Vale had reached nearly £17,000.[107]

By this date there had been some changes in the partnership. The three Porritt brothers had twelve sons between them (John Austin was childless) and a dispute arose about the position in the firm of Joseph's eldest son, William John. He was dismissed from his post in the mill and, shortly afterwards, Joseph, feeling that the future of his others sons in the firm could not be settled to his satisfaction, withdrew from the business. Taking his share of the partnership's assets with him, partly in cash, partly in goods and machinery, he set up in business with his sons, first at Ramsbottom and then at Helmshore. The three remaining partners bought new equipment and carried on together until 1866 when Samuel who had five sons

Stubbins Vale Mill in 1874. This extremely fine photograph shows many interesting details, including the quarry behind the chimney from which stone for the mill and houses was taken; lengths of woollen cloth drying on tenterhooks on the hillside behind the tentering tower (which later had a second storey added); and the houses of the three Porritt brothers. Bottom left is Stubbins Vale House, the home of James Porritt; The Cliffe (Samuel) stands above the trees centre right; and Green Mount (Joseph) is on the extreme right.

decided that he too would withdraw and set up on his own. Taking £30,000 in cash and bills as his share he left Stubbins Vale and moved to Bamford. James Porritt and John Austin were left in charge and changed the name of the firm to Porritt Brother and Austin. Within three years their assets had a greater value than when Samuel left and James's sons, Richard and John, were taken into the partnership.

During the first half of the 1870s, about £16,000 was spent on installing new machinery at Stubbins Vale, but from 1877 until James Porritt's death in 1896 less than £2,500 was laid out on new plant. Similarly the building programme temporarily came to an end and no new property was bought. All this changed when James's son, Richard, and then his grandson, Austin Townsend Porritt, took over. They bought new machinery, including a twenty-eight foot dry felt woollen loom that was then the largest in the world. A new weaving shed was added to the mill complex in 1907 and in the following year electric light was installed throughout the mills. Austin Porritt also made the firm into a limited company and included fifty employees in the list of shareholders.

In 1914, Porritt Brother and Austin became one of the constituent firms of a new company, Porritts and Spencer Limited.[108] To avoid duplication, some reorganisation took place and Stubbins Vale became the centre for producing white washers, worsted warps and card cloth for weaving and shared in the manufacture of steaming blankets, grey washers, winders' listing, linen warps and sizing cloth. A.T. Porritt planned to make several changes to the buildings, including the demolition of some of the buildings between the road and the railway. These were to be replaced by a three-storey block to house wide felt looms and warping machines. A bridge over the road would link this new building to the first floor of the original mill that would be used for spinning and storing yarn. Another weaving shed was also to be built over a filled in lodge almost opposite the mill gates.

The First World War meant that these plans had to be shelved and it was not until the 1920s that some additions and alterations were made to the mill, including the new weaving shed. In 1926 another new building was put up on the site of another filled in lodge on the north side of the main mills. It was known as the cotton warehouse, but also housed new looms weaving cotton dry felts sold under the trade name of Arrow Dryers. More additions followed in 1936 and 1937 with a cotton picking room and an extension to the cotton weaving shed.

The Second World War brought a shortage of raw materials and manpower and some parts of the mill had to be closed down. Demand for papermakers' felts,

Workers in the cotton winding room at Stubbins Vale in the 1930s. The buildings that were used for the production of the firm's cotton goods were nicknamed 'The White City.'

however, continued to be high and Porritt Brother and Austin made a special contribution to the war effort by manufacturing felt that was used to seal bullet holes in aircraft tanks. They opened a canteen at the mill and the workpeople found that holidays with pay became one of the normal conditions of employment. Throughout the war the company also paid special allowances to the dependants of employees who were serving in the Armed Forces.

In May 1940, the Porritt family and Stubbins Vale suffered an irreparable loss when Austin Porritt's only son, Richard, was killed during the retreat of the BEF to Dunkirk. He had joined the firm in 1936 after spending some months at Stubbins Vale to gain practical experience of working in the mill. He took a keen interest in the welfare of the Lancashire cotton workers during the economic depression of the 1930s. Eager to try to improve the lot of the working classes, he stood for parliament in 1935 and was elected MP for the Heywood and Radcliffe Division. On the outbreak of war he had joined up and was just thirty years old when he lost his life. A year after Richard Porritt's death, Stubbins Vale Mill and Stubbins Vale House were damaged when two heavy explosives were dropped nearby. Nearly every window in the mill was blown out, but nevertheless work continued as normal the next morning.[109]

For some time after the war, shortage of manpower and materials continued to be a problem. However, Porritts and Spencer soon began exporting felts to those markets that had been closed during the war and this led to further expansions at Stubbins Vale. A new weaving shed equipped with Northrop looms appeared in the late 1940s and in 1951 spacious new offices were built to mark the centenary of the mill, using stone from the demolished Stubbins Vale House. It was also during the 'fifties that the mill began to use synthetic fibres (nylon and terylene) side by side with the traditional cotton and wool, not only in felts but also in filter cloths for the laundry industry. Terylene blankets made at Stubbins Vale even found their way to the Antarctic when they were used by an expedition led by Vivian Fuchs.[110]

By the mid-1960s, despite all the changes that had taken place, papermakers' felts were still the most important product manufactured at Stubbins Vale. In March, 1968 when J.L. McArthur, chairman of Porritts and Spencer, wrote his annual report he was able to announce another important change: merger terms had been agreed with the Scapa Group Ltd. and two years later the new company became Scapa Porritt Ltd. Meanwhile, Stubbins Vale continued growing and in October 1970 a new single storey building was opened by Ronald Bray, MP for Rossendale. This extension was to house machinery for making synthetic wires and fabrics for paper machines, the whole project costing nearly £250,000.[111]

A few years later, as part of the continued reorganisation of the Scapa Group mills, production of yarn was moved from Stubbins Vale to Mossfield Mill. This sounded the death knell for James Porritt's magnificent five-storeyed mills, which were not suitable for housing modern machinery. They stood empty for twelve months before demolition began on 1st September 1978. The 180-foot chimney was

The end of a landmark: Stubbins Vale chimney topples into the partially demolished mill in April 1979.

the last to go and was felled on a bitterly cold April day in 1979 when more than 200 people gathered on the nearby hillside to watch the giant felled. The demolition of the oldest parts of the mills did not end Stubbins Vale's links with the textile industry entirely. Those buildings that had once housed the cotton side of the business and that had been nicknamed 'The White City' became the home of Scapa Synthoform Ltd. This company, which later became Unaform Ltd. and then Voith Fabrics, continued the Porritt tradition of producing paper machine forming fabrics using some of the most up-to-date machinery, including a Jäeger loom that cost over £1 million.[112]

In 1982 some of the buildings on the other side of Stubbins Vale Road were acquired by TNT Express (UK) Ltd., part of the international transport organisation. They took over what was left of the 'mill bottom' (that had housed the fulling stocks), a drying room and two weaving sheds built in 1874 and 1926 and transformed them into the administrative head office for the entire company.

HOPE MILL ('THE BLACK FACTORY')

Hope Mill was built in 1860 on a piece of land fronting Bury Road just beyond the bridge over Dearden Clough Brook. Its site was taken on a 999-year lease from Lord Derby by James Warburton at an annual rent of £18 15s. Warburton went into partnership with James Nuttall and they called their new mill India Mill. Success for them was short-lived and by 1865 the mill had been renamed Hope Mill and was being run by Thomas Nelson who had previously been one of the tenants of Bridge Mills. In 1871 he was employing fifty-two people at the little mill.[113]

Thomas Nelson sold up in 1874 when the mill consisted of a weaving shed with preparation rooms, engine and boiler houses and a warehouse and contained 108 powerlooms. For a couple of years the mill was run by Henry Musgrave Briddon and Craven Charles Goring, merchants, commission agents and manufacturers, who were also in business at Burnley and Manchester. By 1876 they too had been replaced by Richard Haworth and Robert Walmsley whose partnership was dissolved in 1878. Haworth continued on his own until 1880 when his business foundered and the mill was put up for sale again.[114]

The new owners of the mill were James Holden and George Alty, towel manufacturers at Holcombe Brook, and they turned Hope Mill over to weaving towels. By 1891, George Alty had sole charge of the mill and ran it until his death in 1917. He added a new tape room at the back of the building in 1912. Hope Mill closed briefly at the beginning of the First World War, was reopened and then closed again in 1918. In the following year, James Alty, George's son, and two other Edenfield men, Harry Minton and John Fort, formed a private limited company, which they called George Alty Ltd., and restarted the mill. By the early 1920s, only the latter two men remained as partners and they and their descendants ran Hope Mill for nearly fifty years, continuing the business of weaving towels of all kinds.[115]

Hope Mill in 2002.

The mill closed in November 1967, but in the following year another new company was set up – the Edenfield Spinning Co. Ltd. – and started production in April 1969 employing about twelve people. They ran Hope Mill until about 1980 when they transferred to Ramsbottom. The Edenfield mill was divided into units and in 1994 much of the original three-storey building fronting the main road was demolished to create a parking area.[116]

UNION MILL AND CUBA MILL

The 1850s and 1860s saw the establishment of a number of co-operative mills in the Rossendale valley and neighbourhood. One of the first, the Bacup and Wardle Commercial Company, paid yearly dividends as high as 62½% and its success prompted other groups of working men to join together to build their own mills. One such body was the Ramsbottom Spinning and Manufacturing Co., which was incorporated on 10th January 1861. Its first shareholders were Thomas Wolstenholme, joiner, from Edenfield; Joseph Hallworth, engineer, and William Butterfield, carder, both of Irwell Vale; James Dearden, farmer, of Bank Lane; William Taylor, coal agent, William Horsfall, book-keeper, Thomas Lund, mechanic, James Garnett, mason, William Ross, warehouseman, all of Ramsbottom; and Robert Ashworth, engineer, of Rose Bank.[117]

The company acquired from Lord Derby a plot of land at Stubbins adjoining Bolton Road North and bounded by Ramsbottom Gas Works on one side and the goit to Ramsbottom Mill on the other. On part of this land they built the four-storeyed Union Mill, a boiler house and an office and added a large weaving shed in 1868. They also built houses for their workers in Bolton Road North and Dale

Street, the latter named after John Dale. He joined the firm as a book-keeper, but became company secretary and then manager, a position he held with only a short break until his retirement in 1898.[118]

The Ramsbottom Spinning and Manufacturing Co. ran Union Mill until 1904 when the business went into liquidation. The mill closed in January throwing about 500 people out of work. The closure, coming so soon after Stubbins printworks had closed down, was a serious blow to the village. The *Ramsbottom Observer* commented, 'Those who know their Stubbins say that the village is quite another place to what it was twelve months ago. Numbers of houses are unoccupied, and, in a few words, things are not what they used to be.' The building and its contents, including 746 looms and mules and ring frames, were put up for sale in June 1904, but there were no takers. At the end of the year the property was assigned over to Ramsbottom Co-op. In 1898 and 1902 the company had issued a number of mortgage debentures to the co-op. By 1904, nearly £20,000 was owing and, following an action in the Chancery of the County Palatine, it was ordered that the property should be transferred to the co-op. After this the mill was divided into two: the weaving shed and associated buildings were let to the Star Manufacturing Company, Ramsbottom, while the spinning section was sold to a new company, Cuba Mill Ltd. From then on the two mills had separate histories, although for some years the boiler and engine houses were shared.[119]

Union Mill

As well as the weaving shed, the Star Manufacturing Co. leased the size mixing, taping, winding and warping rooms, a warehouse and cloth store, twisting room, mechanics' shop, roller covering house and boiler, economiser and engine houses. The plant they also rented included a pair of horizontal steam engines, various size becks, three tape sizing machines, warping and winding machines and 746 calico looms. A new boiler and economiser were installed in 1906, the same year in which electric light was fitted throughout the mill.[120]

The company leased the mill for ten years, but at the beginning of 1909 they returned it to its owners. Two years later, the co-op sold Union Mill to John Brandwood, owner of the Elton Cop Dyeing Co. Brandwood and several other manufacturers and businessmen, set up a new company called the Union Manufacturing Co. (Ramsbottom) Ltd. to run the mill. This business had only a short life and went into voluntary liquidation in 1917. The mill was bought for £5,000 by another new company, the Union Manufacturing Co. (Stubbins) Ltd. Shortly before the sale, a fire broke out in the four-storey part of the building, causing the roof to fall in and gutting the top three storeys. In all about £15,000 worth of damage was caused, although the weaving shed was saved.[121]

Like its predecessor, the second Union Manufacturing Co. enjoyed a fairly brief spell at Stubbins. In January 1920 the mill passed to the Holme Manufacturing Co.

Stubbins from above Stubbins Vale Mill in about 1925. Cuba Mill is the large building to the right of the tall chimney. The smaller building next to it is the warehouse section of Union Mill, with the roof of the weaving shed just visible behind the Ramsbottom Gas Co.'s gasometer.

Ltd. of Cliviger. New looms were installed and the old ones shipped to Japan. Again the story of the new business at Union Mill was not one of lasting success: the company was wound up in January 1924. Six years later the mill was said not to have run 'for a considerable time' and it was demolished in 1939.[122]

Cuba Mill

To begin with, Cuba Mill had a more settled history than its neighbour. The company that bought it in 1904 was set up by a group of Oldham businessmen and worked the mill without serious difficulty until the late 1920s. The buildings were extended several times and in 1913 ring frames driven by electricity rather than steam were installed. The picture of prosperity had faded by the summer of 1929 when Cuba Mill was among those closed during the cotton strike of that year. It had not re-opened by early 1930 when it was sold to the Lancashire Cotton Corporation (LCC). This was an amalgamation of businesses formed at the instigation of the Bank of England in order to save the Lancashire banks that were owed huge sums by the cotton firms. The Cuba Mill Company had liabilities of £51,000 and assets of nearly £78,000 that were transferred to the LCC. By the autumn of 1931, the mill was at work again, but as part of the Corporation's attempts to turn itself into an efficient and profitable business it had to reduce the number of machines it had at work throughout the county. Cuba Mill fell victim to this paring down operation and when a *Ramsbottom Observer* reporter visited the mill early in 1936 he found that it had been idle for some time and that scrap merchants were busy smashing up the old ring frames.[123]

Turnbull and Stockdale bought the mill, but, as we shall see in a later chapter, it had various non-industrial uses during the Second World War. Afterwards it became the quilting department and the company added a single-storey printing shop in 1961. Seven years later, however, Cuba Mill was one of the sections closed by Turnbull and Stockdale's parent company. It was offered for sale at £43,000, but there no takers. Two years later the asking price had fallen to £29,000 and this time Cuba Mill was taken over by the Traditional Leather Upholstery Co. and N.C. Brown Ltd., storage equipment manufacturers. Following a fire in 1974 the first company moved to Rose Bank. A second disastrous fire occurred in December of the same year. At the height of the blaze more than thirty fire engines were in Stubbins trying to put out the fire at Cuba Mill as well as the one at Rose Bank. Over 200 people in Bolton Road North and Dale Street were evacuated and took refuge in the Railway Hotel. The whole of the main part of the mill was destroyed, leaving just the office block and two single-storey extensions standing. The site was developed as an industrial estate of small units housing a variety of businesses, including SPR Stainless Steel Products whose mini breweries were installed in pubs all over the world.[124]

CHATTERTON WEAVING SHED

In 1908 William Turnbull and William Stockdale, the Rose Bank printers, set up a new company to allow them to manufacture their own cloth. Originally to be called the Rose Bank Manufacturing Co., the name was quickly changed to the Chatterton Weaving Co. and it was in a field at Chatterton that they built a completely new weaving shed. The building took just four months to complete and went into production in March 1909 with sixty-four fancy looms driven by electricity supplied by the Lancashire Electric Power Co. The mill was extended several times and by the late 1940s housed 208 looms. Like Turnbull and Stockdale Ltd., the Chatterton Weaving Co. was taken over by Arthur Sanderson and Sons Ltd. They decided to close the Chatterton shed in 1966 and transfer weaving to another mill in Nelson. In the following year, the Tunstead Needlefelt Co. Ltd., manufacturers of underfelts, bought the building and installed broadlooms to weave needleloom carpets. The company still runs the mill.[125]

SPRING VALE MILL

Spring Vale Mill began life as the Edenfield brewery, which was closed following its acquisition by John Kenyon Ltd. of Cloughfold in 1913. Three local men, James Richard Nuttall, joiner and builder, James Kay, butcher, and William Greenwood went into partnership in 1915 as the Edenfield Size Manufacturing Co. and started making

Turnbull and Stockdale's Chatterton Weaving Shed in the late 1920s.

size in the old brewery. Their company received a licence to store petrol in 1929 and, trading as Edenfield Motor Services, it opened a garage on the open space at the front. The buildings themselves were used by James Pate's carriers business until 1940.[126]

In 1940 Thomas Aitken and Son Ltd. of Irwell Vale Mill acquired the property, which they remodelled and renamed Spring Vale Mill. They ran the mill for more than twenty years. The only incident of note during that time took place in November 1949 when a blocked drain deep underground forced water up through an old well into the ground floor and flooded the weaving shed. It took several weeks to excavate the drain and make repairs. In 1958, the company decided to close the mill and transferred the machinery to Lumb and Irwell Vale Mills, but in the following year Spring Vale was re-opened as the winding and doubling section. It closed again in May 1962 and was bought by the CWS for use as a warehouse in connection with their footwear factory at Britannia Mill, Haslingden. When they too decided that they no longer needed the mill, Brown and Forth, a small firm of chemical merchants moved in. This was in 1972 and the firm stayed until 1999 when the old brewery buildings were again put up for sale. There are currently plans to build houses on the site and demolition began in March 2002.[127]

Spring Vale Mill awaiting redevelopment after the departure of Brown and Forth Ltd. in 2000. The building in the photograph dates from 1940.

BRITANNIA ROPEWORKS

In 1886, village man William Warburton set up in business making rope in a building that he had erected on a plot of land off Gin Croft Lane. He called his business the Britannia Rope and Twine Co. and he ran it until about 1901 when he seems to have leased the works for a time to John Blakey who also ran a ropeworks in Radcliffe. By 1904, however, Warburton had taken over the Edenfield ropeworks again in partnership with Joseph Riley, an overlooker who lived at Thorn Bank on Bolton Road North. They took a thirty-year lease on the buildings in May 1904, but in August of the following year Riley bought Warburton's share and continued on his own. He ran the business until 1911 when he sold out to three brothers, Walter, Josiah and Frank Jackson from Glossop who were already in partnership as ropemakers. They made the Britannia Rope and Twine and Co. into a limited company and this concern ran the ropeworks for the rest of its working life. In its heyday, the company employed sixty people and produced sixty miles of washing line per week. When the business closed in September 2001, it was Britain's last cotton rope manufacturer.[128]

A 1948 advertisement for the ropework's products.

On the rope-walk in June 1998.

NOTES

1   Manor of Tottington records (LRO: DDHCL liber K, folio 42)

2   Manor of Tottington records (LRO: DDHCL liber M, folio 446); Manchester Mercury 25th March 1777

3   Manor of Tottington records (LRO: DDHCL liber Q, folio 110; liber W, folio 139)

4   Sun fire insurance policy (Guildhall Library: MS 11937/1, entry no. 619123)

5   Manor of Tottington records (LRO: DDHCL liber Z, folio 229; liber GG, folio 738; Liber KK, folio 207) Bolton Chronicle 29th March 1828

6   James Stott's stock book for trade (Helmshore Local History Society collection)

7   PP, *A return of the number of power looms used in factories …* 1836 (24) XLV

8   Manor of Tottington records (LRO: DDHCL liber AB, folio 311)

9   A.Muir, *The History of Porritts and Spencer*, [typescript] (1966), p. 56; BT 15th February 1879; 1851 census Tottington Higher End (PRO: HO 107/2249)

10 A.V. Sandiford and T.E. Ashworth, *The Forgotten Valley*, (1981), pp. 18-19

11 BT 31st July 1858; 1861 census Tottington Higher End (PRO: RG 9/3059); RO 27th April 1917

12 BT 26th April 1873

13 Dissolved companies files (PRO: BT31/16343/65047)

14 BT 24th October 1871

15 BT 13th January 1872; Mill valuations 1880-82 (LRO: PUH/5/2)

16 RFP 20th November 1982; Records of George Clegg (1920) Ltd. (Companies House, Cardiff)

17 Manor of Tottington records (LRO: DDHCL liber KK, folio 207)

18 Manchester Guardian 28th February 1849; P. Ewart and T. Ashworth, *Observations on the mills, power and waterfalls of the Irwell and its tributaries 1833* (Bolton archive service: UWR/3); BT 12th December 1868; Mill valuations 1880-82 (LRO: PUH/5/2); 1861 census Tottington Higher End (PRO: RG 9/3059); 1881 census Tottington Higher End (PRO: RG 11/4136); Kelly & Co, *The Post Office Directory of Lancashire*, (1873); BT 17th November 1877

19 RO 20th April 1923; Edenfield parish records: 1790 survey (MCL: MF PR 117a)

20 G.H. Tupling, *The Economic History of Rossendale*, (1927), p.199; Manchester Mercury 6th February 1821, 10th April 1821

21 P. Ewart and T. Ashworth, *Observations on the mills, power and waterfalls of the Irwell and its tributaries 1833* (Bolton archive service: UWR/3)

22 T. Newbigging, *History of the Forest of Rossendale*, (1893), p. 316; 1851 census Tottington Higher End (PRO: HO 107/2249)

23 Copy conveyance 26th May 1852 (LRO: DDX/1777 uncat); Manor of Tottington records (LRO: DDHCL liber BD, folio 654; liber BP, folio 350); BT 25th January 1868

24 BT 24th December 1881; M. Starkie, *Mineral water manufacturers in Rossendale* [typescript], (1987) (Rawtenstall library: RC 663.62 ROS); RO 27th July 1962, 20th April 1923

25 Exchequer bills and answers, Trinity term 32 George III (PRO: E112/1530/233)

26 G. Turnbull, *A history of the calico printing industry of Great Britain*, (1951), p. 100; Manchester Mercury 23rd June 1789, 13th March 1792

27 Manor of Tottington records (LRO: DDHCL liber X, folios 455-6); Rough plan of Mr. Edmd. Sagar's woollenworks … 1817 (Bolton archive service: ZAL/188)

28 Manchester Mercury 19th July 1814; deed of covenants 1st February 1806 (LRO: DDX 1350 uncat Box 8)

29 Lease 16th July 1839 (LRO: DDX 1350 uncat); London Gazette 6th December 1839; J. Graham, *History of printworks in the Manchester district 1760-1846*, (1846) (MCL: BR66 667.3G1)

30 1851 census Tottington Higher End (PRO: HO 107/2249); Seyd & Co, *The Manchester and district commercial list*, (1881-1882); BT 12th August 1882

31 J.W. Barber-Lomax, 'Barcelona and Stubbins', *Ramsbottom Heritage Society News Magazine*, (Winter 1992-3) 5-7; BT 19th February 1870. Rumney also had a long running dispute with the Porritts over water rights and was co-respondent in a divorce case.

32 BT 12th August 1882; Seyd & Co, *The Manchester and district commercial list*, (1881-1882); 1881 census Tottington Higher End (PRO: RG 11/4136); Dissolved companies files (PRO: BT 31/5850/41062); G. Turnbull, *A history of the calico printing industry of Great Britain*, (1951), pp. 324-332; RO 20th February 1903, 17th March 1911

33 RO 16th December 1904, 30th December 1932; Valuation list – Ramsbottom (North) 1895 (LRO: PUB 8/105); Valuation list – Ramsbottom (North) 1910 (LRO: PUB 8/162)

34 RO 2nd November 1962; RFP 16th April 1967

35 RFP 26th October 1968, 21st March 1970; BT 19th February 1993, 10th June 1997

36 J. Graham, *History of printworks in the Manchester district 1760-1846*, (1846) (MCL: BR66 667.3G1); Ewood Bridge deeds (Helmshore Local History Society collection); Bankruptcy order book (PRO: B1/86, pp. 204-209); Manchester Mercury 26th July 1791, 19th November 1793

37 Manchester Mercury 19th November 1793

38 Manchester Mercury 19th March 1799

39 Manchester Mercury 3rd August 1802

40 Ewood Bridge deeds (Helmshore Local History collection); G. Coupe, *Tottington Hall through five centuries*, (1987), pp. 21-23

41 Manchester Mercury 14th March 1815, 23rd March 1819

42 J. Graham, *History of printworks in the Manchester district 1760-1846*, (1846) (MCL: BR66 667.3G1); Ewood Bridge deeds (Helmshore Local History Society collection); P. Ewart and T. Ashworth, *Observations on the mills, power and waterfalls of the Irwell and its tributaries 1833*, (Bolton archive service: UWR/3); Absalom Watkin's diary 11th November 1844 [Courtesy of Magdalen Goffin]

43 Bolton Chronicle 14th November 1829; C. Aspin, *Haslingden 1800-1900*, (1962), p. 21; Blackburn Standard 8th May 1844

44 1861 census Haslingden (PRO: RG9/3061); Dissolved companies files (PRO: BT 31/1864/7347); RO 12th October 1894

45 T. Skinner & Co. (Publishers) Ltd, *Skinner's Cotton Trade Directory of the World*, (1940-41); Haslingden Observer 18th April 1959; Haslingden Borough Council, General Works Committee minutes 27th June 1901 and 12th March 1962; GPO telephone directories, Blackburn area, 1962-1975

46 RFP 16th November 1985, 25th July 1987

47 Lease to Lawrence Rostron 1st August 1801 (LRO: DDK leases, box 196); Manor of Tottington records (LRO: DDHCL liber DD, folio 346, liber WW, folio 111); P. Ewart and T. Ashworth, *Observations on the mills, power and waterfalls of the Irwell and its tributaries 1833* (Bolton archive service: UWR/3); PP, *Reports of the inspectors of factories for the half year ending 31st December 1841*, 1842 (31) XXII

48 Manor of Tottington records (LRO: DDHCL liber AG, folio 340; liber AP, folio 479; liber AY, folio 476); Blackburn Standard 1st August 1849; 1851 census Tottington Higher End (PRO: HO 107/2249)

49 Mannex & Co, *History, Topography and Directory of Mid-Lancashire*, (1854); E. S. Drake, *Commercial directory of Bolton, Bury, Wigan ... and adjoining townships*, (1861); 1861 census Tottington Higher End (PRO: RG 9/3059)

50 Haslingden Chronicle 11th January 1868; Counterpart lease of Edenwood mill 24th April 1883 (LRO: DDX/1777 uncat)

51 Conveyance 11th October 1900 (LRO: DDX/1777 uncat); *Turnbull and Stockdale 1881-1931*, (1931), p. 31; RO 17th June 1955; RFP 22nd July 1967, 19th October 1968

52 Manor of Tottington records (LRO: DDHCL liber WW, folio 111; liber XX, folio 653); P. Ewart and T. Ashworth, *Observations on the mills, power and waterfalls of the Irwell and its tributaries 1833* (Bolton archive service: URW/3)

53 J. Graham, *History of printworks in the Manchester district 1760-1846*, (1846) (MCL: BR66 667.3G1); PP, *Children's employment commission. Appendix to the second report, part 1*, 1843 (431) XIV; Manchester Guardian 13th April 1850, 25th July 1884

54 BT 26th July 1879; RO 29th January 1892, 3rd November 1905

55 B.R. Law, *Fieldens of Todmorden*, (1995), pp. 122-4

56 Conveyance 11th October 1900 (LRO: DDX/1777 uncat); RO 11th November 1904, 2nd July 1915, 9th May 1924, 25th June 1937, 17th August 1951; *Turnbull and Stockdale 1881-1931*, (1931), p. 17

57 RO 10th February 1905, 7th July 1905, 19th January 1945; *Turnbull and Stockdale 1881-1931*, (1931), p. 25

58 RO 27th November 1964; RFP 17th September 1966, 22nd July 1967, 17th August 1968, 29th November 1969

59 Burnley Evening Star 21st December 1974; RFP 4th January 1975, 1st May 1976, 14th June 1980; Rossendale Borough Council minutes 6th January 1989

60 Lease 6th September 1813 (LRO: DDX/1350, uncat. box 8); Abstract of the conveyance to John Rostron

(LRO: DDX/1777 uncat. box 1); Duplicate demise 29th July 1834 (LRO: DDX/1777 uncat. box 2); Walmersley-cum-Shuttleworth valuation list 1876 (LRO: PUB/8/45)

61 RFP 17th August 1968, 16th November 1968, 7th August 1971, 10th May 1980; C.L. Tweedale, 'The Turnbull Tale', *Ramsbottom Heritage Society News Magazine*, (Summer 1993), 2-6

62 Manor of Tottington records (LRO: DDHCL liber AA, folio 493; liber GG, folio 583)

63 Manor of Tottington records (LRO: DDHCL liber ZZ, folio 360; liber AK, folio 259); 1851 census Tottington Higher End (PRO: HO 107/2249)

64 Manor of Tottington records (LRO: DDHCL liber BZ, folio 595; liber CB, folio 733; liber CM, folio 750); Bacup Times 20th March 1869; Haslingden Chronicle 17th December 1870; BT 18th September 1875, 8th February 1879

65 Manor of Tottington records (LRO: DDHCL liber EW, folio 523); BT 23rd April 1887, 12th October 1889; RO 5th March 1909

66 Manor of Tottington records (LRO: DDHCL liber Y, folio 569); Royal Exchange fire insurance policy (Guildhall Library: No. 179638); Will of John Haworth of Edenfield 1804 (LRO: WCW); Tottington Higher End land tax returns 1806-1830 (LRO: QDL); T. Rogerson, *Lancashire General Directory*, (1818), p. 104; Wheeler's Manchester Chronicle, 17th February 1827

67 P. Ewart and T. Ashworth, *Observations on the mills, power and waterfalls of the Irwell and its tributaries 1833* (Bolton archive service: UWR/3); 1851 census Tottington Higher End (PRO: HO 107/2249); 1861 census Tottington Higher End (PRO: RG 9/3059)

68 Dissolved companies files (PRO: BT 31/547/2219); BT 17th December 1864; Bacup Times 9th July 1870; Haslingden Chronicle 10th December 1870

69 Manor of Tottington records (LRO: DDHCL liber CH, folio 712; liber CL, folio 656); Mill valuations 1880-1882 (LRO: PUH/5/2)

70 Manor of Tottington records (LRO: DDHCL liber DR, folio 684; liber ES, folio 698); 1910 valuation list – Ramsbottom [North Ward] (LRO: PUB/8/162); RO 18th August 1916

71 Dissolved companies files (PRO: BT 31/24677/155639); RO 5th May 1939

72 Manchester Mercury 6th September 1791, 24th January 1792, 17th May 1802; Lease 16th February 1824 (LRO: DDFo/41/4)

73 E. Baines, *History, directory and gazetteer of the County Palatine of Lancaster*, (1824-5); J. Pigot & Co, *New commercial directory for Cheshire, Derbyshire and Lancashire*, (1828); Bolton Chronicle 24th March 1847; Estate memoranda book (LRO: DDFo/44/16)

74 Manchester Guardian 5th September 1835

75 BT 5th February 1859, 20th June 1874, 13th February 1875, 28th August 1886, 26th February 1887, 10th December 1887; The Simmons collection of records relating to Lancashire water wheels [Copies at the Lancashire Library Local Studies department, Preston]; P. Mannex & Co, *History, topography and directory of Mid-Lancashire*, (1854); 1861 census Tottington Higher End (PRO: RG 9/3059); Manor of Tottington records (LRO: DDHCL liber BW, folio 501); Mill valuations 1880-82 (LRO: PUH/5/2); Abstract of title of A.T. Porritt (LRO: DDX 1586 uncat)

76 Dissolved companies files (PRO: BT 31/4422/28774)

77 Dissolved companies files (PRO: BT 31/10766/81614; BT 31/11796/91562); Valuation Office field book 1910 (PRO: IR 58/15368); Abstract of title of A.T. Porritt (LRO: DDX 1586 uncat); RO 16th December 1904

78 Abstract of title of A.T. Porritt (LRO: DDX 1586 uncat); 1910 valuation list – Ramsbottom [North Ward] (LRO: PUB/8/162); Haslingden Guardian 25th September 1914; Dissolved companies files (PRO: BT 31/23545/145975); RO 22nd August 1919, 13th April 1923, 9th March 1928, 9th April 1937, 11th December 1942; Lancashire Evening Telegraph October 1991

79 GPO telephone directories, Blackburn area, 1967-1973; RFP 3rd May 1975; BT 19th October 1872

80 Manor of Tottington records (LRO: DDHCL liber PP, folio 496); W. Robertson, *Rochdale Past and Present*, (1876), p. 305

81 W. Turner, *Riot! The story of the East Lancashire loom-breakers in 1826*, (1992), pp. 38-39; PP, *A return of the number of power looms used in factories... 1836* (24) XLV; P.Ewart and T. Ashworth, *Observations on the mills, power and waterfalls on the Irwell and its tributaries 1833* (Bolton Archive Service: URW/3)

82 Manchester Guardian 6th February 1836, 24th June 1837; PP, *Reports of the inspectors of factories for half year ending 31st December 1841*, 1842 (31) XXII

83 Manchester Guardian 4th September 1841, 29th March 1845; PP, *Reports of the inspectors of factories for half year ending 31st December 1841*, 1842 (31) XXII; Manor of Tottington records (LRO: DDHCL liber AI, folio 701)

84 BT 21st March 1857; 1861 census Tottington Higher End (PRO: RG 9/3059)

85 Accrington Times 1st January 1876

86 BT 24th November 1877

87 Manor of Tottington records (LRO: DDHCL liber CT, folio 1287); RO 9th July 1897

88 RO 9th June 1905, 15th September 1911, 7th December 1917, 25th December 1931, 6th January 1950

89 RO 2nd August 1929, 23rd January 1931, 2nd September 1932, 16th February 1934, 6th January 1950; The late James Dewhurst *pers. comm.*

90 RO 7th March 1951, 19th October 1956, 8th February 1957, 1st August 1958, 15th January 1960; RFP 27th November 1976, 17th September 1977; Records of John Schofield (Textile Machinery) Ltd. (Companies House, Cardiff)

91 Bury rentals 1822-1840 (LRO: Derby estate records DDK/1813/77, etc.); Survey and valuation of the township of Walmersley-cum-Shuttleworth 1842 (LRO: PUB/8/3)

92 Derby estate instructions for leases book 1853-1856 (BAS: BWO/T1908); Survey and valuation of the township of Walmersley-cum-Shuttleworth 1842 (LRO: PUB/8/3); BT 17th July 1875; RO 26th February 1892, 26th June 1896

93 RO 19th July 1907, 24th January 1908, 19th May 1933, 27th August 1937; T. Skinner & Co, *Skinner's cotton trade directory of the world*, (1923 and 1930-31)

94 Manchester Guardian 28th January 1832

95 PP, *Correspondence and return relative to the removal of labourers from agricultural districts to manufacturing districts*, 1843 (254) XLV; Manchester Guardian 29th July 1837, 15th June 1839; 1851 census Tottington Higher End (PRO: HO 107/2249); Bacup Times 21st July 1877

96 Mill valuations 1880-82 (LRO: PUH/5/2); RO 6th September 1912, 5th March 1915; Records of Thomas Aitken and Son Ltd (Companies House, Cardiff)

97 Daily Despatch 27th November 1930; RO 1st January 1937

98 RO 18th December 1936, 27th September 1946

99 RO 1st November 1940; Records of W. and E. Products Ltd, Edenfield Soap and Toiletries Ltd and Sigma Soap Ltd (Companies House, Cardiff); E. Fogg and A. Jennings, 'Mercury peril from soap manufacture', *New Scientist*, (16th May 1985), 9

100 Manor of Tottington records (LRO: DDHCL liber AC, folio 542); 1841 census Tottington Higher End (PRO: HO 107/540/1); PP, *Report from the select committee appointed to inquire into the administration of the relief of the poor, 48th report*, 1837-38 (579) XVIII, part III 457; I. Slater, *Royal national classified commercial directory and topography of the county of Lancashire*, (1851)

101 Derby estate instructions for leases book 1846-1850 (BAS: BWO/T1908); BT 24th January 1863

102 Walmersley-cum-Shuttleworth valuation list 1864 (LRO: PUB/8/9); BT 21st September 1889

103 T. Skinner & Co, *Skinner's cotton trade directory of the world*, (1940); RO 7th September 1923

104 RFP 28th January 1966

105 Most of this section is based on Augustus Muir's unpublished *The history of Porritts and Spencer* (1966)

106 BT 15th February 1879

107 BT 6th December 1873; *Lancashire. Part First. The premier county of the kingdom. Cities and towns, historical, statistical, biographical, businessmen and mercantile interests, wealth and growth. An epitome of results.* (1889-90), p. 306

108 The others were Joseph Porritt and Sons, Samuel Porritt and Sons and J.H. Spencer and Sons, a firm founded by a former Porritt manager in 1903

109 RO 9th May 1941

110 RO 16th May 1958

111 Porritts and Spencer Ltd. press release (author's collection)

112 BT 25th February 1977, 14th April 1979; RFP 23rd September 1978, 19th February 1993

113 Derby estate instructions for lease book 1861-1863 (BAS: BWO/T1909); E. S. Drake, *Commercial directory of Bolton, Bury, Wigan ... and adjoining townships*, (1861); Walmersley-cum-Shuttleworth valuation list 1864 (LRO: PUB 8/9); 1871 census Tottington Higher End (PRO: RG 10/4139)

[114] BT 28th February 1874, 30th March 1878, 26th June 1880, 24th July 1880; P. Mannex & Co, *Directory and topography of north-east Lancashire*, (1875-6); Walmersley-cum-Shuttleworth valuation list 1876 (LRO: PUB/8/45); Seyd & Co, *The Manchester and district commercial list*, (1881-1882)

[115] I. Slater, *Royal national commercial directory of Bury, Heywood, Radcliffe, Ramsbottom and districts*, (1888); J. Worrall, *The cotton spinners and manufacturers' directory*, (1891); RUDC building regulations plans, no. 433 (BAS: ARM/T1991); Haslingden Guardian 28th August 1914; RO 8th August 1919; T. Skinner & Co, *Skinner's cotton trade directory of the world*, (1923 etc.)

[116] RFP 21st Oct 1967, 12th April 1969; Edenfield Spinning Co. Ltd. records (Companies House, Cardiff)

[117] C. Aspin, *Mr. Pilling's short cut to China and other stories of Rossendale enterprise*, (1983), pp. 5-8; Dissolved companies files (PRO: BT 31/525)

[118] Derby estate instructions for leases book 1861-63 (BAS: BWO/T1909); Walmersley-cum-Shuttleworth valuation list 1864 (LRO: PUB/8/9); BT 25th January 1868; RO 1st July 1910

[119] RO 8th January 1904, 17th June 1904, 9th December 1904, 16th December 1904; Lease 7th May 1908, (BAS: GRI/T1676)

[120] Lease 7th May 1908 (BAS: GRI/T1676)

[121] RO 28th July 1911, 6th July 1917; Dissolved companies files (PRO: BT 31/20294/118496); Assignment 24th September 1917 (BAS: GRI/T1676)

[122] Assignment 2nd June 1920 (BAS: GRI/T1676); RO 19th December 1919, 1st September 1939; Haslingden Guardian 10th January 1930

[123] Dissolved companies files (PRO: BT 31/17346/82901); RO 31st January 1913, 2nd August 1929, 6th November 1931, 13th March 1936; Haslingden Guardian 10th January 1930, 7th February 1930; M. Rose (ed.), *The Lancashire cotton industry – a history since 1700*, (1996), p. 275

[124] Ramsbottom valuation list 1938 (BAS: ARM/T1870); RO 17th August 1951, 11th August 1961; RFP 17th August 1968, 4th January 1975, 27th October 1984; Burnley Evening Star 21st December 1974

[125] Chatterton Weaving Co. Ltd. records (Companies House, Cardiff); RO 5th March 1909; J. Worrall Ltd, *The Lancashire textile industry*, (1948); RFP 26th August 1967; *Greenwood & Coope Limited Fiftieth Anniversary*, (1974)

[126] RO 17th October 1913, 15th October 1915, 29th July 1932, 27th January 1933; RFP 11th January 1963; RUDC register of petroleum licences 1926-1969 (BAS: ARM/T960)

[127] RO 11th November 1949, 25th November 1949, 9th May 1958, 2nd October 1959, 11th January 1963; RFP 11th June 1999

[128] The Britannia Rope and Twine Co. Ltd. records (Companies House, Cardiff); Manor of Tottington records (LRO: DDHCL liber DX, folio 576; liber EW, folio 483; liber EY, folio 637; liber FL, folio 612); Kelly's Directories Ltd, *Directory of Lancashire*, (1901); RFP 20th July 2001; Lancashire Evening Telegraph 10th August 2001

QUARRYING AND COAL MINING

QUARRYING

THE PEOPLE OF EDENFIELD and district had the right to quarry stone out of their ancient copyhold land and to use it to build their houses, barns and walls or to sell it as they wished. If they wanted to quarry stone from the former common land that had been enclosed in the 17th century, they had to seek the permission of the Lord of the Manor. Many farms had a small stone pit in a corner of a field from which they supplied their own building needs. At the end of the 18th century as nearby towns and villages began to grow, as mills were built and as new turnpike roads cut across the district, the demand for stone also grew. Quarrying became an increasing important way of making money. People like the Haworths who had farmed at Horncliffe for generations started to quarry the splendid sandstone that lay under their ancestral fields. In the case of the former common land, the Lord of the Manor granted leases to men who set themselves up as quarry owners. In 1785, for instance, James Dewhurst the elder, James Dewhurst the younger, both of New Hall, and John and James Lord of Spotland took out a lease on 'all the slate mines and slate pits and quarries of stone, slate and flags' at Foe Edge. Quarrying also started to expand on Scout Moor and Turf Moor above Turn. Here in about 1799 George Haworth leased a plot of land to build a stone mill 'near Mr. Bamford's Yate.' This seems to have been the beginning of the stone-rubbing mill on New Gate Brook in which rough flagstones were given a smooth surface to make them suitable for floors and pavements.[1]

By the 1840s the main quarries were at Horncliffe, Foe Edge, Great Height (not far from Whitaker Pasture Farm), Scout Moor and Fecit End. There were smaller ones too at Sheffield Gate (near Horncliffe), Bank Nook, Elton Banks, New Hall (near the junction of the old highway and Sand Beds Lane) and Hollins (just south of Brook Bottom Brook). Even the largest of these quarries were still relatively small-scale affairs. In 1851, for instance, James Walton who had taken over Horncliffe Quarry in about 1846, was employing only twenty men. The main limit on expansion was the difficulty and cost of moving stone by road much beyond a few miles from where it had been quarried. All this changed with the coming of the railways. One of the reasons given to support the building of the railway was the existence of thirty quarries between Bury and Rawtenstall producing 'building stone of the first rate quality' and 'the finest stone ... anywhere in the neighbourhood of Manchester.' The new railway meant that stone could be exported to Manchester, Preston, Liverpool, Birmingham, parts of Yorkshire and even London.[2]

Working in an area of Scout Moor Quarry known as the 'Boggart Hole' in about 1905.

In the second half of the 19th century the quarry workings began to expand, eating further and further into the hillsides. The excavations at Foe Edge, for example, met up with Cragg quarry above Cowpe as the hill between the two was worked away by the firm of Butterworth and Brooks (later Brooks and Brooks) who also ran Great Height quarry as well as several others elsewhere in Rossendale. Some of the quarries like Bank Nook became increasingly difficult to work because of the amount of overburden that had to be removed to get at useable rock. (In the mid-1870s, John Spencer, the agent for Butterworth and Brooks, calculated that there was a thickness of 45 ft. 6in. to be removed to get at stone suitable for flags at Bank Nook). At Horncliffe and Scout Moor quarries the problem was partly solved by mining the stone. Tunnels were driven into the hillside for some considerable distance to get at the best stone, leaving the upper surface undisturbed.[3]

The quarry engine 'James' pictured near Cowpe Lowe with its drivers, Messrs. Spencer and Dobbs. It had a dark green livery with polished brass fittings.

To facilitate the movement of stone away from these vast workings, the quarry owners built narrow gauge railways or tramways. The first to be completed was that at Horncliffe, which opened in 1863, followed by Great Height and Foe Edge as far as Ding quarry in 1866-67 (which was some five miles in length) and by Scout Moor in 1880. Here the tramway climbed from a stone staithe on Rochdale Road up the Dearden Brook valley before running back on itself at a higher level into the quarry. The Horncliffe tramway seems to have used locomotives from its beginning, since in July 1863 James Walton offered for sale twenty draught horses 'in consequence of completing of a new tramway.' The Great Height tramway, however, used horses at first, although they were later replaced by locomotives including 'James', built in 1887. Locomotives such as 'Excelsior' also ran the Scout Moor tramway.[4]

In the case of Horncliffe and the Great Height/Cragg quarries, stone was taken down from the edge of the workings on inclines to sidings on the main railway. Trains of fully loaded wagons pulled up the empty wagons, which were then hauled into the quarries themselves to be filled with stone. At Scout Moor the stone was carried away by road from the stone staithe on Rochdale Road. The *Bacup and Rossendale News* for 29th September 1877, for example, noted that,

During the last week one of the traction engines of Messrs. Whittaker & Sons, of Scout Moor Quarry, has been daily taking to Bury six wagons loaded with sett stones for paving, weighing 50 tons, or equivalent to about 23 or 24 horse loads.

By the last decades of the 19th century, quarrying was an important employer of labour in the Edenfield area. In 1871, for instance, James Whittaker had forty-seven men working for him at Scout Moor, while in 1861 James Walton at Horncliffe employed between ninety and one hundred men. Ten years later his workforce had risen to 250 men and twenty boys. When James's son, Richard, married in 1879, he treated 700 of his employees, their wives and sweethearts to a trip to Blackpool, but within a few years he had been declared bankrupt. His debts amounted to over £23,000. Horncliffe remained in the hands of the Walton family, however, for by the end of December 1885 James's three sons, Richard, James Frederick and Edwin, had taken over the business. The three men ran Horncliffe until 1905 when their lease expired, but they re-opened it in May 1907. The *Rossendale Free Press* said, 'Previous to the recent stoppage the stone was obtained by mining, but workmen are now engaged baring the top soil, evidently preparatory to getting at the rock from the top.'[5]

By the early years of the 20th century, the time of high prosperity and activity for local quarries was coming to an end. The reserves of stone nearest the surface were exhausted making it more costly to get at the remaining supplies, while at the same time other building materials, including brick and concrete, were becoming more

The remains of Whittakers' stone staithe at Turn in 1951.

popular. Some quarries closed completely at about the time of the First World War and have lain disused ever since. Those in the Edenfield district have had a more chequered history. The Waltons were at Horncliffe until about 1916, but in 1919 a new company, the Rawtenstall Quarries Limited, set up by a group of engineers from Ashton-under-Lyne and Radcliffe and John Phillipson, an Entwistle quarry owner, acquired the quarries. They planned to use the stone to make concrete. The *Haslingden Guardian* reported in December 1919 that:

> An opinion has been expressed that only half of the bed rock has been worked and it is the intention of the new company to resume operations in this direction. At present the preliminary operations are in progress, and for a little over a fortnight a gang of men have been engaged in digging a road for the conveyance of the hewed rock from the hill to the railway siding. The new track is being cut about 50 yards away from the cutting used by the old company which will also be utilised for transferring the rubble for concrete. This work is being pushed forward as quickly as possible in order to enable plant to be installed on the hill for the actual quarrying. This plant alone cost £10,000 and is now lying in Yorkshire until such time as it is required. Unlike most disused quarries the rubble has not been disposed of for road making purposes, hence its value for the concrete making industry. Shafts are to be driven into the hill, as it is estimated that hundreds of thousands of tons of rock are still to be got, and so far as quarry stone is concerned it will not be worked out for generations to come.

The task of installing the new plant and making the quarry ready to work took some time and no stone was sold until October 1921. It was not an auspicious start and the company was voluntarily wound up in 1925. The liquidator found that there were liabilities of nearly £29,000 and assets of a mere £84 4s 11d. A period of long disuse followed for the quarries (they were worked briefly after the Second World War by J. Barcroft (Horncliffe Quarries) Ltd) until 1978 when they began to be used as a landfill site.[6]

At Scout Moor the Whittaker family bought the quarry from Lord Derby in the 1920s and continued to work it until the early 1950s. Like Horncliffe, the quarry was then used for tipping trade refuse, but re-opened in 1968 when the motorway building programme brought a huge demand for stone for filling. Soon the quarry resounded to blasts of gelignite as forty men worked around the clock to excavate 1,200 tons of rock a day. By May 1969 more than one million tons of rock had been taken out of Scout Moor to build parts of the M1 and M62 and the Rawtenstall-Edenfield bypass. The quarry fell quiet once more in 1970 and was again considered as a tipping site. However, quarrying operations started again in 1983 and have continued ever since.[7]

COAL MINING

Like quarrying, coal mining has a long history in Edenfield. People who described themselves as colliers and coalminers appear in parish registers and other records in the 17th century, and their small-scale abandoned workings survived to be recorded

STONE QUARRIES

AT

RAWTENSTALL

TO BE SOLD BY AUCTION AS A GOING CONCERN

BY

F. S. AIREY, ENTWISTLE & CO.

AT THE

ESTATE EXCHANGE, FOUNTAIN STREET, MANCHESTER,

On Tuesday, the 1st day of October, 1929,

At 3 o'clock in the Afternoon prompt.

Subject to the Conditions of Sale of the Manchester Law Society and to Special Conditions.

All that Freehold (formerly copyhold) Estate known as " The Horncliffe Estate " situate near Rawtenstall in the County of Lancaster and containing 73 acres 3 roods and 3 perches of land or thereabouts.

Together with the Stone Quarries thereon known as " The Rawtenstall Quarries " now being worked by the Vendors.

The Stone is of first class quality and suitable for making Flags, Kerbs, Sets, Cubes and Edgings for street paving, and random stone can be crushed with a portable crusher.

There are good facilities for loading and transporting, the Quarries being close to a main road

---

Further particulars and permission to view can be obtained from :—**THE AUCTIONEERS** 10, Norfolk Street ; **Messrs. R. B. BATTY & CO.**, Solicitors, 4, Clarence Street ; **Messrs. JOHN ADAMSON & CO.**, Chartered Accountants, 30, Spring Gardens, all of Manchester ; **Messrs. BULCRAIG & DAVIS**, Solicitors, Amberley House, Norfolk Street, Strand, London, W.C.2., or at the office of the undersigned, where the Particulars and Conditions of Sale may be inspected 7 days prior to the Sale.

G. C ADAMS,

Solicitor,

29, Princess Street,

Manchester.

Horncliffe Quarry offered for sale in 1929 after the failure of Rawtenstall Quarries Ltd.

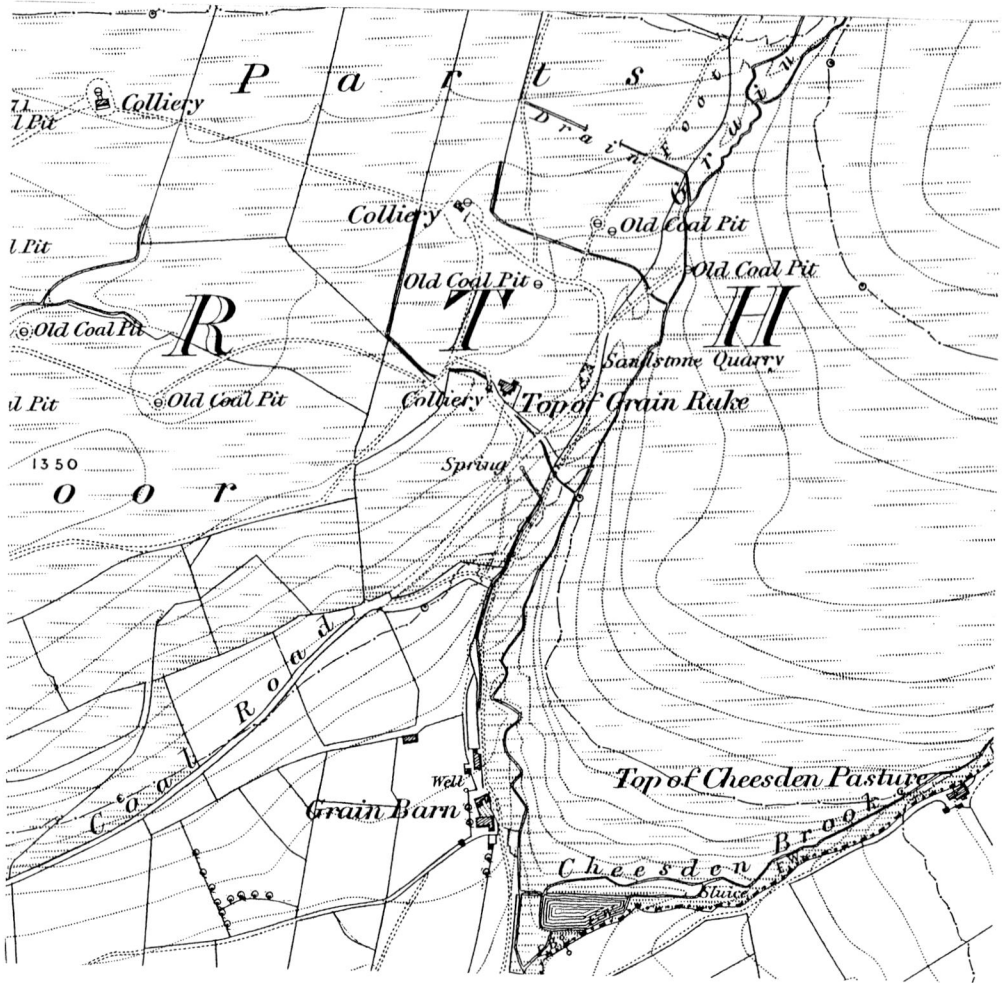

Collieries and abandoned coal pits on the south-east end of Scout Moor in the 1840s.

by the Ordnance Survey in the 1840s. On Dearden Moor coal was never mined on a commercial scale, although during the coal strike of 1921 a seam of eight to ten inches thickness was worked by about a dozen men. The outcrops on Scout Moor and Turf Moor were more commercially viable and in the 1840s there were five collieries in operation. Scout Moor colliery was to the east of Further Barn Farm, near the quarry, with two other pits on the south side of the moor in areas called New Grounds and Ten Acres. The remaining two collieries were near Top of Grain Rake at the head of the Cheesden valley.[8]

By the end of the 19th century the name Scout Moor colliery had become attached to a new pit opened on the hillside about half a mile east of New Gate. Here a drift went into the ground and under Whittle Pike, while coal from another pit at the east end of Turf Moor above Fecit arrived at the same point on a tramway. A small steam winding-engine hauled the full trucks of coal out of the Scout Moor mine before they were sent down to New Gate on an incline, the weight of the full trucks pulling up the empty ones. When the miners working at the pithead were ready to send down a load of full trucks they alerted their co-workers at the bottom of the hill by giving a tug on a handle attached to a system of wires and pulleys. This made a heavy iron bar fall against another piece of metal shaped like a frying pan mounted on the wall of the building at the foot of the incline. The collieries at New Grounds, Ten Acres and Top of Grain Rake had been worked out by the 1890s, although a small pit had been opened near the latter in the banks above Grain Brook.[9]

Scout Moor colliery was worked by Lawrence Duckworth who lived at Sheep Hey until his death in 1865 when his widow and executors took over. The Scout Moor Colliery Co., whose directors included the Ramsbottoms of Lodge Mill, followed them. The colliery supplied not only this mill, but also several others in the district as well as the households of Turn and the surrounding area. The coal was slow burning and it was even said that it was possible to build up your fire with Scout Moor coal, go on the annual week's holiday and return to find your fire still burning. Eventually the colliery was taken over by the Whittaker family, but they worked the pit only intermittently. It had fallen into disuse by the late 1920s, but was being worked again in 1939, although by then the tramway had been abandoned. The mine

The derelict pithead buildings at Scout Moor Colliery in the 1950s.

closed again in 1941, and apart from working briefly in 1952, has been disused ever since.[10]

In 19th century Turn a fair number of men and boys found work in the coalmines. If we take the 1871 census as an example, there were forty-three miners in the village and the surrounding farms and cottages. Ten of these were boys aged under fifteen, including James Yates, Robert Hill and Thomas Haworth who were all just ten years old. Since 1842, the employment underground of children under the age of ten had been prohibited, but even in 1861 one eight-year-old boy – James Holden of Kay Barn – was working in the Turn mines. Children were usually employed as 'drawers', whose job it was to push or pull tubs of coal from the coalface to the pit entrance.[11]

Given the primitive working conditions in the mines, it is not surprising that accidents were not unusual and occasionally fatal. In June 1872, for instance, John Hamer and William Hill were working in a tunnel in Scout Moor colliery. They had finished mining the coal and were pulling up the rails and 'drawing' the props prior to abandoning the workings. As Hamer knocked out a prop, part of the ceiling collapsed and killed him. Three years later, Thomas Lee, a boy aged about twelve who worked as a drawer, was travelling down the pit in an empty wagon. He got entangled in a rope, was crushed between a pulley wheel and its frame and was killed instantly.[12]

NOTES

[1]   Counterpart lease 1st April 1785 (LRO: DDHCL uncat. Box 133); Bury and Pilkington Field Book 1798-1800 (LRO: DDK 1768/7)

[2]   1851 census Tottington Higher End (PRO: HO 107/2249); Bacup and Rossendale News 8th August 1885; S. Hamilton, 'The historical geography of south Rossendale 1780-1900', M.A. thesis, University of Manchester, (1974), p. 175

[3]   Surveyor's report on minerals in Butterworth and Brooks' district, c. 1875 (LRO: DDHCL uncat. Box 120); J. Davies, 'Quarrying in Rossendale', (1985), pp. 39, 74

[4]   BT 4th July 1863; B. Roberts, *Railways and Mineral Tramways of Rossendale*, (1974) pp. 16, 23-25; Bacup and Rossendale News 19th March 1870

[5]   1871 census Walmersley-cum-Shuttleworth (PRO: RG 10/3948); 1861 census Tottington Higher End (PRO: RG 9/3059); 1871 census Tottington Higher End (PRO: RG 10/4139); Bacup Times 21st June 1879; Bacup and Rossendale News 8th August 1885; RFP 26th December 1885, 25th May 1907; B. Roberts, *op. cit.*, p.16. I have been unable to trace the 1905 sale notice referred to.

[6]   Dissolved companies file: The Rawtenstall Quarries Ltd. (PRO: BT 31/25901/167270); Haslingden Guardian 26th December 1919; Liquidator's report: The Rawtenstall Quarries Ltd. (author's collection); J. Davies, *op. cit.*, pp. 108, 110; RFP 14th November 1987

[7]   Burnley Evening Star 22nd May 1969; RO 13th December 1957; RFP 16th May 1970, 27th August 1983

[8]   RO 20th May 1921

[9]   Sketch of the Scout Moor incline drawn by F. Sanderson (Rawtenstall library: RC 622.33EDE)

[10] RO 1st June 1923, 19th September 1939; W. Beswick, *Memories of Turn Village*, (n.d.), p. 4; A. Todd, *Around Ramsbottom*, (1995), p. 92

[11] 1871 census Walmersley-cum-Shuttleworth (PRO: RG 10/3948); 1861 census Walmersley-cum-Shuttleworth (RG 9/2839)

[12] BT 22nd June 1872, 15th May 1875

SHOPS

THE BUSINESS TALENT or instinct seems to run in many families, and in the last five years it has taken decisive wings. A walk through the lengthy highway which connects Holcombe Brook, Ramsbottom, Stubbins and Edenfield almost forces the conviction that, locally, "We are a nation of shopkeepers." In numerous instances the front rooms of houses and cottages have succumbed to the commercial idea of the occupiers, with a result that the shop-cum-dwelling has sprung up as a new factor in the community … The little out-of-the-way emporium accessible in a cluster of houses, and open almost at any hour, cannot help thriving. It has come to be a strong rival of the bigger shop in the town, much in the same way as the gramophone has become the competitor of the cottage piano.[1]

This passage was written in 1909 when the proliferation of shops in front rooms had obviously made an impression on its author, but his comments could equally apply to any part of the 19th century. If the evidence of census returns, trade directories and the number of former shop buildings still standing is to be believed, Edenfield had been a 'village of shopkeepers' for many years. Stubbins too could boast a variety of shops by the end of the 19th century, while smaller places like Turn, Strongstry, Irwell Vale and Ewood Bridge all had at least one general store.

It was towards the end of the 18th century that several Edenfield people first began to describe themselves as shopkeepers and to put up buildings that combined living accommodation with a purpose-built shop. One of the earliest surviving examples is the house now numbered 46 and 48, Bury Road, which dates from the 1790s. In the early 19th century it was joined by the block of property in Market Street, which still houses some of the village shops, including the chemist, news-agent and fish and chip shop. Elsewhere some former shops betray their origin by their outward appearance. They usually have large windows on the ground floor set to the side of, or flanking, the front door. A good example is 49, Market Street, one of a pair of houses built in 1846 by John Pickup, grocer, and formerly called Heelis Place. A large window takes up most of the front wall on the ground floor, while on the gable end the blocked taking-in door was probably used to allow goods to be put into storage on the first floor. The 1851 census shows that this building was a grocer's shop kept by George Duckworth, with the man who built it living in retirement next door.[2]

In the second half of the 19th century, purpose-built shops began to appear in some of the other villages as well. Among the earliest were the shop at the end of North Street, Strongstry, built in 1854 and the large double-fronted grocer's shop built in Milne Street, Irwell Vale at about the same time by Jonas Hollis. Not many years later the shop that eventually housed Turn Co-op was built, while in 1867 a branch of Ramsbottom Co-op made its appearance in Bolton Road North, Stubbins.

Market Street shops in the 1970s, with Hill's draper's nearest the camera.

Just across the road, the terraces built in the 1880s by William Rumney and Co. included three shops. The largest of the new shops built in the second half of the 19th century was Edenfield Co-op on Market Street dating from 1868, which housed the various departments on the ground floor with an assembly room above. Not many purpose-built shops were put up in the 20th century. In 1900 James Dewhurst, draper, demolished some of the old property in Market Place near its junction with Exchange Street and replaced it with Exchange Buildings, housing two shops. Two branch co-ops were built in 1922; one in Bury Road and one in Bolton Road North, and these were joined by another shop at 54, Bolton Road North in 1932.[3]

At the opposite end of the scale from substantial stone buildings like Edenfield Co-op were shops in simple wooden huts. All sorts of businesses have been run from them. At Stubbins, for example, there was a butcher's shop and a fish and chip shop next to the Railway Hotel in the 1880s and at the turn of the century they were joined by another fish and chip shop further along the road towards the river. At about the same time, Peter Nuttall built a wooden clogger's shop in Bury Road, Edenfield. At Lumb in the 1920s Charles Reeves had a sweet shop and tobacconist's next to the cottages at Lumb Bridge End, while Turn had two hut shops. One on Rochdale Road was kept by William Harris, barber, and the other at the end of

Lodge Mill Lane housed the clogging and shoemaking business of John Pickup (Jack o' Jinnies) and Thomas Wisdom. Many people also have fond memories of the tea hut at Scout Fold kept by the Wain family.[4]

Before the detailed census returns begin in 1841, we do not have a very clear picture of what kinds of shops were to be found in Edenfield and its neighbours. For example, although an 1818 trade directory notes a grocer, a grocer and butcher, and a confectioner in Edenfield, it does not specify what the other seven shopkeepers who are listed were selling. From the middle of the century we get a much clearer idea. In 1851, for instance, there were twelve grocers, three greengrocers, six butchers, two tea dealers and two drapers in Edenfield itself, with grocers also at Ewood Bridge, Rose Bank, Turn and Irwell Vale. There were the same number of grocers in 1891, along with a fruiterer, three butchers, two drapers, a tea dealer and two newsagents. By the late 1880s Stubbins had two butchers, three grocers, a newsagent and a 'fried fish dealer'.[5]

The fish and chip shop was not the only newcomer to make an appearance in the second half of the 19th century. Changes in the standard of living and education as well as improved communications via the railway were reflected in the different kinds of shops that opened. For instance in the 1830s and 1840s, newspapers were

MAGNALL'S
FISH AND CHIP RESTAURANT.

Full of nutrition, fresh from the sea,
Rich in sweet flavour, good as can be;
In quality only our custom relies,
Excellence always will win the first prize.
Depend on experience, here at your wish:
Fresh as the morning we serve our Fried Fish.
In rich golden hue our Potatoes are dressed,
So are our Hake and Cod, all of the best.
Here is the place to appease every wish,
In beautiful Potatoes and splendid Fried Fish.

Market Street, Edenfield.

The power of advertising: the Magnall family extol the virtues of their fish and chips in verse in 1928.

not a common sight in the village. James Taylor (1832-1913) recalling his youth commented, 'Few indeed were the papers that reached Edenfield then, and on a Saturday it was a regular occurrence for the villagers to gather at [my] father's place to hear the news read.' By 1861, there was sufficient demand for newspapers for at least one villager (Joseph Garbett) to combine selling newspapers with keeping a draper's shop. By the end of the century there were two newsagents in Edenfield, with a third in Stubbins. The latter village had also acquired a jeweller's shop by 1891.[6]

Until after the Second World War, Edenfield and its neighbours still had numerous small shops. Given the *Ramsbottom Observer*'s comments that are quoted at the opening of this chapter, it is no surprise to discover that a poor rate valuation made at the same time lists no fewer than thirty-eight shops in the village. Nearly half of these were in Market Place or in Market Street between the end of Exchange Street and the Manchester and County Bank (no. 21). Stubbins had eight shops and there were odd ones in the smaller villages and hamlets like Strongstry and Stubbins Vale. By 1938, if we exclude the co-ops, there were forty shops in the Edenfield, thirteen in Stubbins, two in Irwell Vale and one each in Chatterton, Strongstry and Turn. As in the 19th century, there were not just the usual butchers, grocers and

Market Place shops in 1906. The shop with the impressive frontage on the left is Robert Gee's bakery, with Richard Holden's tailor's shop next door and Eli Elton's butcher's nearest the camera.

bakers, but also specialist shops selling a variety of goods. In 1924, for example, Mary Alice Elton sold china at 14 Market Street and Mary Ann Taylor kept a ladies' outfitters at 49, Market Street. A few years later they were joined by Joseph Bolderson at 115, Market Street who sold gramophones and records 'at such prices and value as would make a journey to town a waste of time and money.'[7]

The number of shops began to decline after the Second World War, but they were not drastically reduced until the 1970s. In 1969, for example, you could have bought your weekly joint at one of three butchers, cakes and bread at two bakers and much of your other shopping at four grocers. By 1978, one of these – Keith and Barbara Scranage's shop at 9, Market Place – was self-service, reflecting one of the greatest changes in shopping in the past fifty years. Currently Edenfield and Stubbins have a butcher, a grocer, a baker, a newsagent, and a fish and chip shop each and there is also a chemist in Edenfield. The smaller villages and hamlets like Turn, Irwell Vale, Ewood Bridge and Strongstry have all lost their shops.[8]

Occasional glimpses of the contents of some of the village stores are offered by sale notices in local newspapers or from other stray documents. James Taylor's drapery business at Turn, which closed in April 1869, must have easily supplied the needs of the housewives in the village and surrounding farms. The list of items given when his stock was sold off included French merinoes, French twills, alpacas, coburgs, skirtings, shawls, handkerchiefs, Dowlas linen, holland, diapers, checks, tablecloths, winceys, flannels, twills, calicoes, dress linings, bed ticks, fustians, carpets, fancy dresses, gentlemen's ties, ladies' ties, collars, kid and silk gloves, stockings, yarn, worsted, velvet and other trimmings, nets, beads, umbrellas, sun shades and stays. Nor is it difficult to imagine the interior of Mrs. Pilling's shop in Edenfield in 1919 where patent medicines rubbed shoulders with butter dishes, tins of Nestlé's milk jostled boxes of candles and the remainder of the stock included canisters, a large number of pans, enamelware, crockery, buckets, brushes, cotton card, paper blinds, mops, soaps, powders, fluids, tea, coffee, tinned foods, ointments and haberdashery goods. Some thirty-five years later a similar mixture of items was on offer at the Stubbins branch of the Ramsbottom Co-op. As well as fresh and tinned foods, there were mop heads, braces, stockings, handkerchiefs, enamel pans, teapots and dolly blue on the shelves. The stock also included a familiar roll call of brand names – Oxo, Ovaltine, Persil, Ribena, Weetabix and Vaseline – as well as goods whose names have passed into memory. Among others were Congress Soap, Lavagene, Three Bears Oats, Bird's Puddena, Scotch Maid milk and Phosferine, 'The Greatest of all Tonics', for spring lassitude, summer debility and winter chills and influenza.[9]

Not every shopkeeper concentrated on selling one particular kind of merchandise or, indeed, made their living solely from shop keeping. To take some examples from the 1861 census: Lawrence Elton in Pindle Place (47-51, Bury Road) was a butcher and grocer, Joseph Garbett in Temple Row was a draper, bookseller and newsagent, and William Wilson, who lived in the East Street area was a grocer and draper. At

J. W. FISHER

HIGH-CLASS

Baker & Confectioner

❖

**WEDDING & BIRTHDAY
CAKES A SPECIALITY**

**Bread & Tea Cakes
Fresh Daily**

❖

Parties catered for

15, MARKET PLACE, Edenfield

A 1929 advertisement for the long established bakery in Market Place.

Michael Sixsmith, third generation of the Market Place bakers, preparing another batch of
bread for the shop.

East View near Stubbins Vale Mill, John Brierley kept a grocer's shop, but also worked as a woollen weaver. Other combinations in different census returns include butcher and innkeeper, draper and tea dealer, baker and beerseller, grocer and gardener, grocer and loom jobber, grocer and knitter, grocer and registrar of births and deaths, hatter and insurance man and confectioner and cotton weaver.

Although some shops had quite short lives, opening and closing within a few years, others served the village for a long time, playing a more significant part in its history. A good example is the bakery at 15, Market Place. Robert Gee set up in business here as a grocer and baker in the late 1860s. (Not surprisingly his fellow members of Edenfield Co-op did not take kindly to his opening of a rival establishment and expelled him). He kept the shop until his death in 1914, after which it was taken over by James Fisher who sold bread and cakes there throughout the inter-war years. He in turn was replaced by James and Hilda Sixsmith whose family still run the business.[10]

Another well-known establishment was the confectioner's shop and café that Jim Haworth kept at the junction of Exchange Street and Market Place for about sixty years until his death in 1942. The lower portion of the building was the café and was usually referred to as 'Jim Haworth's bottom'. It was connected to the shop by a

Jim Haworth and his assistant at the Market Street door of his shop and 'refreshment rooms.' As well as running this establishment, Jim took a keen interest in the village cricket club and firmly believed that the earth was flat.

speaking tube, down which mischievous boys would blow peas after calling Jim supposedly to give their order. People have fond memories of buying glasses of sarsaparilla here, or of watching entranced as Jim cut paper-thin slices of boiled ham.[11]

In the history of Edenfield shop keeping, Jim Haworth had the unique distinction of seeing one of his own products on sale in the village and nearby towns. This was his invention the 'Patent Quick Easy Washer' manufactured by the Quick Easy Washer Co. The washers were large earthenware discs with irregular surfaces that

---

A USEFUL NEW YEAR'S PRESENT.

A MERRY CHRISTMAS AND A REAL PRACTICAL GENUINE HAPPY NEW YEAR

IN ALL HOMES WHERE THE

PATENT QUICK EASY WASHER

IS INTRODUCED.

Christmas only comes once a year, but Washing Days come once a week, or 52 times a year. Why disfigure your hands with rubbing. Make short work of your Washing, and use the most up-to-date method.

Any sensible woman knows that you cannot wash clothes without rubbing, despite arguments to the contrary. This new invention is rubbing all the time; it makes your washing day the easiest day of the week; costs you only 3s. 6d.; lasts a life-time; and is never out of order. You will use less soap, less water, less time, less work, and have less worry. Your washing better finished; takes no extra room; always ready for work; without doubt the best of all Washers, and can be had from the following Dealers:—

RAWTENSTALL:—

Messrs. WHITTAKER & TAYLOR, Bank-street.
CONSERVATIVE STORES AND BRANCHES.
W. H. HORNE, Queen's Buildings.
P. GREGORY, Newhallhey.
J. KAY, Ironmonger, Bacup Road.
W. JOHNSTON, Burnley-road.
A. CANE, Cabinet Maker, Crawshawbooth.
I. LAW, 32, Baltic, Waterfoot.

EDENFIELD:—

CO-OPERATIVE STORES
CHATTWOOD SUPPLY STORES.

RAMSBOTTOM:—

CO-OPERATIVE STORES AND BRANCHES.
YATES BROS., Bolton Street.
OLDHAM AND CO., Bridge Street.
A. ROSTRON, Shuttleworth.

HASLINGDEN:—

CONSERVATIVE STORES.
J. WHITELEY, Manchester-road.
C. BARLOW, 24, Blackburn-road.
W. H. HALSTEAD, Blackburn-road.

THE QUICK EASY WASHER CO.,
1, Market St., Edenfield, Nr. Manchester.

The housewives of Edenfield and district were alerted to the merits of the Edenfield Patent Quick Easy Washer in a series of advertisements that appeared in the *Ramsbottom Observer* early in 1904.

fitted into the bottom of dolly tubs. They were designed to rub clothes as they were swished around by a 'dolly', thereby dispensing with the need to bend over a rubbing board to carry out the same task. The advertisements for this new device appeared regularly in local papers for a few years in the early 1900s telling local housewives that it could make 'washing day the easiest day of the week.' By 1904 they also included testimonials from satisfied customers from as far away as Farnworth: 'I would not be without your Patent at three times the cost' (Helmshore lady); 'Your Patent is worth a Guinea' (Ramsbottom lady); 'I have never come across anything near, let alone equal, to your Washers.' (Edenfield lady). We do not know how long the quick washers remained in production, but numbers of the discarded earthenware discs can still be seen making unusual ornaments in several Edenfield gardens.[12]

THE CO-OPS

The Edenfield Industrial and Provident Society Ltd. was formed at a public meeting towards the end of November 1859 and held its first general meeting a month later. In the meantime, the society had opened its first shop in Crown House at the corner of Gin Croft Lane and Market Place. They traded from here until 1869 when they moved to their own newly built premises in Market Street. James Porritt laid the foundation stone of the co-op hall on 28th November 1868 and the building opened in August of the following year. It had been designed by the Bury architects, Maxwell and Tuke, and comprised a grocery department, draper's and butcher's facing Market Street with a clogger's shop in Elizabeth Street. The warehouse was behind the shops on the ground floor. The second floor was taken up by an assembly room with smaller rooms off it, some of which became the headquarters for the Edenfield Liberal Club until they built their own premises in 1911.[13]

By the time the new shop was opened, two more co-ops had appeared in the district. Ramsbottom Co-op opened a branch at Stubbins in 1867, while Haslingden had a branch at Ewood Bridge from about 1869. A clog and shoe department was added at Stubbins in 1878 with, from 1882, a reading room over it. Another co-op branch made an appearance in 1876 when the Rawtenstall Conservative Co-op took over the grocery store of the Hollis family in Milne Street, Irwell Vale. The Ramsbottom Co-op opened a branch at Turn in 1873, but it closed ten years later. In the following year the people of Turn decided to set up their own co-op and formed a society that began trading from two cottages on Rochdale Road near the Plane Tree Inn. (They later expanded into a third cottage).[14]

For nearly forty years these five co-ops served their village communities with no further additions until the extraordinary events of 1921-22. The first hint of what was to come appeared at the quarterly meeting of the Edenfield society in October 1921 when it was revealed that the idea of opening a new branch in the Bury Road area had been proposed. The question had been raised whether Ramsbottom Co-op

Edenfield's former co-op store in 1988. Although the ground floor shops have been occupied by a number of businesses, most of the building has failed to find a use since the co-op closed.

rather than Edenfield should control it and the matter had been put before the Co-op Union for arbitration. This body had decided that, since Ramsbottom was the larger society, it should run the new branch. The decision did not please the Edenfield co-operators and at their December meeting they decided to build their own branch shop in Bolton Road North. The two branches opened within a fortnight of each other in April 1922.[15]

In the early days of the Edenfield society, shop hours were fixed at 7.30am to 9pm on weekdays and 7.30am to 11pm on Saturdays, opening for a total of seventy hours. Their prices included ham at 10d, 6½d for a large loaf and 5½d for 2 oz. of tobacco. Any committeeman heard swearing during hours of business was fined 1d for each offence. By the late 1890s, membership stood at 221 and in 1922 'something like half' the population of the village were members. When the society celebrated its centenary in 1959 there were 535 members. Turn, the other self-contained co-op in the district, had a membership of eighty-five in 1895. This rose to over 100 in the years just before the First World War. In the 1890s and early 1900s they regularly paid a dividend of over 3s in the pound, reaching 3s 6d in 1899 and 1911. Edenfield's

Edenfield Co-op committee in the inter-war years. Henry Freeman (who is in the middle of the front row) served on the committee for thirty-two years, twenty-seven of them as president.

dividend reached 3s in the pound in the 1860s, but fell to about 2s in the pound in the inter-war years and to between 1s and 2s in the 1940s.[16]

The various co-ops began to close in the 1950s, beginning with the branch at Ewood Bridge whose building was demolished in 1958-9. Turn put up its shutters for the last time in August 1959 because of declining trade, and by the end of the following decade it had been joined by Stubbins, Irwell Vale and Edenfield. The branch shop in Bolton Road North was the last to go, surviving until 1970.[17]

NOTES

1.   RO 22nd January 1909
2.   Manor of Tottington records (LRO: DDHCL liber W, folio 407; liber AL, folio 846); 1851 census Tottington Higher End (PRO: HO 107/2249)
3.   Manor of Tottington records (LRO: DDHCL liber CI, folio 611); RO 29th March 1912, 28th January 1898, 21st December 1921, 10th June 1932; I. Slater, *Royal National Commercial Directory of Bury, Heywood, Radcliffe, Ramsbottom and districts*, (1888); BT 5th December 1868
4.   I. Slater, *Royal National Commercial Directory of Bury, Heywood, Radcliffe, Ramsbottom and districts*, (1888); Valuation list 1895 – Ramsbottom (North) (LRO: PUB 8/105); RO 11th June 1926; W. Beswick, *Memories of Turn village: Its life, activities and characters 1907 - 1933*, (n.d.), p. 5
5.   T. Rogerson, *Lancashire General Directory*, (1818); 1851 census Tottington Higher End (PRO: HO 107/2249); I. Slater, *Royal National Commercial Directory of Bury, Heywood, Radcliffe, Ramsbottom and districts*, (1888)

6   RO 8th November 1912; 1861 census Tottington Higher End (PRO: RG 9/3059); 1891 census Tottington Higher End (PRO: RG 12/3352)

7   Valuation list 1910 – Ramsbottom (North) (LRO: PUB 8/162); Ramsbottom valuation list 1938 (BAS: ARM/T1870); Kelly's Directories Ltd., *Directory of Lancashire*, (1924); Diocese of Manchester – Parish church, Edenfield blotter 1929 (author's collection)

8   Rossendale Productivity Association, *Classified Rossendale Directory*, (1969); M. Gray, *Edenfield – Church, parish and village 1778 - 1978* (1978), p.16

9   BT 24th April 1869; RO 21st March 1919; Ramsbottom Co-op stock sheets, Stubbins branch, 6th March 1954 (BAS: Ramsbottom Heritage Society archive. MAINARCH 0166).

10   RO 13th November 1959, 2nd October 1914; Kelly's Directories Ltd., *Directory of Lancashire* (1924); Trades' Directories Ltd., *North-Western Counties of England Trades Directory* (1936, 1939, 1966, 1969); Lancashire Evening Telegraph 19th April 2000

11   *Pers. comm.* the late James Dewhurst; J. G. Hillis, 'Childhood memories of Edenfield', *Ramsbottom Heritage Society News Magazine*, (Spring 1997), p.13

12   RO 8th January 1904, 22nd January 1904, 22nd May 1904

13   RO 13th November 1959; BT 5th December 1858

14   Ramsbottom Co-op Magazine - centenary issue 1958 (BAS: Ramsbottom Heritage Society archive. MAINARCH 0163); RO 11th April 1952; RFP 6th May 1922; RO 28th August 1958, 30th June 1922

15   RO 7th October 1921, 21st December 1921, 14th April 1922, 28th April 1922

16   RO 13th November 1959, 13th October 1899, 3rd March 1899, 17th February 1911

17   RO 28th August 1959, 14th December 1962; GPO Classified Telephone Directory – Blackburn and Preston Areas 1962 - 1971

PUBLIC HOUSES AND EDENFIELD BREWERY

L YING AT THE JUNCTION OF SEVERAL ROADS, Edenfield found itself ideally placed to offer a drink and a place to stop and rest to travellers. The village's two oldest public houses – the Pack Horse and the White Horse (now the Horse and Jockey) – were already open for business in 1770. In 1792 they were joined by a 'new erected messuage or dwelling house … now used as a wine tavern', which was christened the Coach and Horses (now the Three Sisters). The fourth of the village public houses, the Rostron Arms, did not make its appearance until the 1830s. It began life in the same building as Thomas Yates's grocer's and draper's shop at 44-46, Bury Road, but in about 1840 moved to the more imposing building in Market Place.[1]

COACH AND HORSES
— *As it was* —

This early 20th century sketch of the Coach and Horses was made by Rawtenstall historian Patrick Stephens, and is the only record of the building before its frontage was altered.

Ewood Bridge was the first of the other villages to acquire a public house. It opened its doors probably in the late 1790s in a printing shop built in 1791 by William Morris. This building was used until 1827 when the landlord, John Ratcliffe, erected a new public house at the bottom of Greens Lane on a site now occupied by 18, Bridge Street. Following changes to the layout of the turnpike road from Ewood Bridge to Haslingden, Ratcliffe built the third Bridge Inn in 1837 (851, Manchester Road). This was used until the late 1990s. Stubbins and Turn did not get their own licensed premises until the 1860s when the Railway Hotel (Stubbins) and the Plane Tree Inn (Turn) were built in 1866 and 1867. There has never been a public house of any kind in Irwell Vale.[2]

With the passing of the Sale of Beer Act in 1830, a new kind of drinking place came into existence. The act was designed to give 'the poor and working classes of the community a chance of obtaining a better, cheaper and a more wholesome beverage' and allowed any householder assessed for the poor rate to buy a licence from the Excise authorities for two guineas a year. In return he could sell beer in his own house, for consumption on or off the premises, without interference from local magistrates. Somewhat unbelievably the act was designed to reduce drunkenness. Beerhouses had shorter opening hours than public houses and it was argued that customers would go home once the beerhouses had shut, rather than make their way to a nearby public house.[3]

Edenfield people quickly took advantage of the act and by 1841 there were nine beerhouses in the village. Like the public houses, beerhouses were usually found next to the main roads, although this was not always the case. In 1850, for instance, Richard Ashworth was selling beer at Sand Beds Farm, as was James Haworth at Alderbottom. Some of the licensees had other jobs as well. They included Thomas Dewhurst, a butcher in Temple Row, and Thomas Gerrard, a blacksmith in Market Place. Later in the century beersellers with other occupations included Henry Ramsbottom (stone quarry man), William Entwistle (music teacher) and George Cryer (loomer). Several beerhouses became well established and were kept by the same licensee or family for thirty or forty years or more. The Kellys, for example, sold beer from their house at Ashenbottom from the 1850s to the 1890s; Mary Rothwell had her beerhouse in the cottages on Bolton Road North near Rose Bank from the 1830s to the early 1870s, while Roshannah Pickstone was landlady at the beerhouse at the junction of Blackburn and Burnley Road from 1887 to 1925.[4]

Most of the beerhouses that did last a long time were given names like their public house counterparts. The five that became well known were the Adelphi Inn (originally the Jolly Carter) at 59, Blackburn Road; the Quarryman's Arms (also known as the West End) at 114, Burnley Road; the Horse Shoe Inn (formerly the Weavers' Arms and the Moulders' Arms) at 5, Burnley Road; the Volunteer Inn (6, Market Street); and the Bird in Hand (12, Gin Croft Lane). Only one beerhouse ever had purpose-built premises. This was the Quarryman's Arms where the original house had become very dilapidated by 1893. It was replaced by a two-storey building with a splendid crenellated porch and its name clearly carved into the wall.[5]

The Wine and Beer House Act of 1869 gave magistrates some control over beerhouses, making the granting of all licences conditional on the justices' approval. Their numbers were gradually reduced in the district as a whole, although all of the main Edenfield ones survived into the early 20th century when the 1904 Licensing Act brought further reductions. The act allowed magistrates to close public houses

Roshannah Pickstone (1842-1926), landlady of the Horse Shoe Inn beerhouse.

Market Place, Edenfield in 1900 with the Volunteer Inn occupying a central place at the corner of Gin Croft Lane.

or beerhouses that they considered to be surplus or redundant and for the owners to be compensated from a fund financed by a levy on the trade. In 1907 the Volunteer Inn and the Pack Horse became the first licensed premises in Edenfield to be considered for closure under this scheme. The former consisted of a commercial room, singing room, (with stage at one end), taproom, snug, serving bar and kitchen, while at the Pack Horse were a bar parlour, top parlour, tap room, bar, kitchen, two cellars and a clubroom. The case against the Volunteer Inn was not proceeded with, while the Quarter Sessions quashed the order to close the Pack Horse. For over seventy years it had been kept by the Haworth family and provided 'baiting' accommodation for more than a score of horses and also had a drawing-up space and watering trough at its front. In addition it was one of the meeting places of the Holcombe Hunt:

> They went to the Pack Horse to feed and not to drink, because at the Pack Horse they could get food prepared by an old lady who had been born in the house, and who gave them good milk and food and butter right off the farm.

Nevertheless, the building was in a very poor state and was completely rebuilt in 1908.[6]

The first beerhouse in the village to close was the Adelphi Inn, which was referred for compensation in February 1908. It was followed in 1917 by the Volunteer Inn and

Edenfield's oldest public house, the Pack Horse. The figures in the older photograph are the owner, Richard Nuttall, and his three sons, John Will, Jim and George. The other picture was taken in 1908 during the pub's rebuilding.

the Bird in Hand whose landlord lamented the fact that his trade had not been as good since the navvies left the district following the completion of Scout Moor reservoir in 1909. The Horse Shoe Inn shut its doors for the last time in 1925, but the Quarryman's Arms lasted until 1962, an odd survival from the dozens of beerhouses that once flourished in the area.[7]

The four public houses in the village remained unaltered until recent times, although attempts were made to declare the Horse and Jockey and the Coach and Horses redundant in 1925 and 1945. When the case against the Coach and Horses was put to the Bury Licensing Sessions, the landlord, seventy-year-old John Entwistle, explained that 'it was a family house, used chiefly by men and their wives. Some of the younger element who were customers were now in the Forces. He had a catering licence, provided teas and had "put up" people.' John Hamer, a retired bricklayer from East Street, said that he had been a customer for forty years, that the pub was a clean and comfortable house and that he liked the landlord. When asked whether he liked what was on offer there he provoked laughter in the court by remarking simply, 'I should not go everyday if I didn't.' Although the licence was referred for compensation, it was renewed in June 1945.[8]

Drastic changes to the Horse and Jockey were proposed in 1965 when plans were put forward to rebuild the pub away from the road with a car park in front. 'A feature of the proposed new inn, which will be of ranch-style construction, will be large windows at the rear to give a panoramic view of the Valley.' said the *Ramsbottom Observer*. The Pack Horse changed its name to the Topham's Arms in 1986 and became an Italian restaurant in 1991; the Railway Hotel at Stubbins changed its name to the Corner Pin, while the late 1990s saw the closure of the Bridge Inn, Ewood Bridge and the Plane Tree, Turn. The Coach and Horses has also had mixed fortunes in the past few years. The building itself had been altered, probably in the early 1900s, but it was not until June 1996 that the old name disappeared to be replaced very briefly by the Bengal Brasserie and Pub and then the Three Sisters, its current name.[9]

EDENFIELD BREWERY

Until well into the 19th century, most local publicans brewed their own beer, and licensed premises generally had a brewhouse adjoining. From 1861, however, Edenfield had its own brewery. It was begun by Thomas, son of James Mercer, landlord of the Horse and Jockey. He bought a plot of land between Blackburn Road and Burnley Road on which he built Spring Bank Brewery using the old lodge from Elton Banks Mill as a water supply. It was quite a modest concern, employing six men and one boy in 1871 and twelve men in 1881. However, in the 1880s Mercer expanded the business by buying up beerhouses (including the Adelphi Inn and the Horse Shoe Inn) and building new public houses such as the Mechanics' Arms, Helmshore.[10]

Mercer ran the business until 1899 when he sold the brewery, the Adelphi Inn, the Horse Shoe Inn, the Volunteer Inn, an off licence at 103, Bury Road and several

The only known photograph of Edenfield brewery before it was extensively altered. The occasion was a Primitive Methodist Whitsuntide procession in the 1920s.

cottages. The purchasers were the Grants Tower Brewery Co. Ltd., incorporated on 16th August 1898 with the intention of taking over Mercer's business as a going concern. The directors included the landlords of the Commercial Hotel and the Swan Hotel, Haslingden and the Clarence Hotel, Ramsbottom as well as a bleacher, colliery proprietor, provision dealer and cigar merchant. The new company paid £5,500 for the brewery and other property and immediately renamed it the Grants Tower Brewery. Using a picture of the tower as a logo, the company produced not only beer, but also mineral waters and ginger beer. An 1893 advertisement for the brewery included a description of its beer from the Essex county public analyst: 'this is a well brewed beer with a comparatively small percentage of alcohol, and is pleasantly flavoured with the extract and aromas of the hop.' In 1908, however, one local man noted, 'The ale brewed by this firm is not well liked, it being of a very purgative nature, as to be known to the old 'topers' of the district as "Sh-t-n Br—ches".'[11]

An 1897 advertisement for Edenfield brewery.

In the following year the Grants Tower Brewery Co. Ltd. went into receivership and the Edenfield Brewery Co. Ltd. acquired the business. In fact this was a return to ownership by the Mercer family since the directors of the new firm were Thomas Mercer and his sons, Thomas and Donald, with the younger Thomas in charge at Edenfield. Another take over a few years later – this time by John Kenyon Ltd. of Cloughfold – marked the end of the brewery, which closed in 1913.[12]

NOTES
[1] Manor of Tottington records (LRO: DDHCL liber W, folio 131); Tottington Higher End valuation 1837 (LRO: MBH 5/6); 1841 census Tottington Higher End (PRO: HO 107/540/1);
[2] Ewood Bridge deeds (Helmshore Local History Society); BT 7th September 1867; Derby estate instructions for leases book 1867-1868 (BAS: BWO/T1909)
[3] P. Jennings, 'Studying beerhouses', *The Local Historian*, (November 1987) 457-464; N. Longmate, *The Waterdrinkers*, (1968), p. 23
[4] 1841 – 1891 censuses Tottington Higher End (PRO: HO 107/540/1, HO 107/2249, RG 9/3059, RG 10/4139, RG 11/4136, RG 12/3352); Tottington Higher End valuation 1837 (LRO: MBH 5/6); RO 13th February 1925
[5] BT 9th September 1871, 11th September 1869; Manor of Tottington records (LRO: DDHCL liber EM, folio 791); RO 26th August 1892, 1st September 1893.

6   N. Longmate, *op. cit.*, pp. 32, 246; RO 8th February 1907, 7th February 1908, 28th February 1908

7   RO 7th February 1908, 9th March 1917, 13th February 1925, 12th January 1962

8   RO 13th February 1925, 2nd February 1945

9   RO 22nd January 1965; RFP 1st November 1991

10 Manor of Tottington records (LRO: DDHCL liber EM, folio 791); 1871 census Tottington Higher End (PRO: RG 10/4139); 1881 census Tottington Higher End (PRO: RG 11/4136); Bacup and Rossendale News 15th January 1881

11 Dissolved companies files: Grants Tower Brewery Co. Ltd. (PRO: BT 31/8115/58574); Rossendale Division Gazette 25th February 1893; P. Stephens, *Notes on Edenfield and Ewood Bridge* (Rawtenstall library: RC 942 EDE)

12 Dissolved companies files: Edenfield Brewery Co. Ltd. (PRO: BT 31/19002/104985); RO 26th September 1913

MAKING A LIVING – A MISCELLANY
PROFESSIONS AND PUBLIC SERVANTS

THE CLERGY

Until 1842, the clergymen who had charge of Edenfield church also took services at Holcombe and lived in a house there. From about 1811 they were helped by assistant curates, beginning with the Rev. John Johnson who moved from Haslingden to lodgings in Hawthorn House. He stayed until the late 1820s and was followed by the Revs. John Clayton and William Verdon. In 1842, the Rev. Matthew Wilson was appointed curate and lived in the village until his death in 1870. He took up residence in the newly built parsonage in the early 1850s and became Edenfield's first vicar when the new parish was formed in 1865. One account of him says that he was a keen 'aborist' who planted many trees in

Rev. Matthew Wilson, Edenfield's first vicar.

the churchyard and vicarage garden. In a pamphlet published in 1867 he complained about a straying donkey that had eaten a weeping willow 'of a rare kind' that he had planted at the head of his mother's grave.[1]

In the second half of the 19th century, the Anglican clergy were joined by the Rev. Thomas Cain, minister at Stubbins Congregational Church from 1865 to 1907. He was born on the Isle of Man and as a boy was taught by a man who had served on HMS Victory at Trafalgar. He trained for the ministry in Manchester and while still at college was appointed pastor of the new Congregational Church. When he first arrived in the area he lived at Hawthorn House, but moved to Stubbins Villa, which was built by his father-in-law, James Porritt, in 1871. This house (renamed Greystones) became the vicarage for St. Philip's church in 1936, while the Congregational ministers moved into the house next door at the end of Eden Bank. The Primitive Methodists acquired no. 86 in 1919 for their manse, so it is not surprising that the houses were given the epithet 'Parsons' Row'.[2]

DOCTORS

From the first half of the 19th century until the early 1970s Edenfield has nearly always had a resident doctor. The first man to hold the position was Joseph Gartside, who was born in Saddleworth, came to the village in the 1830s and stayed until his death in 1862. He described himself as 'surgeon and accoucher' [man mid-wife], but villagers could also call on Ann Pilling, the village mid-wife in the 1860s. Several of the men who came after Dr. Gartside were from Scotland and included James Galloway (1871), who held the degrees of Batchelor of Medicine and Master of Surgery from the University of Glasgow, and William Decus (1881), a graduate of Aberdeen University. One of their successors who was a well-respected figure in the village was also a Scot. He was Dr. Henry Deans who was in partnership with his brother, William, in the 1890s and early 1900s with surgeries both in Edenfield and Ramsbottom. William had come to Edenfield in about 1875 as assistant to Dr. Galloway and had taken over the practice in the mid-1880s when he moved to Ramsbottom. After his death in 1912, his brother went into partnership with Dr. Ralph Crompton of Carrbank, Ramsbottom and remained so until his own death in 1925. His obituary noted:

> Of a genial disposition, Dr. Deans had evinced a keen interest in ambulance classes, having been divisional surgeon to the local corps. Many who served in the Great War as well as the South African War received their training at the hands of 'Dr. Henry,' as he was familiarly known in Edenfield.

After Dr. Deans came Dr. John H. Struthers, who left the village in 1939 and emigrated to South Africa, and Dr. Ian G.L. Ford, both of whom had their surgery in Acres House. Dr. Ford had qualified in Dublin in 1931 and went into practice first with Dr. Crompton, then with Dr. Edward W. Gleeson and finally with his wife, Bridget. He gave up general practice when he became a consultant surgeon at Bury and Rossendale hospitals. From the early 1970s, Edenfield's surgery has been at 53, Market Street and has been in the care of the Rawtenstall practice started by Dr. John Archibald. In the 19th century, for anyone who distrusted doctors there were some practitioners of more traditional medicine, one of whom was Ellen Chattwood, a 'bleeder with leeches', who lived in the village in the 1850s.[3]

THE POLICE

Until the establishment of a police force in Lancashire in 1840, law and order in Edenfield was in the hands of the officials of the township of Tottington Higher End. They could not detain any wrongdoers in the village itself until the early 1830s when a lock-up was built at the bottom of Gin Croft Lane. By the early 1840s this building was also doing duty as the police station. The first man to be stationed there was P.C. David Nagle, a native of County Cork who had joined the new police force in June 1840. He probably arrived in Edenfield towards the end of the year or early in 1841, but his stay in the village was quite brief since he resigned from the force in December 1841.[4]

The building at Gin Croft Lane remained in use until the 1860s, but when the 1871 census was taken the police station had moved to 24, Market Street where it

Two of the police constables who were stationed in the Edenfield area in the late 19th century. Robert Kirkpatrick (*left*) was at Stubbins when the 1881 census was taken, while Alexander Chisholm was living in the police station at 24, Market Street a few years later.

stayed until its closure in the late 1930s. By 1881 there were two constables in Edenfield, with a third, Robert Kirkpatrick, living at Stubbins. One of P.C. Kirkpatrick's successors was P.C. John Reeves who joined the force in 1882. He transferred to the Bury Division in 1897 and went to live at Stubbins. Early in August of the same year, three boys were playing on some islets in the River Irwell near Stubbins Bridge. There had been a storm a short while before and the river began to rise rapidly. Two of the boys scrambled to the bank, but ten-year-old Arthur Haworth was cut off by the water. The *Bury Times* recounts what happened next:

> People who began to assemble at the river's bank in considerable numbers made ineffectual attempts to throw ropes to the boy left on the islet, whose position was rapidly becoming dangerous. Police-constable Reeves, who resides near, came on the scene in his slippers and shirt sleeves and taking one end of the rope, and leaving the other with the crowd, he dashed into the strongly-rushing water at some peril and managed to reach one of the islets near where the boy was standing. Making a slip noose at the end of the rope Reeves threw it to Haworth and shouted to him to pass it beneath his arms. The boy did so and was then dragged safely on to the bank by the people.

In the meantime, another would-be rescuer had got into difficulties so P.C. Reeves waded into the river again until the water was up to his shoulders and helped the man to the bank. The constable was awarded the Royal Humane Society's medal for his bravery. He was stationed at Stubbins until his retirement in 1907.[5]

In the first half of the 20th century, two policemen served in the village and stayed for some years. P.C. John Turnbull joined the force in 1894 and was transferred to the Bury Division in 1898. He was based in Edenfield until his death from influenza in 1918. His colleague, P.C. Thomas Woods, joined the force in 1906 and spent his entire career first in Summerseat and then in Edenfield. He retired in 1931, but lived in Stubbins until his death in 1964.[6]

P.C. Thomas Woods and villager Joseph Jackson at the gates of Acres House in the 1920s.

NEW JOBS, NEW OPPORTUNITIES

The 19th century saw the creation of a number of new kinds of jobs. The coming of the railways, for instance, meant that by the time the 1851 census was taken there were railway porters, clerks, plate layers and even an 'inspector of carriages' in Edenfield, Ewood Bridge and Lumb. Similarly, in 1854 the Ramsbottom Gas Co. was set up to build a gas works with six gasholders on land at Stubbins. Once complete, the works provided jobs for a number of men as stokers and by the 1880s, when most houses were lit by gas, at least one man, Ralph Shaw who lived in Bury Road, made his living as a 'gas meter inspector.' Not many years later, another local man turned his attention to a different source of energy. John Henry Hindle was born in 1869, the son of the book-keeper at Irwell Vale Mill, and lived in a house whose site is now occupied by The Grange. After attending Ewood Bridge National School, he qualified as an electrical engineer and installed the first electric lights in the village at Bridge Mills in 1894. Later he founded a firm making electrical presses, but his real passion was for astronomy. He began making telescopes in 1910 and by the 1930s was recognised as a world authority on the grinding and optical figuring of large telescope mirrors. He was rewarded for this work by being made a Fellow of the Royal Astronomical Society and his gravestone records that, 'He helped them to look at the stars.'[7]

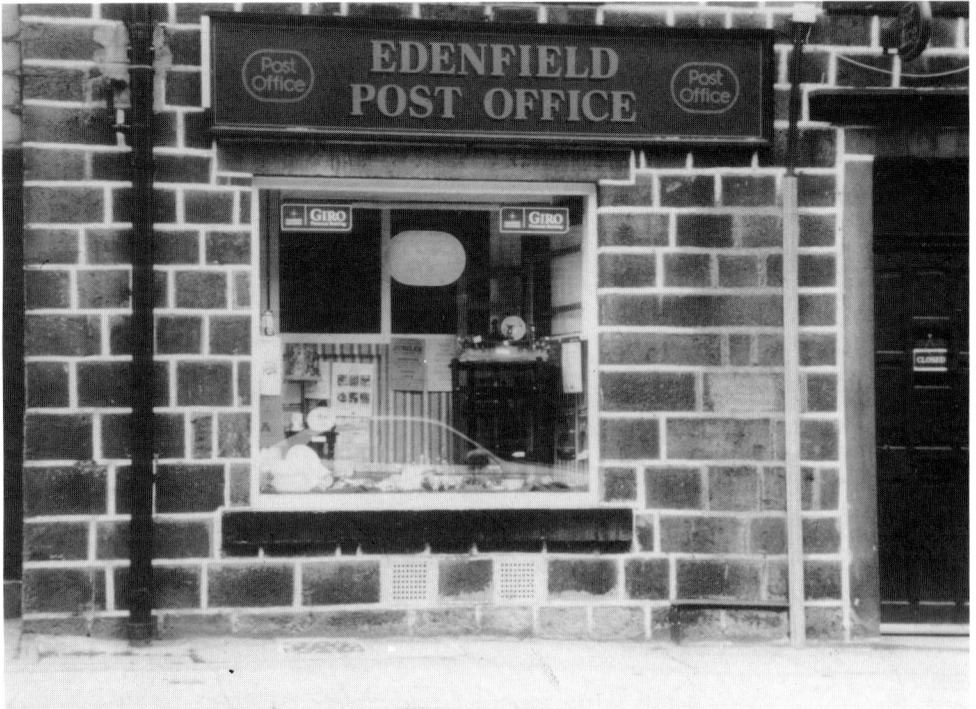

Edenfield Post Office at 123, Market Street, its home for more than 100 years.

Changes at national level also brought new jobs for village people. The introduction of civil registration from 1st July 1837 created the post of registrar who had to record the births, marriages and deaths that took place in the locality. The men who held the position usually combined it with some other job: Richard Pickup, registrar in the 1850s also kept a grocer's shop, John Darwen, registrar in 1871 was also a barber, while in 1861 and 1871 Edmund Chattwood and Thomas Emmett also acted as assistant overseers of the poor. Another example of a new job created by changes brought in by the government was that of postmaster. Until the 1850s, letters either came in the mail gig from Manchester and were left at the Horse and Jockey or were carried on foot from Bury, arriving at 11.30am and departing at 2pm. The postman who had walked from Bury demanded 6d or 7d for the delivery of a letter. This changed when Edenfield got its first post office. It opened on 4th December 1852 in a building at the Market Place end of Commercial Row where Abel Hall, the new postmaster, also kept a grocer's and druggist's shop. In about 1870 the post office moved to 64, Market Street when James Taylor became postmaster. It has since been at 17, Market Place and 121, Market Street, before settling at 123, Market Street in the early years of the 20th century. When Stubbins grew in the second half of the 19th century, it too acquired a sub-post office. It opened in 1884 at 292, Bolton Road North where Richard Barlow had a grocer's shop and has subsequently found a home in various houses beside the main road until reaching 288, Bolton Road North. Turn also had its own post office at 267-269 and 312, Rochdale Road in the early years of the 20th century.[8]

TRADES AND CRAFTS

Throughout the 19th century and well into the 20th century, Edenfield and its neighbours had a multitude of people who made their living by some trade or craft. Some of them, like shuttle makers and heald and reed makers, were dependent on the demands of a particular industry, while others supplied not only industry, but also agriculture and individual households. Blacksmiths, for instance, may have found themselves shoeing horses one day, making a part for a machine the next, and repairing a fire shovel on a third. Some of these men were independent craftsmen with their own smithy who employed several men. James Pilling, for example, took over the smithy at Barnett Place (now partially occupied by Heycrofts View) in the late 1830s when he was in his twenties. By 1861 he was employing two men, including his son, Henry, who carried on the business when his father retired in the 1870s.[9]

Other craftsmen labouring away in small workshops, either on their own account or for small masters, included tinplate workers and nail makers who appear in the census returns for both Edenfield and Ewood Bridge. Richard Mason who lived in Market Place until the 1870s was a tinplate worker who had three apprentices bound to him in 1851. His business ran into difficulties in 1858, but had recovered by 1861 when he described himself as a master coppersmith and iron and tinplate worker employing two men and two boys, including his sixteen-year-old son. He moved to Ramsbottom in the 1880s to set up a new works in Irwell Street. When his stock was sold in 1858 it included coal and candle boxes, trunks, trays, tea and coffee canisters, iron pans, iron and cast fenders, scales, candlesticks, chisels, milk kits, watering cans, buckets 'and other articles usually kept at an ironmonger's shop.'[10]

People connected with the building trade, included not only builders and joiners, but also carpenters, plumbers and glaziers, painters and plasterers, paperhangers and white-washers. Again some of these individuals built up small businesses in which they employed other people. One example was James Lord who lived at 44, Market Street in 1871 and who was a master painter employing six men and two boys. Some of these small firms became well established and made a significant contribution to village history. Two such concerns were the joinery and building firms established in the 1830s by John Pilling and Thomas Wolstenholme. Pilling built his own sawmill near the Guide Post, while Wolstenholme traded from premises in Bury Road. Both firms helped to build many churches and other public buildings in the area, including Stubbins Congregational church and the Wesleyan Methodist chapel, as well as dozens of houses. The two firms merged in 1933, continuing as H. Wolstenholme and Son, joiners and undertakers.[11]

Guide Saw Mill, the home of John Pilling's joinery business. It was demolished in 1995.

Many people, especially in the 19th century, made a living by providing some kind of service for their neighbours. They included barbers, tailors, milliners, shoe-makers and cloggers, some of whom became well-known figures in the places in which they lived. James Ramsbottom, for example, made and repaired the clogs and shoes of the people of Turn for over thirty years in the mid-19th century from his workshop at Lime Leach. In the early 1900s his place was taken by John Pickup ('Jack o' Jinney's') who worked from a wooden hut at the end of Lodge Mill Lane. His hut was shared by Tom Wisdom who made boots and shoes, including riding boots for members of the Holcombe Hunt. Many of these small businesses flourished: John Bentley, a tailor in the 1850s living in Temple Row employed two men in 1851 and three in 1861 and Alice Brooks of Irwell Vale, milliner, dressmaker and straw bonnet maker, had two employees. More often than not, however, they were simply individuals and in the case of dressmakers were often unmarried daughters in a family still living at home and taking in dressmaking as means to add to the household income. Such workers proliferated in the 19th century: the 1851 census, for instance, records thirteen dressmakers or milliners in Edenfield, two in Ewood Bridge and one in Stubbins.[12]

IN SERVICE

For most of the 19th century and into the 20th century, some of the more well-to-do people in Edenfield and district found work for their contemporaries by employing them as servants. Until the middle of the 19th century, local landowners like the Haworths at the original Horncliffe House and the Eltons at Elton Banks, and textile manufacturers including the Rostrons at Chatterton Hey and Acres House, the Porritts at Dearden Clough House and Hawthorn House and the Parkinsons at Ewood Bridge made do with just one or two servants living with them. Servants were also found in the homes of the more prosperous tradesmen: in 1841, for instance, grocer Lawrence Duckworth had Thomas Duckworth and Mary Grimshaw as servants in his household at Crown House. In the second half of the century, professionals like the Rev. Thomas Cain, Congregational minister, and Alfred Booth, the village schoolmaster, also employed servants.[13]

The second half of the 19th century also brought with it textile manufacturers' huge houses, which needed a full of staff of servants to look after them. Top of the list were the Hardmans of Horncliffe House who employed a butler, cook, housemaid, nurse, general domestic servant, coachman and gardener. The term nurse usually meant a female servant whose job it was to look after the young children of the household. They were often in their teens or early twenties, although in 1851 John Ruthven, an assistant railway secretary who lived in Milne Street, Irwell Vale, was employing ten-year-old Priscilla Heaton, while John Aitken, cotton manufacturer, had eight-year-old Susannah Farnel as nurse for his infant daughter, Lucy Jane.[14]

Susannah Farnel was born in Halifax and many of her fellow servants were also from outside Lancashire. Most came from small villages or towns in the more rural counties of England and Wales where employment opportunities were limited. To take the servants who were working in the area in 1891 as an example, their places of birth included Croughton (Northamptonshire), Pawlett (Somerset), Stone (Staffordshire), Ludlow (Shropshire), Calder Bridge (Cumberland), Hanworth (Norfolk), Candlesby (Lincolnshire) and Holywell.[15]

NOTES

[1] RO 8th August 1924

[2] RO 26th November 1926; 1871 census Tottington Higher End (PRO: RG 10/4139); BT 13th May 1871; P. Dunne, *St. Philip's Church, Stubbins*, 1927-1977, (1977) p. 9; Stubbins Congregational church record book (BAS: CST/1); Edenfield Primitive Methodist trustees' minute book 1900 - 1923 (BAS: CRR/T1490)

[3] 1841 - 1881 censuses Tottington Higher End (PRO: HO 107/540/1, HO 107/2249, RG 9/3059, RG 10/4139, RG 11/4136); RO 12th July 1912, 30th January 1925, 11th August 1939; *pers. comm.* the late Eleanor Graham; J. and A. Churchill, *The Medical Directory*; J. Heap, *The Bury Directory*, (1850); RFP 24th December 1971

[4] 1841 census Tottington Higher End (PRO: HO 107/540/1); Police examination book (LRO: PLA 11/3)

[5] 1871 census Tottington Higher End (PRO: RG 10/4139); 1881 census Tottington Higher End (PRO: RG 11/4136); Police examination book (LRO: PLA/11/24); BT 7th August 1897, 23rd October 1897; RO 27th September 1907

[6] Police examination book (LRO: PLA 11/28); Police pensioners book (LRO: PLA 14/19/9); RO 18th January 1918, 31st July 1931

[7] 1851 census Tottington Higher End (PRO: HO 107/2249); 1881 census Tottington Higher End (PRO: RG 11/4136); Manchester Evening News 7th January 1936

[8] 1851 - 1881 censuses Tottington Higher End (PRO: HO 107/2249, RG 9/3059, RG 10/4139, RG 11/4136); RO 30th September 1927; J. Heap, *The Bury Directory*, (1850); RO 8th November 1912; Information on the early history of Edenfield post office courtesy of John Winter of Burnley; BT 21st June 1884; 1901 census Walmersley-cum-Shuttleworth (PRO: RG 13/3634); R. Barlow, *The diary of Richard Barlow, a Ramsbottom postman 1882 to 1925*, (n.d.), p. 13

[9] Tottington Higher End valuation 1837 (LRO: MBH/5/6) Tottington Higher End tithe award and plan 1838 (LRO: DRM 1/97); 1841 - 1881 censuses Tottington Higher End (PRO: HO 107/540/1, HO 107/2249, RG 9/3059, RG 10/4139, RG 11/4136)

[10] 1851 census Tottington Higher End (PRO: HO 107/2249); 1861 census Tottington Higher End (PRO: RG 9/3059); BT 15th May 1858; P. Barrett & Co., *General and commercial directory of Bury...Ramsbottom and adjacent villages and townships*, (1883)

[11] 1871 census Tottington Higher End (PRO: RG 10/4139); RO 7th July 1933

[12] 1851 - 1881 censuses Walmersley-cum-Shuttleworth (PRO: HO 107/2212, RG 9/2839, RG 10/3948, RG 11/3852); 1851 census Haslingden (PRO: HO 107/2250); 1851 census Tottington Higher End (PRO: HO 107/2249); 1861 census Tottington Higher End (PRO: RG 9/3059); W. Beswick, *Memories of Turn Village*, (n.d.), pp. 5-6

[13] 1841 census Tottington Higher End (PRO: HO 107/540/1); 1891 census Tottington Higher End (PRO: RG 12/3352)

[14] 1871 census Tottington Higher End (PRO: RG 10/4139); 1851 census Tottington Higher End (PRO: HO 107/2249)

[15] 1891 census Tottington Higher End (PRO: RG 12/3352)

TRANSPORT

TURNPIKE ROADS

AS THE TEXTILE INDUSTRY GREW in the 18th century, so too did the need to move larger and larger quantities of raw materials and finished goods. The old roads soon proved unequal to carrying increasing amounts of wheeled traffic and moves were made to remedy the situation by setting up turnpike trusts. Each trust was empowered to build and maintain certain lengths of road (often laid out along new routes that by-passed the old circuitous highways) and to charge tolls to pay for repairs. Trustees were usually prominent local men – manufacturers, merchants and landowners – who stood to gain from better roads. Members of the trust that oversaw the building of the road from Haslingden through Edenfield to Bury, for instance, included John and Lawrence Hoyle, woollen merchants and manufacturers, with mills at Dearden Clough.[1]

Not everyone was in favour of spending money on new roads. For example, at the second reading of the bill to allow the building of the Edenfield and Little Bolton turnpike on 10th May 1797 a petition against it was placed before the House of Commons. It was signed by the inhabitants of the townships of Tottington Higher End and Tottington Lower End who said that the proposed road began in a small village in a thinly populated township:

> ... and the said intended Turnpike Road cannot lead from Bolton through Edenfield ... in a direct or good Line, to any other Market Town or Place of great Population; and that the whole Line of the same intended Road lies at a distance from the populous Villages between Bolton and Edenfield, and leads through a Country having few Inhabitants, and has in many Places a bad Bottom, that is distant from Materials for making and repairing the same, is very circuitous, and in many Places rises and falls very rapidly, and it will be no Accommodation to the Public.

A second petition on 16th May added that the road would be 'serviceable only to a very few interested Individuals, to whose Lands it will form a good Occupation Road maintained at Public Expense.' Despite these objections the bill was passed and received the royal assent on 19th June 1797.[2]

The Edenfield-Little Bolton road was only one of four turnpikes to meet at Edenfield. The earliest of the four was that built by the Bury, Haslingden, Blackburn and Whalley turnpike trust under an act of 1789. This trust improved the old road through the centre of the village and laid out new stretches of highway from the church to Ewood Bridge and south from Market Place. The Rochdale-Edenfield turnpike trust (1794) took responsibility for a new route from the junction of Michael Wife Lane and the old road to Bury across the fields towards Cheesden, incorporating a short stretch of the old road between Turn and Fecit. At the north end of the village, another new road cut across farmland after the Burnley and Edenfield turnpike trust was granted powers in 1795. This is the present main road to Rawtenstall. The Edenfield and Little Bolton trust's contribution to the network of roads was to link the village and Stubbins with a road at a gentler gradient than the steep and narrow Chatterton Lane.

Once a turnpike trust had been set up, its first task was to engage surveyors who viewed the existing road or proposed route and reported on their condition. The trustees then decided on the lengths of road to be built or repaired and invited contactors to tender for the construction of particular sections of road. One of the most well known of such men was John Metcalf ('Blind Jack of Knaresborough') who, despite having been blind from the age of six, could lay out new lengths of road with considerable skill. He was responsible for building about seven miles of the road belonging to the Bury, Haslingden, Blackburn and Whalley trust. This included the stretch from Ewood Bridge to Bent Gate and he is said to have lived at Ewood Bridge while he carried out this work.[3]

After the work of construction had been completed, the trustees continued to employ surveyors to keep the road in good repair. In April 1793, for instance, Richard Walmsley of Edenfield was appointed surveyor of the stretch of road from Haslingden to Dearden Cough at an annual salary of thirty guineas on the understanding that he would work on the road every day. Repairs were to be paid for out of toll revenues. The rate of tolls was fixed by the act that established each trust and could not be raised without a new act. Foot passengers and certain other kinds of traffic such as post horses carrying the mail were exempt from tolls, but all other traffic had to pay. The tolls set by the Edenfield and Little Bolton trust in 1797 began by levying 2s on every 'Coach, Berlin, Landau, Chariot, Chaise, Calash, Curricle, Hearse or Litter' drawn by six horses, with a descending scale on the number of horses so that a single-horse vehicle paid only 6d. There were different rates too for wagons and carts depending on the size of their wheels. Later acts that renewed some of the turnpike trusts allowed tolls to be revised to take account of developments such as steam traction engines.[4]

Tollhouses were built at intervals along the roads to house the toll collectors. There were six around Edenfield, two of which survive. Number 9, Market Place, which formerly projected into the road to reduce the space for the tollgate to span and to allow the toll collector to keep a watchful eye on the passing traffic, was built by the Blackburn, Bury, Haslingden and Whalley trust, while 113, Burnley Road, was built in 1826-7 by the Burnley and Edenfield trust. The others were at Ewood Bridge at the junction of the new road and Ewood Lane (now Greens Lane); on Rochdale Road at the bottom of Plunge Road; at Turn where the old lane from Bleakholt met the new road; and at Stubbins a short distance from the west end of the bridge over the Irwell. At first toll collectors were paid by the turnpike trusts. For example, in 1791 James Holden of Ashenbottom was appointed toll collector at

Crow Woods tollhouse (113, Burnley Road) in 1938. The board listing the various tolls would have been fixed on the front of the building between the windows. A number of boards are preserved at Whitaker Park Museum, Rawtenstall.

Ewood Bridge at a weekly wage of 9s 11d. Later it became more usual for the collection of tolls to be let by tender to the highest bidder who paid a fixed sum in return.[5]

Apart from the toll bars, the other most visible remains of the turnpike era are the milestones, which the trusts had to set up along their roads. They were found on Rochdale Road near Brass Row; outside no. 18, Market Street; near Elton Banks House; and at Rose Bank, near the end of Chatterton Lane. Only the Market Street example survives. It once gave the distances to Bury, Manchester, Haslingden, Blackburn and Whalley, but was defaced during the Second World War.

Where the new roads crossed streams or rivers as at Dearden Clough the trusts had to build and maintain bridges. It was a different matter when the turnpike used an old bridge maintained by the county. There were two on the roads approaching Edenfield, one at Ewood Bridge and one at Stubbins. In the early 1780s both these bridges were single arch structures with a fifty-six foot span. Ewood Bridge, which lay partly in Salford Hundred and partly in Blackburn Hundred, was in good repair but New Bridge at Stubbins was anything but. The county surveyor found,

> The foundation bad and the bridge much sunk, and in so ruinous a situation that it is expected to fall every flood or even when a carriage passes over, which is not very often.

Ewood Bridge was rebuilt with two arches in 1792-3 and New Bridge probably a few years later. Both were subsequently altered to allow the roads to be widened.[6]

Construction methods on the new roads were often fairly crude, usually consisting of laying a compacted surface of small stones and gravel. Nevertheless, the turnpikes were an improvement on the old highways and could accommodate the increasing and changing traffic that used them. It became possible for manufacturers to move raw materials and goods in carts and wagons instead of by packhorse. Eventually some of the larger concerns had their own teams of horses and fleets of wagons to cart goods to Manchester. For example, in 1858 Greenhalgh and Rumney at Stubbins printworks had five horses used for the journey to Manchester in the early hours of the morning.[7]

The increased amount of traffic also opened up opportunities for local people to make a living as carriers, both to neighbouring towns and to Manchester. By the mid-19th century there were four master carriers in the village, employing between four and twenty-one men. The Whittakers of Crow Woods and Chapel House ran the most successful and long lasting of these concerns. The business was founded in 1825 by James Whittaker who carried goods from Burnley in the north and Church in the west through Rossendale to Manchester. Even after the railways opened in the 1840s the firm continued to carry goods to and from Manchester by road. For instance, in 1847 they delivered 142 bales of cotton to the Helmshore firm of James and Thomas Rawstron and took away over 9,000 finished pieces of cloth to the

Carters in the employ of J. and J. Whittaker, the Edenfield carriers, pose proudly with their horses and a huge block of stone at Ramsbottom station in the early 1900s.

Manchester markets. Similarly, from the end of July to the beginning of September 1852 they carried 2,350 pieces of cloth for James Rostron of Ravenshore Mill and over 13,000 pieces for him in the first half of 1854. They also delivered bales of raw wool to W. and R. Turner of Helmshore, as well as other items such as boxes of soap, sacks of malt and loads of turnips.[8]

Their competition with the railways was so successful that in about 1853 they were approached by the Lancashire and Yorkshire Railway Co. who asked them to withdraw from the Manchester route. In return they were granted exclusive rights to carry goods from all the stations between Ramsbottom and Bacup. Part of their success lay in the fact that in 1850 James Whittaker made an agreement with the trustees of the Burnley and Edenfield turnpike road. Under this he paid any tolls for the following twelve months in advance and in return the trustees allowed that he would not be liable to pay more than half of the toll he was then paying on carts and wagons carrying goods and merchandise. Just over twenty years later, the family paid £2,600 for all the tolls on the road for a twelve-month period when they were offered for sale by auction.[9]

The business continued to prosper: in 1885 when John Whittaker, who was then the senior partner, died he had 'upwards of 100 of the finest draught horses in England' and a few years previously had been employing 114 men. Whittakers continued to use horses for carrying until the early 1950s, but made their first move into the mechanical age in 1877 when they began using traction engines. The trial trip of one engine carrying cloth and other goods between Rawtenstall station, Crawshawbooth and Loveclough Printworks was made in April 1877 and was 'eminently satisfactory'. In October of the same year the first traction engine ever to be seen in Bacup made its appearance when Whittakers delivered cotton to Forest Mill.[10]

The success of the Whittaker family business was later matched by the firm founded by Richard Nuttall. Richard's father, George, was a farmer, but also carried goods locally, specialising in carting stone from Scout Moor Quarry. His son followed him into farming, but one winter in the early 1880s when his horses were standing idle because of a frosty spell of weather he decided to put them to work carrying to and from Manchester. His first customers were the Ramsbottom Spinning and Manufacturing Co. at Stubbins and he later carried for the Starks and Turnbull and Stockdale's at Rose Bank. Richard took his five sons into partnership and extended his business in the early years of the 20th century by buying the business of James Schofield in 1902 and of his own brother, John, in 1904. When he died in 1934, as befitted a man who had worked with horses all his life, his coffin was taken to Edenfield churchyard on a dray drawn by a team of horses. Richard Nuttall and Sons Ltd. still operate from their garage next to the former Pack Horse public house, which Richard had bought in 1906.[11]

As well as easing the movement of large loads of raw materials and merchandise, the turnpike roads made it easier to carry letters, parcels and passengers. The first

The funeral procession of Richard Nuttall, founder of the carrying business that still bears his name, making its way along Market Street in July 1934.

coach from Clitheroe to Manchester via Accrington and Haslingden started running in 1815 and was soon joined by others with names like 'The Commercial', 'The Traveller', 'The Independent Highflyer' and 'The Invincible'. The towns of Clitheroe, Blackburn, Haslingden, Burnley, Rochdale and Bury were linked to Manchester and each other by coach services, many of which passed through Edenfield because of the way the different turnpike roads met there. Some of them broke their journey at the Horse and Jockey.[12]

Although the railways killed off much of the long distant travel by road until the 20th century, there were still plenty of opportunities for passenger travel on a smaller scale – even if only to and from the nearest railway stations. Horse buses passed through the village several times daily by the late 1850s and in 1867 the Edenfield, Shuttleworth and Bury Omnibus Co. Ltd. was set up to carry passengers and parcels. Many villages were shareholders, but the venture did not enjoy long-lasting success: it went into liquidation in 1872 and its assets were sold. They included seven horses, two omnibuses, a mourning 'bus and a brougham. Other people stepped into to provide public transport from the village. In 1876, for instance, an omnibus left the Horse and Jockey for the Knowsley Hotel, Bury twice a day. It may have been operated by Thomas and Edwin Howard whose stables were at Pinfold and whose business ran until Edwin retired in 1887. Their omnibus could carry thirty-three passengers and they also had a wagonette for twenty people, a brougham, phaeton and dog cart.[13]

The turnpike system was not a complete success. Trusts had to borrow money to finance their road-building schemes and often found that their income could not pay off these loans and the interest on them. For example, in 1834 the Edenfield and Little Bolton trust claimed they were unable to pay for any road repairs because toll receipts had proved insufficient even to pay the interest on the debt. The abolition of statute labour in 1835 did not help matters and the clerk of the Rochdale and Edenfield trust complained in 1840:

> The abolition of statute duty has caused the inhabitants to refuse to perform it, or to pay rates in lieu of it for the repair of this road, which has caused extreme litigation by indictments to compel them to repair, and a great expenditure of the trust money.

As the 19th century wore on, turnpike trusts had to seek fresh legislation to extend the terms of their original acts, but with a growing demand for the abolition of tolls and the financial difficulties of many trusts, continuations were allowed only on certain conditions and for limited periods. Gradually turnpike trusts lapsed – the Blackburn, Bury, Haslingden and Whalley Trust going in 1875, for instance – and the turnpike era came to an end in 1890 when the last trust was abolished.[14]

RAILWAYS

Despite improvements brought by the turnpike trusts, road transport remained slow. In the early 1840s, for instance, carriers were taking five hours on average to cart goods from Edenfield to Manchester. Local manufacturers, merchants and businessmen felt that a railway would speed up the shipment of raw materials and goods. They met together in Bury in September 1843 to consider a scheme to build a railway from Manchester to Rawtenstall. The minutes of the meeting explain their interest in the proposed railway:

> The most important matter in connection with this part of the undertaking seems to the Committee to be the opening it will give for the traffic of the active manufacturing district around Haslingden, Accrington, Blackburn, Newchurch, Rossendale, Bacup, etc., which do not even possess the facilities of a canal navigation to Manchester and must of necessity have a large and increasing traffic to that town.

One of the largest subscribers to the scheme was Thomas Aitken, the Chatterton and Irwell Vale cotton manufacturer. He put up £2,500 and became one of the original twelve directors of the company.[15]

In May of the following year, a second company, the Blackburn, Burnley, Accrington and Colne Extension Railway Company, was set up to build railways that would link these towns with the Rossendale line. The two concerns merged in 1845 to form the East Lancashire Railway Company. In the meantime, the work of construction had begun. The new railways had an enormous impact on the face of the local landscape as thousands of tons of earth were moved to carve out cuttings or raise embankments. Two wooden trestle viaducts at Alderbottom carried the lines over the Irwell (they were rebuilt in 1893), while the line to Accrington crossed the river

How the *Illustrated London News* saw the Alderbottom viaducts in September 1848. That in the foreground carried the newly built Stubbins to Accrington branch of the East Lancashire Railway over the Irwell, while its neighbour did the same for the Stubbins to Rawtenstall line.

again at Lumb over an impressive nine-arch viaduct. Stations with simple wooden buildings were set up at Stubbins and Ewood Bridge. They were later rebuilt in stone and included not only booking offices and waiting rooms, but also a station-master's house. Ewood Bridge (which changed its name to Ewood Bridge and Eden-field Station in 1891) also had a siding with goods warehouse, weighing machine and crane. In 1869 the well-to-do inhabitants of the district sent a request to the directors of the Lancashire and Yorkshire Railway Co. (which had taken over the East Lancashire Railway Co.) asking for a separate waiting room for first class travellers to be provided at Ewood Bridge because, 'At present time, passengers of any class are compelled to use the same waiting room.' They also asked for a tele-graph office to be set up and for 'the consideration of the directors to adherence to the time of arrival of trains mentioned in their time tables.'[16]

The construction of the lines was not without its problems. At Lumb, for instance, while the viaduct was being built several landslips occurred carrying immense masses of earth down towards the river. Problems of a different kind were caused by the influx of hundreds of navvies into the district. At the beginning of 1846 almost 700 men were working on the line between Bury and Rawtenstall. The presence of such a large number of men in the neighbourhood was said to have 'created evils (touching both the welfare of the labourers employed and the interests of society) the taint of which seems not unlikely to survive their original cause.' In May 1846 a quarrel about wages started among the railway workers in Ramsbottom and escalated into a riot involving nearly 2,000 men.[17]

The line to Rawtenstall opened in September 1846 when a train of thirty-three carriages painted sky blue and bearing the East Lancashire Railway Co.'s coat of arms steamed into the station. Bradshaw's *Railway Gazette* described the scene:

Arrived at Rawtenstall, the band struck up the national anthem, and the passengers alighted, after a remarkably pleasant and interesting trip. Almost the whole population of the district were assembled around the train on its arrival. At first the feeling was one of vacant admiration, which, however, soon quickened into enthusiasm, and at last vented itself in tremendous cheering.[18]

The company entertained about 500 guests to 'a splendid collation, champagne being in the greatest abundance' in the weaving shed of a nearby mill. By October, five trains each way passed through Ewood Bridge and Stubbins every day, with four on Sundays. Coaches from Blackburn, Haslingden, Accrington, Whalley and Clitheroe met trains at Ewood Bridge until the Stubbins to Accrington line opened in August 1848.[19]

The new railways were not welcomed by everyone: some old men in Edenfield thought that they sounded the death knell for the village and said that it would 'never do any good, now that the railway has come; it would take everything from here, and we might as well shut up.' In general, however, the new means of transport became immensely popular especially at holiday times when, through the agency of the cheap trip, hundreds of people from the locality could stir beyond their native

Ewood Bridge and Edenfield station in the early 1900s. The station buildings on the left included a stationmaster's house above the booking office and waiting rooms.

place with relative ease. Within a few years of the opening of the lines the officials of the Edenfield Wesleyan Methodist Sunday School decided that,

> In consequence of cheap Railway trips at the Whitsuntide Holidays we think it necessary to change the Whitsuntide festival to some other day say Good Friday or has [sic] the Committee at some future meeting may determine.

The day of the railway excursion had arrived. Trips were organised at holiday times – not only by the railway company, but also by local employers – to places like Belle Vue, Blackpool, Southport, Liverpool and, by the 1880s, Edinburgh, Glasgow and Ireland. Some of the outings were truly astonishing in size. For instance, in 1879 when Richard Walton, son of the Horncliffe quarry owner, got married, his father treated 700 of his workmen and their wives and sweethearts to a day out in Blackpool. A special train took the party to the resort where, after a sail on a steamer, the multitude made their way to Raikes Hall Gardens. At the head of the procession came the band of the Raikes Hall Guard, followed by over 200 women 'two deep of all ages and complexions, and in the most charming variety of attire.' After them came the band that had accompanied the trippers, with the quarry men bringing up the rear.[20]

Even larger numbers went on the trips organised by Turnbull and Stockdale's early in the 20th century: 800 on a day trip to Blackpool in July 1914 and 900 in July 1920. Workers at Stubbins Vale Mill had a similar outing in September 1932, when a mere 270 caught the special to Blackpool. After an enjoyable day the party arrived back in Ramsbottom at 11.15pm. These were the days when the railway company were prepared to lay on a 'little special' to take some of the trippers home to Helmshore. Workers at Turnbull and Stockdale's occasionally organised trips for themselves that lasted a couple of days, although this usually involved a gruelling schedule. Take the outing to Scotland in 1910, for example. A group of thirty set off from Stubbins on the 8.21pm train to Manchester one Friday night in June. They caught the 10.45pm train to Edinburgh where they arrived at 4.30am. Before breakfast they visited Calton Hill and later stopped at various places in and around the city, including the Forth Bridge. The 10.40am train took them to Glasgow for a quick tour before they caught another train to Balloch for dinner. This was followed by a three-hour cruise on Loch Lomond and supper at a nearby hotel. They left Balloch at 9pm and arrived back in Stubbins at 10.30am on the Sunday morning.[21]

Over the years there have been a number of accidents on the line between Stubbins and Ewood Bridge. One of the most serious took place on 4th August 1856 when temporary alterations had been made to the railway near Alderbottom before work began on laying a second set of rails. When the 7.50pm train from Ramsbottom to Bacup pulled by the 'Aurora' reached the spot, the engine left the rails and fell down the embankment. The carriages too were derailed and badly damaged. John Fielding, the driver, was killed on the spot and the fireman and a passenger fatally injured. Eight other passengers were also seriously injured. Other accidents were caused by people treating the railway line as a convenient short cut. One of the first of these took place in March 1847 when a young man called James Cawthorn and his father were walking on the line near Stubbins station when a train from Rawtenstall approached. The younger man tried to help his father out of the way, but in doing so was struck by the engine and died almost immediately. Another accident was narrowly avoided in July 1873 when Margaret Davenport was walking on the line at Alderbottom. A train came down the line from Bacup and the driver blew his whistle to alert her. She took no notice, even when the train pulled up only a few inches away. Indeed, it was not until the driver threw a piece of coal at her that she turned around and leapt out of the way because she thought the engine was still moving. She later recovered enough to be able to walk home to Lumb.[22]

Apart from people using the line as a short cut, there were others who treated the railway in an even more cavalier fashion. Thomas Parkinson, cotton manufacturer at Ewood Bridge, in collusion with Thomas Pilling, who worked for the East Lancashire Railway Co., used the line to shift the materials of an old building down to Bury in

LMS

Ramsbottom & District Holidays.

PERIOD EXCURSIONS.

FRIDAY, AUGUST 12th for any Period up to 17 days.
SATURDAY, AUGUST 13th, for any Period up to 16 days.
SUNDAY, AUGUST 14th
MONDAY, AUGUST 15th } for any Period up to 15 days.
TUESDAY, AUGUST 16th

TO BLACKPOOL 6/6
LYTHAM 6/6 ANSDELL 6/6 ST.ANNES 6/6

By any Train or by the following Special on Saturday—
Ewood Bridge .... dep. 9-34, Stubbins 9-40, Ramsbottom 9-43, and
Summerseat dep. 9-49 a.m.

TO SOUTHPORT 6/3

By any Train or by the following Specials :—
Saturday—Ewood Bridge dep. 7-59, Stubbins 8-4, Ramsbottom 8-8, Summer-
seat 8-11 a.m.
Join through train at Bury.
Monday — Ewood Bridge dep. 8-8, Stubbins 8-13, Ramsbottom 8-19, Summer-
seat 8-23 a.m.   (Through Train).

TO FLEETWOOD 7/-
POULTON 6/6 THORNTON 6/6

By any Train each day.

To Morcambe 8/6 Lancaster 7/9 Arnside 10/-
Carnforth 9/- Grange-o-Sands 10/6 Kents Bank 10/6
and Silverdale 9/6

By any Train having a Through Connection
(With certain exceptions).

To Prestatyn 12/6 Rhyl 13/- Abergele 14/- Colwyn
Bay 15/- Llandudno Junction 15/6 Deganwy 15/9 and
Llandudno 16/-

any Train (with certain exceptions).

Off to the seaside: the LMS offering trips to the coast during the annual wakes week holiday
in 1932.

Contrasts on the Stubbins-Rawtenstall line. The first diesel locomotive arriving at Ewood Bridge station in 1956 and the Flying Scotsman at Irwell Vale halt in 1993.

December 1847. They always ensured that the wagons ran at night and when morning came shunted them into a siding at Ewood Bridge. On one occasion, however, the points failed to close properly so that when the 8 o'clock train to Rawtenstall arrived at Ewood Bridge it steamed into the siding and hit the wagons. Parkinson and Pilling were sent for trial at the Salford Quarter Sessions in January 1848, but we do not know the final outcome of the case.[23]

For a little over one hundred years, steam trains worked the lines through Stubbins and Ewood Bridge, but diesel multiple units were introduced for passenger services to Rawtenstall in 1956 and to Accrington in 1961. This step towards modernisation came too late, however, and under the recommendations of the Beeching Report the Stubbins to Accrington line closed at the end of 1966. Passenger services on the line to Rawtenstall continued until the summer of 1973 and coal trains used the line for a few more years after that. When these were withdrawn in December 1980, the line effectively closed. This was not the end of the story, however. The track from Bury was not dismantled and the East Lancashire Railway Preservation Society stepped in to save it as a steam railway. It reopened as far as Ramsbottom in 1987 and to Rawtenstall in 1991, since when the members of the society have run regular weekend services along the line.[24]

THE MOTOR AGE

The means of transport that would ultimately oust the railways made its first appearance in Edenfield in 1902. Dr. Henry Deans and his brother, William, who lived in Ramsbottom, brought the first car into the village in March of that year. The *Ramsbottom Observer* said, 'Their new vehicle is a real beauty, and it has been the object of much curiosity and interest as it has been driven about the district.' Other early motorists included A.T. Porritt who 'motored' to Scarborough in the summer of 1907 and was involved in one of the first car accidents in the area when he ran down a child at Bent Gate.[25]

In the meantime, locals had been able to get further glimpses of cars in August 1904 when General Booth drove through the district. Spectators watched as half a dozen cars sped along Whalley Road and Market Street, ploughing up the muddy surface as they did so.

> Not at Peel Brow or Edenfield did the motors give evidence of having slackened their speed, and their annihilation of the distance right up to Rawtenstall left the villagers profound in speculation and wonderment.

said the *Ramsbottom Observer*. By 1908 the paper could remark that, 'The motor car is steadily taking the place of horseflesh all over the country, and in our own district the elimination of the horse from the service of the well-to-do people is becoming marked.'[26]

Private cars were soon joined by other motor vehicles. Nuttalls, the Edenfield carriers, had invested in a petrol driven lorry by the outbreak of the First World War and at the same time William Whittaker, newsagent and stationer, of 11, Market Street, organised the first tour by motor coach from the area. The coach, a twenty-eight-seater with solid rubber tyres, carried a party of holidaymakers on an eight-day tour of Scotland in July 1914. The itinerary included stops at Edinburgh, Oban, Loch Lomond, Dumbarton and Glasgow. Breakfast and a table d'hote dinner were provided every day and a cold lunch served on the Sunday, all for a total of £4 17s 6d. Following the war, coaches and charabancs replaced wagonettes as the mode of transport for church and works outings.[27]

The gradual increase in motor traffic brought several changes to the villages. Cars needed somewhere to be kept and in 1911 Dr. Deans' home, 'Newlands', was the first in the area to acquire a 'motor car house'. More garages were added on to houses or built wherever there was some spare land throughout the inter-war years. By the late 1920s, there was enough motor traffic passing along the roads to make it worthwhile for people to make a living supplying petrol and carrying out vehicle repairs. Frederick Birch was the first to set up petrol pumps at Stubbins in 1927. His enterprise was short-lived, but a couple of years later the Edenfield Size Manufacturing Co. was granted a licence to store 500 gallons of petrol in an underground tank at the old brewery. By 1932 the company was trading as Edenfield Motor Services with a licence to store 5,000 gallons. Whittaker Spencer started selling petrol at his Whalley Road Service Station, next door to Hope Mill, in 1930 and in 1933 the Central Garage opened in old buildings next to the Horse and Jockey with two petrol pumps on Market Street.[28]

Whalley Road Service Station in the 1930s.

Increased traffic brought changes to the roads themselves. Ramsbottom Urban District Council was responsible for the upkeep of the main roads in its district and by 1906 found that cars and lorries were causing problems. Councillors drafted a memorial to send to the government drawing its attention to 'the terrible nuisance and damage' caused by motor vehicles. They asked that the cost of repairing the roads should be paid for out of an additional tax on vehicles rather than out of local rates and added that 'serious danger accrues to persons using the highways from the Motor Vehicles raising such great clouds of dust as render the sight of other vehicles almost impossible to give time to get out of the way.' A second petition in 1908 called the government's attention to the 'grave and increasing evils caused by the road Motor Traffic.' Similarly, when Haslingden Borough Council applied for a loan to repair the road from Ewood Bridge to Bent Gate in 1912, the Town Clerk said that 'the traffic of heavy motors had increased so much on that road that the expense of maintenance was continuously increasing.' Ramsbottom Urban District Council borrowed money in 1902 and 1906 to finance its road repairs and by the end of 1907 considerable lengths of the highway through Edenfield and in Bolton Road North had been macadamised or paved with setts. The inter-war years brought further changes to the roads, including the laying of a pedestrian crossing in Market Place in 1935. In the following year plans for two others at the day school and Stubbins school were proposed, but these were never carried out. To ease the flow of traffic at the junction of Market Place, Rochdale Road and Bury Road an island was built in 1935 and replaced by a mini roundabout in 1993. The Blackburn Road/Burnley Road junction remained unaltered until 1956 when it too got a traffic island, which was replaced by traffic lights in 1966.[29]

PUBLIC TRANSPORT – TRACKLESS TRAMS AND BUSES

While the well-to-do were taking their first drives in motor-cars, moves were being made by Ramsbottom Urban District Council to provide transport for the masses. The government granted the council powers to operate a tram service in 1903, but largely because of the cost of laying tracks and providing electricity the scheme was put off from year to year. Eventually, after procrastinating for ten years, the council decided to go ahead with a scheme for 'trackless trams' (trolley buses). The service began in August 1913 with the arrival of two trams looking resplendent in a vermilion and cream livery picked out in gold. Their seats were upholstered in rattan cane 'well sprung, so as to minimise any possible vibration which may be occasioned as the result of unevenness of road surface', for, as the *Ramsbottom Observer* said, the roads over which the trams were to run could not 'in any sense be compared to a billiard table.' Following a Board of Trade inspection, No.1 tram went into service carrying passengers to Holcombe Brook and back. 'There were crowds of people to see it away, and all along the route people rushed to their doors and gateways to witness the novel spectacle.'[30]

Passengers queuing up to ride on Ramsbottom Urban District Council's tram no.2 during the first week of its service in August 1913. The photograph was taken on Market Street, Edenfield, outside Chapel House Farm.

There were stages at approximately every quarter of a mile along the route, those between Stubbins and Edenfield being Stubbins station, Chatterton Lane, Chatterton Old Lane, Nimble Nook, Elizabeth Street and Edenfield church. Request stops also operated at Industrial Street, Rose Bank, Thorn Bank, Market Place and the Post Office. Passengers paid 1d for any quarter mile stage and ½d for every two stages over the mile.[31]

To begin with, the new trams were very popular. Officially they had twenty-eight seats, but one old driver later recalled, 'Twenty-eight! We sometimes carried nearer fifty-eight!' One Saturday in June 1914 over 4,000 passengers were carried and by 1917 passenger numbers averaged 10,000 a week. One man was even inspired to write a poem in praise of the trams:

OUR CARS

If you are downhearted,
And deep thoughts have started
To traverse and trouble your mind;
Then just listen to me
I've a good recipe,
And the cheapest one of its kind.

Forsake you the fireside,
And go out for a ride
Upon the merry, merry car.
You will not forget it,
You will not regret it.
When once more on your hearth you are.

You're sure to wax jolly,
You'll find out 'tis folly
To walk and then say you feel done;
For the car is the thing
That unto you will bring
What you long for – jolly good fun.

At Edenfield get on,
What tho' you are treat on,
You'll forget e'en your lightest care;
If you sit down behind,
Oh! You will have to mind,
Or else you will find yourself, where?

Why! Going down Rose Bank
With a clatter and clank,
If you do not hold tight you will,
I'll bet you a "fiver",
Be nearer the driver
Than you were when you set down the hill.

The seats they are splendid,
I'm sure they're intended
To constantly make you rebound;
I know that you'll bless them,
And that you confess them
Better than the "merry-go-round."

The "figure eight's" no good,
The "water chute", who would
Ever again think of that, pray;
Allow me, in one sense,
The "houses of nonsense,"
Do travel our roads every day.

They quake and they quiver,
They shake and they shiver,
As o'er the black river they go.
When you look on that river
You feel that your liver
Is creeping inside you as slow.

But hold fast in your nook
Till you reach Holcombe Brook,
You cannot but say "You like it."
It is better by far
Than a grand motor car,
Better by far than to bike it.

Oh, no! Do not get out!
The car will turn about
And bring you right home for threepence.
It beats steeple chasing,
It's grand, it's embracing;
I'm sure you will say, "It's immense."[32]

Two new trams were added to the fleet in 1915. They were built to run more smoothly than the original four, but still had solid rubber tyres that did little to ease the journey over the stone setts. From the wear and tear caused by the continual jolting, the trams were often in need of repair and by 1917 only two were running. Following the First World War, attempts were made to improve the tram service by buying a seventh tram in 1922 and in 1925 by fixing indicators along the route to show whether or not a particular tram had gone. However, by this date the council were relying more and more on motorbuses as a means of public transport. The trams were gradually phased out and in June 1928 the *Ramsbottom Observer* commented:

> One will have observed during the past few weeks that very little is seen nowadays of the trackless trolley cars which have been a feature of Ramsbottom's public life for the past fifteen or sixteen years. We are given to understand that the two or three cars of that type possessed by the District Council are only put into service at rush periods ... Motor 'buses, the modern mode of travel, now cope with the traffic demands and there is a likelihood that ere long the trackless cars will be a thing of the past in Ramsbottom.

In fact, the trams were not withdrawn completely until the end of March 1931.[33]

BUSES

Ramsbottom Urban District Council's first bus – a twenty-six-seater single-decker Thorneycroft – began running between Rawtenstall railway station and the Bury tram terminus at Walmersley in August 1923. The new service was inaugurated with none of the ceremony that had attended the introduction of the trams ten years earlier, but immediately proved popular. The bus ran at ninety-minute intervals throughout the day and in its first fifteen days of operation carried over 11,000 passengers. Encouraged by this success, the council immediately ordered a second bus that arrived in January 1924 and allowed them to run a forty-five minute service.[34]

In the meantime, Ribble Motor Services had applied to the council for a licence to ply for hire within the Urban District. This had been refused, which meant that

The first bus to run through Edenfield pictured outside the Duckworth Arms in 1923.

when Ribble started a service from Blackburn to Rochdale through Edenfield passengers could get on in the village only if they had bought a return ticket outside the Ramsbottom area. Further problems were caused when Ribble started to run a service from Burnley to Bolton through Edenfield, Shuttleworth and Ramsbottom at the end of 1925. The dispute was solved in the following year when it was agreed that the council would not operate its own buses between Ramsbottom and Bolton and that Ribble would not cover the Ramsbottom-Bury route. On 18th November 1926 a new half-hourly bus service from Edenfield to Bury via Ramsbottom was started by the council. A year later this service, and the one from Rawtenstall to Bury, began to be run jointly by Ramsbottom, Bury and Rawtenstall councils. This allowed cheap return tickets to be issued, the fare between Bury and Ramsbottom, for instance, being 1s 2d return.[35]

By the late 1920s, the local bus services were well established and well used, although travellers sometimes had cause for complaint. One correspondent to the *Ramsbottom Observer* in September 1928 said he was

> ... amazed and ... disgusted at the manner in which some of our school children misbehave themselves in the 'buses. On Monday evening about a dozen boys entered a Rawtenstall bound bus at Edenfield, and the noise they made by singing ditties and shouting, in spite of reprimands from the 'bus conductor, was, to say the least, disgraceful. This is only one

One of Ramsbottom Urban District Council's post-war fleet of buses at Edenfield in July 1949. The bus was bought in 1947 and ran until 1961. Note the supports that formerly carried overhead cables for the trackless trams.

of several instance I have come across where local children, especially those returning from school, seem to make our 'buses a place for revelry by the way they skip about.

It was not until the beginning of the following year that timetables were displayed along the route. 'Now we have got time tables let us have an efficient service and one run to time, if possible', was the *Ramsbottom Observer*'s comment.[36]

After the Second World War, Ramsbottom Urban District Council continued to run buses and, had some of the post-war development plans come to fruition, Edenfield would have become the centre of the council's transport department. One proposal was to build a new bus station on the triangle of land formed by Rochdale Road, Bury Road and a new road to link the two. The plan came to nothing and the nearest the village got to acquiring a bus station were the bus bays and shelters built in Bury Road in 1951 and 1952. By 1969 Ramsbottom was the only urban district council in the country with its own bus service that operated at a profit. In the autumn of that year it was swallowed up by the huge SELNEC transport company and many people mourned its passing.[37]

THE EDENFIELD BY-PASS

One of the post-war schemes that eventually became a reality was a road to reduce the amount of traffic passing through Edenfield. Locals first heard of the new road

Building the Rawtenstall-Edenfield by-pass in 1968. The photograph shows the construction of the Stubbins roundabout.

in a lecture given by the council's surveyor in January 1945, but it was not until 1957 that the Ministry of Transport provisionally selected the scheme for forward planning. Two twenty-four foot carriageways were to be built on the hillside to the east of Market Street stretching for about a mile, although early in the following year the route was changed to the west side of the village. In the next few years plans were adopted to up-grade the road to motorway status, but this idea was dropped in 1963, saving about £15,000. Work began on 1st June 1967 and villagers saw changes to the landscape that had not been witnessed since the railways had been built 120 years earlier. The by-pass took two years, one month and nine days to build, cost £3¼ million, and was opened on 9th July 1969.[38]

NOTES

[1] 29 Geo. III, c. 107 (1789) An Act for amending, widening ... the Road from a House in Bury ... to Haslingden and Blackburn

[2] House of Commoms Journal, (1797), pp. 561, 578

[3] G.H. Tupling, 'The turnpike trusts of Lancashire', *Memoirs and proceedings of the Manchester Literary and Philosophical Society*, 94 (1952-3), 7; Bury, Haslingden, Blackburn and Whalley turnpike trust minutes 7th January 1790 (LRO: TTA/1); P. Stephens, *Notes on Edenfield and Ewood Bridge*, [manuscript] (1908) (Rawtenstall library: RC 942 EDE)

[4] 37 Geo.III, c. 174 (1797) An Act for amending, widening, altering and keeping in Repair, the Road from or from near Edenfield Chapel ... to the township of Little Bolton ...; 29 & 30 Vic., c. lxxix (1866) Rochdale and Edenfield Road Act

[5] Blackburn Mail 20th June 1827

[6] E. Holme, *An account and measurement of the public bridges within the hundred of Salford*, (1782); Bridgemaster's reports, July 1792, October 1792, July 1793 (LRO: QSP/2310/2, 2314/37, 2326/23); Plans and sections of the bridges belonging to the hundred of Salford, c. 1803 – 1805 (LRO: QAR/6/6)

[7] G.H. Tupling, *op. cit.*, p.8; BT 18th December 1858

[8] 1851 census Tottington Higher End (PRO: HO 107/2249); RFP 17th October 1953; Information from the Whittaker family business records courtesy of Mrs. E. Whittaker via Chris Aspin

[9] BT 4th July 1885, 13th April 1872; Burnley and Edenfield turnpike trust minutes, 31st August 1850 (Burnley library: N14)

[10] BT 4th July 1885; 1881 census Tottington Higher End (PRO: RG 11/4136); BRN 28th April 1877, 6th October 1877

[11] RO 7th July 1934

[12] RO 4th April 1913, 21st August 1914

[13] BT 15th January 1859, 16th November 1872, 7th October 1876, 13th October 1880, 1st October 1887; Dissolved companies files (PRO: BT 31/1377)

[14] PP, *Appendix to the report of the commissioners appointed to inquire into the state of the roads in England and Wales*, 1840 [280] XXVII; S.W. Partington, *The toll bars and turnpike roads of Bury and Rossendale*, (1921), p. 4; G.H. Tupling, *op. cit.*, p.22

[15] H. Hanson, 'The railway comes to Bury – communication developments in south-east Lancashire.' B.A. dissertation, University of Manchester (1966), appendix II; C. P. Meredith, 'Transport developments in east Lancashire 1780 - 1860.' M.A. thesis, University of Manchester (1978), pp. 116, 119

[16] Illustrated London News 30th September 1848; Haslingden Guardian 12th August 1893; Mill valuations 1880-1882 (LRO: PUB/5/2); BT 3rd January 1885; RO 26th June 1891; Haslingden Chronicle and Ramsbottom Times 3rd July 1869

[17] Manchester Guardian 23rd August 1848, 20th May 1846; H. Hanson, *op. cit.*, pp. 35-6

[18] Bradshaw's Railway Gazette 3rd October 1846

[19] C. Aspin, *Lancashire, the first industrial society*, (1969), p. 26; Manchester Guardian 23rd August 1848, 3rd October 1846

²⁰ RFP 20th May 1905; Edenfield Wesleyan Methodist Sunday School committee minute book, 25th May 1849 (BAS: CRM/T1267); BT 6th June 1885, 28th June 1879

²¹ RO 24th July 1914, 16th July 1920, 30th September 1932, 24th June 1910

²² PP, *Report ... upon the accidents which have occurred on railways during the year 1856*, 1857 Session 2 [2287] XXXVII; Blackburn Standard 6th August 1856; Manchester Guardian 17th March 1847; BT 26th July 1873

²³ Manchester Guardian 5th January 1848

²⁴ M. Bairstow, *The East Lancashire Railway*, (1993), p.32

²⁵ RO 7th March 1902, 26th July 1907, 23rd August 1907

²⁶ RO 26th August 1904, 25th September 1908

²⁷ RO 7th August 1914, 29th August 1949

²⁸ RO 10th February 1911, 29th July 1932, 10th February 1933; RUDC register of petroleum licences 1926-1969 (BAS: ARM/T960)

²⁹ RUDC minutes 10th May 1906, 6th August 1908 (BAS: ARM/T206); Haslingden Guardian 7th June 1912; BT 14th December 1907; RO 13th March 1936, 16th March 1956; RFP 19th November 1965, 17th September 1993; RUDC pedestrian crossings file 1934-1970 (BAS: ARM/T1177)

³⁰ B. Palmer, 'Ramsbottom trolley buses', *Ramsbottom Heritage Society News Magazine*, (Winter/Spring 1992) 12-16; RO 15th August 1913

³¹ RO 13th June 1913

³² RO 18th July 1952, 11th December 1914; B. Palmer, *op. cit.*

³³ RO 28th May 1915, 21st August 1925, 25th June 1928, 10th April 1931; B. Palmer, *op. cit.*

³⁴ RO 10th August 1923, 24th August 1924, 1st January 1924

³⁵ RUDC minutes of traction committee 29th November 1923, 21st December 1925 (BAS: ARM/T2026); RO 15th August 1924, 11th December 1925, 18th November 1927; RUDC Transport Department – 56 years of municipal passenger transport 1913 - 1969 (BAS: Ramsbottom Heritage Society collection. MAINARCH 0100); RUDC Memoranda 1938 (BAS: Ramsbottom Heritage Society collection. MAINARCH 0521)

³⁶ RO 7th September 1928, 18th January 1929

³⁷ RO 2nd February 1945, 30th August 1946, 3rd August 1951, 21st November 1952; Daily Express 19th September 1969

³⁸ RO 2nd February 1945, 22nd November 1957, 21st February 1958, 31st July 1959, 1st February 1963; RFP 12th July 1969

EDUCATION
DAY SCHOOLS

EDENFIELD CHURCH OF ENGLAND SCHOOL

EDENFIELD SCHOOL STARTED LIFE in the early years of the 18th century in a building in a corner of the churchyard, facing the main road. A second wing fronting Church Lane was added in about 1825 and these two buildings did service until the present school opened on 8th May 1861. One afternoon shortly before the new school was completed, the children lined up on the footpath outside the old school and watched breathlessly as the new spire was hauled into position. Once it was in place, they gave three rousing cheers, although this may have been as much for the fortnight's holiday they had been given as for the safe fixing of the school spire. This wood and lead steeple survived until 1909 when it was rebuilt in stone. There have been few other major changes to the school, apart from the addition of classrooms in 1890 and the late 1970s.[1]

Edenfield School in April 1961. The children line up to have their photograph taken as the building celebrates its centenary.

In 1761 Edenfield school received its first endowment when a small field called The Green at the bottom of Gin Croft Lane was placed into the hands of trustees. The rents and profits from the land were to be paid to the village schoolmaster for instructing a specified number of poor children. The first tenant of the land was a man called John Brooks who built a small cottage on it. An investigation into endowed charities in Lancashire in 1828 reported that,

> a person of the name of Sarah Nuttall lived with John Brooks as his wife, and had children by him, and many years having elapsed since his death, she claimed this property as part of the waste, on which she stated she had built a house.

One villager later recalled Sarah as 'a quaint sort of body' who used her cottage as a toffee shop to which young men and their sweethearts flocked on a Sunday evening.[2]

Seeing that Sarah was an old woman in 1828, the trustees did not evict her, but after her death, her son Thomas handed back the property. As we have seen the land was subsequently built on, but the ground rents continued to be collected by the trustees and a payment made to the schoolmaster. After the new school was built, the money went towards paying the 'school pence' of poor children chosen by the trustees. Once school fees were abolished in the early 1890s, plans were made to use the trust's funds to promote night classes in Edenfield, but the scheme foundered. Instead in 1899 it was decided to use the income to provide exhibitions for higher education for children from the township of Tottington Higher End. Changes brought by the 1944 Education Act again altered the charity's remit and its activities were temporarily suspended. However, the committee met again in 1954 when they decided to use some of their income towards the payment of travelling expenses of a scholar attending a secondary school at some distance from the village.[3]

Like many parish schools Edenfield became associated with the National Society for the Education of the Poor in the Principles of the Established Church, which was formed in 1811. For most of the 19th century and the early years of the 20th century, the school received grants from the society and was generally known as Edenfield National School. It continues to have strong Anglican links but has seen a number of changes, particularly in the last fifty years or so. From 1947, under the terms of the 1944 Education Act, it no longer took children of all ages, only those aged from five to eleven years. In the following year, a new development plan, which was designed to fit the proposals of the act, suggested that Edenfield school should be closed and its children sent to a new school at Stubbins. The plan provoked a strong reaction from the villagers who petitioned the Minister of Education. Lancashire County Council, however, reaffirmed their decision to close the school and for a time it seemed all was lost. Following a few years of uncertainty the proposal was dropped and in 1951 the school was granted 'aided' status, partially relieving its managers of the cost of its upkeep. Greater authority was given to the County Council in 1975 when Edenfield became a 'controlled' school.[4]

More than sixty years separate these two groups of children at Edenfield School. The older photograph dates from about 1905. William Greenwood, headmaster, taught in the village between 1896 and 1930. The teachers in the other photograph (taken in 1971) are Margaret Taylor (*left*) and Pat Wolstenholme.

The second National School in the area was at Ewood Bridge where it also doubled as St. Peter's Mission Church. Unlike Edenfield, however, it was linked with the National Society from its very beginning. In 1836 the Rev. William Gray of Haslingden, the Rev. William Holt of Edenfield and John Parkinson, senior, of Ewood Bridge first applied for a grant towards the establishment of a school. They stated that the school was intended for seventy boys and seventy girls who would be taught in one room. The parents of each child were to be asked to make a small weekly payment of 1½d or 2d per week. In a letter accompanying the application, the Rev. William Gray made very clear why he thought it of the greatest importance that a Church of England school should be built in the village:

> The dissenters, who now occupy a temporary room in what may be called the Ewood Bridge district, as a Sunday school, are doing all they can to raise the means of erecting a building to be permanently occupied in the same way. This I am anxious to prevent; and I have hitherto succeeded in nullifying all their applications to the Landowners for a site.[5]

The school was built in 1839 on land given by John Parkinson and opened on 15th March 1840. The *Blackburn Standard* described it as a 'neat and commodious building, erected at a cost of about £200' and went on to say that the school 'newly lighted up with gas from the neighbouring works of Mr. Parkinson, exhibited in the evening a most beautiful appearance.'[6]

In 1883, when there were about ninety scholars, two new classrooms were added on a piece of land on the north side of the building. Since it was rather hilly, the villagers had to set about to remove tons of earth to form a level space for the classrooms and a playground (previously children had played in the road). The extension opened at Easter 1885 and created a building of three rooms. One was used as the church and the other two as a main schoolroom and an infant schoolroom. There was a gallery in the main room, which meant that it could hold about 200 people.[7]

Disaster struck the little school in the spring of 1902. On Monday 17th March the village held a meeting to plan celebrations for the coronation of Edward VII in the summer. At the end of the evening Thomas Walker, the headmaster, turned off the gas and left everything apparently safe. However, in the early hours of the following morning, the school was seen to be on fire and the alarm was raised. Despite the best efforts of the villagers and Haslingden Fire Brigade the building was completely gutted and daylight revealed a smoking roofless ruin. Nothing of its contents was saved except a few old registers and, ironically, some bundles of firewood.[8]

A couple of days after the fire the villagers held a meeting in the Reading Room in Bridge Street and decided that, despite the fact that the school had not been insured, they would rebuild it. Plans were drawn up and a fund started, receiving loans and donations from the Diocesan Church Building Society, the National Society and the mill owners Anderton and Halstead Ltd. A three-day bazaar held in

Ewood Bridge National School after the 1902 fire.

Haslingden in October 1903 also raised nearly £400. By this date the school had been completed and lessons began there on 27th April. In the interim the infants had been taught in the Board Room of the Outfall Sewage Board at Ewood Hall and the older scholars in the Reading Room. The 1902 fire was in some ways a blessing in disguise since it allowed the school to be remodelled to meet the requirements of the new Education Act.[9]

The 1902 Act brought another change to the school since it was placed under the care of the Education Committee of Haslingden Borough Council, although the managers were still responsible for the building. It continued to take all children up to the age of fourteen until 1929 when those over the age of eleven transferred to schools in Haslingden, Rawtenstall and Edenfield. Numbers were further reduced in 1947 with the transfer of the juniors to Haslingden C. E. school. Perhaps partly because of its small size, even before these changes, Ewood Bridge seems always to have been a school with a happy atmosphere, something that visitors commented on. The 1922 Diocesan report, for instance, said: ' This school is like a large family, the members of which have an affectionate trust in one another and are bound together by mutual interests and aims. Hence there is an excellent tone in the school.' No doubt some of the long-serving staff helped to create this family atmosphere. They included Thomas Walker, headmaster from 1898 to 1930, and Mary Alice Butterworth who taught there from 1910 until 1950, becoming head in 1944.[10]

Pupils at Ewood Bridge School with their teacher Miss Butterworth in July 1950.

The school was granted aided status in 1951, but it became increasingly clear that it did not have a long-term future. In the following year there were fourteen children attending, but only four of them were of compulsory school age. The school eventually closed in January 1959.[11]

STUBBINS CONGREGATIONAL DAY SCHOOL

The third of the local schools with strong church ties was Stubbins Congregational Day School. It opened in February 1868 and shared the Sunday school building, using one large room and a classroom with a gallery at one end. There was just one teacher, James Fraser, to begin with and the first school inspectors' report found that 'the children were many of them very raw, having had no previous schooling.' Ten years later the school had 'improved considerably in every respect and bears testimony to the industry and care of the Master.' Some sixty years later another school inspector thought that:

> The happy and active atmosphere which pervades this school is largely due to the very friendly relations existing between the teachers and the children. The curriculum provides generously for a number of stimulating and attractive activities into which the children enter with pleasing industry and application...The Head Teacher and his staff deserve

commendation on the attainments of the school and particularly for the fostering of such a healthy corporate spirit.[12]

In 1883, Stubbins was transferred to the newly formed Tottington Higher End School Board and continued under their care until they were superseded by the Lancashire Education Committee under the 1902 Act. A proposal to rebuild the school in 1914 came to nothing, but almost became necessary in the following year when a fire broke out, destroying most of one wing of the building. It is perhaps surprising that the damage was not greater since the Ramsbottom Fire Brigade were out on a practice run when the call was put through to the Fire Station. When they eventually arrived at the fire and connected their hose to the water main from Scout Moor they found that it had been turned off for the night. Instead water had to be pumped from Rose Bank and Edenwood mill lodges.[13]

Following repairs to the building it continued to house the school for more than fifty years. After the Second World War plans were put forward for a completely new school on an adjoining site. Work began in 1967 when two infant classrooms were erected. A further three classrooms, an assembly hall, kitchen and staff room were completed in 1970 and the old school building closed in the summer of that year. Stubbins County Primary School has flourished in the new building ever since.[14]

Pupils at Stubbins School in 1930 with their headmaster, Mr. Renwick, and teacher, Mrs. Booth.

The reception class at Stubbins County Primary School with teacher Mrs. Dewar in March 1996.

TURN BOARD SCHOOL

The school in which children from Turn were taught for nearly ninety years owed its existence to one of the provisions of the 1870 Education Act. England was divided into districts managed by School Boards who had the authority to establish elementary schools in areas where school provision was insufficient. The Walmersley and Shuttleworth School Board decided that a school was needed in Turn village. The building, which could hold 150 children, was designed by a Bury firm of architects and built by local man, James Holt of Shuttleworth. It opened in August 1880 with 100 pupils. One of the first inspectors to visit the new school 'admired the building very much and thought it was one of the nicest he had seen in this part of the district.'[15]

Turn school began steadily with one headmaster, John H. Gornall, and a mistress, Susan Butterworth. The first HMI report in May 1881 said: 'The Children over seven have done as well as could have been expected and those under seven will not improbably know something next year.' Succeeding reports, however, found little to praise and condemned many of the lessons as merely moderate or adequate. The blame was laid squarely with the teachers. The 1887 report said that the infants 'are

Turn Board School in the early 1900s.

as backward as they can well be: the late Mistress can have paid them but little attention.' while in 1889 the inspector considered the staff 'though sufficient for the annual average would be weak anywhere.'[16]

Perhaps because of the continued criticism by school inspectors, the headmaster at Turn felt compelled to write to members of the School Board in April 1891 to offer some explanation. His letter is worth quoting at length for the picture it paints of life in the village:

Since November last, the weather here has been of the most severe wintry type. The consequence is that the attendance has been very irregular, and the routine of the school has been interfered with in a most exceptional manner. In addition there has been a great amount of sickness during the past few weeks. – Scarlet fever, sore faces and heads, chicken pox, rheumatic, and other complaints, all preventing that progress which we should have been making under other circumstances. Under the new code great importance is attached to "general intelligence." Turn children, of course, see very little beyond their own little world. As instance of this I give the following: – Seven children only have ever seen the sea, and only one has seen a regiment of soldiers. Many other similar instances could be quoted. Such children naturally are very ignorant to a highly-cultured man like an inspector of schools. They have also very few reading facilities. I know of many houses where there are no books whatever, and where not even a weekly paper is taken in, and in many instances the parents can neither read nor write. The inspector goes one day to a school where the parents are fairly educated – tradesmen, mechanics, &c. In their homes are books, newspapers, magazines, &c; the parents are able to answer the children's inquiries. The next day he comes to us, where scarcely one house in ten is provided with any amount of reading matter. The parents are ill-informed, and the children's vocabulary is not a tithe of the vocabulary of the children in the former school, and the consequence is we seem woefully behind. All are examined and judged alike, and we have to suffer on account of circumstances and conditions over which we have no control whatever.[17]

The class of 1951 at Turn School.

A few years later it became clear that the misgivings of the inspectors were justified. In the spring of 1894 the School Board learnt that Mr. Gornall had been sending children to the Plane Tree Inn for beer for him to drink during school hours and in the following year he was asked to resign over irregularities about the school penny bank, which had been set up in 1891. Under the new headmaster, Alfred Briggs, the school quickly improved and won praise from the inspectors.[18]

Like Stubbins, Turn passed under the jurisdiction of Lancashire County Council in 1903. It continued to provide an educational home for the village children until July 1968 when its forty pupils were transferred to the new school at Stubbins and the building was abandoned. It was demolished in 1977.[19]

PRIVATE SCHOOLS

In the 19th century Edenfield was home to a number of small private schools. The earliest of these was kept by the Rev. John Johnson, the village curate, who supplemented his income by teaching 'a few Parlour Boarders' along with his own children at Hawthorn House. His fees for 'Education in general' were a guinea a quarter in 1813, with 'use of the Globes and French' 10s 6d per quarter extra. More than fifty years later Hawthorn House became the College School under the headship of Joseph Peers. A native of Bury, Mr. Peers moved to Ramsbottom as a young man to work in a mill. He won a scholarship, which enabled him to teach, and he set up his first school in London. By 1868 he had moved to Edenfield and established his school at Hawthorn House. His advertisements promised, 'Education thorough, situation healthy and delightful, numbers of pupils limited, charges moderate.' The school had moved again by 1871, this time to Bass Lane.[20]

A third private school that lasted a good deal longer than either of the two that had made their home in Hawthorn House was kept by members of the Harrison family who lived on Bury Road. It began in the 1830s and was open for more than thirty years. Thomas Harrison, its founder, took a few boarders into his house, but the school itself was taught in the room at the top of the stairs between 11 and 13, Market Street. Later it transferred to an empty room at Dearden Clough Mill. Thomas Harrison's daughters, Elizabeth, Eliza and Sarah also taught with him and after his death his sons, Harry and Joseph, took over. Joseph was a keen gardener with a passion for rhubarb and was generally known as 'Rhubarb Joe'. His crop is said to have thrived on the contents of the village cesspits. The Harrison family school was not the only one to be taught in a mill: in 1863 William Pickles was employed by Sarah Rostron partly to teach the half-time children in her employ in a room in Bridge Mills. Such a system was easily abused and in December 1863 Pickles was fined £5 and costs for stating that Jane Walsh had been in the school from nine o'clock until noon on 13th October when he in fact did not open the school until ten that day. A similar school opened at Stubbins printworks in 1869.[21]

There were two more private schools in the village in the second half of the 19th century. One of these, a 'select ladies' school' for both boarders and day pupils was established by G.H. Walle at Chatterton Hey in 1887. Its success was short-lived and it seems to have closed in the following year. More long lasting was a similar establishment run by Miss Jane Wilson (1828–1905), cousin of Edenfield's first vicar. She began her teaching career at the village school, but in the 1870s started her own school in a modest way in a house in Holly Mount (1-5, Blackburn Road). By 1881 she had moved into Acres House. The larger premises allowed her to take more pupils and to employ visiting masters as well as resident mistresses (who had been trained by the College of Preceptors. The same body also set the exams for the school). Although Acres House was advertised as a ladies' boarding school, boys were admitted as well as girls. In 1881, for instance, the boarders included Emil and Reginald, sons of Monsieur Emil Quack, a Liverpool wine merchant and shipper. In addition, one of the day pupils who attended between 1881 and 1885 was Austin Townsend Porritt. The school closed in 1890 when Miss Wilson moved to Accrington. The gap left by its closure may have been filled by the Misses Butterworth who placed an advertisement in the *Ramsbottom Observer* for their ladies' school and preparatory school for boys at Lodge View, Ramsbottom and Market Place, Edenfield in September 1891.[22]

SECONDARY AND ADULT EDUCATION

Edenfield has never had a secondary school, but it might have had if post-war plans had been carried out. In 1948, the Rossendale Divisional Education Executive approved the acquisition of some thirty-eight acres of land to the west of Market Street. This was to be the site of a Secondary Technical School, a County College and a Secondary Modern School. The plan had been considerably scaled down by 1952 when only the secondary school remained a possibility. This proposal for a new three-form entry secondary school for the Ramsbottom area seemed to have been given the green light in 1959, but the Rawtenstall-Edenfield by-pass would have cut through the site. An alternative location on the sloping land on the eastern side of Market Street was suggested, but the scheme was finally abandoned in 1960.[23]

For much of the 19th century, steps were taken to provide elementary education for adults who had had little or no schooling as children or to provide training for trades and crafts. As early as 1833 there was an evening school in the village attended by about thirty adults and the Mutual Improvement Societies at the various churches had a strong educational role. In addition, in the 1860s at the Primitive Methodist chapel, night schools taught reading, writing, arithmetic and grammar. The teacher's salary was paid out of subscriptions from the scholars, but the Sunday school officials agreed to pay for gas, coal, room hire and copybooks. 'Continuation classes' or night schools teaching elementary subjects began at both Stubbins and Turn schools in the 1880s and 1890s. They were taught by the headmasters and their assistants and, for a fee of 2s 6d for a course of lessons or 3d per week, students could take subjects such as reading, writing, arithmetic, history, drawing, physical exercise and millinery. In a letter written in November 1893, Mr. Gornall, the headmaster at Turn, said that more women could be attracted to his continuation classes if they could choose from singing, dress making or 'laundry work.' In the following year a sixteen-week course of dressmaking was taught at the school.[24]

This course was set up by the Technical Education Committee of the Lancashire County Council, which had been established under the terms of the 1889 Technical Instruction Act to promote various kinds of adult education. Before the passing of the act a similar kind of service was provided by individual teachers under the banner of the Department of Science and Art, South Kensington. Several courses of lessons in elementary science and art were taught at the Wesleyan Methodist Sunday School in Edenfield in the early 1880s. The teachers were J. M. Stocks and James Halliwell who lived at 118 Market Street and who also taught in Bury and Haslingden. Subjects included magnetism and electricity, inorganic chemistry, building construction, geometry and perspective.[25]

THE 'THREE RS' AND MORE

The education a pupil might receive at any of the local schools in the 19th century consisted of much more than just the three Rs. Any boy attending the Rev. Johnson's school at Hawthorn House in 1813, for example, could learn Greek, Latin and French 'in the grammatical methods practised in our best schools'. He could also take arithmetic, merchants' accounts, mensuration, dialling, plain and spherical trigonometry, navigation, practical astronomy, and algebra. The third part of the curriculum was made up of geography, chronology, history and the principles of the Established Religion. Later in the century the girls at Acres House were offered history, geography, arithmetic, grammar, scripture, French, drawing and painting, dancing and piano or violin lessons. They also had a tennis lawn to play on.[26]

Pupils at the village school were almost as well served. An advertisement for a master in 1825 stressed that he must have 'a thorough knowledge of the English Grammar and also of the Arithmetic', while in the 1860s under the headmastership of George Sutcliffe, the senior class studied algebra, mensuration, Euclid, book-keeping, Latin, astronomy, elocution and the piano. They learnt handwriting by copying 'Be careful how you entertain strangers for they may be angels unawares' and other mottoes into their books. In music lessons any scholar could write a few bars of music on the board and ask someone else to sing it. On Friday afternoons there were two-hour singing lessons of popular songs of the day, including 'Annie Lisle', 'Rosalie, the Prairie Flower', 'Waken, Lords and Ladies Gay' and 'Now pray we for our country.' For physical exercise the boys were drilled by Sergeant Seymour of the LRV and played cricket on Wednesday afternoons. Needlework for the girls made an appearance in the 1870s and an object lesson in elementary science was introduced in 1896.[27]

The curriculum at Stubbins and Turn schools was mainly centred on the three basic subjects, but also included needlework, religious instruction, geography, history, drawing and elementary science. In 1905-6, for instance, the infants practised drawing, clay modelling and paper folding and hemmed pieces of calico. The children in standards I and II studied forty-four stories from English history from Julius Caesar to the death of Queen Victoria and the pupils in standards III-VI learnt to recite 'An order for a picture', 'The Pipes at Lucknow' and 'Faithful Unto Death.' Music and singing lessons also had their place in the timetable. The tonic sol-fa system of instruction was used until the purchase of pianos in 1889 (Stubbins) and 1898 (Turn) helped lessons along. Some of the songs taught at the two schools in the 1870s and 1880s included 'Awakening from sweet slumber', 'The Burlesque Band', 'Home, Sweet Home', 'The harp that once through Tara's halls', 'The last rose of summer' and 'Woodman, spare that tree.' Poems the children learnt at about the same time included 'The prisoner of Chillon', 'The Inchcape Rock', 'The child's first grief', 'Marmion' and 'Father coming home from work.'[28]

The quality of some of the lessons at Stubbins and Turn sometimes fell short of the standards expected by the school inspectors. In 1883 the inspector who called at Turn noted '... the Arithmetic is incorrect ... the character of the Handwriting is ragged and irregular in the extreme and mistakes in spelling are numerous.' Six years later matters had improved slightly, but still did not please the inspectors:

> Discipline is satisfactory and needlework is much improved. Reading is tolerably fluent and accurate, but very few questions on the meanings were answered. Writing is poor, especially in the Upper Standards. Spelling is very poor and arithmetic and English are barely fair.

Comments in the reports on Stubbins school were often similar. In 1884, for instance, the inspector found the reading of many of the pupils to be 'unintelligent, monotonous and not even mechanically correct.' A few years later another inspector found the reading fluent, but complained that 'the absence of voice training is to be regretted, and makes the exercise unpleasant.'[29]

The picture was not totally gloomy, however, and where improvement had been made or good work done, the inspectors were ready to praise pupils and teachers. Stubbins school received a particularly glowing report in 1896:

> The good management and methodical teaching in this school have had their natural effect. In all the subjects the several classes have secured high marks. Reading in the third and fourth standards, and arithmetic in the fourth standard, being almost the only exceptions, and these are very fair. The children are neat and alert, and the Board has good reason for satisfaction.

The report on Turn school a couple of years later was also very favourable: 'The elementary work is well taught, and the order is good. Needlework deserves the highest grant and Geography is satisfactory.'[30]

With a new century came new lessons to add to the curriculum. At Edenfield school, for instance, a garden was established, although in 1912 it was reported to be

Stubbins School cricket team, 1928.

in a 'very backward condition'. The children of Ewood Bridge were also encouraged to take an interest in matters horticultural by entering a competition for growing pot plants run by Haslingden Natural History Society in 1905. A similar scheme was tried for a few years in the 1960s at Edenfield. Other changes brought in during the First World War and the 1920s and 1930s included cookery, woodwork, dancing, nature study and swimming lessons.[31]

In 1924 Ewood Bridge and Stubbins schools had their first taste of wireless broadcasts. On 23rd April the Ewood Bridge scholars and a good many parents listened to the King's speech at the opening of the British Empire Exhibition at Wembley. In the following month a broadcast consisting of selections by Besses o' th' Barn brass band, solos by local singer James Savin, a talk on bird songs and the news bulletin entertained the senior class at Stubbins. The *Ramsbottom Observer* noted that 'the children proved good "listeners-in" and eagerly showed their appreciation of the various items rendered.' The sets used in 1924 were merely on loan and it was not until 1935 that both schools acquired wirelesses of their own. Soon the children found themselves part of the national audience for music lessons, stories and nature talks, as well as sharing the Armistice Day service and hearing the proclamation and abdication of Edward VIII. Turn school did not acquire a wireless until 1942. It was replaced by a more up-to-date radio in November 1950 and the weekly timetable was altered so that the children could listen to Singing Together,

Music and Movement, Nature Study, Travel Talks and Let's Join In. Some fifteen years later, the pupils had their horizons expanded even further when they began watching schools programmes on a second-hand television set. The man responsible for acquiring the television was John Stothard, Turn's enthusiastic headmaster from September 1964 to December 1965. During that short time he began piano, recorder and violin lessons, held French classes and cookery sessions and introduced hamsters, stick insects, terrapins and tropical fish into the school.[32]

As well as being re-arranged to accommodate new subjects, the timetable was also occasionally interrupted on special occasions or for lessons on particular topics. From the late 19th century onwards, each school usually received an annual visit from a representative from the Lancashire and Cheshire Band of Hope Union who lectured on the merits of abstinence. In the 1920s and 1930s lectures and essay writing on health – 'How do cleanliness and fresh air make the home healthy?' – and on 'Safety First' joined talks on temperance. Until the Second World War, Empire Day (24th May) was observed by singing patriotic songs, raising and saluting the flag and talks on the vastness of the British Empire. Other anniversaries were celebrated too. They included the centenary of the Battle of Trafalgar in 1905 when

Time to read at Edenfield School in 1973 for (*left-right*) Sarah Wolstenholme, Rosie Trippier and Gillian Barlow.

Playtime at Edenfield School, October 1996.

Ewood Bridge children were given a talk on Lord Nelson before singing the National Anthem, and the ter-centenary of Shakespeare's death in 1916, which they marked with a recreation of the trial scene from 'The Merchant of Venice'. Edenfield and Stubbins children learnt about the League of Nations in November 1921, while at Ewood Bridge in April 1931 the usual history lesson was given up in favour of a talk on the census.[33]

On a more light-hearted note, children took part in concerts and were treated to the occasional outing. The annual concerts were often combined with the distribution of prizes for regular attendance and good schoolwork. Typical of such events was that held in Edenfield National School in January 1902 when the entertainment consisted of songs, recitations, a 'stump speech' and a flag drill, after which prizes of books and 'other useful articles' were presented by the vicar. At a similar occasion at Ewood Bridge in the previous year the programme included ' a capital rendering of the rustic operetta 'Merryton Market' and phonograph selections during the interval. In the late 1950s and early 1960s the Christmas treat for the children at Turn was a trip to Manchester to see a play at the Library Theatre. Occasional visits to the cinema also broke the usual round of the school year. In December 1919 some of the Stubbins children went to Ramsbottom to see 'a series of pictures bearing on the life of Lord Nelson and the growth of the British Navy', while in November 1935 eighteen children from Turn saw 'David Copperfield'[34]

For school trips, children were either taken for walks in the locality or on outings further afield. The walk to Grant's Tower, which 350 children from Turn and Shuttleworth Board Schools were supposed to enjoy in August 1894, had to be abandoned because of bad weather. Instead they ate their picnic in Shuttleworth school before spending the evening playing games. In October 1920 Mr. Walker, the Ewood Bridge headmaster, took thirty pupils on a ramble over Musbury Tor, across Musbury valley and home through Grane. Visits to the coast (Blackpool or Southport) and Belle Vue were popular, and by the early 1930s trips were also being made to North Wales, Edinburgh and London. Early one morning in June 1927 the Ewood Bridge staff and nine boys went by bus to Longridge Fell to see the eclipse of the sun, arriving home at 8.35am.[35]

NOTES

[1] Edenfield parish records (MCL: MF PR 117a); Manor of Tottington records (LRO: DDHCL liber QQ, folio 709); L. Longworth, *Edenfield Church and School History Notebook*, (1989), p. 62; RO 12th September 1924, 17th December 1909; Longworth, *op. cit.*, p. 63

[2] *Return comprising the reports made to the Charity Commissioners, in the results of Inquiries in the Administrative County of Lancaster...into Endowments...Vol. IV, Salford Hundred*, (1910); Archdeacon Rushton's visitation returns (MCL: MSf 942.72 R121 vol. 15); RO 15th April 1892

[3] *Return comprising the reports made to the Charity Commissioners, in the results of Inquiries in the Administrative County of Lancaster...into Endowments...Vol. IV, Salford Hundred*, (1910); RO 1st April 1892, 17th March 1899, 13th August 1954

[4] RO 28th April 1961, 6th August 1948, 27th August 1948, 22nd July 1949, 9th November 1951; Longworth, *op. cit.*, p. 72

[5] Letter from Rev. William Gray to the National Society, 26th May 1836 (National Society archives, Church of England Record Centre, South Bermondsey)

[6] *St. Peter's, Ewood Bridge. Memoir of Centenary Celebrations*, (1939), pp. 6-7; Blackburn Standard 18th March 1840

[7] RO 30th June 1933, 21st March 1902

[8] RO 21st March 1902

[9] *St. Peter's, Ewood Bridge. Memoir of Centenary Celebrations*, (1939), pp. 6-7; RO 9th October 1903; Ewood Bridge National School log-book, 14th April 1902 (LRO: SMHs/2/1)

[10] *St. Peter's, Ewood Bridge. Memoir of the Centenary Celebrations*, (1939), p. 9; Ewood Bridge National School log-book, 17th February 1922 (LRO: SMHs/2/1); RO 26th May 1950; Haslingden Guardian 28th March 1930

[11] RO 9th November 1951, 8th February 1952; Musbury Parish Magazine, February 1959 (LRO: PR 3067/14/12)

[12] HMI reports 1869 and 1879, Stubbins Congregational records, Education Department correspondence portfolio (BAS: CST/11/1); *Stubbins County Primary School – Extracts from the school log book 1868 - 1988*, (1988), pp. 25-26

[13] Tottington Higher End School Board minute book 1882-1888 (LRO: SBT/1); RO 21st May 1915

[14] RFP 6th May 1967, 20th June 1970

[15] Walmersley and Shuttleworth School Board minutes 1878-1886 (LRO: SBW/1)

[16] Walmersley and Shuttleworth School Board minutes 1878-1886 and 1886-1893 (LRO: SBW/1 and SBW/2)

[17] RO 24th April 1891

[18] Walmersley and Shuttleworth School Board minutes 1886-1893 (LRO: SBW/2)

[19] RFP 11th February 1967, 10th February 1968

[20] Manchester Mercury 5th January 1813; RO 29th January 1915; BT 11th July 1868; 1871 census Walmersley-cum-Shuttleworth (PRO: RG 10/3948)

[21] 1851 census Tottington Higher End (PRO: HO 107/2249); 1861 census Tottington Higher End (PRO: RG 9/3059); Tottington Higher End valuation 1837 (LRO: MBH 5/6); RO 22nd April 1932; Accrington Free Press 15th September 1860; Manchester Courier 5th December 1863; *Stubbins County Primary School - Extracts from the school log book 1868 - 1988*, (1988), p.3

22 BT 5th March 1887, 22nd August 1885, 9th February 1889; RO 11th September 1891, 31st March 1905, 20th April 1923; Kelly & Co., *The Post Office Directory of Lancashire*, (1873); 1881 census Tottington Higher End (PRO: RG 11/4136); B. Guiness Orchard, *Liverpool's Legion of Honour*, (1893), p. 563; Accrington Times 2nd August 1890

23 RO 26th November 1948, 11th January 1952, 5th January 1959, 10th July 1959, 22nd January 1960

24 PP, *Abstract of answers and returns relative to the state of education in England and Wales 1833*, 1835 (62) XLI; Primitive Methodist Sunday School teachers' meeting minute books 1857-1866 and 1867-1877 (BAS: CRR/T2561); Stubbins continuation evening school: preliminary statement, Stubbins Congregational records, Education department correspondence portfolio (BAS: CST/11/1); RO 24th November 1893; Walmersley and Shuttleworth School Board minute books 1878-1886 and 1886-1893 (LRO: SBW/1 and SBW/2)

25 BT 15th July 1882, 12th August 1882, 28th July 1883, 25th July 1885

26 Manchester Mercury 5th January 1813; BT 1st May 1886, 9th February 1889

27 Blackburn Mail 7th September 1825; RO 12th September 1924; L. Longworth, *Edenfield Church and School History Notebook*, (1989), p. 65

28 Turn Board School log-book (LRO: SMR/2/1); *Stubbins County Primary School – Extracts from the school log book 1868 - 1988*, (1988)

29 Walmersley and Shuttleworth School Board minutes 1878-1886 (LRO: SBW/1); Tottington Higher End School Board minutes 1882-1888 and 1888-1895 (LRO: SBT/1 and SBT/2)

30 Walmersley and Ramsbottom School Board minutes 1895-1898 (LRO: SBX/1)

31 RO 28th June 1912, 5th April 1963; Turn Board School log-book (LRO: SMR/2/1); Ewood Bridge National School log-book (LRO: SMHs/2/1); Longworth, *op. cit.*, p. 69

32 Ewood Bridge National School log-book, 28th April 1924 (LRO: SMHs/2/1); RO 30th May 1924; Turn Board School log-book (LRO: SMR/2/1)

33 Longworth, *op. cit.*, p. 68; Ewood Bridge National School log-book (LRO: SMHs/2/1)

34 RO 31st January 1902, 15th November 1901; *Stubbins County Primary School – Extracts from the school log book 1868 - 1988*, (1988) p.21; Turn Board School log-book (LRO: SMR/2/1)

35 RO 31st August 1894, 28th July 1905; Ewood Bridge National School log-book (LRO: SMHs/2/1); Turn Board School log-book (LRO: SMR/2/1)

CHURCHES AND CHURCH LIFE

EDENFIELD PARISH CHURCH

FOR MORE THAN THREE HUNDRED YEARS Edenfield church was a chapel-of-ease in the huge parish of Bury and did not become a Parish Church in its own right until 1865. By the 1770s the original 16th century building was showing signs of its age and in 1774 the villagers decided to apply for permission to rebuild it. The faculty they were granted is dated 30th July 1777 and says that the church was 'a very ancient and decayed Building and in so ruinous a condition that the Inhabitants could not with safety longer assemble themselves for Divine Service.' Moreover, 'through the great increase of the Inhabitants ... the old Chapel was become much too small to contain the Number of Inhabitants usually resorting to Divine Service there.'[1]

The new building – the present Parish Church – replaced the old chapel entirely, with the exception of the tower. It was a plain structure with a small chancel for the

Edenfield Parish Church in the 1950s. The lych-gate was built in 1904 in memory of the Rev. James Yeo who committed suicide in the vicarage in 1901.

communion table at the east end. The congregation went in through one of two doors at either end of the south wall and found themselves in a church packed from end to end with rows of box pews. The pulpit, probably of the two or three-decker variety, stood prominently at the east end in the middle of the nave.

The 'new, handsome and convenient pews or seats' were sufficient for the congregation for some time, but by the early 19th century the increasing population of the district had begun to overflow them. The solution was to build three galleries: one at the west end in 1811 and two on the north and south sides in 1829. This brought the total number of seats in the church to 736. Further alterations were made to the interior in 1870 when more up-to-date pews replaced those in the middle of the nave. In 1909, Thomas Aitken, the Irwell Vale mill owner, offered to give a new organ to the church. In order to make room for it, the congregation decided to rebuild the east end so that it would encompass an organ chamber, chancel and vestries. When it became clear that they could not raise the money for this scheme, an alternative plan was followed whereby part of the south gallery was taken away and the organ installed in the space.[2]

Stained glass windows were set in the chancel and elsewhere in the church in 1890, 1911 and 1948, but much of the building's charm lies in the small panes of plain glass that fill its windows. Clearly the Parish Church has not stood completely unchanged since it was built at the end of the 18th century, but it manages to give the impression that it has, prompting Sir John Betjeman's well-known description of it as 'unspoilt, unspruced Georgian.'[3]

EDENFIELD EVANGELICAL SUNDAY SCHOOL

Shortly after the Rev. James Yeo became vicar of Edenfield in 1870 some of his parishioners left the Parish Church to set up a new church of their own. We do not know exactly what caused the breach, although one contemporary later said that the break away group had found fault with Mr. Yeo 'in connection with the management of the school and other matters.' It may be that Mr. Yeo's political views were too Conservative and his taste in religious services too High Church for men like James Pickup, one of the founders of Edenfield Co-operative Society and one of the people who left the Parish Church in 1870. Whatever the case, a new church – the Edenfield Evangelical Sunday School – was established and held regular Sunday services and a Sunday school in a room over the co-operative stores. For the next fifteen years the new church met with some success, holding tea parties, entertainments and so on, but it closed in June 1885.[4]

ST. PHILIP'S, STUBBINS

St. Philip's began life as a mission church to serve the part of Edenfield parish that lay at some distance from the church. The mission opened at 4, Stubbins Street in

The newly completed St. Philip's Parish Church, Stubbins, in 1927.

1906 and remained there until 1927. The two rooms in the building were made into one in 1908, a small organ installed in 1912 and an old pulpit from St. Paul's, Ramsbottom added in 1920. Two legacies from parishioners allowed the vicar to employ an assistant curate to look after the little church at Stubbins.[5]

A.T. Porritt took an active interest in the Stubbins cause and in 1922 offered a piece of land near Stubbins station as the site for an iron or concrete mission church. In the following year, however, the congregation decided to continue to raise money for a more permanent building. By the spring of 1926 sufficient funds had been gathered to allow work to begin at a new site in Chatterton. Mrs. Porritt laid the foundation stone on 5th June 1926 and at the end of May in the following year the church was consecrated by the Bishop of Hulme. Six years later a procession left the old mission room in Stubbins Street and made its way to St. Philip's. The occasion was the opening of a new stone-built Sunday school by Col. Porritt. The building had cost £1,383 and housed a schoolroom with stage and cloakrooms. A kitchen was added in 1949 and ten years later an old pre-fab house was used to make a further extension. St. Philip's continued as a Parish Church in its own right until 1984 when the Stubbins and Edenfield parishes were joined together to create a united benefice.[6]

ST. PETER'S, EWOOD BRIDGE

The National School at Ewood Bridge opened in 1840 was also used as a place of worship. Known as St. Peter's, it became part of the new parish of Musbury in 1844. Services continued in the building after the day school closed in 1959, but eventually the church too closed and the building was sold in 1976. In the 1880s and 1890s,

St. Peter's, Ewood Bridge was housed in the National School seen on the left in this picture in 1908. The occasion was the funeral of John Walmsley, a Crimean War veteran who lived in the village.

cottage and out-door services were also occasionally held at Irwell Vale by the vicar of Musbury.[7]

WESLEYAN METHODISTS

According to tradition, Methodism took root in the district in the 1740s. Paul Greenwood, an early Methodist evangelist, is said to have preached in one of the farms at Fecit, near Turn in 1747. Services continued to be held in that out-lying district until the mid-1850s.[8] By this date, Wesleyan Methodism was a powerful force in the district, but its early days were not without their setbacks. In 1778, for example, the Rev. John Smith, incumbent of Holcombe and Edenfield chapels-of-ease, noted that:

> The Methodists have much decreased within the 14 years last past, owing principally, as I think, to a certain Instability of Temper, and a rivetted Ignorance predominant among them, which will not suffer them to fix upon and adhere long to any particular Principles of Religion.[9]

By 1790, however, Fecit was recognised as one of the preaching places in the Blackburn Circuit whose records tell us that there were seventeen members in the little society in that year. By the end of 1793 a separate society had been set up in Edenfield and in May of the following year John Schofield's cottage at Pinfold was licensed as a Nonconformist place of worship. In 1796 fifty-three members of the society were listed, although numbers fluctuated over the next few years, falling to fifteen in 1801.[10]

Services continued to be held at John Schofield's until 1827 when John Wallwork, who ran Plunge Mill, rented two rooms above cottages at Bridge Mills. These served as both chapel and Sunday school, although later the school transferred to the room in the top storey of the houses in Market Street reached by the long flight of steps between numbers 11 and 13. A small, plain chapel was built in 1832 on a piece of land in Rochdale Road at a cost of £454 19s. (Its site is now occupied by 25 and 27, Rochdale Road). It was enlarged in 1857. Services also continued to be held in farms and cottages in places like Ewood Bridge and Irwell Vale.[11]

By the 1850s, the Sunday school classes were being taught in both the room in Market Street and the chapel itself. The number of pupils had grown to such an extent (there were said to 308 children attending in March 1858, for example) that the Wesleyans decided to build a completely new school. They chose a site just off Market Place, near its junction with Rochdale Road, and here the foundation stone was laid on 12th June 1869. The school was opened in the following year. The building stood back from the road leaving enough room in front for a chapel. The corner stones of this imposing new building were laid in May 1876 and it was opened two years later. It was typical of many Victorian Nonconformist chapels in its size and interior decoration. It could seat nearly 600 people in pews of varnished pitch pine and had a mahogany pulpit, 'a remarkably handsome fixture … with special

The imposing frontage of the Wesleyan chapel overlooking Market Place pictured in about 1959.

arrangements for accommodating the height of desk to ministers of varying stature.' The chapel and Sunday school were designed by the Bury firm of Maxwell and Tuke, who were later the architects for Blackpool Tower. Both buildings were demolished in 1960 following amalgamation with the former Primitive Methodist chapel in Rochdale Road.[12]

PRIMITIVE METHODISTS

Primitive Methodism found a foothold in the area in the early 1830s at Irwell Vale where services were held in a cottage in Bowker Street. In Edenfield itself Richard Mason, a tinsmith who lived and worked at 21, Market Street, allowed part of his workshop to be used as a place of worship. The land on the north side of his property was then an open space with a well in its centre that became known as Teetotal Well, presumably because of the Methodist connections with the neighbouring house. This Market Street meeting room was superseded in 1841 when a one-roomed school-chapel was built on the north side of Exchange Street. The Irwell Vale Primitive Methodists (who became a separate society from Edenfield in 1850) had to wait until 1853 before they could afford to build their own small chapel at Hardsough. They also held cottage meetings at Lumb.[13]

Both the Edenfield and Hardsough chapels were used for exactly forty years before being replaced by larger buildings. J.D. Mould, a Bury architect with Primitive Methodist connections, designed the second chapels. The corner stones of the Edenfield chapel were laid at a site on Rochdale Road on 15th April 1881 and the new chapel and Sunday school opened in January of the following year when the Rev. Charles Kendall, President of the Primitive Methodist Conference, preached. Irwell

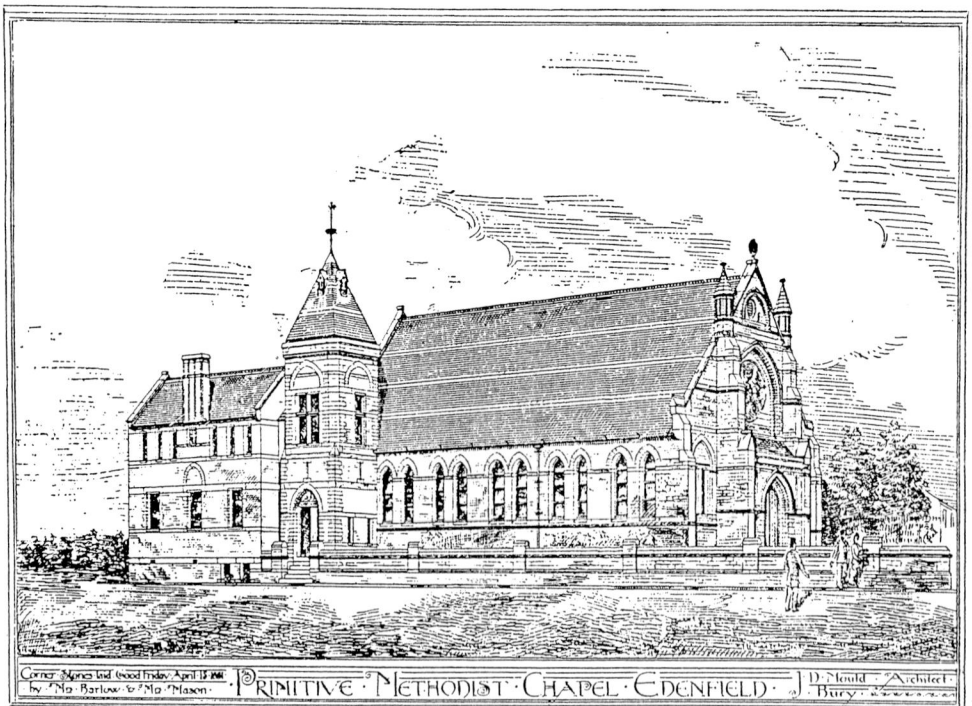

J.D. Mould's drawing of Edenfield Primitive Methodist Chapel made when the Sunday School was added to the rear of the building in 1911.

How Irwell Vale Primitive Methodist Chapel might have looked. Lack of funds meant that the congregation could not afford to build the Sunday School at the rear. It was not until 1992 that a much smaller extension was added to the chapel.

Vale's chapel was completed in 1893 and opened in October of that year. A primary department was added to the Rochdale Road chapel in 1911, but plans for a Sunday school at the rear of the Irwell Vale chapel never came to fruition.[14]

CONGREGATIONALISTS

Apart from the Methodists, the Congregationalists were the other main Non-conformist denomination in the district. The Porritt family were prominent supporters of Park Chapel, Shuttleworth and continued to attend after they moved to Edenfield and then to Stubbins Vale. By 1860, however, they felt that the Stubbins area needed a separate place of worship. The Rev. John Anyon, minister at Park, perhaps realising that he would lose some of the wealthiest members of his congregation, at first refused to entertain the idea. Eventually, however, he agreed that some of the members from Park should form the nucleus of a new church. A room in Stubbins Vale Mill was boarded off and, once suitably furnished, was opened as the Stubbins Congregational Sabbath School and Preaching Room at a tea meeting held on 2nd September 1861. The Sunday school began on 8th September and the first sermons were preached on the following Sunday.[15]

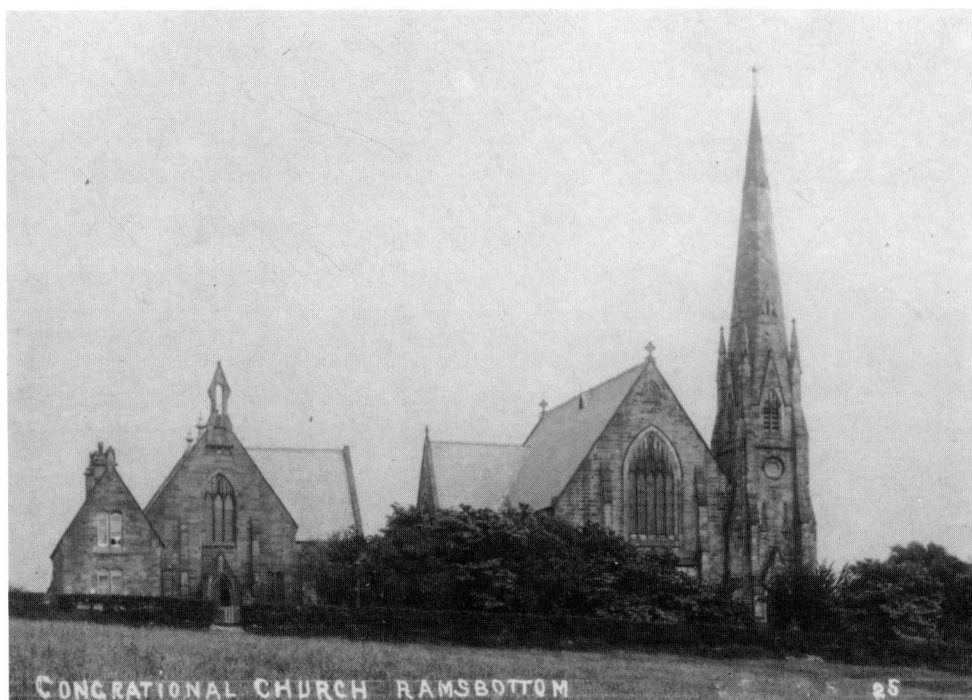

Stubbins Congregational Church, with the school and chapel keeper's house next to it. Only the latter building survives.

Stubbins Vale Mill served as a church and Sunday school for a few years, but in 1865 work was begun on a new church on a prominent site at the side of the road between Stubbins and Edenfield. The school was completed first and opened on 30th April 1866, followed by the church on 14th April 1867. Both buildings were made of stone quarried from the hillside above the mill and a 120 ft. spire at one corner completed the church. James Porritt made a gift of a £5 note to the man who finished off the building by fixing the weather vane to the top of the spire. The church could seat 750 people, while the school could cater for 600 scholars.[16]

Like many Nonconformist chapels built in the 19th century, Stubbins Congregational Church eventually became too large and costly to maintain for its dwindling congregation. The problem of dry rot in the church led to its demolition in 1983-4. The school building was used as a church until it too closed in April 1991. It was subsequently demolished and houses built on the site.[17]

CHURCHES AT TURN

There has never been a purpose-built church at Turn, but the little village and its surroundings have not been totally abandoned by religion. We have already noted its early Methodist connections and each Sunday morning in the early 19th century a handful of men and women could be seen walking along the moorland roads between Turn and Rochdale. Their destination was Hope Baptist Chapel and in 1820 the Rev. John Kershaw, minister there, decided to visit the distant members of his congregation once a month. He preached to them in the large room on the third storey of the hand-loom weaving shop at Lime Leach and in another room at one of the farms at Fecit.[18]

One of the Baptist congregation was George Ramsbottom, co-partner in Cheesden Pasture Mill. He and his brother, James, allowed a room at the mill to be used as a day school and preaching room. The Rev. Kershaw preached there on many occasions, particularly each New Year's Day when there was a large congregation and choir. The Rev. John Anyon, minister of Park Congregational Chapel, also preached at Cheesden Pasture because James Ramsbottom was one of his flock. James and his fellow-worshippers walked from the houses and farms around Cheesden and Fecit across Harden Moor to Park each Sunday 'carrying their dinners and cheering the way with songs of Zion.'[19] John Kershaw continued to visit Lime Leach and Cheesden Pasture until his death in 1869. By this date, a Particular Baptist chapel had been built in Haslingden and people from the area around Turn started to attend so that eventually services at the outlying farms were abandoned.

At the beginning of the 20th century, the Rev. Peter McMillan, pastor at St. Andrew's Presbyterian church, Ramsbottom, ran a mission at Turn. In June 1914, he started holding services in a room possibly in Turn mill. By December, so many people were attending these Sunday afternoon events that they moved into Turn school. For the next few years the mission held weekly services as well as anniversaries, harvest festivals, tea parties, recitals and whist drives. They continued until the mid-1920s, but presumably did not outlive the mission's mother church, which was demolished in 1926. The Church of England, represented by St. John's, Shuttleworth, ran a mission in the 1930s and held monthly services in the 1950s. These had to be abandoned for a time in 1957 when petrol rationing made it difficult for the vicar to travel up to the village.[20]

SUNDAY SERVICES AND CHURCH ATTENDANCE

In 1778, John Smith, the long-serving incumbent of the chapelries of Edenfield and Holcombe, noted that services were held at the two chapels-of-ease every other Sunday and that he preached two sermons on each occasion. Prayers were also read on Good Friday, one of the four days during the year in which he administered the Sacrament of the Lord's Supper to about forty of his congregation. This pattern of services continued until the Rev. Smith's death in 1810. His successor, William Holt, began to make changes, partly helped by the fact that he had a curate to assist him. By the 1820s, two services were held at Edenfield every Sunday as well as on Christmas Day, Good Friday and Public Fasts. Sacrament continued to be a quarterly affair with an average attendance of between twelve and sixteen. The Rev. Holt said that usual Sunday congregations averaged a staggering 300 or 400 in 1821 and 200 or 300 in 1825.[21]

THE

WESLEYAN METHODIST PREACHERS' PLAN,

FROM OCTOBER 28TH, 1838, TO APRIL 21ST, 1839.

PLACES AND TIMES.	PREACHERS' NAMES.
HASLINGDEN, Monday Evening	1 SMETHAM, 2 LEIGH, 3 RODHAM, 4 Robt. HOLDEN, 5 LANG, 6 HEYWORTH,
GRANE, Monday Evening	7 HARGREAVES, 8 RISHTON, 9 Jno. HOLDEN,
ACCRINGTON, Monday Evening	10 Jas. HOLDEN, 11 SUTCLIFFE, 12 GREENWOOD,
HIPPINGS, Monday Evening	13 GILL, 14 DAVY, 15 HUTCHINSON,
EDENFIELD, Wednesday Evening	16 LAW, 17 ENTWISTLE, 18 WALKER,
RAMSBOTTOM, Monday Evening	19 BARNES, 20 CLEGG, 21 PARKINSON,
FACIT, Tuesday Evening	22 PRIESTLEY, 23 SHUTTLEWORTH, 24 WADDINGTON,
GREENHAWORTH, Tuesday Evening	25 HORSFALL.
BAXENDEN, Tuesday Evening	ON TRIAL. 26 TAYLOR.
HUNCOTE, Wednesday Evening	EXHORTER. 27 KIRKBRIGHT.
STANHILL, Thursday Evening	
EWOOD-BRIDGE, Wednesday Evening	REFERENCES.
BANK-LANE	B—Bacup Chapel.
HALLEY CROSS	S—Lord's Supper.
HOLKHAM	L—Lovefeast.
IRWELL VALE	M—Collection for Missions.
OAKENSHAW	Q—Quarterly Collection in aid of the Circuit.
FLAXMOSS.—Tuesday Evening	C—General Chapel Fund Collection, in aid of embarrassed Chapels.
OAKENHEAD-WOOD.—Tues. Even.	
HELM-SHORE.—Tuesday Evening	Every Preacher is expected punctually to fulfil his own appointments, and commence the worship of God at the hour specified; or in case of unavoidable absence, to get his place supplied by one whose name is on the Plan.
SHIRFIN-NOOK.—Wednesday Even.	
SYKE-SIDE.—Thursday Evening	
CRIBDEN-SIDE.—Thursday Evening	
CHURCH-BRIDGE.—Thursday Even	

LESSONS TO BE READ AT THE MORNING SERVICES.

OCT. 28, Prov. 11...Luke 15	DEC. 30, Isai. 37...Acts 28	MAR. 3, Gen. 39...Luke 9
NOV. 4, — 13... — 21	JAN. 6, — 44...Mat. 6	— 10, — 43... — 16
— 11, — 16...John 4	— 13, — 51... — 12	— 17, Exo. 2... — 18
— 18, — 17... — 11	— 20, — 55... — 19	— 24, — v...John 6
— 25, — 19... — 11	— 27, — 57... — 25	— 31, Gen. 22... — 18
DEC. 2, Isai. 1...Acts 4	FEB. 3, Gen. 9...Mark 6	APR. 7, Num 10... — 20
— 9, — 5... — 10	— 10, Exo. 22... — 8	— 14, — 28...Acts. 6
— 16, — 25... — 11	— 17, Gen. 19... — 12	— 21, Deu. 4... — 13
— 23, — 32... — 24	— 24, — 27...Luke 2	— 28, — 5... — 20

The Quarterly Meetings will be held in the Vestry of Haslingden Chapel, January 1st, and April 2nd, at 1 o'clock. The Local Preachers' Meetings will be held on the same days, in the same place, at 11 o'clock.

On the first Friday in every month, missionary prayer meetings will be held in all the places, to commence at eight o'clock in the Evening; when extracts from the missionary Notices will be read, and special supplication offered to God in behalf of the heathen world.

The Methodist Magazines, Hymn Books, and all other works published at the Conference Office, (the profits of which are applied in aid of various Funds connected with the Wesleyan Itinerancy in Great Britain and Ireland, and especially in support of aged Preachers, and Preachers' Widows,) may be had by application to the Itinerant Preachers.

W. Hutchinson, Printer, &c. Accrington.

A preaching plan from the Haslingden Wesleyan Methodist Circuit for October 1838 to April 1839. The preachers visited not only Edenfield, but also Fecit (Facit on the plan), Ewood Bridge and Irwell Vale.

Some of the congregation at the church in the early 19th century were undoubtedly Methodists. The Rev. Smith noted in 1804 that there were some Nonconformists in his chapelries, 'mostly of the weaving & laborious Class of People', but that he could not 'properly divide many of them from those of our own Church as they occasionally attend our Churches & Chapels & are baptized & buried with us.'[22] Nevertheless, as we have seen, the Methodists were holding their own services. By 1812, when Edenfield was part of the Bury Circuit, a service was held at five o'clock every other Sunday. Their frequency increased to two every Sunday once the rooms at Bridge Mills had been taken over in the 1820s. In the late 1830s, the new chapel saw services held every Sunday at 2.30pm and 6.00pm, every other Sunday at 10.30am and every other Wednesday evening at 8.00pm. The Primitive Methodists probably followed a similar pattern. Certainly by 1851, the Edenfield chapel was used for worship in the morning, afternoon and evening of each Sunday, while at Irwell Vale there were afternoon and evening services. Both chapels also had weeknight services, a practice that continued at Irwell Vale until at least 1902.[23]

When the religious census was taken in 1851, the Anglicans and Wesleyan Methodists were also holding three services each Sunday. Those in the afternoon were the most popular: average attendances at the Parish Church were 150, at the Wesleyans 120, at the Primitives seventy and at Irwell Vale forty. Eighty years later, by which time the Anglicans had abandoned afternoon services, most people attended evening worship. The Rev. Ernest Ottley thought that in 1930 his congregation at an ordinary Sunday evening service at the Parish Church usually numbered from 280 to 300, compared with 160 at a morning service. Similarly, the Rev. Charles Wynne at St. Philip's said that he usually had about 100 people at his Sunday evening service, with eighty in the morning.[24]

We should not perhaps accept the rosy picture painted by these figures without looking at some of the evidence for the difficulties faced by the various churches in attracting people to them. In 1804, the Rev. John Smith gave the following account to his bishop:

> There are many Persons in these Chapelries … who, by their Conduct, appear to disregard several of the inestimable Duties [Christ]ianity would impose upon them; & who commonly, if not altogether, absent themselves from the public Worship of God on the Lord's Day; The No. of whom seems rapidly encreasing, since training of Soldiers, fifing, druming &c. &c. on that Day began to be the Order of it.

He continued:

> Another great Cause of want of Principle & Encrease of Irreligion is the Want of proper Instruction amongst the lower Classes of People, in their Youth. They are capable of working when 4 or 5 years of Age, at our Factories & Print Shops; & therefore are frequently sent thither at those Ages to earn something towards their Maintenance & for ever afterwards deprived of necessary Tutorage unless it may be taught on Sundays, or at Nights after the Labour of the Day…[25]

Just over one hundred years later at the annual meeting of members of Stubbins Congregational Church in 1910 an appeal had to be made for 'more faithful service on the part of the members so that the church might be a light amid the darkness of sin & sorrow.' Somewhat later in the 20th century, Irwell Vale Methodists found that attendances at their Sunday afternoon services were falling off: at the beginning of 1957, for instance, there were only between 5 and 8 adults there, with the rest being children. They cut down the number of such services to one a month, before abandoning them altogether in May. Most churches made a determined effort to broaden their appeal to young people. Following the amalgamation of the two Methodist churches, for example, a monthly family service was introduced, while at St. Philip's in 1965 a fortnightly service for parents and their children under school age was started. At these events the vicar entertained the children with a glove puppet named 'Timothy Tot.'[26]

It is difficult to imagine what 19th century churchgoers would have made of such events, although their own services could be lively affairs, particularly in the first half of the century. Recollections of some of the Nonconformist services in particular convey something of the vigour with which they were conducted. At the old Primitive Methodist chapel in 'Jammy Loyne' [Exchange Street], for example, Richard Mason emphasised his words while at prayer by thumping one end of the form so forcefully that the other end flew up. Similarly, the Rev. John Kershaw while preaching at Lime Leach on one occasion brought his arm down so fervently that he broke the oil lamp, leaving the meeting room in darkness. At Irwell Vale in the 1850s the Rev. Daniel Jowett 'preached with such fervour that the sweat ran off his temples down his face' and 'so earnest and excited did he become whilst preaching that without doubt it undermined his health, brought on consumption, and an early death.' Another preacher at Irwell Vale was Edward Fletcher of Radcliffe. On one occasion he based his sermon around the story of the eunuch of Ethiopia (Acts 8, 27-40) concluding with the observation that 'he went on his way rejoicing, he's rejoicing yet for anything I know; at least he was the last time I heard anything about him.' Nonconformist services were also often punctuated by loud exclamations from the congregation, a practice known as 'clerking'. One character known as 'Dicky-'bout-hat' who attended Irwell Vale often shouted, 'That's it lad, go on!' whenever the preacher said something of which he approved.[27]

ANNIVERSARIES AND OTHER SPECIAL SERVICES
THE SERMONS

Should you speak of "school sermons" to a south country or even a Midland parson he would ask you what on earth you meant. I was in a like ignorance before migrating to Lancashire, but after my experience on May 1st, I shall be in a position to reply at length to the queries of clerics who "dinna ken". Firstly, I gathered from observation that the local dressmakers and milliners must have had a somewhat busy time during the preceding weeks, likewise painters and paperers for every house must not only be swept but garnished for the great occasion, whilst for the appearance sake of the churchyard, one could almost wish that the sermons were a quarterly instead of an annual event.[28]

The Sunday School Sermons – described here by the Rev. Ernest Ottley in 1921 – and the Church or Chapel Anniversary Sermons were among the most important occasions in the life of the various churches. They were immensely popular events, attracting huge congregations, not only from the actual church that was celebrating the anniversary, but also from neighbouring churches in the village or elsewhere. Typical of such occasions were the Wesleyan Sermons of 1887 when, 'The chapel in the evening was crowded, there being near upon 800 persons present. The hymn tunes were generally speaking of the old style and were heartily taken part in by the congregation.'[29] There were usually three services on Sermons days, with sermons preached at at least two of them. Preachers were invited to take these services from far and wide. At the Parish Church in June 1865, for instance, the Sermons were conducted by the Rev. H.M. Birch, Chaplain in Ordinary to the Queen, Chaplain (and former tutor) to the Prince of Wales and Rector of Prestwich, while at St. Peter's, Ewood Bridge in 1895 one of the visiting preachers was Captain Chamberlain of the Church Army.[30]

The third service often took a somewhat different form. Sometimes it was a 'service of song' (see below) or an 'address' to the children and increasingly the Sunday school scholars were encouraged to take part of the service. At Irwell Vale in 1898, for example, the children gave a cantata entitled 'The child counsellor', as well as recitations and a solo rendition of 'Rock of Ages'. This pattern was followed by most of the churches for many years to come. One later example comes from the two Methodist churches in Edenfield after their amalgamation in 1960. Their first united Sermons had a special children's service in the morning at which Stephen Jeffreys, Jennifer Main, Miriam Davies and Roger Dawson sang solos, and Anne Entwistle and Leslie Hallam read lessons.[31]

Just as important as the actual services at Sermons weekends were the 'tea meetings' and lectures, which were held either on the Saturday or on the Monday evening. The audiences at these events heard the visiting preachers speak on a wide variety of topics including 'Scottish Covenanters' at the Primitive Methodist Chapel Sermons in 1878 and 'Dreams' at Irwell Vale in 1886. On other occasions, especially in the 20th century, the subjects chosen by speakers often reflected issues of the day and included 'What is democracy?' (1942); 'Rock and Roll Call' (1957 – the problem of getting young people to support the church); and 'Black and White' (1960 – on the racial problems of Africa and the USA).[32]

MUSIC AND MUSICAL SERVICES

By the end of the 18th century an enthusiastic choir accompanied by a small band led the singing in Edenfield Parish Church. The singers were paid for their work. For example, Richard Hoyle, churchwarden for 1781-82 paid 2s for 'singers on Good Friday'. As well as receiving payment for singing, it was traditional for the choir to be supplied with drink: 'ale for singers' is a frequent entry in the accounts, although few churchwardens paid out as much as the 18s that Richard Turner spent in 1813-14 on 'liquor for different singers.' The churchwardens were also responsible for buying instruments for the band. They included a base fiddle and ordinary fiddles, a base viol (predecessor of the cello) and a bassoon purchased in 1786 for £1 11s 6d. In 1781, James Holt also bought a pitch fork to help the singers find and maintain the right pitch. When the new church was completed in 1780, the singers and the band were allocated a pew at the west end underneath the tower, and after the building of the west gallery in 1811 they occupied one of the front seats in it. This meant that the congregation would have followed what was then the usual practice of turning to 'face the music' during the singing of hymns and psalms.[33]

The various Nonconformist chapels had arrangements similar to those at the Parish Church with small groups of singers and musicians to lead the congregational singing. The first chapels had 'singing pews'. In the Primitive Methodist chapel in Exchange Street, it stood in front of the pulpit so that the singers faced the congregation. Musical accompaniment was provided by various combinations of instruments. At Irwell Vale, for instance, at the Sunday School Sermons held in an empty room in Hardsough Mill in 1846 there were violins, clarinets, trombones, cellos and basses, while services at Cheesden Pasture Mill also had string accompaniments. At Edenfield Primitive Methodist chapel in 1858 it was decided to have a single bass and a double bass and that John Ramsbottom was to play the violin. Harmoniums and pipe organs eventually sounded the death knell of the small bands of musicians who played each Sunday, but they continued to make their appearance at special services in some Nonconformist churches into the early 1930s.[34]

In the 18th century the singing of hymns in Anglican churches was generally frowned upon and congregations were supposed to sing only metrical versions of the psalms. Edenfield churchgoers used both the 'Old Version' of Thomas Sternhold and John Hopkins (originally published in 1562) and Nahum Tate and Nicholas Brady's *A New Version of the Psalms of David* dating from 1696. Hymns became more popular in the early 19th century and from about 1814 we find that the Edenfield church-wardens were buying new hymn-books. By 1825 the congregation were using Thomas Cotterill's *A Selection of Psalms and Hymns for Public Worship*, a book that had received the approval of the Archbishop of York in 1820 after much controversy. Nonconformist congregations did not face the same difficulties and all of them, especially the Methodists, were enthusiastic hymn singers with their own hymn-books.

Learning new hymns and tunes was not left to chance and as early as 1826, the Anglicans were paying a man called William Warburton to teach the Sunday school children to sing one night every week for six months. Somewhat later in the 19th century, the Primitive Methodists resolved to spend one afternoon every month practising singing and at the same time their Wesleyan brethren employed their choirmaster, John Taylor, to come into the Sunday school every six or seven weeks to teach the scholars new tunes. Members of both Methodist congregations were given further encouragement to take part in the musical life of their churches in the 1870s and 1880s by teachers of the tonic sol-fa system of sight-singing. Brother Bridgehouse was allowed to start a class in the Primitive Methodist Sunday school in 1870, while in 1884 members of the Wesleyan Tonic Sol-fa Singing Class gave a service of song entitled 'Poor Mike' and a concert of part-songs and duets.[35]

By the time the sol-fa singers were performing, important changes had taken place in the musical life of all the churches. At the Parish Church, for instance, payments to the 'singers' stopped in the 1830s and instead by the early 1870s the 'choir' were the recipients of collections made on their behalf. They also wore surplices and were led by a choirmaster who received a salary. The most important change, however, was found in the way in which music was provided to accompany the hymns. The Parish Church led the way by installing an organ sometime before 1846. It was rebuilt and enlarged in 1866 by Gledhill and Wild of Rochdale whose alterations produced 'a sweetly toned' instrument that was opened by J. Randle Fletcher of Bury who played 'with great ability and good taste.' The present organ was installed in 1911 and dedicated at a special service on 22nd April when the Bishop of Burnley preached and Arthur Nuttall, organist of Haslingden Parish Church, gave a short recital that included pieces by Bach, Haydn, Mendelssohn and Wagner.[36]

Several of the other churches did not change directly from string bands to pipe organs, but instead installed cheaper harmoniums or 'American organs'. The Primitive Methodists bought theirs in 1861, transferred it to the new chapel in 1881 and used it in the Sunday school from 1887 until 1924. St. Peter's, Ewood Bridge acquired its first harmonium in 1897. A replacement had to be bought after the 1902 fire and this second instrument did duty until 1930 when a two manual reed organ was dedicated as a memorial to Thomas W. Walker, headmaster of the day school for thirty-one years. The Wesleyans were the first Nonconformists in the area to have a full pipe organ put into their chapel. It was opened in 1858 and replaced by a larger instrument in 1891. When the chapel closed in 1959, moves were made to sell the organ to a Methodist chapel in Freetown, Sierra Leone, but it was found that it would cost too much to export and that the instrument was not suitable for the tropical climate. Instead it was sold to St. Chad's church, York.[37]

Stubbins Congregationalists followed the Wesleyans' lead, installing a two-and-a-half octave organ with seven stops in their preaching room at Stubbins Vale mill in February 1865. This was replaced by a new Henry Willis organ in the church in 1874 when Frederic Archer, organist of Alexandra Palace, gave two recitals that included some of his own compositions. The Primitive Methodists at Irwell Vale acquired their first organ in the chapel at Hardsough in 1885, which they transferred to the new chapel in 1893. Edenfield Primitives installed their first proper organ in the Rochdale Road chapel in 1887 at a cost of £300; it was rebuilt in 1949. Music at St. Philip's church and its predecessor, Stubbins Mission, was provided first by a harmonium that was bought in 1912 and used until 1930. Its successor came from a church in Manchester and did duty until 1955 when it was replaced by a second-

The organ at Rochdale Road (former Primitive Methodist) Church. It was built by George Benson of Manchester and opened in February, 1887. The opening recital included pieces by Mendelssohn, Beethoven, Bach and Gottschalk.

hand Hammond organ. This too was replaced in 1968 by a smaller electronic organ, partly paid for by money raised by the vicar who had walked to London.[38]

With their newly installed pipe organs the churches were able to offer recitals as an additional part of their musical life. The Congregational church in particular attracted several skilled performers over the years. They included Henry Stafford Trego of London whose recital in January 1879 comprised works by Mozart, Weber and Bach and 'selections from Handel's sublime compositions'. The audience at another recital forty years later enjoyed 'a rare musical treat' when Dr. Thomas Keithley, organ professor at the Manchester College of Music, visited Stubbins. At the Methodist churches in the 1880s and 1890s 'Services of Song' became popular. They consisted of readings from the biography of some national figure – General Gordon was the subject at the Primitive Methodist chapel in April 1885 – or from some edifying story. The title of the service of song given at Irwell Vale in December 1897 was 'A Dark Night', which recounted the life of a man from Bamford whose twelve children all died before him and whose experiences carried the moral, 'Trust in Providence'. At appropriate points in the readings the choir or soloists sang hymns or anthems.[39]

Musical services became increasingly popular at the Methodist churches and Stubbins Congregational church from the beginning of the 20th century and were later introduced at the Parish Church. Like services of song, they consisted of hymns and solos but did not have 'connective readings'. Many of the guest soloists travelled some distance to take part in these services and the Congregationalists were particularly successful in bringing in some big names, culminating in the visit of Norman Allin, 'England's finest bass singer' in 1928. 'His rendering of "The Midnight Review" (Glinka) and "The Clock" (Carl Loewe) simply captivated the assembly, the tone being beautiful, and no artiste could have sung them to better advantage.' said the *Ramsbottom Observer*.[40]

The big musical event at the Wesleyan chapel was the performance of 'Messiah' at Christmas. It was given intermittently in the 19th century, but became established as an annual event in the 1920s and was performed every year until the chapel closed. Again soloists were brought in from elsewhere, although one of the best performances to be given was in December 1940 when all the soloists were from the locality. On this occasion the choir 'showed good balance and tonal qualities for a chapel combination.' The Wesleyan 'Messiah' had a predecessor at Cheesden Pasture Mill where the preaching room was used for some years in the 19th century for the Cheesden Tea and Oratorio. On these occasions music was provided by a harmonium that had been carried to the mill on two mop handles.[41]

OTHER SPECIAL SERVICES

From the late 19th century onwards more and more special services were introduced to fill the church year. Sometimes these innovations were short-lived. For a few years

METHODIST CHURCH, Market Place, EDENFIELD.

SUNDAY, DECEMBER 16th, 1934.

HANDEL'S "MESSIAH"

Part II and III.   **Evening at 6-0.**

Presided over by Rev. W. POLLARD.

Principals :

Soprano : Miss A. BUCKLEY, A.R.M.C.M., of Oldham.
Contralto : Miss MARY ROSCOE, of Bolton.
Tenor : Mr. JAMES H. VAUSE, of Edenfield.
Bass : **Mr. HAMILTON HARRIS, F.R.M.C.M.**
of Manchester.
Organist ; Mr. V. W. Hill.   Conductor : Mr. J. S. Alty.

HYMN I.   PRAYER.
The " Messiah."   **Parts II and III.**

22	Chorus ...	...	"Behold the Lamb of God"
23	Aria	... Alto ...	"He was despised"
24	Chorus ...	...	"Surely He hath borne"
25	Chorus ...	...	"And with His stripes"
26	Chorus ...	...	"All we like sheep"
27	Recit	... Tenor ...	"All they that see Him"
28	Chorus ...	...	"He trusted in God"
29	Recit	... Tenor ...	"Thy rebuke"
30	Aria	...	"Behold, and see if there be any sorrow"
31	Recit	...	"He was cut off out of the land of the living"
32	Aria	... Tenor ...	"But Thou didst not leave His soul in hell"
33	Chorus ...	...	"Lift up your heads, O ye gates"

HYMN II.

38	Aria	...Soprano...	"How beautiful are the feet"
39	Chorus ...	...	"Their sound is gone out"
40	Aria	... Bass ...	"Why do the nations"
41	Chorus ...	...	"Let us break"
42	Recit	... Tenor ...	"He that dwelleth"
43	Aria	...	"Thou shalt break them"
44	Chorus ...	...	"Hellelujah"
45	Aria	...Soprano...	"I know that my Redeemer"
46	Quartet ...	...	"Since by man came death"
47	Chorus ...	...	"By man came also the resurrection"
48	Quartet ...	...	"For as in Adam all die"
49	Chorus ...	...	"Even so in Christ"
50	Recit	... Bass ...	"Behold, I tell you a mystery"
51	Aria	...	"The trumpet shall sound"
56	Chorus ...	...	"Worthy is the Lamb"

HYMN III.

A handbill for one of the annual performances of 'Messiah' at the Wesleyan Chapel.

in the 1890s, for example, the Primitives and Wesleyans held an early morning service in Market Place on the first Sunday in May. They assembled at 6.30am, walked through the village singing hymns and returned to Market Place for the service itself. Somewhat longer lived were services for Foreign Missions, Choirs, Christian Endeavour and Men's Weekends. Outdoing all of these for popularity were the Harvest Festivals. They were taken up by some of the Nonconformists in the 1880s and 1890s and were later adopted by the Anglicans. Churches were often filled to overflowing at Harvest weekends, even a small place like Turn Presbyterian Mission attracting a congregation of more than two hundred in October 1914. The Primitive Methodists were pioneers of the Harvest Festival in the village and the following description of their 1891 service gives us a good idea of how the event was celebrated:

> The decorations which the chapel had undergone made it look particularly beautiful. In front of the pulpit the display of plants, fruit and vegetables was exquisite, and the group of decorations at this place was appropriately crowned with half a loaf. Hanging from the gaspipes were pedlar's baskets, and the window recesses were also set off appropriately. A number of pretty bunches of dahlias and asters mixed were effectively placed … In the morning and evening, sermons were delivered by the Rev. W. Dinning, who also read the connective readings in the afternoon's service with much propriety. In the morning he delivered an able sermon on the parable of the sower. A service of song entitled "Joyful Harvesters", was gone through by the choir in a very praiseworthy manner.

Harvest weekends often concluded on the Monday evening with a 'fruit banquet', another evening of recitations, songs and addresses.[42]

THE SUNDAY SCHOOLS

> It will give real Pleasure to every Friend of Religion and Humanity, to read the following Account of the Number of Children taught in the several Sunday Schools established in the Hundred of Salford.

said the *Manchester Mercury* for 19th August 1788. The list that followed included Edenfield's first Sunday school – at the Parish Church – that had ninety scholars. This school subsequently went into a decline, but was restarted in 1811 when the Rev. William Holt reported that there were 130 children attending and that it was 'expected to be much increased.' And indeed it was, for by 1825 there were said to be about 300 children in the Sunday school. Just over one hundred years later, there were 178 children belonging to the Sunday school and catechism class.[43]

In the 19th century all of the other churches in the district started their own Sunday schools with membership figures that are truly astonishing. The Wesleyans, for instance, reported 180 scholars and fifty teachers in 1832. By 1848, the number of scholars had reached 245, twenty-two of whom had 'been brought to a knowledge of the truth as it is in Jesus in Connexion with the School and a Preached Gospel in this place.' Almost thirty years later, the Sunday school had grown to 365 scholars with fifty-three teachers.[44] Similar figures were recorded for the other Sunday schools.

Children and teachers from Market Place Methodist Sunday School in about 1950.

The Congregationalists claimed 227 scholars in their first year at Stubbins Vale Mill and by the mid-1880s they had one of the largest Sunday schools in the area with 366 children and thirty-nine teachers. For a time in the 1870s the Primitive Methodists did not do so well and in February 1874 offered rewards to 'those scholars who bring in the most outcasts or scholars that do not go to any other school.' In 1878 the school had a respectable seventy scholars, and by 1885 this had increased to 134. Even the smaller churches had sizeable Sunday schools: the Irwell Vale Primitive Methodists counted 149 children in 1875; the Evangelical Sunday School had 91 scholars in 1879 and St. Peter's, Ewood Bridge recorded 101 scholars and ten teachers in 1896.[45]

RELIGIOUS EDUCATION

From the end of the 18th century, children at the Parish Church received some rudimentary religious instruction by learning the catechism: the Rev. John Smith said in 1778 that the children attended church three or four times a year to be catechised and on these occasions he adapted his sermon to illustrate the catechism. The Nonconformist churches did not introduce catechism classes until the 1870s and 1880s, but their Sunday school scholars received religious instruction in other ways. For example, in the 1840s and 1850s, the Irwell Vale Primitive Methodists held a twenty minute Bible class before teaching their children how to write. Secular and religious education stood side by side in a similar way at the Edenfield Primitive Methodist Sunday school in 1865 when the Superintendent was asked to order three dozen spelling books and one dozen Testaments. A few years earlier both the Primitives and the Congregationalists had set up Tract Societies.[46]

In the second half of the 19th century, other small changes were made to the way in which the Sunday schools were taught. At Irwell Vale in 1882 all of the teachers were to 'mention to each Scholar the desirability of repeating the Lord's Prayer after the Superintendent when opening the School.' The Edenfield Primitives introduced the same practice in 1889 and two years later they also started to read out the Ten Commandments once a month. By this date there were all sorts of help for Sunday school teachers. National organisations provided special hymn-books, magazines and courses of lessons. The Wesleyans, for instance, adopted the Wesleyan Sunday School Union Code of Lessons in 1896, with scripture books and object lessons for the younger children. Visiting lecturers also provided variety during the week, expounding on topics such as 'The Tabernacle and Its Witness Illustrated by Diagram', which the Irwell Vale Sunday school heard in 1888.[47]

In addition to religious education and preparing children for church membership in adulthood, the Sunday schools played an important role in providing basic instruction in reading and writing. We have seen that at Irwell Vale in the 1840s and 1850s the Sunday morning Bible class was followed by twenty minutes or half an hour of handwriting, and in 1862 the Wesleyans decided, 'That we begin to spell in the classes every Sunday from 10 o'clock & 2 o'clock until closing time.' Similarly, the Primitive Methodists had both alphabet and spelling classes into the early 1890s.[48]

Most of the Sunday schools had their own library. The Wesleyans opened theirs in 1841 and by 1851 had 224 books to which both teachers and scholars had free access. The Primitives Methodists in both Edenfield and Irwell Vale had libraries of similar size, but it was the Congregationalists who had the largest one of all with 760 volumes in 1885. Each church appointed a librarian to look after its books and drew up sets of rules governing their use. The Primitive Methodists, for example, decided in March 1871 that any one keeping a book longer than a fortnight should pay 1d for the first fortnight, 2d for the next fortnight and so on until the book was returned. A selection of books in the Wesleyan library at Christmas 1887 included 'The city: its sins and sorrows', 'Sketches of Glasgow Necropolis', 'Life and times of Alexander Von Humboldt', 'No gains without pains', 'The traffic in strong drink' as well as several novels including 'Uncle Tom's Cabin', 'Persuasion' and 'Northanger Abbey'. Some of the Sunday school libraries survived into the 20th century, that at Stubbins Congregational Church being dispersed in June 1929.[49]

Strict rules governing the behaviour of both the teachers and the children had to be obeyed. The minute books of the various Sunday school teachers' meetings include complaints of unpunctuality on the part of the teachers, and when preparing for the Whitsuntide celebrations in 1862 the Wesleyans decided that fines should be levied on all teachers who arrived late for the procession. All married teachers were to be fined 6d each, while unmarried male teachers were to be fined 2s 6d each, unless a satisfactory reason could be given for their tardiness. Children attending the Sunday school at Irwell Vale in 1873 had to be cautioned 'against lounging about the School door when they ought to be inside', while in 1866 the Edenfield Primitive Methodists found the attendance and attention of the first class of boys was satisfactory, 'but their Morals and religious Desires are not so good as desirable.' Some years later, in 1913, the vicar of Edenfield found he had to make an appeal for more Sunday school teachers because some of his staff had resigned owing to the rudeness of some of the children. In his letter in the parish magazine he said:

> It is distinctly hard lines on teachers who have taken the trouble to get up a lesson and devote well-earned leisure to helping other people's children, when they find their efforts repaid by insolence.[50]

WHITSUNTIDE AND CHRISTMAS

WHITSUNTIDE

The Sunday school year was punctuated by a number of special occasions that were eagerly anticipated by both scholars and teachers. We have already noted the Sermons and of equal importance were the Whitsuntide festivities. Until the 1950s each church or chapel usually held its own procession, although Market Place and Rochdale Road Methodists occasionally joined forces in the 1930s. St. Philip's and Stubbins Congregationalists began holding joint processions in 1951 and the Parish Church and the Methodists followed their example in 1959. Irwell Vale and St. Peter's, Ewood Bridge always held separate walks, although in 1959 Irwell Vale joined the two other Methodist churches in Edenfield.

A substantial part of the population of Edenfield and district participated in the Whit Walks. In the 1870s, for instance, small churches like Irwell Vale and Ewood Bridge regularly numbered over 100 and 200 in their respective processions. On Whit Friday 1903, when the Whit Walks were at the height of their popularity, more than 450 people took part in the Parish Church procession, 400 walked for the Wesleyan Methodists and 240 for the Primitives. Numbers began to fall after the Second World War, although in the 1950s the St. Philip's/Congregational procession could still number over 300 and in 1999 there were more than 200 in the Parish Church/St. Philip's walk. The nature of the Whitsuntide celebrations had also begun to change in the 1930s: at a meeting in October 1938 the Rochdale Road congregation decided that there was no point in going on with the traditional arrangements. The main reasons given were the difficulties caused by increased traffic, shortage of help for catering, a lack of interest among the young people in either the procession or the following field sports and finally the extended holiday giving people the opportunity to go away. The Parish Church gave a similar reason in 1949 when they too abandoned the Whit Friday Field Day.[51]

Each church had clearly defined routes for their walks. In part these were determined by topography: for example, Irwell Vale tended to walk to Lumb or Ewood Bridge and back simply because the situation of the village made it difficult to follow a circular route. The new housing estates at Edenfield and Stubbins built in the inter-war years and the 1950s also acted as magnets, drawing the processions off their old routes so as to include people living in the new houses. A second factor that determined where the walks went and where halts were made to sing hymns was the location of the homes of the well-to-do members of the congregations. Until the 1920s, most of the processions were planned to take in as many of these houses as possible. At the beginning of the 20th century, for instance, the Primitive Methodists called at The Mount, then the home of the Barlows who ran Bridge Mills, while the Parish Church called at the vicarage, Hawthorn House (home of Richard Walton, vicar's warden) and Horncliffe House (home of the Hardmans who owned New Hall Hey Mills). Similarly, the Congregationalists stopped at Rose Bank House, Green Mount and Stubbins Vale House (where they were allowed to walk through the extensive greenhouses and where oranges were given out). After the Second World War the processionists tended to stop to sing hymns at the homes of aged and sick members of the congregations, but the custom of calling at the homes of the local mill owners lingered on for some time. In 1957, for example, the united procession of the Stubbins Congregational Church and St. Philip's stopped at Highbury where Mrs. Turnbull gave out bags of sweets to the children.[52]

Although Whit Walks in the 20th century could be quite long, they were nothing compared to the marathons of the 19th century. In June 1874, the Ewood Bridge procession visited Ewood Hall and Horncliffe House before returning to the school for lunch at twelve o'clock. They then set off again to call at Bent Gate and Musbury vicarage at Gregory Fold before returning to a field near the Woolpack for sports. One participant in the Parish Church procession a few years earlier in 1868 later recalled:

> Leaving the school at 9.30, our first halt was at Elton Banks, the residence of the late Mr. John Aitken, where we sang a hymn and our teachers and elders partook of refreshments, then through the grounds of Horncliffe House, which was being rebuilt and on to Mr. Richard Hardman's of Cliff Tower (hymns and refreshments). We next ascended "The Rake", and visited Mr. James Walton, then via Balladen to "The Carr", the temporary home of Mr. Henry Hoyle Hardman (more hymns and refreshments). Returning through Townsendfold to Edenfield our next objective was Chatterton Hey, then inhabited by Mr. James Rostron (more hymns and refreshments). The next stage was down Bolton-road, through Chatterton and Strongstry to the late Mr. John Austin's house. On our return journey we were driven to shelter under Stubbins railway arch by a heavy thunderstorm which the writer has cause to remember, for he was the proud possessor of a new velvet coat which liberally spread its dye over his neck and hands thus imparting a striking resemblance to a tiger. The storm having abated we dragged our weary footsteps to Mr. John Duckworth's, Sheep Hey (more hymns and refreshments), then back through Brown Bent and Nimble Nook to the school, where we did ample justice to the tea awaiting us.

Whitsuntide processions over the years. Teachers and pupils of St. Peter's, Ewood Bridge pose outside the school in about 1900. Rochdale Road (ex-Primitive) Methodists stop to sing a hymn on the council house estate in the early 1930s. St. Philip's on Bolton Road North in the 1950s. The Parish Church procession setting off from Church Lane in 1997.

Those who were capable of walking then visited the Rev. Matthew Wilson, at the vicarage, returning to a field behind the school to spend the evening in playing "kiss and turn", "shy widow" and other popular games of those bygone days.[53]

The Whit celebrations did not end when the processions broke up, for the participants usually adjourned to a nearby field for an afternoon of sports and games. The band that had led the procession often stayed to provide music, although the Wesleyans would not allow them to play for dancing. Games of cricket and football were usually on the programme, while in 1874, St. Peter's, Ewood Bridge also held sack and wheelbarrow races. The Congregationalists had an even more varied programme in 1916:

> In addition to races for members of the primary and junior departments of the Sunday school, an egg and spoon race had been arranged for the young ladies, while a blind-folded carriage race for mothers evoked much fun, as did a pillow-slip fight for men.[54]

At the end of the afternoon the walkers made their way back to their respective Sunday schools for tea. Huge amounts of food had been prepared to feed the multitudes. The Wesleyans in 1842, for example, bought 3 lbs of treacle, 12 lbs of currants, seeds, cinnamon, lump sugar, brown sugar, and tea, coffee, butter and milk. By 1886 the Provision Committee decided that they needed 80 lb of plain bread, 80 lb of teacakes, 36 lb of currant bread, 32 lbs of butter, 52 lbs of sugar, 3 lbs of tea, 6½ lbs of coffee and 750 buns. The other churches provided similar kinds of foods in similar quantities, although in 1861 the Primitive Methodists washed down their meal with Henry Wallwork's 'cowfoot and nettle drink.'[55]

An evening's entertainment of songs and recitations given by the scholars usually ended the day. Recalling such an event at Dearden Clough Mill in the 1840s one former Sunday school scholar at Park chapel said:

> A room in the mill would have been cleared of machinery, and temporary tables erected, and tea was served to all the children, and any members of the congregation were also made welcome. After the cloths had been removed it was the practice to give from a platform a miscellaneous entertainment. The scholars would sing, and recite their pieces – Mr. Joseph [Joseph Porritt] took a keen interest in training them – and altogether these events were very enjoyable.

In the 1870s two churches – Ewood Bridge and Stubbins – ended the day's proceedings by letting off balloons.[56]

Whit Saturday was often the occasion for scholars to be treated to a trip out, either to a local picnic spot like Waugh's Well or to somewhere further afield. These could be long days: when the Parish Church Sunday school went to Preston in three wagonettes in 1901 they left Edenfield at seven o'clock in the morning and did not get back until after midnight. Similarly in 1916 Stubbins Congregational Sunday school walked all the way to Sunnyhurst Woods at Darwen, caught the tram to Blackburn 'where a short time was spent in shop-gazing', travelled by train to Helmshore and then walked back to Stubbins.[57]

CHRISTMAS

At the opposite end of the calendar from the Whitsuntide celebrations stood the annual Christmas or New Year parties. Again these were hugely popular events, often thrown open to the general public and attracting large numbers. Four hundred people sat down to tea at the Evangelical Sunday School's party in 1876, 440 at the Primitive Methodists in 1891, 350 at the Wesleyans in 1906, 250 at Irwell Vale in 1909, 344 at Ewood Bridge in 1916 and 300 at the Parish Church in 1939. The crowds of partygoers were served tea in relays, a Primitive Methodist minute in 1857 noting that the boys were to be given their food first, but that the tablecloths were not to be put on until they had finished. Like the Whit teas, astonishing amounts of provisions had to be bought to cater for the multitudes. To take just one example: in 1866 the Wesleyans bought 60 lbs of flour for plain bread, 50 lbs for teacakes, 45 lbs for currant bread, 25 lbs of currants, 20 lbs of beef, 46 lbs of ham, 22 lbs of mutton, 22 lbs of new butter, 28 lbs of lump sugar, 4¾ lbs of tea, 15 qrts of milk and 3 qrts of cream. To ease the task of preparation slightly the Primitives asked their Superintendent to try to get a machine for slicing bread in readiness for their New Year's Day party in 1868.[58]

Typical of the scene that must have greeted the partygoers on these occasions was that found at Stubbins Congregational church in December 1872 described here by a reporter from the *Bury Times*:

> From the rafters were suspended festoonings of evergreens interspersed with a choice variety of artificial flowers. The large gasoliers were artistically ornamented with trimmings of coloured paper, and in the space between these a pendant of evergreens hung from the ceiling, to each of which there was attached a cluster of beautiful flowers. The walls were relieved with several seasonable mottoes, including "Unto us a child is born; unto us a son is given", "A Merry Christmas", "A Happy New Year", &c. enclosed with a rustically arranged bordering of holly, &c. The two pillars in front of the platform were decked with a spiral wreathing of holly &c., and extending from one pillar to the other was the proclamation "Glory to God in the highest, and on earth goodwill towards men" in white letters on a red ground.[59]

The entertainment that followed the tea was at first quite serious in character. On Christmas Day 1867, for instance, the Congregationalists heard 'an interesting and instructive address' on Sunday school tuition, while in 1870 no less than four clergymen gave talks to the Primitive Methodists. In 1876, the Ewood Bridge party began with an exhibition of 'dissolving views' [lantern slides] given by the Padiham Musical and Dissolving View Company, which included 'scenes of the late Ashantee war', and in the same year the teachers and scholars of the Evangelical Sunday school performed a sacred drama entitled 'Joseph and His Brethren'. In the late 19th century the after-tea concerts became more varied and light-hearted. Typical of the many that were given over the years was that performed by the Primitive Methodists in 1891, which was watched by over five hundred people. The programme included glees, action songs, humorous songs, duets, recitations, a violin

Children at Irwell Vale Methodist Chapel performing a nativity play as part of the Sunday service in December 1973.

solo and two dialogues entitled 'The confidential clerk' and 'The wedding at the mill'. In the years just before the First World War short musical plays (usually referred to as 'cantatas' or 'operettas') became a popular item at most of the Christmas concerts. Many were based on well-known fairy tales or had similar stories and included 'Snow White' at Irwell Vale in 1908 and 'The Butterfly Queen', 'Red Cap in Fairy Land', 'The Magic Ruby or the Rajah of Rajahpore' and 'The Little Man in the Moon' at Ewood Bridge and Stubbins during the war and the 1920s. These productions were still being performed at the Parish Church in the early '30s, but elsewhere were being replaced by full-scale pantomimes. As we shall see, pantomimes tended to be staged separately from the Christmas party, but the Parish Church combined the two, beginning with 'Robinson Crusoe' in 1936.[60]

From the 1860s the Primitive Methodists made their annual party the occasion for the presentation of prizes for good attendance. The Congregationalists and Evangelical Sunday school soon followed their example, but it was not until the 20th century that the practice became usual at all the local churches. Another innovation introduced at Stubbins in the 1920s and later copied by the other Sunday schools was the appearance of Father Christmas to give out presents to the children. At Ewood Bridge in the early 1930s he heralded his arrival by walking through the village ringing a bell or blowing a trumpet.[61]

MUTUAL IMPROVEMENT SOCIETIES

As well as educating and entertaining their children, the churches also provided opportunities for both education and recreation for young adults. They set up various organisations – generally known as Mutual Improvement Societies – whose aim was to encourage their members to spend their time in a worthwhile manner. Indeed, when the Primitive Methodist Young Men's Literary Society was established in 1877 it was declared that it was 'for the improvement of their minds' and that all members were to 'try to cultivate their minds and acquire information.'[62] The first of these societies – The Edenfield Young Men's Institute – was set up at the Wesleyan chapel in 1856 and by the end of the 1880s had been joined by similar organisations at Stubbins Congregational church, the Primitive Methodist chapel, the Parish Church and Irwell Vale chapel. Although each society was attached to a particular church or chapel, they were non-sectarian and welcomed all denominations to their meetings.

The chance survival of the first minute book of the Wesleyan society gives us a good idea of how the Mutual Improvement Societies operated. Modest quarterly subscriptions of 2s 6d (for those over 21), 2s (16-20) and 1s 6d (under 16) gave members access to a newsroom stocked with various papers and periodicals, including *The Examiner*, *The Times*, *Preston Guardian*, *London Evening Star*, *Illustrated London News*, *Punch*, *Leisure Hour*, *Sun at Home*, *Band of Hope*, *London Journal*, *British Workman*, *Bury Miscellany* and *Musical Times*. At the end of 1856 the *Bury Times* and *Cassells' Illustrated Family Paper* were also bought for junior members. In March 1867 the Stubbins Mutual Improvement Society reported that it was 'hoped shortly to have a good public library which would be useful not only to the members but for general reading for every person who wished to become a subscriber.' A year later there were some one hundred books in the library.[63]

Shortly after the Wesleyan Institute began, its members decided that young women should also be allowed in for one night a week on the payment of a quarterly subscription of 1s. The activities of all the societies were broadly similar and had a strong educational slant. The programme for the Wesleyans in April 1856 was: -

> Monday – arithmetic and writing
> Tuesday – reading and discussion
> Wednesday – grammar and dictation
> Thursday – arithmetic and writing for females
> Friday – arithmetic and writing

Six villagers were appointed teachers and supplies of copybooks, pens and penholders were bought. 'What are the causes of thunder and lightening?' was the first subject that they chose for discussion. In February 1858, drawing was added to the curriculum one night a week for a month. As well as the weekly classes, the Mutual Improvement Societies also organised lectures given by visiting speakers. Villagers were thus given the opportunity to learn something of wide variety of topics. In

1857, for example, those who went along to the Wesleyan Sunday school heard about old proverbs, vagrancy in old times, Shakespeare and his writings and money and its mysteries. Some years later, Robert Brown of Haslingden brought along a nest of ants to illustrate his talk on the intelligence of ants, while in 1889 the Edenfield Church Schools Young Men's Association heard a lecture about the telephone from Dr. J.L. Kerr of Crawshawbooth. In October 1867, when the Rev. Robert Best lectured to the Stubbins Mutual Improvement Society he illustrated his talk on a recent view of Rome with 'photographic pictures and inscriptions from the catacombs.' So delighted were his audience that they cheered frequently during his speech. In the 1890s the same society heard lectures on the evolution of religion, the life of Cromwell, stamps and their peculiarities, the antiquity of man, and the Remington typewriter. Questions they debated included 'Is war justifiable?' and 'Should child labour be abolished?' At Stubbins the programme of self-improvement and education was taken a step further in 1888 with the formation of an ambulance class taught by Dr. William Deans of Ramsbottom.[64]

Like most of the other church organisations, the Mutual Improvement Societies put on entertainments for their members. The Wesleyans, for example, had three tea parties in their first year and were treated to a performance of a drama entitled 'The teetotal chairman in a fix' at one and songs by the Edenfield Glee Singers at another. There were glee singers too at the first annual tea party and soiree of the Stubbins Mutual Improvement Society at the Congregational Church in March 1867 when four hundred sat down for tea. At another party in 1903 the programme included songs, games and gramophone selections.[65]

Most of the Mutual Improvement Societies came to an end in the years before the First World War, but their spirit lived on in similar organisations. The Congregationalists opened an institute in 1907 to provide games and reading material each night from six o'clock to ten. The Young Men's Class at the Primitive Methodist chapel heard talks on many different topics well into the 1950s. They included capital punishment, South Africa, radar, penicillin, tobacco smoking and its effects and the life of Handel. In 1921 the members of the class decided to form themselves into a branch of the League of Nations Union and as such they held meetings and talks until the Second World War. Lighter moments at some of the other churches included a lecture by 'Romany' (the Rev. Bramwell Evans) at Market Place Methodists in January 1942 and a series of lantern lectures at Irwell Vale in 1950, which included views of the Lake District and Switzerland.[66]

TEMPERANCE

In the second half of the 19th century, all of the local churches took up the fight against strong drink and drunkenness by instilling a desire for sobriety among their children and young people. First into the fray were the Congregationalists who set up a Band of Hope while they were still meeting at Stubbins Vale Mill. It was short-lived, but was re-established in 1882 and soon had 260 members. When its majority was celebrated in 1903 several ex-members wrote 'expressing heartfelt thanks for the words of encouragement they received whilst attending the meeting held in connection with the society which had enabled them to withstand the temptations of strong drink.'[67]

The Wesleyans had copied the Congregationalists' example by 1864 and the Primitives at Edenfield and Irwell Vale followed suit in 1873. The Parish Church does not seem to have been so enthusiastic in championing the temperance cause, although by the beginning of the 20th century it had set up a branch of the Church of England Juvenile Temperance Society. In 1889 and 1890 a United Gospel Temperance Mission helped the efforts of the churches in the village: in August 1889 a procession of about 380 people walked from one end of the village to the other 'and a kindly invitation thrown out to all who had not yet taken the pledge', after which buns and coffee were served in the Co-op hall and there was dancing, cricket and football in a nearby field. Other organisations that were separate from the churches also played their part in the fight against strong drink. They included a branch of the Independent Order of Rechabites (a teetotal benefit society) and visits from the Blue Ribbon Army, a temperance movement whose members wore a blue ribbon as a mark that they had signed the pledge.[68]

Like many other church organisations, the activities of the Bands of Hope were a mixture of entertainment and edification. Members heard lectures with titles such as 'Objections to teetotalism answered', attended prayer meetings at 7.30am on Temperance Sunday and received prizes of books entitled 'The Methodist Temperance Manual' and 'Alcohol – what it is and what it does'. The entertainment after tea parties often consisted of a mixture of songs, recitations and addresses, although in 1877 the Wesleyans listened to the Bacup Temperance Handbell Ringers. Somewhat lighter in tone were the annual picnics to local beauty spots. In May 1904, for instance, the Parish Church Juvenile Temperance Society picnicked at Waugh's Well where tea was followed by three-legged races and games of football, hymn singing at a nearby farmhouse and the distribution of oranges, nuts and sweets. Interest in the temperance societies declined after the First World War, but the Band of Hope at Irwell Vale lingered on until 1939. As late as 1937 at the annual meeting it was noted that some of the children had signed the pledge.[69]

UNIFORMS AND YOUTH CLUBS

In the early years of the 20th century some of the churches decided to provide entertainments for their young people outside of Sunday school activities. At the Parish Church a Lads' Club was formed in 1904 to provide lectures and gymnastic exercises; it was revived during the First World War to teach physical drill. In the meantime, Boy Scout troops had made their appearance in the district. The Edenfield troop held their first paper chase in March 1911, taking a route up to New

Edenfield Brownies and Guides helping to celebrate the bi-centenary of the building of the Parish Church in 1978.

Hall, Scout Moor Reservoir and Scout Moor Quarry. Tea was followed by drill, a gymnastic display and camp amusements and in the evening the troop paraded through the village, 'a considerable crowd ... assembling to see them off, whilst groups of people lined the streets and bursts of admiration were heard on every hand.' In August of the same year, the Stubbins troop camped at Castleton in Derbyshire. They walked the forty-two miles to their destination, setting off one Friday night at nine o'clock and arriving on Sunday. At the end of the week they were supposed to travel home by train, but a railway strike put paid to their plans and they had to walk all the way. 'There were no complaints, however, the lads facing the task with the pluck that tells.' In the inter-war years and after the Second World War the Scouts were joined by Cubs, Brownies and Guides at Rochdale Road and Irwell Vale Methodists, the Parish Church and St. Philip's.[70]

Other efforts were made to cater for the needs of young people in a less formal way. The ex-Wesleyans were pioneers in this field when in 1935 they set aside one of the classrooms for 'use of a young person's social evening to play table tennis and lexicon, &c.' In April 1943 one of their events was a screening of the film 'The Romance of Cotton' produced by David Whitehead and Sons of Rawtenstall. Six years later a youth club at Stubbins Congregational Church started to meet every Friday night providing badminton, billiards, table tennis and arts and handicrafts for its members. In September of the same year, St. Peter's Youth Club at Ewood Bridge opened in the old village reading room, which had been equipped with a dart board and billiard table. The *Ramsbottom Observer* commented:

> For the young people, hitherto deprived of such facilities, the club should provide a blessing, particularly during the long winter evenings and affords great opportunities for communal recreation as well as the many other facets of Youth Club activity.[71]

A 'good news' club for boys and girls opened at Rochdale Road chapel in October 1951 and at the same church in 1959 Edenfield Youth Club got under way with ten members. By the beginning of the following year membership had risen to fifty and the club provided a programme of visiting speakers as well as facilities for playing games. The Rochdale Road example was followed in the early 1960s by St. Philip's and Irwell Vale Methodists, both of which started their own youth clubs.[72]

ORGANISATIONS FOR ADULTS

Each church also had groups aimed solely at the adults in their congregations. The Mothers' Union at the Parish Church, St. Philip's and St. Peter's, for example, was matched by the Ladies' Guild at the Primitive Methodist chapel, and the Ladies' Aid at the Wesleyans and Irwell Vale Primitives. Similarly, St. Philip's had a Men's Guild and later a Men's Fellowship, while the Parish Church set up a branch of the Church of England Men's Society. Whatever the title of these groups, their activities were often similar, providing entertainment for their members and making the churches the very centre of the social life of the villages.

A few examples of events organised by the ladies at the various churches give us a flavour of the variety of amusements on offer. In January 1913, the members of the Parish Church Mothers' Union sat down to a 'surprise tea':

> All of them took certain eatables to the schoolroom, and these were mixed up one with another, those who attended subsequently partook of whatever delicacies happened to come their way. It proved a "surprise tea" in every sense of the word, and, needless to say, there was much merriment and general enjoyment.

During the 1920s and 1930s, short plays or 'Lancashire Sketches' became very popular. With titles like 'Anastasia joins t' Domino Club' and 'Custard and Rhubarb i' Paris', these productions usually played to full houses. In October 1932 Edenfield could even boast a world premiere when the Rochdale Road Methodist Ladies' Guild, helped out by a few of their husbands, presented 'Nowt so queer as folk', written by their minister, the Rev. William Killcross. During the summer months there was also usually a trip out to look forward to.[73]

Edenfield Methodist Ladies Guild enjoying a cup of tea at their meeting on
14th November 1995.

FUND RAISING AND FUN FOR EVERYONE

Most of the church activities we have looked at so far were intended for the different
sections of the congregations or Sunday schools, but on many occasions all the
churchgoers came together to raise money for their particular church or simply to
enjoy themselves. More often than not, of course, they did both at the same time.
Fund raising events came in all sorts of shapes and sizes, although as late as 1928 the
trustees of the Wesleyan chapel decided that they did not 'desire our people to raise
money for church and school purposes by Dancing.' Until the 1950s, whenever a
church needed to raise large sums for a major scheme of alteration or to pay off
money owing on the building, they usually held a bazaar. These events lasted three
or four days and took months of planning, often with small events to raise money for
the bazaar itself. Many were given a theme that allowed the participants to give free
rein to their imaginations. At the Wesleyan bazaar in December 1870, for instance,
there were five stalls:

> Each stall was semi-circular, the roof being of the tent pattern, and covered in with
> artistically arranged pieces of red, white and blue calico, while muslin pieces were
> suspended along the whole length.

The ladies of the Parish Church chose a 'Bon Marché Boulonais' as the theme for their event in October 1918. The occasion opened with 'a charming tableau' entitled 'Preparing for the Market', followed by a prologue in verse, set to music, after which the market room was thrown open to reveal the stallholders dressed in 'the Boulonnais costume.'[74]

When the members of Stubbins mission were raising money to pay for the church that became St. Philip's, they held a three day bazaar in 1924 and taking their cue from the recently held British Empire Exhibition at Wembley, they called it 'Wembley in Edenfield'. This event raised over £1,000 in two days. Similarly, the Congregationalists christened their 1934 bazaar 'A Winter Cruise' with the stage set out as a ship's deck. Children were dressed as sailors and each of the five stalls represented a different port of call. As well as being able to spend freely on all sorts of items, bazaar goers were usually entertained with songs and short sketches and, of course, tea was always available. Somewhat unusual was one of the attractions at the Wesleyan bazaar in December 1870 that included a museum of 'curious articles' among which were ashes from Vesuvius, a pair of Prussian clogs, a Persian lady's pipe, a case of sea monsters, part of the first steam boat 'The Lady Charlotte Dundas' and a bayonet from the field of Waterloo. In contrast, almost one hundred years later the biggest draw at a bring and buy sale organised by the Parish Church was the appearance of Margot Bryant who played Minnie Caldwell in 'Coronation Street'.[75]

While bazaars were usually held in the winter, the summer months brought opportunities for other activities. Outdoor events were the particular forte of St. Philip's and Stubbins Congregational Church and were variously styled garden parties, country fairs, galas or fetes. They were usually held in the grounds of one of the large houses in the district such as Chatterton Hey or Rose Bank House or in a field adjoining the church. Though each occasion had its own flavour, they generally offered a variety of stalls and sideshows, fancy dress parades, sports and games, and music provided by a local brass band or other group. Over the years additions were occasionally made to this well tried mixture, but not always with success: a beauty show at the Congregational garden party in 1910 had to be abandoned 'as only two or three of the ladies came forward despite the complimentary suggestion that there were many more beautiful persons in the gathering.' Baby shows proved more successful when introduced by the Congregationalists and St. Philip's in the late 1930s. Great ingenuity went into devising new sports to join the usual flat races, egg and spoon races and so on. They included a tug of war between married and single ladies at Irwell Vale Primitive Methodists in 1916 (the married ladies won) and a slow cycle race and clock golf competition at St. Philip's in 1929. Attractions at some of the post-war events included tableaux on lorries, knobbly knees competitions and, at St. Philip's in 1960, a 'novelty feature' of the afternoon was a stall 'where hot-dogs were cooked barbecue style and served on the spot.'[76]

An increasingly important part of the summer fetes in the 1930s and more so after the Second World War, was the Rose Queen crowning ceremony. Stubbins Congre-

Two Rose Queens. (*Left*) Ivy Haworth at Stubbins Congregational church in 1931 and (*Below*) Margaret Smith at the Parish Church in 1950. With Margaret are her attendants Jean Quinton, Hazel Dearden, Patsy Kay and Julia Kay and cushion bearer Roger Barlow.

gationalists were pioneers in choosing one of the Sunday school girls as queen for a year. Their first one was Ivy Haworth in 1931. She and her successor, Esme Lewis, were called Cotton Queens in imitation of the *Daily Dispatch* competition that started in 1931, but the title Rose Queen was used from 1933 onwards. In the following year the idea was taken up enthusiastically by St. Philip's, Irwell Vale followed suit in 1935 and the Parish Church in 1936. Rose Queen ceremonies were interrupted by the war, but were revived at the Parish Church in 1947, St. Philip's in 1948, briefly at Irwell Vale in the mid-1950s and at the Congregational church in the late 1960s.[77]

Concerts, plays and pantomimes brightened many a dark winter's evening. Variety concerts were always popular and over the years included songs, recitations, dances, and sketches. As tastes and fashions changed so did the content of these shows. The entertainment given by Stubbins Congregationalists in March 1869 consisted of 'a judicious selection of vocal music and recitations … very creditably gone through by the choir and scholars.' From the 1890s to the 1920s, 'minstrel entertainments' were popular and troupes were formed at the Parish Church, Stubbins Congregational Church and the Primitive Methodist chapel, while in March 1917 the 'Au Courant' Pierrot Troupe from Ramsbottom entertained the members of Turn Mission. 'Tableaux vivants' made regular appearances on concert programmes until the early 1900s. At the event organised by the band and banner committee of the Wesleyan chapel in February 1906, for instance, the tableaux included 'The Village Wedding', 'The Gypsy Warning', 'She Wore a Wreath of Roses' and 'Before and After Marriage.' The tableaux often had a religious theme and somewhat similar were sacred plays or pageants that were given occasionally. At the Parish Church in November 1909 for instance, 'a storyette symbolic of the introduction of Christianity to this country' entitled 'The Coming of the Dawn' was performed before a large audience. Some fifty years later there were full houses at St. Philip's and Rochdale Road Methodist Church when they staged 'By Thy Glorious Resurrection' and 'Pictures Come to Life'.[78]

It was a short step from some of the comedy sketches to full-scale pantomimes, something at which Rochdale Road Methodists excelled. In the 1930s their resident playwright, the Rev. William Killcross, wrote no less than six three-act pantomimes, all of which were immensely popular. For example, one Saturday evening in 1935 the audience began queuing to see 'Babes in the Wood' ninety minutes before curtain up and more then one hundred people had to be turned away because the show had sold out. Mr. Killcross's pantomimes often included original songs and a script with a local flavour 'which caused shouts of laughter.' Villagers have fond memories of Tom Hillis as the dame with Albert Kendall as his comedy partner. These two men took over the job of writing and producing the pantomimes after the Rev. Killcross had left the village, beginning with 'Aladdin' in 1938. The success of the Rochdale Road pantomimes was later emulated by the Parish Church and St. Philip's whose productions continued until the early 1960s. In the early 1990s, the Parish Church revived its annual pantomime with great success.[79]

Two of the many pantomimes that have been staged in Edenfield over the years. The older picture shows the cast of 'Aladdin' at Rochdale Road Methodist Chapel in 1938, while the Parish Church gave the production of 'Snow White' in 1994.

NOTES

1.   Edenfield parish records (MCL: MF PR 117a)
2.   Archdeacon Rushton's visitation returns (MCL: MSf 942.72 R121 vol 15); L. Longworth, *Edenfield Church and School History Notebook*, (1989), pp. 14, 29-30; RO 28th April 1911
3.   L. Longworth, *op. cit.*, p.28; J. Betjeman (ed.), *Collins Pocket Guide to English Parish Churches: The North*, (1968), p.153
4.   RO 4th November 1898, 18th July 1919; BT 6th June 1885
5.   RO 10th July 1908, 8th November 1912, 24th September 1920, 5th December 1924
6.   RO 25th August 1922, 5th October 1923, 4th June 1926, 3rd June 1927, 26th May 1933, 29th April 1949, 7th August 1959; L. Longworth, *op. cit*, p.52
7.   Blackburn Standard 18th March 1840; Musbury parish magazine February 1959; S.J. Winward, *Musbury Crown: story of school and church 1815 - 1977* (1977); Musbury parish magazine June 1889, November 1891
8.   RO 30th June 1893
9.   Articles of Enquiry preparatory to Visitation, 1778 (Cheshire Record Office: EDV7/1, vol. 2)
10.   Register of dissenters' meeting houses (LRO: QDV/4); 'History of Methodism in Edenfield' (LRO: MAc uncat.)
11.   BT 19th June 1869, 25th May 1878; Haslingden Circuit. The Wesleyan Methodist Preachers' Plan 1838-1839 (author's collection)
12.   Wesleyan Methodist Sunday school committee minute book 1841-1866 (BAS: CRM/T1267); BT 19th June 1869, 3rd June 1876, 25th May 1878; RO 1st January 1960
13.   Bury Primitive Methodist Circuit Quarter Day minute book 1836-1852 (BAS: CBP/T1268); J. Simpson, *Irwell Vale. A centenary history of the Methodist church*, (1993), pp. 5, 8-9; RO 17th July 1925
14.   BT 16th April 1881, 18th October 1890; RO 29th September 1911; Haslingden Guardian 4th November 1893
15.   Stubbins Congregational Church record book 1860-1928 (BAS: CST/1); W.E. Harding, *The history of Park Congregational church, Ramsbottom*, (1931) p. 85;
16.   Harding, *op. cit.*, p. 87; P. Barrett & Co., *Directory and topography of Bury, Heywood, Ramsbottom ... and adjacent villages and townships*, (1880); RO 4th March 1932
17.   J. Barnes, *Historical Notes on Stubbins Congregational Church* [typescript], (1985), pp.12-13; Rossendale Herald and Post 11th April 1991
18.   B.A. Ramsbottom, 'Limey Leach and Cheesden Pasture', *The Strict Baptist Historical Society, annual report and bulletin*, (1974); A survey and valuation of the township of Walmersley cum Shuttleworth 1842 (LRO: PUB/8/3)
19.   Harding, *op. cit.*, p. 80
20.   RO 25th September 1914, 9th October 1914, 19th February 1915, 25th February 1916, 24th January 1919, 31st December 1937, 4th January 1957; BT 19th December 1914
21.   Articles of Enquiry preparatory to Visitation, 1778, 1821 and 1825 (Cheshire Record Office: EDV7/1, vol. 2; EDV7/6, vol. 3; EDV7/7, vol. 2)
22.   Articles of Enquiry preparatory to Visitation, 1804 (Cheshire Record Office: EDV7/3, vol. 2)
23.   J. Stott, *Notices of Methodism in Haslingden*, (1898), pp. 54-55; 'History of Methodism in Edenfield' (LRO: MAc uncat.); Haslingden Circuit. The Wesleyan Methodist Preachers' Plan 1838-1839 (author's collection); Census of religious worship, 1851 (PRO: HO 129/477); Bury Primitive Methodist Circuit quarterly minute book 1899-1913 (BAS: CBP/T1477)
24.   Census of religious worship, 1851 (PRO: HO 129/477); Episcopal visitation returns 1931 (MCL: M39/97)
25.   Articles of Enquiry preparatory to Visitation, 1804 (Cheshire Record Office: EDV7/3, vol. 2)
26.   Stubbins Congregational church meeting minute book 1896-1974 (BAS: CST/2/1); Irwell Vale Methodist church trustees' minute book 1949-1964 (LRO: MAc uncat.); RO 2nd December 1960; RFP 9th July 1965
27.   RO 28th July 1899, 17th July 1925; B.A. Ramsbottom, 'Limey Leach and Cheesden Pasture', *The Strict Baptist Historical Society, annual report and bulletin*, (1974)
28.   RO 20th May 1921
29.   Wesleyan Methodist Sunday School minute book 1881-1889 (BAS: CRM/T1482)
30.   BT 10th June 1865; RO 2nd August 1895
31.   RO 13th May 1898; 15th April 1960
32.   BT 26th October 1878; Irwell Vale Methodist church trustees' minute book 1853-1947 (LRO: MAc uncat.); RO 17th April 1942, 12th April 1957, 15th April 1960

33 Edenfield parish records [churchwardens' acounts and plan of church 1777] (MCL: MF PR 117a); Archdeacon Rushton's visitation returns, letter dated 30th August 1852 (MCL: MSf 942.72 R121 vol 15)

34 RO 17th July 1925; J. Simpson, *Irwell Vale: a centenary history of the Methodist church*, (1993), p.6; W.E. Harding, *The history of Park Congregational church, Ramsbottom*, (1931), p.76; Primitive Methodist Sunday school teachers' meeting minute book 1857-1866 (BAS: CRR/T2561); RO 10th April 1931.

35 Articles of Enquiry preparatory to Visitation 1821 and 1825 (Cheshire Record Office: EDV7/6, vol. 3; EDV7/7, vol. 2); Edenfield parish records [churchwarden's accounts 1826-7] (MCL: MF PR 117a); Primitive Methodist Sunday school teachers' meeting minute books 1867-1877 and 1873-1884 (BAS: CRR/T2561); Wesleyan Methodist Sunday school minute book 1881-1889; BT 8th March 26th 1884, 26th April 1884.

36 Churchwardens' accounts (MCL: MF PR 117a); Archdeacon Rushton's visitation returns, p.19 (MCL: MSf 942.72 R121 vol 15); BT 17th February 1866; RO 28th April 1911

37 RO 17th July 1925, 27th November 1959; *St.Peter's Ewood Bridge 1839 to 1939* (1939), p.8; Haslingden Guardian 19th September 1930; BT 3rd July 1858; Market Place Methodist church finance committee minutes 1929-1959 (BAS: CRM/T2574)

38 BT 25th February 1865, 21st March 1874; J. Simpson, *op. cit.*, p.11; RO 17th July 1925, 8th November 1912, 2nd September 1955, 30th November 1968; Rochdale Road Methodist trustees' minute book 1940-1976 (BAS: CRR/T2561); P. Dunne, St. *Philip's church, Stubbins 1927-1977 Souvenir Brochure* (1977), p.6

39 BT 1st February 1879, 25th April 1885; RO 10th December 1897, 10th October 1919

40 RO 27th July 1928

41 RO 6th December 1940; Rochdale Observer 14th July 1938

42 RO 6th May 1898, 19th October 1914, 28th September 1891

43 Articles of Enquiry preparatory to Visitation, 1811 and 1825 (Cheshire Record Office: EDV7/4, vol. 1; EDV7/7, vol. 2); Episcopal visitation returns 1931 (MCL: M39/97)

44 C. Hill, *The history of Wesleyan Methodism in Edenfield*, (1928), p.8; Wesleyan Methodist Sunday school minute book 1848-1878 (BAS: CRM/T1267); BT 30th May 1885

45 BT 30th August 1862, 30th May 1885, 7th June 1879; Primitive Methodist Sunday school teachers' meeting minute book 1873-1884 (BAS: CRR/T2561); Irwell Vale Primitive Methodist teachers' meeting minute book 1872-1894 (LRO: MAc uncat.); RO 29th May 1896

46 Articles of Enquiry preparatory to Visitation, 1778 (Cheshire Record Office: EDV7/1, vol. 2); RO 7th July 1933; Primitive Methodist Sunday school teachers' meeting minute book 1857-1866 (BAS: CRR/T2561); Stubbins Congregational church record book 1860-1928 (BAS: CST/1)

47 Irwell Vale Primitive Methodist teachers' meeting minute book 1872-1894 (LRO: MAc uncat); Primitive Methodist Sunday school teachers' meeting minute book 1885-1892 (BAS: CRR/T2561); Wesleyan Methodist Sunday school committee minute book 1892-1896 (BAS: CRM/T1267)

48 RO 7th July 1933; Wesleyan Sunday school minute book 1848-1878 (BAS: CRM/T1267); Primitive Methodist Sunday school teachers' meeting minute book 1885-1892 (BAS: CRR/T2561)

49 Wesleyan Methodist Sunday school committee minute book 1841-1866 (BAS: CRM/T1267); Wesleyan Methodist Sunday school minute book 1848-1878 (BAS: CRM/T1267); BT 30th May 1885; Primitive Methodist Sunday school teachers' meeting minute book 1867-1877 (BAS: CRR/T2561); Wesleyan Methodist Sunday school minute book 1881-1889 (BAS: CRM/T1482); Congregational teachers' meeting minute book 1905-1934 (BAS: CST/10/1)

50 Wesleyan Methodist Sunday school committee minute book 1841-1866 (BAS: CRM/T1267); Irwell Vale teachers' meeting minute book 1872-1894 (LRO: MAc uncat); Primitive Methodist Sunday school teachers' meeting minute book 1857-1866 (BAS: CRR/T2561); RO 7th November 1913

51 BT 25th May 1872, 14th June 1873; RO 5th June 1903; Primitive Methodist Leaders' meeting minute book 1929-1945 (BAS: CRR/T1490); RO 10th June 1949; RFP 28th May 1999

52 RO 14th June 1957

53 BT 8th June 1874; RO 13th June 1924

54 BT 8th June 1874; RO 23rd June 1916

55 Wesleyan Methodist Sunday school committee minute book 1841-1866 (BAS: CRM/T1267); Wesleyan Methodist Sunday school minute book 1881-1889 (BAS: CRM/T1482); Primitive Methodist Sunday school teachers' meeting minute book 1857-1866 (BAS: CRR/T2561);

56 BT 9th August 1913, 10th June 1871, 7th June 1873

57 RO 7th June 1901, 23rd June 1916

58 BT 15th January 1876; RO 9th January 1891, 31st December 1909, 4th February 1916, 6th January 1939; Primitive Methodist Sunday school teachers' meeting minute books 1857-1866 and 1867-1877 (BAS: CRR/T2561); Wesleyan Methodist Sunday school minute book 1848-1878 (BAS: CRM/T1267)

59 BT 4th January 1873

60 BT 28th December 1867, 8th January 1870, 15th January 1876; RO 9th January 1891, 1st January 1909, 2nd February 1917, 7th February 1919, 4th February 1921, 16th December 1927, 1st January 1937

61 Primitive Methodist Sunday school teachers' meeting minute book 1857-1866 (BAS: CRR/T2561); RO 20th December 1929, 16th December 1932, 8th December 1933

62 BT 6th October 1877

63 Edenfield Young Men's Institute Minute Book 1856-1858 (BAS: CRM/T1482); BT 23rd March 1867, 18th April 1868

64 BT 19th March 1887, 3rd November 1888, 16th November 1889; Haslingden Chronicle and Ramsbottom Times 2nd November 1867

65 BT 23rd March 1867; RO 6th February 1903

66 RO 14th February 1907, 13th May 1921, 23rd January 1942, 13th January 1950; Primitive Methodist Sunday school men's class minute book 1919-1953 (BAS: CRR/T1490)

67 BT 22nd November 1862; RO 20th March 1903

68 RO 20th May 1904, 16th February 1912; BT 3rd August 1889; Accrington Gazette 8th April 1882

69 Primitive Methodist Band of Hope minute book 1894-1918 (BAS: CRR/T2574); BT 27th November 1875, 17th March 1877; RO 20th May 1904; Irwell Vale Primitive Methodist Band of Hope minute book 1929-1939 (LRO: MAc uncat)

70 RO 11th November 1904, 17th March 1911, 25th August 1911

71 Wesleyan Methodist trustees' minute book 1882-1938 (BAS: CRM/T1482); RO 16th April 1943, 18th March 1949, 30th September 1949

72 RO 5th October 1951, 15th January 1960, 21st August 1961; Irwell Vale Methodist trustees' minute book 1949-1964 (LRO: MAc uncat)

73 RO 24th January 1913, 1st December 1933, 28th January 1938, 28th October 1932

74 Wesleyan Methodist trustees' minute book 1882-1938 (BAS: CRM/T1482); BT 24th December 1870; RO

SPORTS, GAMES AND PASTIMES

UNTIL THE SECOND HALF of the 19th century, most recreations enjoyed by the people of Edenfield and its neighbourhood were usually fairly simple and often quite brutal. Cock fights, dog fights and fistfights were popular, especially at Holcombe. In November 1839, for instance, a crowd of between two and three thousand people gathered on Holcombe Hill to watch a prize fight between Charles Jones and Samuel Pickstones, two Manchester beersellers. The contest was for £50 a side and lasted for about thirty rounds. Both men 'got a pretty good drubbing', but Jones was declared the winner. On Christmas Day 1849, two Edenfield men, Edward Hunt and another man named Suthers, who were both 'in liquor', began an impromptu wrestling match in one of the beerhouses. Hunt was thrown by Suthers and so badly injured that he died later the same day. Changes in moral standards, wrought by better education and the influence of the churches and Sunday schools, gradually put paid to such events being held openly. Instead they retreated to out of the way places. Thus, while in 1831 a cock fight could be held at a public house in the centre of Holcombe in front of a 'numerous and respectable crowd', by 1900 the organisers of a similar event chose the disused Cheesden Lumb Mill, just beyond Turn, as their venue. On this occasion they were disturbed by the police and more than two hundred spectators fled from the scene.[1]

Possibly a little less cruel than the cock fights, but still fairly savage were the Sunday afternoon rat hunts that took place in Stubbins in the early years of the 20th century. Commenting on one held in October 1904 the *Ramsbottom Observer* said that over one hundred people had made their way to the riverbank to watch 'with great excitement how the dogs do their work.' The reporter felt that 'votaries of the sport might better employ their time.'[2]

Cock fights and so on allowed local gamblers to indulge their passion. They had other opportunities too. The game of pitch and toss was played fairly regularly throughout the district. Indeed, one description of Haslingden in 1873 suggested that the town's inhabitants could not take a walk on to the hills in any direction without meeting gangs of men playing the game. Pitch and toss involved throwing coins at a marker. The man whose coin landed nearest to it was allowed to toss all the coins in the air and keep those that fell face up. Since this game was illegal, players chose quiet spots in which to play it. Even so they were sometimes caught as in October 1892 when Patrick Mulvee, Henry Mosely, John Lonsdale, John Pringle, James Pickstone, Joseph Birtwistle, Joseph Hill and George Morgan were playing at the bottom of 'St. James Street', Edenfield (probably Church Lane). Since most of them were merely spectators they escaped prosecution, but Morgan was fined 5s and costs and 'severely cautioned.'[3]

Money changed hands too on the outcome of an unusual event held in February 1887 when a field near the church was the starting point for a race between two Haslingden cats. The object was to see which cat reached home the quickest. On being let out of their baskets, the cats made off towards Irwell Vale.

> It then dawned upon the owners and handicapper for the first time that they had not made any arrangements at the other end for recording the arrival of the contestants. The three men took to their heels and reached home (three miles distant), utterly exhausted, in something less than 30 minutes.

They need not have been concerned for nearly a fortnight went by before the first cat appeared back in Haslingden.[4]

Races of a more conventional character were popular, as John Wolstenholme who was born in 1850 later recalled:

> There were not the attractions in the way of sport and entertainment when I was a lad, but I, along with Eli Elton and one or two others, used to challenge the lads about Shuttleworth and other parts of the district. We had some really good team and miniature cross-country races from which we derived a good deal of sport.

By the 1880s a race was held almost every Saturday somewhere in the district. The Spindle Pad (the road from Ewood Bridge to Irwell Vale, which was destroyed when the sewage works were built) was a popular venue. On one occasion a race was going to be held on the main road between Haslingden and Rawtenstall but the police put a stop to it and the runners moved to the Spindle Pad. One spectator later said, 'Just as they were getting ready, old Hopwood the farmer turned up and objected, but a big burly delph chap from Haslingden caught hold of him in his arms like a child and put him down in the dyke bottom and sat on him until the race was over.' Crowds of spectators made their way to Turn one Monday night in April 1886 when a race was held between a quarryman and a local mill owner:

> The quarryman duly stripped for the race and put his best foot forward, but the factory master, although ten years older than his opponent, beat him by a considerable distance, the run being for 300 yards.[5]

Foot races and other sports were also popular with members of the Manchester Literary Club who visited Edenfield in the 1860s when Edwin Waugh, the Lancashire dialect poet, was staying at Foe Edge. After Waugh's death, his friend Ben Brierley wrote:

> Our literary club picnics were glorious times. On these occasions we had all kinds of sports. Waugh's favourite game was wrestling, Lancashire fashion…But Waugh, not being satisfied with wrestling, would race anyone of the party. Dick Bealey took up the challenge, and the competitors stripped. The course was a long field behind the "Horse and Jockey", Edenfield. Waugh had no chance with Bealey, being heavily handicapped. His legs lumbered away like two automaton pop bottles, the machinery of which had not been properly wound up.[6]

Another feature of local sporting life were the horse races held until about the middle of the 19th century around a course laid out on Cowpe Lowe, high above the village. The name of the public house the Horse and Jockey was changed from the White Horse in the early 1800s and may commemorate these races. Later in the century, probably in the 1850s and 1860s, horse races were run on the main road through the village over the short distance between the Pack Horse and the Horse and Jockey. One of the reasons why horse races on the moors came to an end was that mill owners began to use them for grouse shooting. A report of the opening of the 1883 season said:

> On Monday about a dozen brace of birds were bagged by three guns on the moor a little to the south of Cowpe Law. Some of the birds were unusually small for the period of the year, but they were plump and fairly strong on the wing. All the old birds shot were also in fine condition.[7]

During the First World War and for a few years afterwards, hound trailing became popular and courses of up to nine miles were laid over Cowpe Lowe, Scout Moor, Turn, Cheesden and Ashworth Moor. The Horse Shoe Inn and less frequently the Bird in Hand and Bridge Inn, Ewood Bridge, were the usual starting points for the trailers. The events were at first run by the Tottington and District or the Rossendale Hound Trailing Associations, but after the war the Edenfield and District Hound Trailing Association was set up to oversee the meetings. For a few years these events attracted a great deal of support and interest as this report of a November 1918 trail shows:

> The popularity of hound trailing in the Bury and Ramsbottom district was fully proved on Saturday afternoon, when there was a gathering of more than a thousand spectators to witness the start and finish of a hound trail from the Horse Shoe Inn, Edenfield. Eleven dogs mainly from Ramsbottom, Bury, Tottington and Rochdale, were started ... The trail was laid over about eight miles of open moorland country, and there was a keen race at the finish, not more than eighty yards dividing the first five dogs. After being out thirty minutes Riley's Bess came in first, about ten yards in front of Ormerod's Fred. Then came Fletcher's Famous twenty yards behind, with Dewhurst's Prince and Chapman's Cracker forty or fifty yards away ... In a puppy trail that preceded the bigger event Taylor's Dinah was the only animal to finish.[8]

THE WAKES

Many of the traditional sports and pastimes were enjoyed at the local wakes. These yearly celebrations originally commemorated the dedication of a nearby church, but by the late 18th century they had lost their religious aspect and had become boisterous junketings. Edenfield wakes were held towards the end of August 'with considerable hilarity' as one old man recalled. Another participant remembered horse races, clog dancing for silk ribbons and two characters, Dick o' Granny's and Will o' Granny's. Dick was a champion sack racer, while Will, who had crooked legs, 'was more in the feightin' line.' By the end of the 19th century the wakes had become the occasion for day trips to the seaside and when mills began to close for several days they became the wakes week holiday. Something of the character of the old wakes lingered on at Holcombe where in 1880 there were foot races, jumping matches, climbing a greasy pole for a leg of mutton and 'the usual sights and doings of a thoroughly old-fashioned country wakes'. By 1890 the Edenfield wakes and annual fair had shifted to early October. Held in a field behind the Pack Horse they comprised 'Hancock's steam galloping horses, exhibitions, shooting saloons and aunt Sallies of every description.' On the final day a prize was given to the boy who could eat a treacle bun the quickest with his hands tied behind his back.[9]

CALENDAR CUSTOMS

Although the traditional wakes changed character and gradually died out, somewhat more tenacious were various activities associated with particular feasts or times of the year. Shrove Tuesday was generally known as 'Blacking Day' when apprentices at the mills blacked up their faces with soot and grease before taking the day off as an unofficial holiday. The custom lingered on into the 1950s, although by then employers did not look kindly on it. In 1954, Porritt Brothers and Austin at Stubbins Vale Mill locked all the doors and gates to prevent apprentices from Ramsbottom gaining entry and collecting their fellow workers. Nothing daunted, the youths found a way in through a trapdoor and the Porritt apprentices, along with other from Stubbins paper mill, Rose Bank printworks and the Chatterton Weaving Company went off to the cinema in Bury.[10]

Blackened faces were also seen at Easter until about the First World War. One villager from Turn recalled 'black-faced mimers who toured the district, stopping periodically to give a mimed play' while another remembered the men wearing ragged clothes with their coats turned inside out and singing:

> We're coming round a pace egging
> To see what you will give;
> If you don't give us anything,
> We's wonder how we's live.
> We have an old triangle.
> A tambourine and a'
> We want a bit more money
> To buy an old banjo.

On another occasion the pace eggers caused alarm when they called at the back door of one Edenfield house. The maid was so startled by their appearance that she rushed to her employer calling out, 'Madam! Madam! The Boers are in the back yard!'[11]

'Garbed in lace-curtain and tissue paper finery, one or two May Queens, each with a small retinue of courtiers, made their advent in Ramsbottom and Edenfield on Monday. Most of the youngsters had their own pole, too, and danced around with improvised steps' said the *Ramsbottom Observer* in May 1944 recording the continuance of one May Day custom. At the same time the paper lamented the death of another:

> Not many carters or farmers, if any, followed what used to be a very popular custom of decorating their horses with coloured ribbon and the shining brass of the harness. Fifty years ago it was a common sight on May Day to see horses with their tails neatly plaited and tied with red, white and blue ribbon. In these hectic days, of course, we have more to do and think about than the gay decoration of horses in order to keep up an old tradition.[12]

CRICKET AND FOOTBALL

> For a while we did not know how to pass our time away. Beforetime, it had been all bed and work; now, in place of 70 hours a week it was reduced to 55½ hours. Cricket and football became the most popular sport of the day.

These words were written by Moses Heap (1824-1913), a cotton spinner who briefly lived at Shuttleworth in the 1830s and attended Edenfield school. He was recalling the passing of the 1847 Ten Hours Act, which reduced the hours of labour for many cotton workers. Cricket was the first of the team games to gain popularity in the area and by the 1860s Edenfield and its sister villages were fielding several teams. They included not only Edenfield Cricket Club (which could muster a second XI by 1875), but also Edenfield Rangers, Nimble Nook, Rose Bank, Turn, and Strongstry and Chatterton United Eleven. In the 1890s teams from the various churches joined them.[13]

The Edenfield village team continued to play into the late 1890s, but by the turn of the century had faded away. Its place was taken by Edenfield United Cricket Club, which was formed at a meeting held in Jim Haworth's refreshment rooms on 12th February 1902. The new club fielded two teams in its first season that began with a match against Holcombe Church on 27th April. The 1902 games were friendly matches only and it was not until the following year that the club played regular fixtures as part of the Rossendale and District League. Their 1903 season was not particularly successful and they finished near the bottom of the table. They more than made up for this disappointing showing in 1904 when they won the league championship. After their final match against Bacup St. Mary's, Jack Heyworth, their captain, received the cup on their behalf and the team and their supporters boarded a couple of wagonettes and set off for home. The *Ramsbottom Observer* described their triumphant return to the village:

> The Green Man Hotel was left amidst cheering and waving of flags, of which the jubilant youths possessed half a dozen of the latter. The beaming skipper displayed the "pot" prominently on the "dickey" in front, and en route the team were frequently applauded, but on entering Edenfield the scene was truly remarkable. The Stubbins Vale Brass Band was awaiting them at the Quarryman's Arms Inn and there the procession was commenced. All the villagers seemed to have turned out, and to the strains of "See the conquering heroes," the champions paraded through the street, preceded by several youths bearing torches. The reception and general rejoicing was something that will not readily be

forgotten. The holding capacity of the cup was tested often, but happily everything passed off without a hitch. The proceedings were kept up with gusto until a late hour, and the "homecoming" will surely be remembered as a red letter day in the annals of the village.[14]

In the following year the club moved to the Ramsbottom and District Amateur League and here too were immediately successful: both teams came top of their division, the second XI winning every game they played. They were league champions again in 1907 and 1908, and in 1909 they moved up to the Bury Amateur League. The team repeated its earlier successes by winning the Bury League in 1914 and 1915, the final year in which games were played until after the First World War. When peace came there was some uncertainty as to whether the club would continue. However, early in 1920 members decided to carry on and two years later were again league champions, having won seven and drawn three of their ten matches. They had been helped to victory by the extraordinary bowling of Allan Smith. In one match against Walshaw in July 1922 he took eight wickets for one run and by the end of the season his average was an astonishing 2.66. The club topped the batting averages with 19.6 and also won the Myles N. Kenyon fielding prize – a bat and leg guards.[15]

The Edenfield CC first XI in 1922, the year in which they were First Division champions of the Bury and District League.

The year is 1963 and Edenfield are again champions of the Bury and District League.

Games in the Bury League had to be suspended in 1943, but resumed in 1947. Edenfield were champions twice in the 1950s and again in 1963, their last season in the league. Thereafter they have played in the Bolton and District Cricket Association League (1964-1968), the North Manchester League (1969-1987) and the Ribblesdale League (1988-1992). An important change came in the 1993 season when the club joined the Premier Division of the Vaux Ribblesdale League and for the first time in its history fielded a professional. The first man to fill the position was twenty-two year old all rounder Andrew Williams, a former England Under 19s international. The '90s also saw the formation of three junior teams, a ladies' team and a third XI.[16]

From the year of the club's foundation, games have been played in a field off Gin Croft Lane. When the opportunity to buy the ground arose in 1928, the club did so for £150. They built a new pavilion in 1912 and in the 1930s added a timber tea tent and toilets. Further improvements were made in the early 1950s when a ladies' toilet block was put up. One doubtless apocryphal account of the preparations for this work says that the committee took the decision to appoint an architect for toilets 'for ladies with concrete bottoms and wooden sides.' A new brick pavilion was built in 1973 and a shower room installed in 1990, while in 1999 a legacy of £97,000 from

John Cort, who had played for the team in the 1930s, allowed the club to embark on an ambitious programme of improvements to the Gin Croft Lane ground.[17]

By the 1870s, football equalled cricket in popularity and teams proliferated. Various leagues were established and reports of matches began appearing in local newspapers. Among the teams taking to the field in the late 1870s were Edenfield FC, Stubbins Rangers and Turn Duffers. By 1891, even a small place like Turn could muster three football teams: Turn FC, Turn FC Reserve and Turn Olympic. Their competitors included Edenfield Albion, Edenfield Young Britons, Ewood Bridge Wanderers, Irwell Vale Young Britons, Strongstry White Star and Strongstry Excelsior.

There was always a keen rivalry between Edenfield and Shuttleworth football teams and it became particularly intense towards the end of the 1893-4 season. Edenfield had played well and had won the Rossendale Charity Shield, not having lost a single match throughout the whole tournament. On a beautifully fine

Edenfield FC, winners of the Bury and District League Cup and Shield, 1894. The players and officials are: (*Back row*): G.H. Dewhurst (*sec.*), G. W. Tattersall, H.J. Whitworth, James Pickstone, A. Edmondson (*Middle row*): Job Pickstone, J.R. Barnes, Sam Buck, Nat Omerod, S. Ormerod, H. Nuttall (*Front row*): M. Haworth, H. Lord (*captain*), L. Ashworth
The name on the football refers to Frank Sugg, sports outfitter, who had offered to give a football to any team in the league that had a goal average of not worse than 100 for and 10 against. Edenfield won it with 100 goals scored and only 9 against.

Saturday afternoon at the end of March 1894 the rival teams met on Ramsbottom cricket ground. More than 3,000 spectators turned up to watch the match. The Edenfield side took to the field first and 'were accorded a very hearty reception, the general opinion being that they would romp home easy winners.' However, 'hearty as was their reception it was nothing to the ovation which greeted the appearance of the Shuttleworth team when they stepped on the ground five minutes later.' The match did not begin well for Edenfield, one of whose players scored a home goal while attempting to head the ball away from the net. By half time they had equalized, but twenty-five minutes into the second half, Shuttleworth scored again 'amidst tremendous cheering.' Edenfield failed to get any more goals, leaving Shuttleworth the winners.

Partisan feelings continued to run high for some days after the match and in the following week the *Ramsbottom Observer* reported:

> We learn that members of Shuttleworth football team had a lively time of it at Edenfield on the Sunday after they had won the Parks Challenge Cup. They were having a drive in a wagonette and all went smoothly until they reached the village where their defeated opponents hold forth. It was there they had to run the gauntlet of a continuous shower of rotten apples, oranges, old codfish heads, &c. and when they had dodged the missiles to the best of their ability, pocket handkerchiefs had to be brought into play to make themselves presentable. We do not by any means infer that the Edenfield Football Club were in any way responsible for this. We should prefer to attribute it to a gang of excited football idiots who know more about that game than they do about good behaviour.

One final match was played in the 1893-4 season before it was over. Towards the end of April, Edenfield lined up to play a team composed of players from the rest of the league. Kick off was at four o'clock, but by then only a few of the 'Rest' players had put in an appearance. At half past four a telegram was received saying that players from Shuttleworth would arrive at five o'clock. In fact, it was after six when they turned up and, as the *Ramsbottom Observer* said, 'the feelings of both spectators and players may be better imagined than described, and the names given to the Emergency Committee of the League were more forcible than polite, and they will not soon forget the reception they received on arrival.' Difficulties in clearing spectators off the pitch meant that kick off did not take place until 7 o'clock with only about half of the 'Rest' team playing. Not surprisingly, Edenfield won 6 - 0.[18]

Within a couple of years the enthusiasm of the '93-94 season had evaporated and Edenfield, Shuttleworth and other local teams had folded. Interest was revived after the turn of the century and the early 1900s again saw crowds of up to 2,000 people turn out to watch the newly formed Edenfield United and Stubbins Albion play in the Bury league. In 1913, following a game 'full of exciting incidents' played at Gigg Lane, Albion won the Parks Challenge Cup. The Ramsbottom and District Amateur League set up in 1908 encouraged the formation of other clubs, which included teams from the Edenfield Liberal and Conservative Clubs, from Turn and Irwell Vale and from Turnbull and Stockdale's at Rose Bank.[19]

Two village teams from the 1920s: Irwell Vale (*above*) and Turn

The local leagues were suspended during the First World War (although junior teams such as Stubbins Brigade continued to play), but were revived when peace came. Edenfield United played in both the Ramsbottom and Bury Leagues, being champions of the former in 1931 and winning the Parks Challenge Cup in the latter in 1933. They joined the Bolton league in 1934 and from 1938 fielded two teams, the second of which was known as Alderwood. When Edenfield United won the Ramsbottom league again in 1939 their medals were presented by Eric Brook, Manchester City's star outside left, and in August of the same year Brook returned to Edenfield to coach the village team. Jackie Bray, City's half back, also turned out to watch the training session. In the following year Edenfield signed no fewer than five players who had all played for senior league sides. They were Miles (Manchester City Reserves), Turner and Walsh (Fleetwood), Wolstenholme (Bury) and Allerton (Lancaster City).[20]

New leagues set up between the wars included a junior section of the Ramsbottom league, the Ramsbottom Sunday School Union league and the Bury and District Woollen Mills league, in which a team from Stubbins Vale Mill played. Some of the teams in these and other local leagues in the 1920s and 1930s included Ewood Bridge Albion, Stubbins Juniors, and Turn Athletic. Both Methodist chapels in Edenfield as well as the Parish Church, St. Philip's, Stubbins Congregationalists and Irwell Vale Primitive Methodists all entered teams in the Sunday School league. Irwell Vale also played in the Haslingden league where they won the Bailey Cup in 1927. Games could be tough for players even in matches organised by the Sunday School Union and following complaints of swearing, betting and 'incitement to rough play' by spectators in 1922 officials of the league appealed for help to 'conduct the game as it should be, in a clean and manly and sportsmanlike way.'[21]

The Ramsbottom league organised matches throughout the Second World War and in 1941 the team from St. Philip's won both the league and the challenge cup competition, the first time in the history of the league that this had happened. Edenfield United were re-formed by the Community Association in 1946 and in 1950 faced Nangreaves in the final of the Ramsbottom League challenge cup. 'In a fast, keen game' Edenfield 'severely hammered the Nangreaves defence' and won the match by three goals to one. A couple of years later, the mantle of the leading team in the district passed to Turn FC, which was revived in 1953. The enthusiastic support for this village team was almost as keen as it had been for Edenfield in the heady days of the 1890s. When they played their first away match at Summerseat it was arranged that the half-time score should be conveyed back to the village by homing pigeon. Henry Martin, the left half, scribbled the score down and dispatched the pigeon to his brother, Alfred, who conveyed the news to his fellow supporters. Unfortunately Turn were two goals down and went on to be defeated 5 – 0. Turn continued to play in the Bury league for a number of years and on Good Friday 1960 played in front of a crowd of nearly 1,000 people when they were beaten by Ramsbottom Youth Club 3 – 0. In recent years, Edenfield FC has enjoyed success

Edenfield FC in 1996 when they were First Division champions of their league. The team included three sets of brothers: Stephen and Peter Valentine, Paul and Karl Stanley, and Gavin and James Richards.

against teams from the Bury and Rochdale area. They won no fewer than three cups and were First Division champions in 1996, the same year in which they were provided with their own shower room at the Rostron Arms.[22]

NEW GAMES AND SPORTS

In the late 19th century and the years before the First World War, people in the Edenfield area found a whole variety of new ways to amuse themselves. Some of these established themselves as long-lasting favourites, while others were short-lived manias, when a particular pastime briefly caught everybody's attention before interest died away completely. Bicycles began to make an appearance in the locality in the late 1860s. At first they were treated as a novelty, but as their construction improved cycling became a popular hobby. The Rossendale Bicycle and Tricycle Club was founded in 1878 and two of its original members had connections with Irwell Vale. Herbert Ruthven was born and brought up in the village, while his

H.J. Whitworth of Irwell Vale, champion tricyclist.

brother-in-law, Henry J. Whitworth, lived there for a time in the early 1890s when he was at the height of his cycling prowess. During his long career, he won many trophies, including two long distance medals, which he picked up in 1891. In May of that year he rode 125 miles in 11 hours 55 minutes on a Beeston pneumatic tricycle and won the gold medal of the Rossendale club. Later in the year he secured a bronze medal by riding from Old Trafford to Shrewsbury and back as far as Hanley (108 miles) in 11 hours 58 minutes.[23]

By 1895 there were sufficient cyclists in the area to make it worth the while of James Halliwell, sewing machine agent, musical instrument dealer and teacher of music, to begin selling bicycles as well. For £12 10s cycling enthusiasts could buy a 29 lbs 'Dunlop' with pneumatic tyres or for £10 an up-to-date roadster. He also carried out repairs. By May 1900 there were said to be 'a considerable number of cyclists in Edenfield and district' and suggestions were made that a cycling club should be formed in the village, but nothing came of the proposal.[24]

During periods of hard frost skating was popular and in January 1891 'almost every mill lodge and sheet of water of any magnitude' was pressed into service by local skaters and the local papers noted that 'quite a fair sprinkling of the gentler sex … have been tempted to don their "No. 3 Acmes" and join in the swift silent race.' The construction of the sewage works at Ewood Bridge offered new opportunities for skaters and in January 1903 the filter beds there were said to have been especially well patronised.[25]

At about the same time, a new pastime reached the village: early in 1902 ping-pong made an appearance at some of the local clubs and by May the *Ramsbottom Observer* could report: 'The all-absorbing game of ping-pong seems to have taken a firm hold up Edenfield way, where they are going in for ping-pong teams, ping-pong matches, ping-pong tournaments, etc. in no half hearted fashion.' The two village teams were set up by the Liberal Club and by Jim Haworth, café owner, confectioner and cricket enthusiast. Their opponents included Calendar Clifford (Ramsbottom) and the Rawtenstall Appolla Male Choir. Several matches were played, but by the end of the year enthusiasm for the game had died. Nothing more was heard of it until after the First World War when it was one of the games taken up by the young people at the various churches.[26]

EDENFIELD BATHS

Of a similar vintage as the ping-pong craze, but somewhat longer-lived, were the Edenfield swimming baths. They were largely the brainchild of Lawrence Elton who got permission from Lord Derby to use a small disused reservoir at Dearden Clough as a swimming pool. Throughout the spring and summer of 1901, the young men from the village worked at the baths preparing for their opening in September. Water was supplied from the Dearden Clough Mill lodge and carried along in a wooden trough about 100 yards in length. The baths leaked quite badly at a trial filling and

Edenfield open-air swimming baths in about 1905. Dearden Clough Lower Mill is in the background.

the walls had to be dismantled so that they could be given a puddled lining. Eventually all was ready; a wooden changing room and a 6 ft. 6 in. fence completing the arrangements.

The baths were officially opened at the first annual gala of the Edenfield and District Swimming Association held on 7th September 1901. A large crowd gathered around the pool and on the hillside above to listen to speeches and watch swimming exhibitions, races, a polo match and a pillow fight across the pool. The baths proved very popular and soon additional changing rooms had to be built. In 1905 the pool was lined with brick and enlarged to twenty-five yards long by twelve yards wide, ranging in depth from 3 ft. 10 in. to 5 ft. 9 in. It was even proposed in 1910 that the baths should be heated but this proved too expensive.[27]

Membership of the Swimming Association rose steadily, reaching 270 in 1906. A ladies' club was suggested in 1908, but it was not until 1913 that the proposal was carried out. Wednesdays were set aside as the day ladies could use the pool, paying a 2s entrance fee (1s for under sixteens). Male members paid 2s 6d or 1s 6d. Since the baths were in the open air, their popularity was partly dependent on the weather. In the good summer of 1903, 300 to 400 bathers a week visited Edenfield, but conversely, a bad summer in 1907 made it the worst season for the club and membership fell to eighty-six. Nevertheless the general success of the baths was regarded somewhat jealously by the people of Ramsbottom and each year they demanded to know when the town was to get its own swimming pool. In 1907 the question prompted a letter to the paper from 'Edenfield Swimmer' singing the praises of the baths and advocating their use by local schools. He came to the tongue-in-cheek conclusion that there was 'as little prospect of getting baths in Ramsbottom to-day as there was fifty years ago. And no wonder! The place is dead!! The people have no enterprise!!!'[28]

The swimming galas, held every summer until 1912, were popular events. In 1904, for example, six hundred spectators came to watch and were 'loud in their praises of the aquatic fare.' Events included handicap races, obstacle races, polo matches, and exhibitions of high diving and life saving. From 1904 onwards a 200 yards scratch race was held for the Barlow Perpetual Challenge Cup presented by Edwin Barlow, while the winner of the fifty yards handicap for boys under sixteen received the Deans Cup, the gift of Dr. Henry Deans, the Swimming Association's president. Various kinds of comic race also won the approval of the crowds. For instance, in 1907 competitors had to swim a length of the baths, get dressed in 'wearing apparel' and swim back to the starting point. One swimmer 'almost lost a portion of his garments owing to not being "braced" up by a sufficient quantity of strings.' On another occasion competitors had to try to sit astride an inflated Ceylon pigskin. 'The innocence with which the pig upset the calculations of the competitors and caused them to perform variants in somersaults was as amusing as the tumblings themselves and everybody enjoyed great laughter out of the event.'[29]

A swimmer grapples with the inflated pigskin at the 1908 gala, much to the amusement of the spectators.

David Billington of Bacup, a regular visitor to the galas, brought the pig to the baths. Born in 1885, he had been declared 'Boy Champion of England' in 1898. At Edenfield in 1906 he gave 'a splendid exhibition of ornamental swimming, as follows: - Like a seal, one leg out of water, shipwreck, revolving, sculling (feet first), somersault, swimming like a porpoise, monkey up a stick, waterwheel, swimming like a crab, a length under the water, a length with feet tied, and like a steam tug.' On two occasions he broke his own records for swimming 500 and 1,000 yards. Another swimmer who appeared at Edenfield baths was Beatrice Kerr, champion of Australia, who came in 1906 and 1907. 'She did all sorts of conceivable performances in the water with a grace and facility which won for her golden opinions.'[30]

Although the 1912 gala was the last one to be held, the swimming club continued using the baths for a couple more years and spent £18 2s in 1914 on a new bridge and general repairs. The First World War put a stop to activities and nothing further was heard of the baths until 1920 when a special meeting was held to decide whether the swimming club should be disbanded. They decided to carry on and it was even suggested that the restoration of the baths could form part of any memorial scheme for the men killed in the war. Within a week or two of the meeting, however, the *Ramsbottom Observer* reported that the baths were having difficulties with the water supply. Two years later the writer of a letter to the paper said he 'was surprised and pained' to see the dilapidated state of the baths. This was the end of the little swimming pool at Dearden Clough, which had seen so much activity for a few years in the early 1900s.[31]

RECREATION GROUNDS AND PLAYING FIELDS

Apart from the swimming baths, Edenfield got another sporting venue in the early 1900s. This was the recreation ground in Exchange Street. The Ramsbottom Urban District Council bought Grindlestone Meadow and two long rows of old houses here in 1901. The *Ramsbottom Observer* thought the site was 'a really capital one in most respects, being high, dry, hard and level. Plenty of fresh air is to be obtained on it and the views from all sides are magnificent.' The houses were demolished in 1902 and the field properly drained. Work on laying out the new recreation ground was completed in April 1905 and swings were set up in 1912 (bought by Edenfield Coronation Committee with funds left over from the previous year), followed by a splendid shelter given in 1914 given by Mrs. Aitken, widow of Thomas Aitken of Irwell Vale Mill.[32]

Other recreation grounds appeared in the neighbouring villages in the years between the wars. In 1920, Col. A.T. Porritt gave a small plot of land between the railway lines at Strongstry as a recreation ground for the people of Strongstry and Chatterton. The land was divided into two parts, one for children, the other for adults and in September 1920 an old army hut opened as a village institute. It was divided into three – a games room, a newsroom and a practice room for Stubbins

The shelter on Edenfield recreation ground in 1914. Bob Pilling (*left*) and Simeon Chattwood oversaw the building work.

A.S. Watson, mayor of Haslingden, presenting a football at the opening of the Ewood Bridge playing fields in 1932. Alderman Jerry Lord stands on the left wearing a trilby.

Vale Band. Throughout the 1920s and 1930s, lectures, whist drives, concerts, garden parties and dances were held at the institute. Col. Porritt was also the donor of land at Chatterton (the site of the old mill and its lodge), which was made into playing fields and a recreation ground with swings, a shelter, seats and 'an elaborately constructed walk between an avenue of trees.' The land was given as a 'peace memorial' and was officially opened in April 1923.[33]

Nearly ten years later, Haslingden Borough Council provided a playing field at Ewood Bridge on land between Manchester Road and Ewood Lane (now Greens Lane). The Mayor, A.S. Watson, opened it in March 1932 and also presented a new football to the village lads. The ceremony was specially arranged for a quarter to two so that immediately it was over Mr. Watson could drive over to Blackburn to see Rovers play at home. Meanwhile, Ald. Jerry Lord, who also attended, dashed down to the railway station to catch a train to take him to the Bury match at Gigg Lane. Towards the end of the Second World War, the newly formed Walmersley-cum-Shuttleworth Ratepayers' Association felt that Turn too should have a playing field and they put their request to Ramsbottom Council. The field between Rochdale Road and Bleakholt Road opened in 1953.[34]

SPORTS CLUBS

As we have seen, local mills had fielded football and cricket teams for many years, but between the wars their organisation was given a solid foundation by the establishment of sports clubs, often with their own premises and grounds. At Irwell Vale, for instance, tennis courts and a bowling green were opened in 1926. Stubbins paper mill also had its own bowling green, while at Rose Bank Turnbull and Stockdale Ltd. made over sixty acres available to the sports club. This allowed them not only to have a playing field behind Stubbins Congregational Church, but also to lay out a nine-hole golf course above Edenwood Mill. By the early 1930s, Turnbull and Stockdale's workers had eight cricket teams (including two for ladies) and two football teams. The Rose Bank sports club did not survive the Second World War, its demise perhaps hastened by the burning down of its pavilion in May 1944. Irwell Vale's club continued into the 1960s, while that at Stubbins carried on until the 1970s.[35]

BOWLS, TENNIS AND BADMINTON

Bowling greens were not only found at the Irwell Vale and Stubbins sports clubs, but were also laid out at the Rostron Arms and behind the Primitive Methodist chapel in the 1920s. The latter green was particularly well used, players competing for the Rodwell Cup and the Barlow Cup. The 1936 final for the Barlow Cup was particularly closely contested and the large crowd of spectators 'witnessed one of the most thrilling duels ever staged on the green.' Eventually, the Methodist minister, the Rev. William Killcross, beat Melvin Crawshaw, secretary of the bowling club, by twenty-one points to twenty. The Rochdale Road green closed in the early 1960s, but the one at Stubbins continued until the demise of the sports club. The bowls team from the paper works won the championship of the Rossendale Parks Bowling League three years in succession between 1958 and 1960 and later also played in the Ramsbottom Mid-Week Bowling League.[36]

Tennis courts were also opened at Rochdale Road in 1922 and matches were played with enthusiasm each summer until the outbreak of the Second World War. Originally membership of the club was restricted to those who attended the chapel, but when the courts were reopened in 1946 anyone living in the village could play. The courts were used until 1956 when a dwindling membership spelt the end of the tennis club. The young people at Market Place Methodist with the large Sunday school at their disposal went in for badminton instead of tennis. For some time they simply played the game among themselves, but in 1938 decided to join the Ramsbottom and District Sunday School League. Badminton clubs were also formed at Rochdale Road in 1941, Stubbins in 1948 and St. Philip's in 1961.[37]

BILLIARDS

By the second of the 19th century, the game of billiards had begun to grow in popularity, partly helped by the establishment of a number of clubs. The success of the Edenfield News and Billiard Co. may have been short-lived – it was forced to sell up in 1873 – but lovers of billiards were soon well catered for elsewhere. Public houses such as the Coach and Horses installed billiard tables, while the game was also played at Irwell Vale Working Men's Club, Edenfield Conservative Club (at 71, Market Street) and Edenfield Liberal Club (in the Co-op Hall). In the billiard room of the latter there was a raised platform so that spectators could get a good view of the games in progress.[38]

Billiard teams from the various clubs played each other occasionally in the 1890s and early 1900s, but more serious competition followed the setting up of the Ramsbottom and District Billiards League in 1923. Ewood Bridge Social Club were league champions in 1928, followed by Edenfield Conservative Club in 1930, '31 and '34. After the Second World War the Conservative Club team joined the Bury league and were among the prizewinners in 1959. One of the winning team, seventy-three year old Frank Taylor, had played for the club since 1923.[39]

PASTIMES

As well as the variety of sports and games we have looked at, local people filled their spare time with a host of other activities. For some people this meant turning their work into a hobby. The Barcrofts who farmed at Scout Moor Bottom and New Hall were one family who did this. Several of them bred prize-winning sheep and on occasion acted as judges of lonks and herdwicks. George Barcroft (1855-1919) specialised in breeding and showing sheep dogs. He first entered dogs in a trial at the Preston Guild of 1882 and from then until his death ran dogs in competitions all over the country. In 1889 he won first prize with his dog White Bob at Bala where Queen Victoria watched the trials. The same dog took first prize and a gold medal at the German Collie Club's annual show in Frankfurt in 1897. On this occasion the Kaiser was among the spectators. By the time of his death, Barcroft had won £2,500 in prize money and trophies.[40]

The Barcrofts were not the area's only breeders of prize-winning stock. In the second half of the 19th century, for example, Edwin Walton, son of the Horncliffe quarry owner, took up poultry breeding. He exhibited at agricultural shows both in the locality and further afield, winning as much as £200 in prizes in a single year. By 1915 there were enough poultry breeders in the village and its neighbourhood for them to get together as the Edenfield Poultry Keepers' Association. They organised a yearly show in the Co-op Hall, egg competitions, lectures and an annual picnic (in 1921 to a poultry farm at Garstang). Although the association disbanded in about 1930, it reformed after the Second World War. Shows held at its headquarters at the Rostron Arms attracted competitors from as far away as Droylesden and Newton Heath.[41]

Competitions for birds of a different kind were occasionally held in public houses in the 1870s and 1880s when canary fanciers brought their birds together for singing competitions. Fifteen birds entered the event at the Coach and Horses in February

1875 and sixteen a similar event at the Railway Hotel, Stubbins in January 1886. Prizes were fairly modest: at the Coach and Horses they included a brass pan, a copper kettle and a metal teapot. An extra prize for the bird that sang the longest time consisted of a purse and gold chain.[42]

Similar prizes were on offer in August 1882 when the Plane Tree Inn, Turn hosted a celery show. Competitors paid an entrance fee of 2s 6d to exhibit their heads of celery for the chance of winning a first prize of £1, second 2s 6d and third a copper kettle. By this date, full-scale flower and vegetables shows were held once or twice a year in neighbouring towns, although some of them were confined to the well-to-do who could afford to pay staff to look after their gardens. Entrants at the Ramsbottom Floral and Horticultural Society's fourth annual chrysanthemum exhibition in 1887, for instance, included Mrs. Rumney (widow of the Stubbins printworks owner), Thomas G. Stark, one of the partners at Rose Bank, and James Porritt of Stubbins Vale Mill. The Porritt family encouraged their tenants to take up gardening by organising the Stubbins Vale Vegetable and Flower Show, which was first held in 1885. Prizes were awarded for the best kept garden as well as for all sorts of vegetables and flowers, including celery, cucumbers, onions, carrots, potatoes, rhubarb, broccoli, leeks, lettuce, gooseberries, hyssop, loosestrife, dahlias, roses, stocks, picotees, pansies and 'window plants.'[43]

Groups like the Ramsbottom Botanical Association and Edenfield Horticultural Society further fostered an interest in plants and gardening. The former was founded in 1891 and held meetings at the Railway Hotel, Stubbins at which collections of ferns, mosses and cultivated flowers were exhibited. The Horticultural Society first met in January 1914 and held their inaugural show in August of the

Contestants at Edenfield and District Horticultural Society's autumn show, September 1992.

same year when there were over 380 entries. One of the exhibits was a marrow weighing 25¼ lbs grown by Edwin Wakelin of Stubbins. In the following year the society awarded two trophies: the Barlow silver rose bowl for the best decorative garden and the Kay challenge cup for the best exhibit in the show. As well as competitions, the society has organised lectures and in 1952 hosted 'Gardeners' Question Time'. Panel members Fred Loades, Bill Sowerbutts and Prof. Alan Gemmel answered questions on topics such as the use of basic slag on onion beds, the best method to combat whitefly and why it was dangerous to handle tobacco while fertilising tomatoes. When introducing Edenfield and its gardeners the chairman told listeners: 'Gardening here is no easy task as so many of the gardens are situated on the windy, rain-swept hills.'[44]

The first winner of the Kay cup was George Lord of Turn, one of three local men who enjoyed national success with the plants they grew. Mr. Lord was manager of Turn Co-op for nearly thirty-four years, but his passion was for growing auriculas, carnations and polyanthus, which he entered in shows organised by the National Auricula Society. He won a cup and silver medal in 1921 when he exhibited a new seedling polyanthus called 'George Lord.' William Halldearn specialised in pansies and violas in his garden at Ewood Bridge and carried off many prizes, including several firsts at the National Viola and Pansy shows during the First World War. Just down the road at Irwell Vale, George Redding, who worked the signal box, cultivated a rose garden in part of the goods yard. He too exhibited all over the country and had many successes.[45]

George Lord, co-op manager and champion auricula, carnation and polyanthus grower.

MAKING MUSIC

Making music has long been an important way of recreation for Edenfield people and by the second half of the 19th century music played some part in the proceedings on almost every occasion when people met together to enjoy themselves. Churches and chapels, football clubs and cricket teams, mill workers and members of the co-op, friendly societies and working men's clubs all held concerts, dances and tea parties where groups or individuals performed.

We do not have many details of what instruments people were playing until the 1860s and 1870s, but in 1839, John Rostron, cotton spinner and manufacturer, insured his instruments and music for £200, while Thomas Southerst, the parish clerk who died in 1810, had built his own 'chamber organ'. By the 1860s, pianos had begun to appear in the homes of the well-to-do such as the Porritts at Stubbins Vale, the Parkinsons at Ewood Hall and the Rostrons at Chatterton Hey. Some of the more substantial tradesmen in the village also bought pianos. For example, when the furniture of grocer Lawrence Duckworth was sold in 1878 it included a seven-octave piano in a black and gold case made by Iliff Rintoul and supplied by Broadwoods. Landlords of the public houses were also among the first people in the village to own pianos – William Taylor had one of 6¾ octaves at the Rostron Arms in 1869 – and gradually they made their way into Sunday schools.[46]

Violins were another popular instrument and made an appearance at many events, including a cricket club entertainment in the Co-op Hall in October 1874 and a tea party and ball in the same venue in February 1879. Thomas Smith (1878-1954) was an electrician by trade, but also played the violin. He taught the instrument at his Irwell Vale home and in Ramsbottom as well as playing in the orchestra at the Princess Theatre, Manchester and with Spielman's Orchestra on Blackpool's North Pier. Other instruments that have provided musical entertainment over the years have included flutes, piccolos and concertinas. On occasion, however, a more exotic note has been sounded: the audience at an Irwell Vale Primitive Methodist Band of Hope concert in November 1883 enjoyed dulcimer solos played by Messrs. Warburton and Sparrow, while in March 1899 guests at a dinner and ball to mark the coming of age of James, son of John Austin Porritt, heard him play pieces on the zitherjo.[47]

Along side individual musicians, small orchestras and bands also performed. They included the Ewood Bridge String Band who played for 200 hundred guests at the Ewood Bridge National School tea party in May 1878 and the Edenfield String Band who enlivened meetings of the Edenfield Gospel Temperance Mission in 1889 and 1890. Of a later vintage was the band formed by Harry Schofield (1876-1933), company secretary at Dearden Clough Mill. Naturally enough the band played for the concert and dance organised by the mill workers at the Co-op Hall in November 1917. Similar small ensembles flourished during the 1920s and 1930s and many an evening's entertainment ended with dance music played by the Amazon Six, the Rhythm Boys, the Florida Band or Edenfield's own Collegians Dance Band.[48]

Brass bands were equally as popular as the smaller ensembles. The Rev. Matthew Wilson encouraged villagers to get together to form a band in about 1864. One of the players later recalled that Bob Wilkinson, the drummer, fell over his drum on more than one occasion and when the band led a Sunday School procession in Helmshore they could play only two tunes. The band broke up following the Rev. Wilson's death in 1870 and the players sold off their 'clever bass instruments and one large drum'.[49]

The Collegians Dance Band in about 1935. (*Left-right*) Ernest Taylor, Teddy Yarrow, Fred Hoyle, Jack Barton, Roland Farnell.

Four years later the brass band baton was taken up at Stubbins Vale when twenty-four young men formed a band at the suggestion of Richard Porritt. Their instruments, which were paid for by Porritt Brothers and Austin, arrived in September 1874 and soon the band members were practising enthusiastically in a room in the mill or in the mill yard in fine weather. Although none of them had played in a band before, by Christmas they felt confident enough to go out playing psalm tunes at the big houses in the district. In later years, it was the custom for the band to assemble near Edenfield church on Christmas Eve. When they heard Musbury church clock strike midnight they set off to play through the village, although there were times when the weather was so cold that instruments had to be thawed out in nearby houses and wrapped in red flannel before they would play. Reporting the Christmas Eve playing in 1906, the *Ramsbottom Observer* noted that their repertoire was 'much appreciated' but added, 'We are much in sympathy with any unfortunate individuals who may have been disturbed of their beauty sleep by a formidable crescendo.'[50]

At first the bandsmen did not have uniforms, although they were required to wear top hats when they went out playing. Later they adopted military style uniforms, which they used until the early 1890s when the government prohibited bandsmen from wearing them. Instead, Richard Porritt supplied lengths of indigo cloth, which were made up into uniforms with white piping. This was to be the colour used by the band until its demise, although the trimmings were later changed to red and gold and then to gold only. The band gave their first concert at a gala on Holcombe Hill in

An early photograph of Stubbins Vale Band taken in 1894.

June 1875 and 'acquitted themselves very well considering the short time they have been training.' Soon they were performing throughout the district, as well as further afield, including Blackpool and Preston. They took part in the celebrations of the Preston Guild in both 1902 and 1922. Nearer home it became a tradition for them to lead the Stubbins Congregational Whitsuntide procession, a duty they carried out almost without missing a year from 1875 until 1957.[51]

Within a few years of their formation, the band were also entering contests and winning prizes so that by the beginning of the 20th century they had become the Stubbins Vale Silver Prize Band. (To the locals, however, they were generally known as 'Hanson's Band' since from 1888 they were conducted by William Hanson and his son, James). Most of the contests they won were held in Lancashire, but in 1935 they travelled to Crystal Palace where they came eleventh out of thirty-three bands in their section. At the 1948 AGM the band appeared to be in a prosperous position with twenty-six members and plans to purchase new uniforms. Their repertoire included pieces from opera and musical comedies, but they did not like 'swing' music that was then in vogue. In the next few years it became more difficult to recruit young people and in 1957 the band amalgamated with Summerseat Prize Band.[52]

Stubbins Vale Band in May, 1935. The photograph was taken in the grounds of The Cliffe at an event held to raise money for the band and the organ fund of St. Paul's, Ramsbottom.

Apart from individual instrumentalists and bands, singers contributed much to the musical life of the district. Songs were part of the entertainment on many an occasion until after the Second World War. Typical of the dozens of concerts given over the years was the one held in the Co-op Hall in January 1900 in aid of the Ramsbottom War Relief Fund. The songs performed on that evening included 'Dreamers', 'Killarney', 'Death of Nelson', 'I seek for thee in every flower', 'Mona', and 'Love's Request' as well as 'Soldiers of the Queen', which was very popular then because of the Boer War. At a somewhat more boisterous sing-song at the Horse and Jockey a couple of years later, Edenfield FC and their supporters heard 'English, Irish and Scotch', 'We've got a long way to go', 'Loggerheads' and 'I wish I were single again'.[53]

Many concerts were given by singing groups of one kind or another. One of the earliest of these was the Edenfield Glee Singers who performed at the 1857 Good Friday tea party for the Wesleyan Young Men's Institute. They were heard again in January 1859 following a dinner of roast beef and plum pudding at the Horse and Jockey for the workers at Irwell Vale Mill to celebrate the wedding of Thomas Aitken. Appropriately on this occasion their programme included the glee 'Roast beef of old England'. During the First World War glee parties were formed at Union Mill, Stubbins and at the Chatterton Weaving Co. and sang at whist drives and dances organised by the workpeople at these mills.[54]

Sometimes songs and musical numbers had an added interest for audiences because they had been written by local composers. Thomas Wolstenholme, a Ramsbottom music teacher and organist at St. Paul's church who performed at concerts throughout the district, was one of the most prolific. One of his earliest pieces, the *Marion Valse*, was dedicated to Marion Oversby and was premiered at her twenty-first birthday party in December 1892. Wolstenholme went on to compose a number of anthems, part songs, a Te Deum and a suite of music to commemorate the 1911 Coronation. In the late 1920s, two men from Stubbins, J.T. Turnbull and R. Duckworth, tried their hand at song writing. One of their compositions, 'the well known valse song *I'm Longing for You*' was published in 1929 and was a big hit in the south of England where it was played by Hal Swain and his band.[55]

INNOVATIONS

At about the same time that people were dancing to the strains of the *Marion Valse*, they also made the acquaintance of the first of a series of new inventions that would profoundly alter the way they spent their leisure time. Early in March 1891, a small audience gathered in the Ramsbottom Co-op Hall to listen to a phonograph. The *Ramsbottom Observer* reporter was not greatly impressed:

> The tin funnel shaped instrument through which the sound was transmitted to the audience gave a metallic and smothered ring which prevented the natural tone being discerned, and to that extent the performance was a disappointment.

He conceded, however, that the machine had clearly demonstrated that 'sound could be recorded and treasured up for endless time, and used whenever required.' Within a few years of this concert, the phonograph and its rival the gramophone had begun to take their place along human artistes on the concert platform. In January 1899, for instance, a gramophone at the Parish Church tea and entertainment 'proved attractive and interesting', while in October 1901 when Edenfield Liberal Club held a social evening, the entertainment consisted of gramophone selections as well as songs and recitations. Similarly, in June 1913 at a garden party held at Stubbins Vale House to raise money for the Stubbins Mission building fund, a zonophone 'proved a great attraction on the tea lawn.'[56]

Another new means of entertainment that was to have lasting appeal made its appearance in the 1890s. In December 1897 the *Ramsbottom Observer* reported a concert given in Edenfield Co-op Hall by the Conservative Association. After providing details of the performers, the report added, 'The programme also included exhibitions of the cinematograph by Quartermaster Sergeant Smylie of Bury.' The paper had nothing further to say about the event, even though the audience were enjoying their first encounter with moving pictures less than two years after the first public screening of a film anywhere in the country. Edenfield saw nothing further of the cinematograph until March 1900 when the Wesleyan Band of Hope held a 'grand cinematograph exhibition' in aid of the local Indian Famine

Relief Fund. Travelling entertainers who visited the district also began to include cinematographs among their attractions and by 1910 people could visit the cinema in nearby Ramsbottom.[57]

Films continued to be shown at other venues, especially Sunday schools, although of course here they usually had a religious content. In February 1938, for instance, the Young Women's Bible Class at the Parish Church sat down to watch a missionary film, partly in colour, 'illustrating native life in Tunisia'. In the same year, films 'of a dramatic nature' were greatly enjoyed by the Edenfield Junior 'Imps' Society at a show in the Conservative Club. The advent of cine film also made it possible for people to have shows in their own homes. These could be unintentionally dramatic affairs as the audience in James Buckley's Irwell Vale home discovered in March 1943 when the projector burst into flames and set fire to the house. Probably the earliest footage of Edenfield itself was shot by Dr. John H. Struthers in 1937 and showed the crowning of the Parish Church Rose Queen, Mary Chattwood. When the film was screened in March 1938 there was so great a demand for seats that a repeat showing had to be given. Similar films of village occasions were made in the 1950s and 1960s.[58]

Following the First World War, another novel means of entertainment appeared. This was the wireless, an early demonstration of which was given at the Primitive Methodist Sunday school in February 1923. In the first half of the event the audience heard a lecture 'explaining in detail the wonders of this great invention' and in the second half listened to concerts 'that were being Broadcasted in different parts of the country.' On the payment of 3d they also had the opportunity for individual 'listening-in' sessions. In the following year schoolchildren at Stubbins and Ewood Bridge heard occasional broadcasts and by the early 1930s had become regular listeners. It was not very long before local people were appearing on the wireless themselves. James Savin, 'a well-known local vocalist', took part in the concert that the Stubbins children heard in May 1924, while George Allen, who worked at the co-op in Irwell Vale, performed in 1946. The studio audience warmly applauded his rendition of a song from Verdi's 'Il Trovatore'. In January 1941, Alexander B. Hillis, his brother, Tom, and nephew and niece, John and Jennie, took part in a broadcast in 'The Family Album' series. They talked about Bridge Mills and the business begun there by their ancestor Alexander Barlow.[59]

Not many years after these wireless programmes went on air, signals of a different kind were received in the locality. In the autumn of 1949 two Holcombe Brook men picked up experimental television broadcasts from the Midlands using a 35 ft. aerial erected on Holcombe Hill. Four years later, the North Regional Director of the BBC warned the audience at Edenfield Men's Fireside discussion group that once having bought a television set 'it was very easy to cease to lead the life of an ordinary human being.' By the following year there was at least one television owner in the village: 'T. J.' wrote to the *Ramsbottom Observer* appealing to 'those who have electrical appliances … not to use them when the television programmes are on. It spoils the viewing on your neighbour's television and causes great annoyance.'[60]

Wireless Broadcasting ! !

The Armature Winding Co. Ltd.,
(OF BURY),

Kindly assisted by the Technical Staff of the
Marconi Telegraph Co. Ltd., will give a

Listening-in Demonstration

With Lantern Illustrations, in the

Edenfield Primitive Methodist Sunday School,

On Wednesday Evening, Feby. 7, 1923.

6 to 7 o'clock for Children under 15, ADMISSION 3d.
7-30 to 9-30 for Adults   ADMISSION 6d.

Chairman   -   -   **Mr. A. B. HILLIS.**

Opportunity for individual Listening-in with explanations'
will be provided in the Primary School from 6 o'clock onwards,
at a charge of 3d. each.

Proceeds to Men's Class Fund.

A. Johnson, Printer, Edenfield.

The wireless makes an appearance in Edenfield at the Primitive Methodist Sunday School in 1923.

CLUBS AND SOCIETIES

Over the years a number of clubs, societies and other organisations have provided opportunities for local people to spend their leisure hours together in the pursuit of a common goal. Some have had fairly serious aims, while others have been solely bent on pleasure.

ST. JOHN'S AMBULANCE BRIGADE

In the late 1890s and early 1900s Edenfield had a flourishing division of the Ramsbottom and Rawtenstall St. John's Ambulance Brigade. The corps was formed in 1896, partly at the instigation of the village doctor, Henry Deans, and owed much of its early success to its secretary William Haslam of Irwell Vale who worked hard on its behalf. The original twenty-five members of the corps sat their First Aid exams in May 1897 and in November of the same year paraded through the village, taking up a collection to pay for uniforms. In subsequent years they held further parades, field days and galas at which they gave First Aid demonstrations. By July 1899, there were thirty members in the brigade who met regularly at their head-quarters in Edenfield Co-op Hall to be drilled by Dr. Deans. As well as kitting themselves out with uniforms, they also bought two stretchers, a litter and six wall boxes 'fitted with first aid requisites.'[61]

In the autumn of 1899 the brigade wrote to the War Office and volunteered to go to South Africa to nurse men injured in the Boer War. The first member to be called up was John Bradley of Top o' th' Lee, Shuttleworth, who left just before Christmas 1899. Hundreds of people marched in a torchlight procession from the Co-op Hall to Ramsbottom station via Shuttleworth singing 'Soldiers of the Queen' and other songs along the way. The *Ramsbottom Observer* described the scene:

> When the station was reached a very large crowd had gathered to witness the Corps, and loud cheers of welcome were raised from all the people. It was with difficulty that a way was pushed through the dense crowd at the station, and it required the utmost efforts of the policemen to keep a clear course.[62]

Similarly enthusiastic scenes witnessed the departure of other members of the brigade in 1900. In all, twelve men went to South Africa and all returned, with the exception of Pte. Thomas Haworth, son of the village postmaster. He died from enteric fever in July 1900. His friends and colleagues decided to erect a memorial to him in the parish churchyard and began raising funds. By April 1903 they had sufficient money to set up a granite obelisk with a carving of the crest of the St. John's Ambulance Brigade on top. On a gloriously fine day towards the end of April 1903 hundreds of people from neighbouring towns and villages converged on Edenfield to witness the unveiling ceremony. The memorial stands in a prominent place in the churchyard and is clearly visible from the road. When one traveller saw it shortly after its erection he was prompted to pen the following lines:

Private Thomas Haworth's memorial in Edenfield churchyard.

When England called her sons to arms, and bade them to no foeman yield,
No braver heroes did she send then those who went from Edenfield.
No sword nor deadly gun did they take forth to slay the foreign foe:
Their mission was in mercy's cause, to render aid, to none say "No".
Like angels on the battlefield they sought for those who were distrest,
And rendered aid to dying sons, who oft in thankfulness they blest.
Brave T. H. Haworth was one of those who left his home and kindred dear
To render aid to England's sons, no thoughts had he of death or fear.
His mission o'er, the Lord him called to dwell in starry skies above,
And loving friends at Edenfield subscribed to honour him they loved.
In silent churchyard stands a cross erected by a people's love
To one of England's noble sons, who reigns in that sweet land above.
And strangers as they pass this way oft shed a tear as they stand by
And read the epitaph of him whose name shall never die.
Give honour to those gallant lads, who to the foeman ne'er did yield;
In letters of bright gold inscribe the deeds of those of Edenfield.[63]

The Brigade carried on for some years after 1903 and in 1905 supported the formation of a Ladies' Sick Nursing Association in the village. However, it did not long survive the First World War and was disbanded in 1920. In the meantime, a division of the St. John's Ambulance Brigade had been set up in Ramsbottom and from September 1935 their headquarters were at the old Church of England mission in Stubbins Street.[64]

WORKING MEN'S CLUBS

Among the organisations set up to provide opportunities for recreation for their members were the Working Men's Clubs. The earliest of these was at Irwell Vale. It opened its doors at 26, Bowker Street in December 1880 and was 'to be used as a place in which workmen could associate together for recreation, mutual help, and moral and mental improvement.' For a modest subscription of half a crown members could read a selection of newspapers, buy minerals, herb beer, tobacco and cigars at concessionary prices and play billiards or dominoes. Card playing, however, was not allowed until the early 1890s. A more formal evening's entertainment was organised on occasion as in February 1893 when Thomas Aitken read a paper on his travels in Norway. A similar event in February 1900 included songs, concertina solos, ventriloquism and a performance by a Mr. J. Holt who is said to have 'manipulated the whistling of birds, calling of chickens, the squealing of pigs, etc.' The club closed in 1938.[65]

Of a similar vintage was Ewood Bridge Working Men's Club whose premises were at the end of a row of cottages at Ashenbottom. The club opened in the 1880s and survived until 1957. Like Irwell Vale, it was to afford its members 'the means of social intercourse, mutual helpfulness, mental and moral improvement, and rational recreation.' It also had a licence for the sale of alcohol, as did Edenfield Working

Men's Club, which opened in the old Bird in Hand beerhouse in Gin Croft Lane in October 1919 when about 100 members and friends enjoyed a hot-pot supper. As well as a bar, the club had a billiard room, social room for darts, dominoes and cards, and a concert room. In the early days, members could also attend lectures on subjects such as botany or hear the local MP give his views on the tax on beer. The club operated for nearly forty years, but was forced to close in 1958 when it could no longer compete with television, the cinema and other attractions.[66]

Similar to the working men's clubs, but somewhat shorter lived were the Turn and District Social Club and the Strongstry Young Men's Social Club. Both flourished for a few years before the First World War providing billiards, bagatelle, lectures, potato pie suppers and musical entertainments, which featured not only songs but also selections on the trombone, mandolin and musical glasses.[67]

EDENFIELD MEN'S FIRESIDE

The Edenfield Men's Fireside began life in October 1939 at Rochdale Road Methodist Church and aimed to 'unite and extend, as far as is possible, the friendly contacts made on the bowling green and tennis courts, and in the institute.' For more than forty years its members met once a fortnight during the winter months to hear speakers – many of whom were Manchester University lecturers – give talks on a wide variety of topics. The 1945 programme, for instance, included 'The Implications of the Atomic Bomb', 'Religion Tomorrow', 'A Poor Man's Life in Rome in the First Century', 'Europe Now', 'The Evolution of Man-Kind' and 'Contemporary Music.' The group moved into the Community Centre in the 1950s, by which time it welcomed ladies into its circle and included visits to museums and art galleries in its programme. It continued to meet until 1981.[68]

EDENFIELD AND DISTRICT COMMUNITY ASSOCIATION AND THE COMMUNITY CENTRE

Edenfield and District Community Association (EDCA) was formed in October 1945 at a meeting held in the Co-op Hall where it was decided to 'establish a centre where all peoples, regardless of class, political outlook, or denomination, could meet together.' The meeting was told that it would be four or five years before such a hall could be erected in Edenfield. However, in the following year, Turnbull and Stockdale Ltd. offered an ex-NAFFI hut as the nucleus for a village hall. The first public meeting was held in the new community centre in October 1948 and it was officially opened in January 1949.[69]

The Community Centre provided a home for organisations such as the Men's Fireside discussion group and Edenfield Young People's Club as well as several new bodies that were formed to use the building. They included a Ladies Club, Sunshine Club (for the over '60s), Music Society, Drama Society, Bridge Club and Jazz Society. Some of these proved to be short-lived, but the music and drama societies in

Edenfield Community Players: the cast of 'Charity Begins' January 1959. On the back row are Elsie Tomlinson, James Whittaker, Ethel Hallam, Kathleen Smith, Kathleen Mather and Frank Chadwick. Front row: Renee Chamberlain, Peter Lonsdale, Elizabeth Pickup and Joy Smethurst.

particular flourished. The music society provided gramophone recitals as well as live performances, which between 1949 and 1954 included Haydn's 'The Creation', Mendelssohn's 'Elijah' and German's 'Tom Jones'. The drama society – or Edenfield Community Players as they were known – used the centre as a rehearsal space, although their productions were performed in Rochdale Road Methodist Sunday School. Between 1951 and 1969 they staged all kinds of plays. The 1959 season, for example, comprised a comedy 'Charity Begins' by Richmal Crompton; a thriller, 'Recipe for Murder' by Arnold Ridley; 'The Only Prison', an all woman play set in a Japanese prisoner-of-war camp, and Stanley Houghton's 'Hindle Wakes'.[70]

Other groups not affiliated to EDCA (such as the Edenfield Fellowship for the Disabled) were allowed to use the building and it also became a child welfare centre. Edenfield branch library opened there in 1950, in part replacing another small library established at Turn in the late 1940s. At first the library opened only on Mondays between 2pm and 7.15pm. It stayed at the Community Centre until 1964 when it moved to 77, Market Street with a stock of 2,500 books. When this library closed in 1977, the books went back to the Centre until a trailer library was brought into service in 1989.[71]

NOTES

[1]   Bolton Chronicle 15th January 1831; RO 2nd March 1900; Manchester Examiner and Times 2nd January 1850
[2]   RO 28th October 1904
[3]   BT 10th May 1873; RO 14th Oct 1892; BT 15th October 1892

4   C. Aspin, *Haslingden 1800-1900*, (1962), p. 168

5   RO 22nd April 1932; Haslingden Guardian 24th October 1930; BT 17th April 1886

6   B. Brierley, *Personal recollections of the late Edwin Waugh*, (n.d.), p. 7

7   E. Baines, *History of the County Palatine and Duchy of Lancaster*, (1836), Vol. II, p. 674; RO 21st August 1914; Bacup Times 25th August 1883

8   RO 22nd November 1918

9   RO 27th January 1933, 21st August 1914; Bacup Times 4th September 1880; BT 8th October 1890

10   RO 5th March 1954

11   A. Seymour, *Pace-Egging in Bury and beyond*, (1994), pp. 16-17; *pers. com.* the late Eleanor Graham

12   RO 5th May 1944

13   M. Heap, *My life and times* (1904) [manuscript], pp. 87-88 (Rawtenstall library: RC 942 ROS); BT 3rd August 1867, 11th July 1868, 1st August 1868; Bacup Times 31st August 1867, 7th August 1875

14   RO 16th September 1904

15   RO 6th November 1908, 23rd January 1920, 20th October 1922; I. Bailey, *Edenfield Cricket Club – 100 not out*, (2002)

16   RFP 19th March 1993, 3rd April 1998; BT 9th September 1994; I. Bailey, *op. cit.*

17   RO 30th March 1928, 7th March 1913; RFP 10th December 1999; I. Bailey, *op. cit.*

18   RO 4th May 1894

19   RO 18th April 1913

20   RO 8th May 1931, 5th May 1933, 22nd September 1934, 3rd June 1938, 25th August 1939, 5th January 1940

21   RO 1st October 1920, 30th June 1922, 22nd April 1927, 17th November 1922; Haslingden Guardian 5th December 1930

22   RO 16th May 1941, 23rd August 1946, 12th May 1950, 11th September 1953, 22nd April 1960; RFP 1st November 1996

23   RO 15th May 1891, 18th September 1891

24   RO 11th January 1895, 11th May 1900

25   RO 9th January 1891, 16th January 1903

26   RO 9th May 1902, 30th May 1902, 13th June 1902, 21st November 1902

27   RO 13th September 1901, 21st July 1905, 28th October 1910

28   RO 23rd March 1906, 24th April 1908, 7th November 1913, 29th July 1904, 1st November 1907, 26th July 1907

29   RO 5th August 1904, 13th September 1907, 7th August 1908

30   RO 3rd August 1906

31   RO 11th December 1914, 7th May 1920, 24th March 1922

32   RO 20th September 1901, 9th May 1902, 21st April 1905, 26th June 1914

33   RO 18th June 1920, 3rd September 1920, 20th April 1923

34   RO 25th March 1932, 23rd February 1945, 4th September 1953; Haslingden Observer 26th March 1932

35   RO 10th September 1926, 26th May 1944; *Turnbull and Stockdale 1881-1931*, (1931), p. 43

36   RO 4th September 1936, 30th September 1960, 26th February 1965; Rochdale Road Methodist Church trustees' minute book 1940-1976 (BAS: CRR/T2561)

37   RO 2nd June 1922, 31st May 1946, 5th March 1948, 19th May 1961; Rochdale Road Methodist Church trustees' minute book 1940-1976 (BAS: CRR/T2561)

38   BT 6th December 1873, 8th November 1884, 12th June 1886, 16th April 1887

39   RO 5th October 1923, 13th March 1931, 2nd March 1934, 5th June 1959; Haslingden Guardian 14th March 1930

40   BT 21st August 1869; RO 16th June 1911, 10th October 1919

41   BT 21st June 1879; RO 24th December 1915, 13th July 1917, 3rd June 1921, 24th February 1922, 13th December 1946, 30th May 1947

42   Accrington Times 13th February 1875; BT 30th January 1886

43   BT 5th September 1885

44   RO 10th April 1891, 28th August 1914, 3rd September 1915, 26th December 1952

45   RO 6th May 1921, 30th June 1922, 16th July 1915, 14th July 1916, 25th August 1916, 19th July 1918, 15th August 1947, 29th July 1949, 29th October 1954

46 Fire insurance policy no. 1299330 (Guildhall library: Sun Fire Company records, vol. 258); Blackburn Mail 16th May 1810; BT 18th April 1868, 24th November 1877, 11th December 1886, 21st September 1878, 29th May 1869

47 BT 31st October 1874, 22nd February 1879, 3rd November 1883, 3rd March 1877, 13th November 1880, 10th November 1883; RO 5th November 1897, Haslingden Observer 31st July 1954; programme for dinner and ball 18th March 1899 (BAS: Ramsbottom Heritage Society collection. MAINARCH 0594)

48 BT 11th May 1878, 7th December 1889; RO 8th September 1933, 16th November 1917, 26th July 1929, 29th January 1932, 8th July 1932

49 RO 21st August 1914; Haslingden Chronicle and Ramsbottom Times 9th July 1870

50 RO 10th November 1934, 4th May 1906, 26th December 1906

51 RO 12th March 1948, 25th December 1959, 4th May 1906, 12th June 1931, 10th November 1934; BT 26th June 1875

52 RO 11th October 1935, 13th July 1917, 4th May 1906, 15th October 1948, 3rd November 1961; RFP 3rd June 1967; BT 8th June 1957, 14th June 1957

53 RO 26th January 1900, 28th November 1902

54 Edenfield Young Men's Institute minute book 1856-1858 (BAS: CRM/T1482); BT 22nd January 1859; RO 22nd December 1916, 26th January 1917

55 Haslingden Guardian 31st December 1892; RO 4th August 1944, 25th October 1929

56 RO 6th March 1891, 20th June 1913

57 RO 17th December 1897, 23rd March 1900

58 RO 11th February 1938, 2nd December 1938, 18th March 1943, 4th March 1938

59 Primitive Methodist Sunday School Men's Class minute book 1919-1953 (BAS: CRR/T1490); Ewood Bridge National School log-book 1902-1937 (LRO: SMHs/2/1); RO 30th May 1924, 21st June 1946, 17th January 1941

60 RO 9th September 1949, 23rd January 1953, 8th October 1954

61 RO 18th April 1902, 21st February 1896, 21st July 1899

62 RO 10th November 1899, 22nd December 1899

63 RO 23rd March 1900, 18th April 1902, 13th November 1903; RFP 2nd May 1903

64 RO 25th June 1920, 5th June 1936

65 RFP 25th June 1966; RO 24th February 1893, 9th February 1900

66 Registers of clubs 1903-1947 and 1956-1962 (LRO: PSRd/13/1 and 13/3); RO 10th October 1919, 18th March 1921, 14th July 1922, 24th October 1958

67 RO 28th December 1906, 5th January 1906, 6th January 1905, 27th November 1903, 15th April 1904, 24th November 1911

68 RO 13th October 1939, 28th September 1945

69 RO 22nd October 1946, 26th October 1945, 14th January 1949, 21st January 1949

70 RO 21st January 1949, 29th April 1949, 21st September 1956, 16th September 1949, 5th May 1950, 19th January 1951, 15th February 1952, 30th January 1959, 17th April 1959, 16th October 1959, 4th December 1959

71 RO 2nd December 1960, 25th February 1949, 12th May 1950, 5th July 1946, 30th October 1964; Rossendale Borough Council Minutes 11th October 1977 and 25th August 1989

AT WAR

THE FIRST WORLD WAR

> Come Britons! Be Britons!
> Wake up, wake up, Britons!
> Never let it be said
> That the spirit of your grandsires
> In your generation is dead.
> Be Britons, and boast,
> For ye still rule the waves;
> Ye never, no never, shall be German slaves.
> Wake up, wake up, Britons!
> As of old – strong and true:
> Sing ye of your "Sailor King",
> And of his "boys in blue."
>
> Germans all, Germans all,
> Be careful what you do.
> Germany, Germany,
> We still have boys in blue.
> And if you're going
> To keep on crowing,
> We shall think respect is owing.
> Our Navy's the best afloat:
> Until that's denied,
> Just bottle your pride,
> And sail in the friendly boat.[1]

These verses were penned by Richard Pickles of Edenfield, whose patriotic poems began appearing in the local newspapers as soon as war was declared in August 1914. Men were also encouraged to join up at recruitment meetings, which were held throughout the area. In July 1915, Miss Jane Kitchener, headmistress of Bury Grammar School for Girls and cousin of Lord Kitchener, addressed two such meetings in Stubbins and on Edenfield Recreation Ground. At Stubbins she said she 'wished she was a man of five and twenty' instead of a woman of sixty so that she could join the army, while she told her Edenfield audience 'that there was nothing greater in this world than to give their life and self for their country.'[2]

If reluctant recruits needed further encouragement they could always follow the example of one man, news of whose exploits reached Edenfield throughout the war. While Commander Charles Rumney Samson did not have the advantage of being Edenfield born and bred, he had family connections that made him an adopted son of the village. His grandfather, William Rumney, had owned Stubbins printworks in the 19th century and his parents were married at the Parish Church in 1881. In 1911, Commander Samson was one of the first naval officers to be trained to fly and pioneered the development of aircraft carriers. On the outbreak of war he went to France to take part in a mixture of cavalry operations, infantry attack and air reconnaissance. He bombed zeppelin sheds at Dusseldorf and Cologne and between March 1915 and early 1917 served in the Dardanelles and eastern Mediterranean. In the last two years of the war he was commander of an aircraft group at Great Yarmouth that was responsible for anti-submarine and anti-zeppelin operations over the North Sea. Samson was awarded the D.S.O. (1914) and bar (1917) and French croix de guerre with palm (1914) and in 1915 became a chevalier of the Legion of Honour.[3]

For civilians, the effects of the war began to be felt as soon as the conflict began. The *Haslingden Guardian* for 28th August 1914 reported:

> All over the country spinning mills and weaving sheds are being closed down, and no date is assigned for the re-opening because their directors are as much in the dark as regards a resumption of operations, as the thousands who have merely to wait silently for the call back to their looms and spindles.

Bridge Mills, Hope Mill, Turn Mill and the spinning section of Cuba Mill all closed for a time during the first weeks of the war, while at Chatterton Weaving Shed weavers were reduced to working two days each. At Turn, children whose parents had been temporarily thrown out of work were given a dinner of meat and potatoes cooked in the school kitchen. This continued until November. Matters improved slightly early in 1915 and some mills like Turn could run full time, but Hope Mill, which had been operating a three-day week, had to close again in May 1915. As well as the cotton trade, other businesses found that the effects of war were immediate. Nuttalls, the Edenfield carriers, for instance, had their motor lorry quickly commandeered and sent away to another part of the country.[4]

People soon found they had plenty to do to help the war effort. A local branch of the Red Cross formed at the end of August 1914 and by early September the ladies of the district were busy in the Conservative Club on two or three afternoons a week cutting out night shirts and other items of clothing for men in the Forces. In a single week at the end of October they sent forty-four pairs of socks, thirty-one body belts, two chest protectors and one helmet to Lord Kitchener to be distributed to the men at the front. By the end of the first year of the war they had made or collected 2,152 articles. They also raised money through house-to-house collections and social events such as the concert and dance in the Co-op Hall in April 1917, which brought in £7 0s 6d. The Red Cross branch continued their work throughout the war, disbanding in April 1919.[5]

Workers at some of the mills organised events to raise money to buy comforts or Christmas presents for their fellow workers who had enlisted or to help some other cause connected with the war. These included combined concerts, whist drives and dances held by Bridge Mills and Union Mill employees towards the end of 1916. At the Bridge Mills event in the Co-op Hall the Brunswick Pink Pierrettes from Bury entertained over 300 people, while the Union Mill event at Ramsbottom Liberal Club attracted about 450 people who enjoyed songs performed by the Union Mills Glee Party and various soloists. A similar event in February 1918 organised by people employed by the Chatterton Weaving Co. included a fancy dress parade.[6]

Children helped the war effort too, either on their own initiative or through their schools. Small groups raised money throughout the war by holding competitions to guess the name of a doll, running small bazaars selling sweets, flowers, cakes and drinks, and, on one occasion in 1915, by parading a donkey through the streets. The children collected money along the way before the donkey itself was raffled off. A branch of the League of Young Patriots was formed at the village school and by the first Christmas of the war had raised £9, the boys by chopping over 800 bundles of firewood and the girls by making paper flowers and dressing dolls. The money was divided between various funds and a shilling was sent to each of the former scholars who were in the Forces. In the summer of 1915, the League turned their attention to the National Egg Collecting Scheme for wounded soldiers. Over seven weeks in June and July they collected and dispatched 1,601 eggs. At Ewood Bridge school in the following spring a penny collection among the children raised 4s for the YMCA Huts for Soldiers Fund, while a few months later Turn children handed over 12s to the 'Jack Cornwall' Ward in the Star and Garter Home. Turn also had a War Savings Association, set up with thirty-eight members in March 1917. By the end of 1919 it had received £1,000 in subscriptions.[7]

Mill owners found several ways to help the war effort. Turnbull and Stockdale Ltd. was one of several firms that from the beginning of the war paid half wages to dependents of their employees who had voluntarily enlisted. When the scheme ended in July 1919, they had paid out £16,435 10s 10d. A.T. Porritt at Stubbins Vale initially allowed his tenants to live on their properties rent-free. He also placed Stubbins Vale House at the disposal of the military authorities. After renovation it was used as a convalescent hospital throughout the war. Its first occupants were ten Belgian soldiers who arrived from Whitworth Street Hospital, Manchester in October 1914. Stubbins Vale began with ten beds, but gradually more were added and in 1917 the total reached fifty when the conservatory and vinery at the back of the house were pressed into service. The conservatory became a dining hall and the vinery was made into wards. The *Ramsbottom Observer* commented that covering the glass roof with felt and darkening the ventilators had created an atmosphere of 'cosy comfort and roominess'. Converting the potting shed into a bathroom completed the improvements.[8]

People were generous in their support of the hospital, providing gifts of food and clothing throughout the four-and-a-half years of its existence. They also enter-tained the convalescent soldiers by giving weekly concerts, beginning in November 1914 with a 'concert pour les soldats belges.' Since all the wounded in the hospital at the time spoke only French or Flemish, care was taken to translate as many song

Some of the staff and patients at Stubbins Military Hospital in 1916.

titles as possible. 'O Who will o'er the downs?' became 'O qui voudres bein traverser le montagne?', the part-song (chanson à part) 'In this hour of softened splendour' became 'Dans ce moment de splendour tendre', but 'Jammy Face' proved too much of a test for local translators. Later concerts included many songs that are still associated with the First World War ('Roses of Picardy', 'Goodby-ee' and the like) as well as forgotten gems such as 'Mary Ann, she's after me' and 'Keep your nose out of my bonnet'. When the soldiers had recovered sufficiently to be able to leave the hospital for short trips, they were allowed free travel on the trackless trams and given free admission to the Empire Picture Palace in Ramsbottom. By the time the hospital closed in February 1919, nearly 600 wounded soldiers had received treatment there. Its contents were auctioned off and the proceeds given to the Red Cross in Manchester.[9]

The wounded Belgians who convalesced at Stubbins at the start of the war were not the only foreigners to find a refuge in the Edenfield area. In November 1914, Stubbins Congregational manse at 90, Bolton Road North was set up as a home for Belgian refugees. It was fitted out with borrowed furniture and from the end of the year became home to two couples. Other families were accommodated in two houses at Ewood Bridge. The refugees soon settled into life in east Lancashire: their children enrolled in local schools and, although the families were at first maintained by collections, the men later found jobs. Two of them who worked as fitters at

Turnbull and Stockdale's are said to have been able to understand the broad Lancashire dialect of their fellow workers because of its similarity to their native Flemish. All of the refugees had returned to their own country by the end of March 1919, although one of them – Louis Volchaert – never saw his homeland again. He died in December 1917 and is buried in Musbury churchyard.[10]

Other visitors were attracted to Edenfield by the open spaces on the neighbouring hills. Part of Dearden Moor was used as a camp for the Rawtenstall Training Corps who were based at the Drill Hall in Cloughfold. On nearby Scout Moor in January 1915, 120 members of the Manchester Grammar School Officers' Training Corps (junior division) took field practice in incessant rain after having marched from Ramsbottom railway station. Members of the Turn Home Defence Corps, who first met together in a room adjoining Turn Mill in November 1914, also used the moors for training.[11]

As the war dragged on it began to affect civilian life in more and more ways. Lighting restrictions were first imposed in March 1915, and made more stringent in February 1916. They prompted Richard Pickles to put pen to paper again in a complaint about the unnecessary black-out which, he felt, only helped spies:

> Aircraft may come say twice a month
> which may do damage termed as "small",
> But every hour of darkness helps
> The sneaking spies unto their goal.[12]

Unrestricted U-boat warfare began in 1917 and soon started to disrupt food supplies. In response, the order came to break up grassland for cultivation, although east Lancashire's weather usually made it impossible to ripen the grain. However, a good crop of wheat is said to have been grown on Lodge Farm on the Lumb Hall estate. Householders too were encouraged to grow food in their gardens, while in 1917 Ramsbottom Urban District Council made arrangements with Turnbull and Stockdale Ltd. for land in Bolton Road North and Chatterton Road to be turned into allotments. These were sub-let by the tenant farmers at 5s per 300 square yards. Schoolboys also helped by cultivating gardens at Edenfield and Ewood Bridge schools. Teachers gave lessons on the country's food supply 'and the absolute necessity for strict economy.' When general food rationing arrived in the last year of the war, staff at a least one school found themselves having to close for a day while they made out meat ration cards.[13]

Fuel rationing also made itself felt. Restrictions on the use of petrol imposed early in the war were steadily tightened, and outings from the churches and mills became rambles rather than char-a-banc trips. In the final weeks of the conflict the workpeople at Hope Mill even had to substitute a social and dance for a planned outing by horse wagonette because of new restrictions on 'joy riding'. The various churches also altered their services and other events: in 1916 the new lighting regulations made the Primitive Methodist Band of Hope abandon some of its meetings, while the Congregationalists changed their evening service first to

5.30pm and then to 3.15pm. As the war was drawing to a close the two Methodist churches and the Congregational church decided to hold united services at each place of worship in turn and again the evening services were moved to the afternoon.[14]

In the autumn of 1916, local people found themselves by accident in the middle of the conflict. During the starlit night of Monday 25th September, the L21, one of seven zeppelins on a raid from Germany, visited the area. The huge craft (almost 600 feet long) flew over the Rossendale Valley, dropping bombs on its way, until it reached Ewood Bridge. Here one bomb fell on the golf course but failed to explode and another seven fell near the sewage works and at Irwell Vale. The railway was slightly damaged (although it was repaired in time for the morning trains), the hillside above Hardsough was cratered and part of the wall adjoining Hardsough Lane was blasted some thirty or forty yards across the field. This bomb was sufficiently near to Hardsough Terrace to shatter nearly every window in the row, blow open doors and tear the window frames out of one house, hurling them into the field. A splinter from the bomb penetrated completely through a ten-inch telegraph pole. As it flew on towards Holcombe, the zeppelin dropped another bomb on the field between Irwell Vale and Lumb (now occupied by Meadow Park) and at Lumb itself, where the windows in the mill were broken.[15]

People flocked out of doors during the air raid, many still in their night attire, either to seek shelter in houses with cellars or to get a good view of the zeppelin and the falling bombs, which were plainly visible in the clear sky. One eyewitness of the raid afterwards said that 'fear and anxiety were quickly succeeded in the excitement of the moment by a sense of curiosity. A desire to see if possible, a raider at work.' Another reported that while the raid was in progress 'many cats in the vicinity developed a cheerful friskiness which they had not got rid of by noon the following day.' When daylight came, crowds of people visited the places damaged by the bombs. Irwell Vale resident, William Riley, cut up pieces of shrapnel and sold them to the visitors at 1s a time. After his supply had run out he simply cut up his 'blower' (a metal plate used to create a current of air in the fire grate) and sold it as souvenirs of the zeppelin raid.[16]

When peace finally came in November 1918 there were enthusiastic scenes throughout the locality as the mills closed to celebrate the Armistice. In Ewood Bridge, a group of young women dashed home from the mill, put on their finest clothes, stopped a passing lorry and rode on it to Haslingden cheering all the way. In the excitement the driver did not stop in Haslingden, but took the women on to Accrington. They had to walk back to Ewood Bridge, 'but … seemed in no way put out by their uncalculated experience.' The workpeople at Dearden Clough Mill were given an extra £1 in their wage packets, while the Armistice was marked in more sober fashion at the Parish Church. A service for all denominations was held on the evening of Sunday 17th November when a large congregation heard the Rev. Arthur Studdy preach a powerful sermon.[17]

Edenfield's Peace Celebrations, 1919. The picture shows some of the crowd in Market Place during the service led by the Rev. A. Studdy (*vicar of Edenfield*), the Rev. J. Cawley (*Primitive Methodist minister*) and the Rev. B. Bevan (*curate*).

How the children of Edenfield celebrated peace: the start of the boys' footrace behind the Horse and Jockey.

The Peace Celebrations in July 1919 were blessed with 'perfect weather [which] enabled the full programme of local rejoicings to be carried out without the slightest curtailment.' In Edenfield the day began with a procession through the village headed by Goodshaw Prize Band and including about 200 soldiers and ex-Service-men. At noon the crowd gathered in the Market Place where a service was held, concluding with the National Anthem. 'Dinner on a lavish scale' provided by Mr. and Mrs. Edwin Barlow was served to all villagers over sixty years of age and all widows and widowers. Each guest also received a quarter of tea from Mrs. Barlow. There were other mammoth meals later in the day when 430 children had a free tea in the church school and 240 soldiers and sailors from the district were fed in the Co-op Hall. Here again there were gifts of cigarettes and sweets for every guest. During the afternoon and evening, sports were held in a field behind the Horse and Jockey. As well as the usual foot races, sack race, egg and spoon race and three-legged race, the programme included a comic costume race, gathering up boots race and (for men over 18) a hobble skirt race. A baby show (open to babies born since the Armistice) was won by Jack Dearnley whose prize was five war savings certificates.[18]

The residents of Irwell Vale joined the Peace Celebrations at Helmshore where the programme included a procession around the village, tableaux and dancing displays by the children and a race to the top of Tor and back. During the afternoon and evening, the various Methodist choirs gave concerts, the Irwell Vale Primitive

The 1919 Peace Celebrations for the children of Ewood Bridge School included a visit from the Mayor and Mayoress of Haslingden, Major and Mrs. Halstead.

Methodist choir opening the programme with 'Let the hills resound.' At Ewood Bridge the celebrations began at 9.30am with an out of doors service. This was followed by a procession in which nearly all of the 300 or so residents of the village took part and that ended in a field at Bent Gate. Here there were sports and games, including a race for ladies over fifty and a hairdressing competition for the men.[19]

No general memorial was built in Edenfield to commemorate all those who had been killed in the war. The Primitive Methodists were the first to have their own memorial in the form of a pictorial roll of honour, which they unveiled in December 1918. A more permanent marble tablet carrying the names of the men from the chapel who had been killed was set up in 1922. By this date other memorial tablets had also been erected at the various churches and chapels and some of the mills. At the Parish Church a white marble tablet on the north wall and a peal of eight bells in the tower commemorates all the men from the parish who were killed, regardless of which church they attended. Over 700 people packed into the church for the dedication of the memorial in March 1921.[20]

THE SECOND WORLD WAR

Like the rest of the country, people in Edenfield and neighbourhood began preparations for war in 1938. Air Raid Precaution schemes, which had lain in readiness for some months, were triggered into action by the crisis over Czechoslovakia in the autumn. On 26th September air raid wardens in the Ramsbottom area were mobilised, although the turn out was not as good as it might have been because it was the middle of the September holidays and several wardens were away. Those who were at home reported for duty and began the task of assembling 14,300 gas masks, which had been stored in the Technical School since the beginning of the month. Their distribution started on the following day when the wardens took them out to people in all of the thirty-six sectors into which the Urban District had been divided. Notices posted in mills and shown on the town's cinema screens asked anyone who had not received their mask to collect one from any of six distribution centres, including Stubbins and Turn schools.[21]

By the end of September nearly everyone over the age of four in the Ramsbottom area had been issued with a gas mask. Early in the following month, people also heard the air raid sirens for the first time when they were tested to see how effective they were. At the same time, the council surveyor and his men waited to be given the go ahead to dig trenches for air raid shelters in the playing fields. The signing of the Munich Agreement eased the international crisis, but it was clear that plans for the defence of civilians in the event of a war were simply inadequate. Partly to remedy the situation, a programme of recruitment and training of volunteers took place in the winter of 1938 and spring of 1939. By May, two hundred wardens, forty-five special constables and an Auxiliary Fire Service were on duty in the Ramsbottom Urban District. ARP post no.1 was established at the Coach and Horses, no.2 at 47,

More than sixty years after it was painted, this sign on a gatepost at Stubbins still points the way to the ARP post in Dale Street.

Bury Road, while no.3 was in a washhouse in Dale Street. Nearby Union Mill was rented from Turnbull and Stockdale Ltd. as an ARP store for five years beginning in February 1939. In addition, the Edenfield section of the AFS had their own station at the Central Garage next to the Horse and Jockey equipped with a large trailer pump.[22]

All of the volunteers were able to put their newly learnt skills to the test during the night of 16th/17th May, 1939 when they took part in a 'black-out' exercise. Members of the Special Constabulary were kept busy directing traffic at the main road junctions, while the wardens and AFS dealt with imaginary emergencies. These included an outbreak of fire at the Pack Horse and a high explosive bomb falling on an electricity substation at Nimble Nook, injuring three people. On the following evening ARP volunteers met again, but this time in the more congenial surroundings of Collinge's Tudor Café, Stubbins. The occasion was the presentation of badges and certificates for those who had qualified in First Aid and anti-gas measures.[23]

When war finally came in September 1939, people dug out their gas masks and were encouraged to carry them at all times 'by persuasion, and to a minor degree, propaganda messages such as "Have you got your gas mask?" having been chalked on the pavement.' Earlier plans to build air raid shelters were put into operation. On the 15th the *Ramsbottom Observer* reported:

> The recreation ground just off the Market Place at Edenfield already gives a good imitation of a battlefield, the trenches there being of a fairly extensive nature, and another plot of land in Bolton Road has been utilised. The trenches at the latter place are about forty yards in extent, and are built on the zig-zag plan, as in the case of a direct hit this would reduce casualties to a minimum. It is estimated that the latter trenches alone should be capable of providing shelter for from 160 to 200 people.

By the summer of 1940 additional shelters – each holding at least fifty people – had been built at Turn, Stubbins (near Robert Street), Esk Street, near the Horse and Jockey, near Oaklands Road and in the school yard. Ewood Bridge had a brick shelter opposite the school, while at Irwell Vale the chapel cellars were used. Some of the shelters were not very comfortable, the one at Ewood Bridge in particular giving the headmistress of the school cause to complain. After a raid in December 1940 she noted:

> The floor was damp and dirty – appeared that dogs had made a convenience of the whole shelter. Children had to go into the field to clean their clogs before returning to school.

Eventually electric light was installed and the shelter improved, but in the meantime the children used the school cellars. Here they whiled away the time singing and reciting their times tables. Several of the shelters long outlasted the war: the one on Oaklands Road, for instance, was not demolished until 1968. In the first year of the conflict the frequent alerts began to affect the children and their schoolwork. In October 1940 the Ewood Bridge headmistress wrote:

> The children are certainly showing signs of strain owing no doubt to the broken sleep and varying bedtimes of the family. Arithmetic instead of beginning at 9.35 will not begin until 10.15 or after 11 o'clock. Reading and oral lessons will be taken instead up to playtime.[24]

"UP HOUSEWIVES AND AT 'EM!"

YOU can have a "smack at 'em." There are war weapons in *your* household waste. Every scrap counts, so save every scrap — of paper, metal, bones. ★

Keep them separate and put them by the dustbin every collection day. They are wanted urgently to make munitions. Let's all get right into action *now!*

★ *Also put out waste food if this is collected in your district.*

Put out your PAPER METAL BONES

PUT THEM OUT CAREFULLY
Follow the instructions you will receive, care saves time, space, money.

THEY WILL BE COLLECTED
Councils in districts with a population over 10,000 must arrange for collection. You can help to see that the collection is well and thoroughly done. Send suggestions to your Councils.

THEY WILL BE USED
Every scrap that is put out according to instructions and efficiently collected will be used for victory.

This is what your back door should look like on collection day.

METAL   BONES   PAPER

ISSUED BY THE MINISTRY OF SUPPLY

The Ministry of Supply encouraged housewives to help the war effort by saving household waste. This notice appeared in the *Ramsbottom Observer* in August 1940.

Other signs of the war also quickly made an appearance. In the autumn of 1939 gas detector posts were set up throughout the Ramsbottom area (they were coated with a special paint that turned bright red on contact with liquid gas). Meanwhile, in the following summer, signposts and direction signs were taken down and stone milestones defaced, buses lost their destination boards and place names on shops, schools and churches were covered up. Later in 1940 iron railings around recreation grounds and open spaces and some of the poles that had carried cables for the trackless trams were taken away and, as the *Ramsbottom Observer* put it, 'changed into shells, bombs or other equally troublesome things.'[25]

Since the Edenfield area was considered to be safe, the village and its neighbours took a share of evacuees who came initially from Manchester and Salford. The first batch of evacuee children travelled by train on 1st September 1939 with more arriving on the following two days. Canteens were set up in various schools and other public buildings, including St. Philip's Sunday school and Edenfield Conservative Club. Thirty evacuee children were admitted to Edenfield school and two Manchester teachers taken on to the staff before it re-opened on 14th September. At Turn ten children from Briscoe Lane Junior Mixed and Brookdale Parks schools came with one teacher, while Stubbins received sixty-eight children and three teachers. Ewood Bridge children and staff shared their school with eighty boys from Salford Open Air school. The local children were taught in the school during the morning while the evacuees took their lessons in the cricket pavilion at Bent Gate. The classes changed places in the afternoon. Most of the evacuees returned home early in 1940, although a Mrs. Robert stayed long enough to give birth to the district's first evacuee baby at the home of Mrs. Buckle in Burnley Road in February. The second group of evacuees came from the Mile End Road district of London in the summer of 1944 and stayed for about a year. Towards the end of the war European refugees also found a home in Edenfield, albeit in houses such as those at Pinfold that had been previously condemned as slums.[26]

The evacuees were not the only new faces to be seen in the district during the war years. From the beginning of hostilities until March 1940, men from the Duke of Lancaster's Own Yeomanry along with 120 horses were billeted in Lumb Mill. The soldiers provided opponents for Edenfield United on at least one occasion in October 1939 when in 'a good clean sporting game' both sides scored four goals. After the army's departure for Derby racecourse, the mill became a Ministry of Supply depot. Cuba Mill at Stubbins also provided a billet for soldiers, while their officers occupied Green Mount, one of the old Porritt homes. Here one day in 1943 arrived a very nervous, newly commissioned lieutenant. His name was Dirk Bogarde. Recalling his time at Stubbins Vale, he was later to write:

> From the terrace of the house, grimed with soot and wind, one looked down into a grey, fogged landscape of endless slate-roofed "back-to-backers" and soaring mills throbbing with trundling looms, glittering with acres of lighted windows (dark in the black out after 3.30 in the afternoon) and huge chimneys trailing and belching smoke endlessly into the

curdled air, which loitered out over the spoiled valleys until, eventually, it was dispersed across the distant moors. Not a very attractive vista. I have known better views from happier terraces. It was sad, cobbled, drab, poor.[27]

For First World War veterans, those in reserved occupations or young men awaiting call up, the Local Defence Volunteers, or Home Guard as they became known, provided an opportunity to help to defend their country. The local Home Guard company was based at the Drill Hall, Ramsbottom, but had members from all over the district. A cadet company for boys aged fourteen to sixteen and a half was set up in 1943 and helped to swell the ranks of volunteers. Training took place on the Holcombe firing range and on the moors above Edenfield and Shuttleworth, where the Home Guard learnt how to throw hand grenades. Soldiers from Cuba Mill gave lectures and demonstrations at the Drill Hall, while some of the younger members of the Home Guard used the assault course set up by the regular soldiers in the wood near Edenwood Mill. This involved crossing the brook on a rope bridge, clambering through smoke filled pipes, scaling high walls and wading through water nearly shoulder deep wearing full kit and carrying a rifle.[28]

The war brought immediate changes to civilian life. First of all there was a curtailment of many activities, particularly at the churches. The introduction of lighting restrictions, for example, meant that evening services had to be cancelled even though black-out curtains were soon fitted (in the case of Market Place Methodists using the same curtains that had done duty in the First World War). Further changes were made in 1942 when the Methodist congregations decided to hold services at each chapel on alternate Sundays in order to save fuel. Stubbins Congregationalists also joined these services, which continued to be held even after the partial lifting of the black-out in November 1944. Social activities also had to be cut back. In his annual report for 1940, the secretary of Rochdale Road Methodist Men's Class noted that travelling restrictions had made it difficult to get speakers from outside the district, while the Market Place Methodist Ladies Aid annual tea in January 1940 was quite different from similar events in earlier years:

> Instead of the usual bright social evening that followed the appetising teas which the Ladies Aid committee have always proudly and happily prepared, we each took our own refreshments and by about six o'clock every one had made for home with an eagerness which is not generally known amongst our Ladies Aid members, but just at this time we were passing through a very dangerous period of our lives, owing to enemy action.

Later the same year the ladies also abandoned their annual trip:

> Talked for a long time about the Ladies Trip and went in imagination to Towneley Park and Southport and to various parks both by bus and coach, but all to no avail. We decided to postpone the trip until we could travel under more favourable circumstances.[29]

Although their social life may have changed, villagers soon channelled their energies into the war effort. As in the First World War, local farmers were able to make a special contribution by growing crops on land that had not seen the plough for generations. In the summer of 1941 nearly one hundred acres of land around Edenfield and Turn had been brought into cultivation. Oats were by far the most widely grown crop and were found in greatest quantities on farms like Chapel House (8 acres), Plunge (5¾ acres), the Pack Horse (5 acres) and Gin Croft (5 acres), as well as the higher farms at Turn, including Acre Nook (2 acres), Fecit (2½ acres) and Close Nook (2 acres). Fodder crops, including kale, turnip and swede were also widely grown. Vegetables for human consumption appeared on only a few farms – half an acre at Brook Bottom, just off Rochdale Road, and Kay Close and one acre at Gin Croft – but potatoes were planted on many farms, ranging from Sky House, where J.W. Skillings had put in about 120 yards of main crop potatoes, to Fecit and Close Nook, which each had an acre of potatoes.[30]

There were many other ways in which people made a contribution to the war effort. Branches of the W.V.S. started up at Edenfield and Stubbins and each year held garden parties, whist drives, bring-and-buy sales and concerts to raise money. 'Magnificent success', for example, attended a bring-and-buy sale held by Edenfield W.V.S. at Chatterton Hey in August 1940 where visitors were also entertained by a lady playing ukulele solos. The event raised £45. At Christmas of the same year, Stubbins W.V.S. sent between forty and fifty parcels containing a pullover, two other woolly garments and a packet of cigarettes to Stubbins men in the Forces. Other groups raised money too: on Christmas Eve 1942 carol singers from Rochdale Road chapel collected £15 for the Prisoner of War Books and Parcels Fund, while in January 1943 Edenfield Tradesmen's Association held concerts and whist drives to raise funds for the Red Cross.[31]

Children were not left out of the war effort and sometimes organised events themselves. In September 1940, for instance, Jenny McLaren, Jenny Smith and Herbert and Allan Rogers from Chatterton gave concerts in streets and backyards to raise £3 0s 2d for the Ramsbottom Spitfire Fund. Children also participated in events organised by or through their schools. One such was the collection of waste paper during the local salvage drive early in 1942. Stubbins school collected 3 tons 6 cwts 98 lbs; Edenfield 1 ton 3 cwt 39 lbs and Turn 10 cwt 86 lbs. Two years later, two hours of 'bright and breezy entertainment' at Edenfield school raised money for the comforts fund for those in the Forces. The concert included choruses, songs, recitations, carols, dances and a 'potted pantomime', "The Babes in the Soup" written by the headmaster, Mr. Critchley.[32]

Local people also contributed to the special fund raising weeks that were held annually between 1941 and 1944. During War Weapons Week in 1941, for example, Ewood Bridge children held a jumble sale, raffles and a maypole and collected empty jam jars, which they sold to a Brierfield firm. In the following year in Warship Week, Ramsbottom aimed to raise £140,000, the cost of a large minesweeper, but in fact raised £158,067, the equivalent of £10 17s per head of the Urban District's population. Just a few of the contributions from Edenfield and its neighbours included £50 6s 3d from the W.V.S., £1,650 from Turnbull and Stockdale's Saving Group, £273 15s from Bridge Mills Saving Group and £467 14s from the Stubbins Ladies Saving Association. (They had hoped to raise just £260, enough for two large mines). Mrs. Walker of Ewood Bridge and Mrs. Smith of Irwell Vale organised a joint effort during the same week and raised £20 10s for the Mayoress of Haslingden's mile of pennies. Ewood Bridge children added another £10, the proceeds of a bring-and-buy sale.[33]

As in the First World War when the zeppelin dropped bombs at Irwell Vale, the Edenfield area suffered only once from enemy aircraft action. This time it was Stubbins that was hit when two landmines were dropped by parachute in the early hours of Saturday morning, 3rd May 1941. One of the bombs fell against the bank of the River Irwell, just upstream from Stubbins Bridge, while the other fell in a newly dug garden at Ox Hey. This made damage to property less than it might have been and no lives were lost. ARP Warden Harold Scowcroft was standing only about fifteen to twenty yards from the river bomb and later said:

> I was on duty when I heard the bomb coming. I shouted to some pals a little further along the road who were on duty as firewatchers at a bleachworks, 'Eh lads, there is a bomb coming down.' I took cover, flinging myself flat on the pavement against a wall with my head resting between my hands. There was then a terrific explosion, and water and stones from the river were scattered all round about. Immediately afterwards I heard a second bomb drop about a quarter of a mile away. I continued to lie prostrate for a minute or two, and then on hearing a thud, which I considered was some distance away, I got up. All I could see for some moments was what appeared to be an atmosphere of blackness – as black as coal – and this blackness then seemed to disappear along the river as though it were a cloud.[34]

He added that a weird sort of scream went up from the village. Another warden, J.H. Collinge, was flung against the gable end of his shop and had his helmet whisked from his head and thrown into the middle of the road by the explosion.

Mr. and Mrs. Harry Warwick and their nine-year-old daughter, Alice, had a very lucky escape. Their bungalow on the banks of the river was very near the first bomb and was badly damaged. The roof collapsed in the middle, but was still supported at the gables. Thus, while it pinned the family into their beds, it also acted as a protection from falling debris. In one house the heads of a bunch of daffodils were cut clean off, leaving the stalks and vase undamaged, while in another a dressing table with a revolving mirror was jerked into the centre of the room, its mirror flipped over and then flung back against the wall.

On the following day, shops and mills went to work as usual and people began salvaging their furniture and belongings. A rest centre opened in St. Philip's Sunday school where W.V.S. workers provided meals throughout the day. Incredibly no one was seriously injured and the only fatalities were a flock of hens roosting near the river. A total of 286 houses were damaged. Most of them were repaired over the next few years, including the Warwick family bungalow, but nos. 244-250, Bolton Road North (next to the bridge) and Stubbins Vale House (where many of the interior walls were blown out) proved too badly damaged and were demolished in 1948 and 1950.[35]

Stubbins, May 1941. A policeman stands guard outside the ruins of the Warwick family's bungalow.

'No scenes of wild rejoicing' was how local people greeted peace according to the *Ramsbottom Observer*. A joint service of thanksgiving organised by Edenfield Youth Club was held in Market Place Methodist Church. Members of the club read the lesson and said prayers for people in the Forces and also sang a special hymn. The Market Place Ladies Aid celebrated on 13th June with a special tea, followed on the 20th by a trip to Southport. The secretary recorded that 'we spent a very enjoyable day, indulging as the Market Place Methodist ladies traditionally do in a sumptuous tea of Plaice & Chips & those who were in a more gluttonous frame of mind went onto strawberries & cream.' Early in October 1945, Ewood Bridge children were given a Victory Celebration party when tea was followed by games and singing. At the end of the evening, each child received an apple and 'all went home happy.' People who were demobilised were usually welcomed home with a party: at Ewood Bridge in May 1947, fifty people sat down to a meal, followed by a whist drive and dancing to music played by the Blue Echoes Band. Similarly in June, members of St. Philip's church were welcomed home with an evening's entertainment and supper.[36]

Since none of the villages had a general memorial from the First World War to which the names of those killed in the 1939-45 war could be added, new memorials were usually set up in the individual churches and mills. At St. Peter's, Ewood Bridge a tablet bearing the names of the four village men killed was unveiled at the end of April

1947, while at St. Philip's the memorial took the form of a bronze cross and vases that were dedicated in May 1950. Later in the same year, nearly 300 workpeople from Stubbins Vale Mills saw a black polished granite plaque unveiled to commemorate six employees of Porritt Brothers and Austin Ltd. – including director R.W. Porritt – who had been killed in action. More general memorials in the form of small gardens were established in Stubbins, Edenfield and Turn in 1953 and 1954. The one at Stubbins was laid out on the site of some of the houses destroyed by the 1941 bomb, Edenfield's memorial garden was placed on a plot of land adjoining Market Street, while the site chosen at Turn was next to the Plane Tree Inn.[37]

NOTES

1 RO 16th October 1914
2 RO 16th July 1915
3 *Dictionary of National Biography 1931-1940* (1949), pp. 781-783
4 BT 29th August 1914, 19th September 1914, 31st October 1914, 3rd April 1915, 29th May 1915; RO 7th August 1914; Turn Board School log-book (LRO: SMR/2/1)
5 RO 21st August 1914, 4th September 1914, 30th October 1914, 27th April 1917, 18th April 1919; East Lancashire Branch British Red Cross Society, *An illustrated account of the work of the branch during the first year of the war*, (1916), p. 239
6 RO 10th November 1916, 22nd December 1916, 22nd February 1918
7 RO 6th August 1915, 11th August 1916, 20th November 1915, 15th January 1915, 4th June 1915, 9th July 1915; Ewood Bridge National School log-book (LRO: SMHs/2/1); Turn Board School log-book (LRO: SMR/2/1)
8 RO 4th July 1919, 3rd August 1917
9 RO 13th November 1914, 4th May 1917, 14th March 1919
10 RO 20th November 1914, 1st January 1915; Haslingden Gazette 2nd August 1919
11 RFP 30th September 1916; RO 8th January 1915; BT 28th November 1914, 16th December 1914
12 RO 12th March 1915
13 RO 23rd March 1917, 16th March 1917; Ewood Bridge National School log-book (LRO: SMHs/2/1); *Stubbins County Primary School – Extracts from the school log book 1868-1988*, (1988) p. 21
14 RO 11th October 1918; Primitive Methodist Band of Hope minute book 1894-1918 (BAS: CRR/T2574); Stubbins Congregational Church Meeting minute book 1896-1974 (BAS: CST/2/1)
15 RO 29th September 1916
16 RO 29th September 1916; Haslingden Gazette 30th September 1916; A. Taylor, *The life and times of John Amos Taylor*, (1997) [typescript], p. 33 (Rawtenstall library: RC921 Tay)
17 Haslingden Guardian 15th November 1918; RO 22nd November 1918
18 RO 25th July 1919
19 Haslingden Gazette 26th July 1919
20 RO 17th July 1925; 25th March 1921
21 RO 30th September 1938
22 RO 28th October 1938, 19th May 1939, 8th September 1939; BT 9th September 1939
23 RO 19th May 1939
24 RO 8th September 1939, 15th September 1939, 8th December 1939, 5th June 1940; L. Longworth, *Edenfield Church and School History Notebook*, (1989), p. 69; RFP 30th November 1968; Ewood Bridge National School log-book (LRO: SMHs/2/2)
25 RO 3rd November 1939, 7th June 1940, 28th June 1940, 13th September 1940, 27th September 1940
26 RFP 15th June 1967; RO 8th September 1939, 16th February 1940; Longworth, *op. cit.*, p. 69; Turn Board School log-book (LRO: SMR/2/1); *Stubbins County Primary School – Extracts from the school log book 1868-1988*, (1988), p. 26; Ewood Bridge National School log-book (LRO: SMHs/2/2); Ramsbottom Urban District Council minutes 27th June 1944

27 Lancashire Evening Telegraph October 1991; RO 13th October 1939, 11th December 1942; Daily Telegraph 4th April 1992

28 F. Entwistle, 'The Home Guard in Ramsbottom, 1941-4', *Ramsbottom Heritage Society News Magazine*, (Winter 1994-95) 15-16

29 RO 15th September 1939, 13th October 1939, 16th October 1942; Primitive Methodist Leaders' meeting minute book 1929-1945 (BAS: CRR/T1490); Primitive Methodist Sunday School Men's Class minute book 1919-1953 (BAS: CRR/T1490); Market Place Methodist Ladies Aid secretary reports 1935-1947 (BAS: CRM/T1482); Market Place Methodist Ladies Aid minutes 1933-1944 (BAS: CRM/T1482)

30 National Farm Survey, parish of Ramsbottom (PRO: MAF 32/564/94)

31 RO 9th August 1940, 13th December 1940, 1st January 1943, 8th January 1943

32 RO 20th September 1940, 13th February 1942, 18th February 1944

33 Ewood Bridge National School log-book (LRO: SMHs/2/2); RO 3rd April 1942, 20th March 1942

34 RO 9th May 1941

35 RO 9th May 1941, 25th June 1948, 14th July 1950

36 RO 11th May 1945, 23rd May 1947, 27th June 1947; Market Place Methodist Ladies Aid secretary's report 1935-1947 (BAS: CRM/T1482); Ewood Bridge National School log-book (LRO: SMHs/2/2)

37 RO 2nd May 1947, 26th May 1950, 14th July 1950, 5th September 1952, 31st July 1953, 6th November 1953, 7th May 1954

BIBLIOGRAPHY

MANUSCRIPT SOURCES

Public Record Office, London
    Bankruptcy order books (B1)
    Census of religious worship 1851 (HO 129/477)
    Census returns (HO and RG)
    Dissolved companies files (BT 31)
    Exchequer records (E112)
    National Farm Survey (MAF)
    Tottington Higher End tithe file (IR 18/4284)
    Valuation Office records (IR 58)

Lancashire Record Office, Preston
    Quarter Sessions Petitions (QSP)
    Plans and sections of the bridges belonging to the hundred of Salford (QAR/6/6)
    Land Tax returns (QDL)
    Register of dissenters meeting houses (QDV/4)
    Petty Sessions records (PSRd)
    Wills (WCW)
    Tottington Higher End tithe award and plan 1838 (DRM 1/97)
    Tottington Higher End valuation 1837 (MBH 5/6)
    Haslingden Rural District Sanitary Authority records (SAH)
    Police records (PLA)
    Bury, Haslingden, Blackburn and Whalley turnpike trust minutes (TTA)
    Bury Poor Law Union records (PUB)
    Haslingden Poor Law Union records (PUH)
    Tottington Higher End School Board records (SBT)
    Walmersley and Ramsbottom School Board records (SBX)
    Walmersley and Shuttleworth School Board records (SBW)
    Ewood Bridge National School log books (SMHs)
    Turn Board School log book (SMR/2/1)
    Accrington and Haslingden Methodist Circuit records (MAc)
    St. Thomas's Parish Church, Musbury records (PR 3067)
    Assheton of Downham [Manor of Tottington] records (DDHCL)
    Formby of Formby papers (DDFO)
    Stanley, Earls of Derby papers (DDK)
    Whittaker family of Broadclough deeds and papers (DDX 1350)
    Rose Bank and Chatterton estate deeds (DDX 1777)
    Stubbins estate deeds (DDX 1586)

Cheshire Record Office, Chester
    Articles of Enquiry preparatory to Visitation (EDV7)

Bolton Archive Service
Irwell Reservoirs Scheme records (UWR)
John Albinson of Bolton, surveyor, records (ZAL)

Bury Archive Service
Bury Primitive Methodist Circuit records (CBP)
Edenfield Primitive Methodist Church records (CRR)
Edenfield Wesleyan Methodist Church records (CRM)
Market Place Methodist Church records (CRM)
Ramsbottom Heritage Society archive
Ramsbottom Industrial and Provident Society Ltd. records (GRI)
Ramsbottom Urban District Council records (ARM)
Rochdale Road Methodist Church records (CRR)
Stubbins Congregational Church records (CST)
Woodcock papers (BWO)

Church of England Record Centre, South Bermondsey
National Society archives

Guildhall Library, London
Royal Exchange Fire Insurance Company records
Sun Fire Insurance Company records

Manchester Central Library
Archdeacon Rushton's visitation returns (MSf 942.72 R121)
Edenfield parish records (MF PR 117a)
Episcopal visitation returns 1931 (M39/97)
Graham, J. *History of printworks in the Manchester district 1760-1846* (BR66 667.3G1)

Burnley Library
Burnley and Edenfield turnpike trust minutes (N14)

Rawtenstall Library
Heap, M., *My life and times* (RC 942 ROS)
Sale particulars for Horncliffe House 1899 (RC 728 HOR)
Sketch of the Scout Moor incline (RC 622.33 EDE)
Stephens, P., *Notes on Edenfield and Ewood Bridge* (RC 942 EDE)
Taylor, A., *The life and times of John Amos Taylor* (RC 921 TAY)

Companies House, Cardiff
Britannia Rope and Twine Co. Ltd.
Chatterton Weaving Co. Ltd.
Edenfield Soap and Toiletries Ltd.
Edenfield Spinning Co. Ltd.
George Clegg (1920) Ltd.
John Schofield (Textile Machinery) Ltd.
Sigma Soap Ltd.
Thomas Aitken and Son Ltd.
W. and E. Products Ltd.

Helmshore Local History Society
Ewood Bridge deeds
Stott and Smith papers

Miscellaneous

Absalom Watkin's diary [Courtesy of Magdalen Goffin]
The Simmons collection of records relating to Lancashire water wheels [Copies at the Lancashire Library Local Studies department, Preston]
Whittaker family business records [Courtesy of Mrs. E. Whittaker]

PRINTED SOURCES

Barlow, R., *The diary of Richard Barlow, a Ramsbottom postman 1882 to 1925*, (n.d.)
Fund for the relief of distress in the manufacturing districts – return from local relief committees, week ending 31st January 1863 [Manchester Central Library, P3339]
GPO Classified Telephone Directories – Blackburn and Preston Areas, 1962 - 1975
Haslingden Borough Council Minutes
Holme, E., *An account and measurement of the public bridges within the hundred of Salford*, (1782)
House of Commons Journal
Return comprising the reports made to the Charity Commissioners, in the results of Inquiries in the Administrative County of Lancaster...into Endowments, Vol.IV, Salford Hundred, (1910)
Rossendale Borough Council Minutes
Seyd & Co., *The Manchester and district commercial list*, (1881-1882)
Stubbins County Primary School - Extracts from the school log book 1868-1988, (1988)

DIRECTORIES

T. Rogerson, *Lancashire General Directory*, (1818)
E. Baines, *History, directory and gazetteer of the County Palatine of Lancaster*, (1824-5)
J. Pigot & Co., *New commercial directory for Cheshire, Derbyshire and Lancashire*, (1828)
J. Heap, *The Bury Directory*, (1850)
I. Slater, *Royal National classified commercial directory and topography of the county of Lancashire*, (1851)
Mannex & Co., *History, Topography and Directory of Mid-Lancashire*, (1854)
E.S. Drake, *Commercial directory of Bolton, Bury, Wigan...and adjoining townships*, (1861)
Kelly & Co., *The Post Office Directory of Lancashire*, (1873)
P. Mannex & Co., *Directory and topography of north-east Lancashire*, (1875-6)
P. Barrett & Co., *Directory and topography of Bury, Heywood, Ramsbottom...and adjacent villages and townships*, (1880)
P. Barrett & Co., *General and commercial directory of Bury ... Ramsbottom and adjacent villages and townships*, (1883)
I. Slater, *Royal Commercial Directory of Bury, Heywood, Radcliffe, Ramsbottom and districts*, (1888)
J. Worrall, *The cotton spinners and manufacturers' directory*, (1891)
Kelly's Directories Ltd., *Directory of Lancashire*, (1901)
J. and A. Churchill, *The Medical Directory*, (1920, etc.)
T. Skinner & Co., *Skinner's cotton trade directory of the world*, (1923 and 1930-31)
Kelly's Directories Ltd., *Directory of Lancashire*, (1924)
Trades' Directories Ltd., *North-Western Counties of England Trades Directory*, (1936, 1939, 1966, 1969)
T. Skinner & Co. (Publishers) Ltd., *Skinner's Cotton Trade Directory of the World*, (1940-41)
J. Worrall, *The Lancashire textile industry*, (1948)
Rossendale Productivity Association, *Classified Rossendale Directory*, (1969)

PRINTED SECONDARY WORKS

anon., *Greenwood & Coope Limited Fiftieth Anniversary*, (1974)

anon., *Lancashire. Part First. The premier county of the kingdom. Cities and towns, historical, statistical, biographical, business men and mercantile interests, wealth and growth. An epitome of results*, (1889-90)

anon., *St. Peter's, Ewood Bridge. Memoir of Centenary Celebrations*, (1939)

anon., *Turnbull and Stockdale 1881 to 1931*, (1931)

Aspin, C., *Mr. Pilling's short cut to China and other stories of Rossendale enterprise*, (1983)

Aspin, C., *Haslingden 1800-1900*, (1962)

Aspin, C., *Lancashire, the first industrial society*, (1969)

Bailey, I., *Edenfield Cricket Club – 100 not out*, (2002)

Baines, E., *History of the County Palatine and Duchy of Lancaster*, (1836)

Bairstow, M., *The East Lancashire Railway*, (1993)

Barber-Lomax, J.W., 'Barcelona and Stubbins', *Ramsbottom Heritage Society News Magazine*, (Winter 1992-3) 5-7

Beesley, G., *A report of the state of agriculture in Lancashire*, (1849)

Beswick, W., *Memories of Turn Village: Its life, activities and characters 1907-1933*, (n.d.)

Betjeman, J., (ed.) *Collins Pocket Guide to English Parish Churches: The North*, (1968)

Brierley, B., *Personal recollections of the late Edwin Waugh*, (n.d.)

Burnett, J., *A social history of housing 1815-1970*, (1978)

Coupe, G., *Tottington Hall through five centuries*, (1987)

Dalton, R., 'Farm sale advertisements as a data source in historical agriculture study: possibilities and limitations', *The Local Historian*, (February 1998) 36-49

Dickson, R., *General view of the agriculture of Lancashire*, (1815)

Dictionary of National Biography 1931-1940, (1949)

Dunne, P., *St. Philip's Church, Stubbins, 1927-1977*, (1977)

East Lancashire Branch British Red Cross Society, *An illustrated account of the work of the branch during the first year of the war*, (1916)

Entwistle, F., 'The Home Guard in Ramsbottom, 1941-4', *Ramsbottom Heritage Society News Magazine*, (Winter 1994-5) 15-16

Farrer, W., & J. Brownbill (eds.), *The Victoria history of the county of Lancaster*, vol. V, (1906)

Fogg, E. and Jennings, A., 'Mercury peril from soap manufacture', *New Scientist*, (16th May 1985), 9

Foot, W., *Maps for family history – a guide to the records of the tithe, valuation office and national farm surveys of England and Wales, 1836-1943*, (1994)

Gray, M., *Edenfield - Church, parish and village 1778-1978*, (1978)

Hall, A.D., *A pilgrimage of British farming 1910-1912*, (1913)

Harding, W.E., *The history of Park Congregational Church, Ramsbottom*, (1931)

Hill, C., *The history of Wesleyan Methodism in Edenfield*, (1928)

Hillis, J.G., 'Childhood memories of Edenfield', *Ramsbottom Heritage Society News Magazine*, (Spring 1997) 12-14

Jennings, P., 'Studying beerhouses', *The Local Historian*, (November 1987) 457-464

Law, B.R., *Fieldens of Todmorden*, (1995)

Longmate, N., *The Waterdrinkers*, (1968)

Longworth, L., *Edenfield church and school history notebook*, (1989)

Luty, M., *A penniless globetrotter*, (1937)

Newbigging, T., *History of the Forest of Rossendale*, (1893)

Orchard, B. Guiness, *Liverpool's Legion of Honour*, (1893)

Orr, J., 'Lancashire and Cheshire', in J. Maxton (ed.), *Regional types of British agriculture by fifteen authors*, (1936)

Palmer, B., 'Ramsbottom trolley buses', *Ramsbottom Heritage Society News Magazine*, (Winter/Spring 1992), 12-16

Partington, S.W., *The toll bars and turnpike roads of Bury and Rossendale*, (1921)

Ramsbottom, B.A., 'Limey Leach and Cheesden Pasture', *The Strict Baptist Historical Society Annual Report and Bulletin*, (1974)

Roberts, B., *Railways and Mineral Tramways of Rossendale*, (1974)

Robertson, W., *Rochdale Past and Present*, (1876)

Rose, M. (ed.), *The Lancashire cotton industry – a history since 1700*, (1996)

Rothwell, W., *Report of the agriculture of the county of Lancaster*, (1849)

Sandiford, A.V., and Ashworth, T.E., *The Forgotten Valley*, (1981)

Seymour, A., *Pace-Egging in Bury and beyond*, (1994)

Simpson, J., *Irwell Vale. A centenary history of the Methodist church*, (1993)

Stott, J., *Notices of Methodism in Haslingden*, (1898)

Todd, A., *Around Ramsbottom*, (1995)

Tupling, G.H., 'The turnpike trusts of Lancashire', *Memoirs and proceedings of the Manchester Literary and Philosophical Society*, 94 (1952-3), 1-23

Tupling, G.H., *The Economic History of Rossendale*, (1927)

Turnbull, G., *A history of the calico printing industry of Great Britain*, (1951)

Turner, W., *Riot! The story of the East Lancashire loom breakers in 1826*, (1992)

Tweedale, C.L., 'The Turnbull Tale', *Ramsbottom Heritage Society News Magazine*, (Summer 1993), 2-6

Winward, S.J., *Musbury Crown: story of school and church 1815-1977*, (1977)

UNPUBLISHED DISSERTATIONS, ETC.

Barnes, J., *Historical Notes on Stubbins Congregational Church*, (1985)

Davies, J., *Quarrying in Rossendale*, (1985)

Hamilton, S., 'The Historical Geography of South Rossendale 1780-1900'. MA thesis, University of Manchester (1974)

Hanson, H., 'The railway comes to Bury – communication developments in south-east Lancashire.' BA dissertation, University of Manchester (1966)

Luty, M., *My life has sparkled*, (1967?)

Meredith, C.P., 'Transport developments in east Lancashire 1780-1860.' MA thesis, University of Manchester (1978)

Muir, A., *The history of Porritts and Spencer*, (1966)

Starkie, M., *Mineral water manufacturers in Rossendale*, (1987)

NEWSPAPERS

Accrington Free Press

Accrington Gazette

Accrington Observer

Accrington Times

Bacup and Rossendale News

Bacup Times

Blackburn Mail

Blackburn Standard

Bolton Chronicle

Bradshaw's Railway Gazette
Burnley Evening Star
Bury Times
Daily Dispatch
Daily Express
Haslingden Chronicle and Ramsbottom Times
Haslingden Gazette
Haslingden Guardian
Haslingden Observer
Illustrated London News
Lancashire Evening Telegraph
Leeds Intelligencer
London Gazette
Manchester Courier
Manchester Evening News
Manchester Examiner and Times
Manchester Guardian
Manchester Mercury
Morning Herald
Preston Guardian
Ramsbottom Observer
Rochdale Observer
Rossendale Division Gazette
Rossendale Free Press
Rossendale Herald and Post
Wheeler's Manchester Chronicle

PARLIAMENTARY PAPERS

House of Lords Committee on the state and condition of children employed in the cotton manufactories of the United Kingdom, 1819 (24) CX

Abstract of answers and returns relative to the state of education in England and Wales 1833, 1835 (62) XLI

Persons summoned for offences against the Factory Act, 1835-6 (278) XLV

A return of the number of power looms used in factories, 1836 (24) XLV

Report from the select committee appointed to inquire into the administration of the relief of the poor, 48th report, 1837-8 (579) XVIII

Number and names of persons summoned for offences against the Factory Act, 1837-8 (12) XLV

Appendix to the report of the commissioners appointed to inquire into the state of the roads in England and Wales, 1840 [280] XXVII

Reports of the inspectors of factories for the half year ending 31st December 1841, 1842 (31) XXII

Children's employment commission. Appendix to the second report, part I, 1843 (431) XIV

Children's employment commission. Appendix to the second report, part II, 1843 (431) XV

Correspondence and return relative to the removal of labourers from agricultural districts to manufacturing districts, 1843 (254) XLV

Report...upon the accidents which have occurred on railways during the year 1856, 1857 Session 2 [2287] XXXVII

Report of the Registrar of Friendly Societies in England, 1875 (408) LXXI

INDEX

Walton, James, 29-30, 116, 118-119, 221
Walton, James Frederick, 119
Walton, Richard, 119, 164, 221
Warburton, Ellen, 27
Warburton, James, 103
Warburton, William, 109, 212
Wardley, John, 62
Warwick, Alice, 292
Warwick, Harry, 292
Watkin, Absalom and Son, 70
Watkin, Alfred, 70-71
Watkins, James, 48
Watson, A. S, 258
Watson, David, 71
Waugh, Edwin, 241
Waugh's Well, 224, 229
weavers, 42, 132
Well Street North, 23
Wesleyan Methodism, 152, 164, 191,
    202-235, 266, 267, 282
West View, 11, 98
Whalley Road, 15, 168
Whalley Road Service Station, 169
Whitaker Pasture Farm, 2, 25, 116
White Croft bleachworks, 62
White Horse *see* Horse and Jockey
Whitsuntide, 220-224, 265
Whittaker family, 11, 120, 123, 158-159
Whittaker, James, 33-34, 36, 119, 158-159
Whittaker, John, 34, 159
Whittaker, Robert, 42
Whittaker, William, 29, 169
Whittam, Henry, 29-30, 33
Whittle Pike, 122
Whitworth, Henry J, 253

Whitworth, James, 38
Wiggins Teape Group, 64
Wilkinson, Bob, 263
William Rumney and Co, 63, 72, 126
William Street, 20
Williams, Andrew, 246
Williams, Richard, 15
Wilson, Jane, 190
Wilson, Matthew, 51, 146, 224, 263
Wilson, William, 129
Windy Harbour Farm, 39
wireless, 193, 268
Wisdom, Thomas, 127, 153
Wolstenholme, H and Son, 152
Wolstenholme, John, 241
Wolstenholme, Thomas, 12, 104, 152, 267
Women's Voluntary Service, 291-292
Woodcock, Samuel, 93
Woodhey Dyeing Co, 77
Woodlands Road, 13
Woods, Thomas, 149
working men's clubs, 52, 272-273
Worsick, Alfred, 12, 18, 20
Wrigley, John, 79
Wynne, Charles, 209

Y

Yates, James, 124
Yates, Thomas, 137
Yeo, James, 199
Yew Street, 23, 42
youth clubs, 230-231, 273, 293

Z

zeppelin, 282